PUBLIC POLICIES TOWARD BUSINESS

Readings and Cases

The Irwin Series in Economics

Consulting Editor   LLOYD G. REYNOLDS   *Yale University*

PUBLIC POLICIES
TOWARD BUSINESS

Readings and Cases

Edited by

WILLIAM G. SHEPHERD

Professor of Economics
The University of Michigan

Revised Edition   1979

RICHARD D. IRWIN, INC.   Homewood, Illinois   60430
Irwin-Dorsey Limited   Georgetown, Ontario   L7G 4B3

To Edward

ISBN 0-256-02236-4
Library of Congress Catalog Card No. 78–72056
Printed in the United States of America

3 4 5 6 7 8 9 0 ML 6 5 4 3 2 1

PREFACE

———————— ✕ ————————

Readings and cases afford the student a first-hand look at the best writings and official decisions dealing with public policies toward business. This book gathers together a wide selection of the leading items in the areas of antitrust policy, regulation, and public enterprise. It is a companion to William G. Shepherd and Clair Wilcox, *Public Policies Toward Business*, 6th ed. (Homewood, Ill.: Richard D. Irwin, 1979). Also, this book can be used effectively with other texts or on its own in a variety of course settings. In this revision, I have expanded the coverage of antitrust policy, pruned out marginal topics, and provided more structure for the whole presentation.

The topics proceed through all of the main parts of antitrust policy, with both landmark historical cases and recent decisions. Some of the cases and scholarly debates presented here are still in progress. The regulation of utilities (Part II) is covered in five subsections, including the three main regulated sectors—electrical power, telecommunications, and transportation. There is also a brief section on public enterprise. The readings and cases are introduced and interpreted briefly, and a bank of review questions is given at the end of each main part.

The coverage of the book is designed to be balanced and fair. I will welcome any suggestions for improving the treatment in later editions. I am greatly indebted to David O. Smith for research assistance and to the authors, journals, and publishers for permission to reprint.

March 1979   **William G. Shepherd**

CONTENTS

—— ❦ ——

PART I.   POLICIES TO PROMOTE COMPETITION

Conglomerate Mergers

C. Behavior

Price Fixing and Related Restraints

Tacit Collusion

Other Collective Activities

Price Discrimination

Tie-ins

E.   Transportation

PART III.   PUBLIC ENTERPRISE

Part I

⹝

POLICIES TO PROMOTE COMPETITION

⹝ THE THREE MAIN LINES of antitrust treatment are toward: (1) existing market structure, (2) mergers, and (3) behavior of various kinds, which may suppress or exclude competition. After a review of the origins of policy, we consider the issues and cases in detail.

First, Hamilton and Till note that the Sherman Act emerged from a confused Congressional setting. The law's "intent" is unclear, despite frequent claims about what Congress really meant it to accomplish. The writers also trace the small resources which antitrust policy has had to work with. Only in the 1970s have the funds begun to approach substantial levels.

Then we move to a series of antitrust topics, beginning with *existing market structure*. Then come *mergers*, in three categories: horizontal, vertical, and conglomerate. There follow six categories of *behavior*. First are three in which firms act together: price-fixing, tacit collusion, and other collective activities. Then come three kinds of actions by individual firms: price discrimination (including "predatory" actions), tie-ins, and vertical restrictions.

Readings are interspersed with cases, in order to bring out the issues and precedents clearly.

Walton H. Hamilton (1881–   )
Irene Till (1906–   )

⚹ 1

Antitrust in Action*

By 1940 it was widely argued that the Sherman Act was a weak law, enforced only by a corporal's guard. Why had this happened? Has it continued?

THE CHARTER OF FREEDOM

Scruples and the Constitution

The Sherman Act is a weapon of policy from another age. As the 80s became the 90s, the Nation was becoming uncomfortably conscious of an industrial revolution. Although dinky little railways were a commonplace, the trunk line was still a novelty. The land was dotted with factories using simple mechanical processes; yet chemistry and biology had not been subdued into technologies and electricity had just ceased to be a toy. The telephone was still a novelty; the electric light had just passed its eleventh birthday; the wonders that lie within the vacuum tube were still to be explored. The automobile was a rather impious hope; the airplane, an adventurous flight in wishful thinking. The motion picture and the radio broadcast were as yet hardly tangible enough to be subjects of fancy. Agriculture, once the foundation of national wealth, was being driven back country. Petty trade had been forced to make a place beside itself for a big business which seemed to masses of the people to be strange, gigantic, powerful.

The unruly times offered opportunity to the swashbuckling captains of industry, whose ways were direct, ruthless, and not yet covered over by the surface amenities of a later age. In sugar, nails, tobacco, copper, jute, cordage, borax, slate pencils, oilcloth, gutta percha, barbed fence wire, castor oil they bluntly staked out their feudal domains. The little

---

*Walton H. Hamilton and Irene Till, *Antitrust in Action*, Monograph No. 16, Temporary National Economic Committee (Washington, D.C.: U.S. Government Printing Office, 1941), excerpted from pages 5–11 and 23–26. Hamilton is an extraordinary writer on public policies, with wit, brevity, and sophistication. Till has worked for several agencies promoting competition.

3

man caught in a squeeze play—the independent crowded to the wall by "the Octopus"—the farmer selling his wheat, corn, or tobacco under the tyranny of a market he did not understand—the craftsman stripped of his trade by the machine—the consumer forced to take the ware at an artificial price or go without—here were dramatic episodes. Industry was in the clutch of radical forces—and of iniquity. It was a period in which the ordinary man was confused, disturbed, resentful.

Of this confusion, disturbance, resentment, Congress became aware. It was led by protest and petition to the necessity of doing something about it. Yet a number of obstacles blurred the vision and arrested the action of the Fifty-first Congress. At the time there had been little experience with administration. The regulatory commission was almost unknown. The Interstate Commerce Commission, but three years old, had not yet found its footing; the dominant purpose behind it was not to regulate the railroads but to put an end to rebates and discriminations upon which favored shippers thrived. Some of the State commissions were a bit older, but they had little to offer in the way of usage, device, invention. Just as little was known about industry, whose curious ways had not yet become a subject of detailed study; a speculative account of how competition was supposed to work was enough. Since, barring collusion, the general theory was applicable to any ware of trade, the bewildering variety of industrial activity was hardly suspected. . . .

In direct attack a great many bills were introduced. In Senate and House Member after Member, with his ear to the ground and his head full of scruples, put on paper his own proposal for banning monopoly from the land. As their authors were unlike in courage, vision, knowledge, forthrightness, so did the bills differ in orbit of influence, range of remedy, agency of enforcement, making life mildly uncomfortable or distinctly disagreeable for enemies to the public good. Directness went straight to the mark with prison sentences for "malefactors of great wealth"; decorum countered with the proposal of a constitutional amendment to ease the way for "a strong measure." Nor could "the thumbscrew of monopoly" be considered as a question apart. As a possible "mother of trusts," at least to free-trade Senators, the protective tariff became a new-born iniquity. Thrusts at scarce money, at high money, at the money trust, at high finance, were constantly in evidence. The urge to trust busting went forward to overtones of the currency, investment banking, the tariff, options in grain, the sins of the other party. . . .

Back to the Common Law

As a creature of such currents of thought the statute took shape. The original Sherman bill was a very tentative proposal. It professed to outlaw all arrangements which prevented "full and free competition," to open the Federal courts to suits by parties damnified by such agreements, to provide for the forfeiture of the charter of the offending corporation. Its terms were uncertain, it invited constitutional attack, its author was timid in its defense. Twice it was rewritten by the Committee on Finance; yet it remained the target for the kind of shafts which the statesmen of that generation loved to hurl. The author, confused, yielding, anxious to placate, time after time would concede objection and accept amendment. As thus from many desks rather incongruous bits came into place, members became quite uncertain as to the objective and content of the proposed measure. After running the gauntlet of "the habitudes of the lawyer," the bill retained its legal ban upon interference with competition and its right of private suit for double the amount of damages and costs. As for implementation, a clause—really a broad sheet of paper whereon judges might freely write—gave to the circuit courts of the United States jurisdiction over "all suits of a civil nature at common law or in equity" and authority to "issue all remedial process, orders, or writs proper or necessary to enforce its provisions." A postscript granted a limited exception to trade unions in their resort to collective action to shorten hours and to raise wages, and to farmers' cooperatives in the sale of their own products.

But a posse of Senators on the warpath was not enthusiastic about so lukewarm a measure. Nor were statesmen from the Grain Belt content to let slip the opportunity to have the law on processors and speculators. . . .

[Various strengthening changes were made.]

Step by step all seemed right. Yet somehow the whole of the resolve seemed different from the sum of the motions. A majority had gone along, yet only a straggling of supporters remained faithful to the completed work. Once—and then again—a motion had been made to recommit the bill, not to the Finance Committee whence in lean form it had come, but to the Judiciary Committee. On former occasions the proposal "to deliver the child for nurture to persons who have most interest in its death" had been voted down and for the time the measure was saved from "this great mausoleum of senatorial literature." Now for the third time the motion for reference was put and carried; and the Judiciary Committee—stung by criticism or avid to exploit an opportunity—within six days returned to the Senate a bill with the same caption. The committee had scrapped all that had been sent along; and with Senator Hoar, of Massachusetts as draftsman had written its own law.

The new bill simply recited for "commerce among the several States," the rule of the common law against restraint of trade. This recitation was deemed necessary for it was believed that there was no "Federal common law." A statute was regarded as necessary to bring the body of ancient usage within reach of the United States courts. The statement was framed in familiar legal symbols, not in the language of industry or the idiom of public policy. The prohibitions, which had grown out of the experience with petty trade, were taken over intact. . . .

After the briefest of discussions the Senate adopted the Hoar bill. Its sponsors were apologetic for the very little distance the statute went; but the zeal for argument had long since been spent. It was accepted as a "first installment," presently to be amended as experience pointed the way. In the House a time limit forced an early vote; leave to print crowded the inaudible debate from the floor into the Congressional Record. A single amendment led to a struggle in conference and was eventually abandoned; the text was left intact. There was no enthusiasm; but here was something at least for the people back home—and the congressional campaign was warming up. Besides there were matters of real consequence, such as the McKinley Tariff Act, which wanted legislative attention. So, with only a single vote in dissent—though in both Houses Members answered "present" or were conveniently absent—on the 2d of July 1890, the bill became the law of the land. It is to this day strangely enough called the Sherman Act—for no better reason, according to its author, than that Senator Sherman had nothing to do with it whatever.

The Intent—if Any—of Congress

A great deal has been said about the purpose of Congress in passing the act. At best legislative intent is an evasive thing. It is wrapped in the conditions, the problems, the attitudes, the very atmosphere of an era that is gone. But aside from saying that the act reflects its date, there is little more in the way of concretion to recite. Instead, as a creation of the process of legislation, the statute bears the confused marks of its origin. . . .

In a search for intent the record has been thumbed through with meticulous care and to little purpose. The debates exhibit heat, passion, righteous indignation against the devil of monopoly. The bills proposed went much farther than the Hoar Act. In learned books and before learned judges, passage after passage has been cited to prove what the framers did—and did not—have in mind. The great bother is that the bill which was arduously debated was never passed and that the bill which was passed was never really discussed. The House, in fact, never had a chance at the measure which provoked discussion.

A ruse, whose cleverness only legislative experts can appreciate, drove a barrier between debate and eventual statute. The matter went to a committee notoriously hostile to the legislation. The committee turned a deaf ear to all that the Senate had said and done and went its own way. Intent, therefore, forsakes the Congressional Record for the capacious recesses of that flexible corpus called the common law. When the bill was reported back, the session was late, interest had died, apathy ruled. Yet the statute—untouched except for the Miller-Tydings amendment of 1937—has for 50 years remained the basic act for the control of American industry.

The Fifty-first Congress sensed the rush of an oncoming industrialism. Its task, facing the future, was to create a barrier against shock, a road to order, a guaranty of justice. In debate it laid bare evils within the emerging national economy but could bring itself to do something about it only in a babble of voices. Except for words, it made no thrust at present dangers; it came to no grip with the trends of the times; it made no attempt to chart a course for American industry. When the voters would no longer tolerate delay, it acted. When the need was to shape the future, it looked to the past. On the eve of the greatest of industrial revolutions, the National Government was fitted out with a weapon forged to meet the problems of petty trade. Out of an inability of Congress to face the economic problems of its day the "charter of freedom" for American industry was born.

BIG ACT LITTLE STICK

The Shortage of Funds

A statute lives by appropriations—and from the first the demands of Antitrust have fallen upon the deaf ear of Congress. Not until its fiftieth year was as much as $1,000,000 appropriated to the purposes of the Sherman Act. For more than a decade no separate staff was charged with its enforcement; and when in 1903 Antitrust became a division in the Department of Justice, it was given only half a million dollars, to be expended at the rate of $100,000 a year over a period of 5 years. Between 1908 and 1935 the appropriation varied between $100,000 and $300,000. In 1936 the figure was increased to $435,000; in 1939, to about $800,000, and for the fiscal years of 1940 and 1941 to an all-high of $1,300,000 and $1,325,000.

It is obvious that the staff has been inadequate to police against restraint the whole of American business. In the famous trust-busting campaign of Theodore Roosevelt, the average number of attorneys in active service was 5. In the Wilson administration when the World War had caused prices to skyrocket, the number had risen to 18. In the 20s when the corporation was evolved into an intricate and evasive structure, and merger, amalgamation, integration, holding company was the order of the day, the number engaged did not exceed 25. Not until 1938 were as many as 50 lawyers actually employed; not until 1939 did professional personnel reach 200 attorneys and a half dozen economists.

For almost its whole life Antitrust has been a kind of a corporal's guard—a small section tucked away in the intricacies of a Government department. . . . The contrast between the miniature staff on duty and the enormity of the job to be done speaks for itself. As well attempt to maintain law and order in Boston, Philadelphia, or San Francisco with the bold police force of Oshkosh or Annapolis.

. . . In fixing its appropriations, year by year, Congress customarily uses as its standard the sums allotted in previous years. Legislative custom has it that this year's appropriation is about right. The sum is a norm, with every presumption in its favor; the burden of proof is upon the demand for more money. Thus ancient thought, frozen into a figure, stands as an obstacle against the appropriation which current knowledge and a later understanding suggest.

But the folkways of the Budget cannot fully account for the neglect. The trickle of funds is symptom as well as fact and cause. In the hurly-burly of industrial movement there has been little conscious appreciation of the character and magnitude of the task Antitrust has to perform. The public can understand a chivalrous adventure in trust-busting in the grand manner. And when a champion of the people rides into the wind, seeks out the octopus in his lair, and brings home the scalp of a trust, it applauds. But it has little appreciation of the detailed, day-by-day drudgery essential to the assertion of the public interest in everyday business. With the shift from market to management, authority can be met only with authority. Thus the safeguarding of the public interest in business becomes a continuous and watchful task. In Antitrust old style, heroic victories were now and then to be won upon the open field. In Antitrust new style, a detail of pedestrian work must be done day by day and a multitude of decisions be made back of the line.

The cause of Antitrust lacks that massed support which causes congressional purse strings to loosen. Its appeal is greatest to the man on the outside who wants to barge in on a trade and needs its help in making his way. It is least to persons who, already established, are wary of interference. The support of labor is not easily enlisted. In many industries it has a vested interest in the maintenance of restraints; the power of its leaders depends upon the maintenance of things as they are. It is more prone to view the Sherman Act as a weapon to be used against the trade-union than as an instrument of a better living. The group of men—and women—of good will, who busy themselves more than most over public affairs, are well disposed; but to them Antitrust is only one among many worthy causes to which fitfully they give their attention. A general opinion may favor all the money needed to put teeth into the act; and interested groups may be lukewarm or even hostile to appropriations. But, under our Government, the pressure of the many is difficult. It is the few who understand how to concentrate their pressure at the focal points that count.

The act, throughout the political community, is held in least favor where power and influence are greatest. A rather instinctive suspicion of Antitrust prevails in high industrial quarters. As a symbol the Sherman Act is grand. It sets down a lofty profession of economic faith; it proclaims industry to be the instrument of the common good; it preached the philosophy which makes the market the rightful agency of business control. The statute holds enough of the raw material of thought, out of which the creed of laissez-faire was formulated, to have high ceremonial value in financial circles. It serves its function best, however, as a generality, left in Olympian aloofness, unsullied by contact with mundane affairs. As a control which might do active duty in his own industry, the ordinary man of affairs views it as suspect. As a scheme of regulation it moves toward diffusion of power and runs directly against the trend toward concentration.

The leanness of the budget has left its lines on the national economy. In 1890 free competition as the way of order for industry was not seriously questioned. Conformity to this standard was an obvious expression of public policy. In the years to come the pattern of industry was to be beaten upon by a continuous industrial revolution; turbulent forces were at large which the law said should be subdued. Yet at no time did Congress choose to do more than equip a few knights to go forth to romantic combat. The negligent oversight under which industry was left to its own devices has confused the problem and multiplied the modern task of Antitrust. Industry might once have been held to its competitive norms; it is now too late to restore the primitive design. The recession of the market, as an instrument of industrial control, has obscured the norms of reference provided by the common law. The situation was allowed to get out of hand before the agency was equipped for its task. Antitrust has never been accorded its chance.

A. MONOPOLY AND MONOPOLIZING

————————————— ✂ —————————————

When an industry has one dominant firm or a tight oligopoly structure, antitrust faces a difficult problem. Restructuring could almost certainly increase the degree of competition, by creating more strong competitors. Yet that is difficult to accomplish. Also, it might sacrifice economies of scale or innovation by the leading firms, according to some observers.

Section 2 actions are usually fought long and hard by the dominant firms. There have been two main clusters of action, in 1906–20 and 1938–52. The first one tackled most of the leading dominant firms in industry, and it proceeded briskly. *American Tobacco* and *Standard Oil* were major victories, leading to dissolution and divestiture. Yet Chief Justice White used the *Standard Oil* opinion to insert a "rule of reason" into Section 2. Such "reasonableness" was used in 1920 to acquit the U.S. Steel Corporation, created by mergers in 1901 with about 65 percent of the industry. That decision closed off most Section 2 actions, until in 1938 Thurman Arnold revived antitrust and started a new series of Section 2 actions.

The *Alcoa* decision of 1945 was a landmark, since it sought to remove the "rule of reason." In 1954, the United Shoe Machinery Corporation was also convicted (some six decades after its monopoly was created) in what was an unusually sophisticated decision and opinion. Structure and behavior were carefully weighed, and moderate actions to reduce USM's market position were ordered. Yet in 1956, du Pont's monopoly of "cellophane" was acquitted on the ground that the true market included all flexible packaging materials and that cellophane's share of that market was low.

There was a pause in Section 2 actions during about 1952–67. Yet by 1960 the Court was ready to take a stricter line on dominant firms, and in 1966 it convicted the Grinnell Corporation for monopolizing the market for "accredited central station protective systems" (that is, burglar alarms). Then after 1968, several major cases were brought by the agencies and private plaintiffs. The Antitrust Division's marathon suit against IBM Corporation, filed in 1969, started trial in 1975 and the defense case began in 1978. The FTC took action against Xerox Corporation in 1972, citing a virtual monopoly in the "plain paper copier" market. After brisk negotiations, a settlement in 1975 provided some access to Xerox patents but little else. The Division sued AT&T in 1974 for excessive monopoly in the telephone industry. Western Electric's vertical integration into the Bell System had been debated for many decades, but now the Division also sought other divestiture. The issues spread to Congress, the FCC and the courts, as our selections note.

In 1973 the FTC started a broad action against major oil companies. In 1977 the issues were narrowed, but in 1978 the case was still enmeshed in slow procedures, and trial appeared to be far off. Like the *IBM* and *AT&T* cases, the oil case seemed to show that large Section 2 cases were no longer workable.

Meanwhile, private antitrust cases were proliferating. Many suits were settled or defeated, but some succeeded, even where public agencies had chosen not to act. The cases also went faster, partly because the plaintiffs had requested jury trials. In that setting, there was a common-sense aversion to stalling and legal hairsplitting. In 1978, Berkey Photo Corporation won conviction of Eastman Kodak Company and $81 million damages (the decision was appealed). And an SCM Corporation suit against Xerox Corporation brought conviction and $11 million damages in 1978 (it too was appealed). In both cases, the juries accepted narrow market definitions and found abusive actions by the dominant firms. The cases did not yield restructuring, but they seemed to apply stronger restraints than the slow and uncertain official cases could.

Details of Typical Cases

A "case" usually involves two parties, "plaintiff" (who first filed a complaint) and "respondent" (the defendant). Trial in District Court involves arguments about facts and points of law, after careful pretrial preparation (often lasting years). Either side may appeal the court's decision to the Appeals Court in its region or ultimately to the U.S. Supreme Court. Appeals can involve only points of law, not new facts: the trial record is the sole source of facts. The decision is announced in an "opinion," written by a member of the majority.[1] It reviews previous steps, facts, points of law, and anything else which explains the decision to "reverse" or "affirm" the court below. If there is a conviction, the case may be remanded down to the original court for devising a suitable

---

[1]Actually, many opinions are drafted by the judge's law clerk, usually a young lawyer just out of law school!

"remedy" (or "relief"). Minority members often write "dissenting opinions," commonly in sharp, even sarcastic, tones. The decision sets "precedent" for future cases which may fit the facts and legal status of the case under review. The dissent often defines the limits of the precedent or even sets the stage for future reversals.

The title of District Court decisions lists the original plaintiff first. Most Antitrust Division suits are cited as "U.S. *versus* Alleged Offender, Inc." (the defendant company). On appeal appellate courts *often* and the Supreme Court *always* lists the appealing party first.

Opinions in important antitrust cases often run 20 to 50 pages or even longer, and some of them make very heavy reading indeed. The excerpts here focus only on the key facts and legal points. Structural and merger cases come first (roughly, Sherman Act Section 2 and Clayton Act Section 7). Restrictive practice cases then follow (roughly, Sherman Act Section 1).

✳ 2

United States v. *Standard Oil Co.*
U.S. Supreme Court
221 U.S. 1, 59 (1911)

The Standard Oil Company achieved its monopoly of the U.S. oil industry during 1870–80 by various pricing tactics, railroad rebates, and other means. By 1910 it was slipping but still dominant, and its 40-year monopoly had been extraordinarily lucrative. A government antitrust case succeeded in winning conviction and an order to dissolve the trust. The Supreme Court affirmed. But Chief Justice White, who had awaited this opportunity, wrote a majority opinion advancing the "rule of reason." (The wording of his opinion, incidentally, is tortured and obscure, hard reading for everyone.) "Unreasonable" acts, the specific intent of Standard Oil, and the role of Section 1 were stressed. Despite Justice Harlan's dissent, this greatest stroke of "trustbusting" was also a statement virtually withdrawing future actions except in extreme instances.

. . . In other words, having by the 1st section forbidden all means of monopolizing trade, that is, unduly restraining it by means of every contract, combination, etc., the 2d section seeks, if possible, to make the prohibitions of the act all the more complete and perfect by embracing all attempts to reach the end prohibited by the 1st section, that is, restraints of trade, by any attempt to monopolize, or monopolization thereof, even although the acts by which such results are attempted to be brought about or are brought about be not embraced within the general enumeration of the 1st section. And, of course, when the 2d section is thus harmonized with and made as it was intended to be the complement of the 1st, it becomes obvious that the criteria to be resorted to in any given case for the purpose of ascertaining whether violations of the section have been committed is the rule of reason guided by the established law and by the plain duty to enforce the prohibitions of the act, and thus the public policy which its restrictions were obviously enacted to subserve. . . .

In substance, the propositions urged by the Government are reducible to this: That the language of the statute embraces every contract, combination, etc., in restraint of trade, and hence its text leaves no room for the exercise of judgment but simply imposes the plain duty of applying its prohibitions to every case within its literal language. The error involved lies in assuming the matter to be decided. This is true because as the acts which may come under the classes stated in the 1st section and the restraint of trade to which that section applies are not specifically enumerated or defined it is obvious that judgment must in every case be called into play in order to determine whether a particular act is embraced within the statutory classes, and whether if the act is within such classes its nature or effect causes it to be a restraint of trade within the intendment of the act. To hold to the contrary would require the conclusion either that every contract, act, or combination of any kind or nature, whether it operated a restraint on trade or not, was within the statute, and thus the statute would be destructive of all right to contract or agree or combine in any respect whatever as to subjects embraced in interstate trade or commerce, or if this conclusion were not reached, then the contention would require it to be held that as the statute did not define the things to which it related and excluded resort to the only means by which the acts to which it relates could be ascertained—the light of reason—the enforcement of the statute was impossible because of its uncertainty. The merely generic enumeration which the statute makes of the acts to which it refers and the absence of any definition of restraint of trade as used in the statute leaves room for but one conclusion, which is, that it was expressly designed not to unduly limit the application of the act by precise definition, but while clearly fixing a standard, that is, by defining the ulterior boundaries which could not be transgressed with impunity, to leave it to be determined by the light of reason, guided by the principles of law and the duty to apply and enforce the public policy embodied in the statute, in every given case whether any particular act or contract was within the contemplation of the statute.

. . . [T]he very genius for commercial development and organization which it would seem was manifested from the beginning soon begot an intent and purpose to exclude others which was frequently manifested by acts and dealings wholly inconsistent with the theory that they were made with the single conception of advancing the development of business power by usual methods but which, on the contrary, necessarily involved the intent to drive others from the field and to exclude them from their right to trade and thus accomplish the mastery which was the end in view. And, considering the period from the date of the trust agreements of 1879 and 1882, up to the time of the expansion of the New Jersey corporation, the gradual extension of the power over the commerce in oil which ensued, the decision of the supreme court of Ohio, the tardiness or reluctance in conforming to the commands of that decision, the methods first adopted and that which finally culminated in the plan of the New Jersey corporation, all additionally serve to make manifest the continued existence of the intent which we have previously indicated, and which, among other things, impelled the expansion of the New Jersey corporation. The exercise of the power which resulted from that organization fortifies the foregoing conclusions, since the development which came, the acquisition here and there which ensued of every efficient means by which competition could have been asserted, the slow but resistless methods which followed by which means of transportation were absorbed and brought under control, the system of marketing which was adopted by which the country was divided into districts and the trade in each district in oil was turned over to a designated corporation within the combination, and all others were excluded, all lead the mind up to a conviction of a purpose and intent which we think is so certain as practically to cause the subject not to be within the domain of reasonable contention.

. . . As penalties which are not authorized by law may not be inflicted by judicial authority, it follows that to meet the situation with which we are confronted the application of remedies two-fold in character becomes essential: 1st. To forbid the doing in the future of acts like those which we have found to have been done in the past which would be violative of the statute. 2d. The exertion of such measure of relief as will effectually dissolve the combination found to exist in violation of the statute and thus neutralize the extension and continually operating force which the possession of the power unlawfully obtained has brought and will continue to bring about.

In applying remedies for this purpose, however, the fact must not be overlooked that injury to the public by the prevention of an undue restraint on, or the monopolization of, trade or commerce, is the foundation upon which the prohibitions of the statute rest, and moreover that one of the fundamental purposes of the statute is to protect, not to destroy, rights of property. . . .

Justice Harlan, concurring in part and dissenting in part:

. . . On reading the opinion just delivered, the first inquiry will be, that as the court is unanimous in holding that the particular things done by the Standard Oil Company and its subsidiary companies, in this case, were illegal under the Anti-Trust Act, whether those things were in reasonable or unreasonable restraint of interstate commerce, why was it necessary to make an elaborate argument, as is done in the opinion, to show that according to the "rule of reason" the act as passed by Congress should be interpreted as if it contained the word "unreasonable" or the word "undue"? The only answer which, in frankness, can be given to this question, is, that the court intends to decide that its deliberate judgment, fifteen years ago, to the effect that the act permitted no restraint whatever of interstate commerce, whether reasonable or unreasonable, was not in accordance with the "rule of reason." In effect the court says that it will now, for the first time, bring the discussion under the "light of reason" and apply the "rule of reason" to the questions to be decided. I have the authority of this court for saying that such a course of proceeding on its part would be "judicial legislation." . . .

. . . To overreach the action of Congress merely by judicial construction, that is, by indirection, is a blow at the integrity of our governmental system and in the end will prove most dangerous to all. Mr. Justice Bradley wisely said, when on this bench, that illegitimate and unconstitutional practices get their first footing by silent approaches and slight deviations from legal modes of legal procedure. . . .

✕ 3

United States v. U.S. Steel Corp.

U.S. Supreme Court
251 U.S. 417 (1920)

Formed in 1901 with two thirds of the industry, U.S. Steel was the greatest of the "trust" consolidations. It established cooperative pricing (the "Gary dinners") and reinforced the basing-point system. But its share dwindled and its predatory behavior was tame compared to many other trusts. By 1920, also, the "rule of reason" stood as precedent and World War I had transmuted trusts into patriotic producers. Even so, the Supreme Court vote to acquit U.S. Steel was only 4 to 3. Was U.S. Steel a "good" trust? Should the Court have looked at 1901–10 rather than 1920?

. . . Our present purpose is, not retrospect for itself, however instructive, but practical decision upon existing conditions that we may not by their disturbance produce, or even risk, consequences of a concern that cannot now be computed. In other words, our consideration should be of not what the Corporation had power to do or did, but what it has now power to do and is doing, and what judgment should be now pronounced—whether its dissolution, as the government prays, or the dismissal of the suit, as the Corporation insists. . . .

The power attained was much greater than that possessed by any one competitor—it was not greater than that possessed by all of them. Monopoly, therefore, was not achieved, and competitors had to be persuaded by pools, associations, trade meetings, and through the social form of dinners, all of them, it may be, violations of the law, but transient in their purpose and effect. They were scattered through the years from 1901 (the year of the formation of the Corporation) until 1911 but after instances of success and failure were abandoned nine months before this suit was brought. . . .

What, then, can now be urged against the Corporation? Can comparisons in other regards be made with its competitors and by such comparisons guilty or innocent existence be assigned it? It is greater in size and productive power than any of its competitors, equal or nearly equal to them all, but its power over prices was not and is not commensurate with its power to produce.

It is true there is some testimony tending to show that the Corporation had such power, but there was also testimony and a course of action tending strongly to the contrary. The conflict was by the judges of the District Court unanimously resolved against the existence of that power, and in doing so, they but gave effect to the greater weight of the evidence. It is certain that no such power was exerted. On the contrary, the only attempt at a fixation of prices was, as already said, through an appeal to and confederation with competitors, and the record shows besides that when competition occurred it was not in pretense, and the Corporation declined in productive powers—the competitors growing either against or in consequence of the competition. If against the competition we have an instance of movement against what the Government insists was an irresistible force; if in consequence of competition, we have an illustration of the adage that "competition is the life of trade" and is not easily repressed. The power of monopoly in the Corporation under either illustration is an untenable accusation. . . .

We have pointed out that there are several of the Government's contentions which are difficult to represent or measure, and the one we are now considering—that is, the power is "unlawful regardless of purpose"—is another of them. It seems to us that it has for its ultimate principle and justification that strength in any producer or seller is a menace to the public interest and illegal, because there is potency in it for mischief. The regression is extreme, but short of it the Government cannot stop. The fallacy it conveys is manifest.

The Corporation was formed in 1901, no act of aggression upon its competitors is charged against it, it confederated with them at times in offense against the law, but abandoned that before this suit was brought, and since 1911 no act in violation of law can be established against it except its existence be such an act. . . . The Corporation is undoubtedly of impressive size, and it takes an effort of resolution not to be affected by it or to exaggerate its influence. But we must adhere to the law, and the law does not make mere size an offense or the existence of unexerted power an offense. It, we repeat, requires overt acts, and trusts to its prohibition of them and its power to repress or punish them. It does not compel competition nor require all that is possible. . . .

But there are countervailing considerations. We have seen whatever there was of wrong intent could not be executed; whatever there was of evil effect was discontinued before this suit was brought, and this, we think, determines the decree. . . . [A] court of equity . . . is not expected to enforce abstractions and do injury thereby, it may be, to the purpose of the law. . . . And it is certainly a matter for consideration that there was no legal attack on the Corporation until 1911, ten years after its formation and the commencement of its career. We do not, however, speak of the delay simply as to its time or say that there is estoppel in it because of its time but on account of what was done during that time—the many millions of dollars spent, the development made, and the enterprises undertaken; the investments by the public that have been invited and are not to be ignored. . . .

In conclusion, we are unable to see that the public interest will be served by yielding to the contention of the Government respecting the dissolution of the company or the separation from it of some of its subsidiaries; and we do see in a contrary conclusion a risk of injury to the public interest, including a material disturbance of, and, it may be serious detriment to, the foreign trade. And in submission to the policy of the law and its fortifying prohibitions the public interest is of paramount regard.

We think, therefore, that the decree of the District Court should be affirmed. . . .

Justice Day, dissenting:

For many years, as the record discloses, this unlawful organization exerted its power to control and maintain prices by pools, associations, trade meetings, and as the result of discussion and agreements at the so-called Gary Dinners, where the assembled trade opponents secured cooperation and joint action through the machinery of special committees of competing concerns, and by prudent prevision took into account the possibility of defection and the means of controlling and perpetuating that industrial harmony which arose from the control and maintenance of prices.

It inevitably follows that the corporation violated the law in its formation and by its immediate practices. The power, thus obtained from the combination of resources almost unlimited in the aggregation of competing organizations, had within its control the domination of the trade and the ability to fix prices and restrain the free flow of commerce upon a scale heretofore unapproached in the history of corporate organization in this country.

These facts established, as it seems to me they are by the record, it follows that, if the Sherman Act is to be given efficacy, there must be a decree undoing so far as is possible that which has been achieved in open, notorious, and continued violation of its provisions. . . .

From the earliest decisions of this court it has been declared that it was the effective power of such organizations to control and restrain competition and the freedom of trade that Congress intended to limit and control. That the exercise of the power may be withheld or exerted with forbearing benevolence does not place such combinations beyond the authority of the statute which was intended to prohibit their formation, and when formed to deprive them of the power unlawfully attained.

It is said that a complete monopolization of the steel business was never attained by the offending combinations. To insist upon such result would be beyond the requirements of the statute and in most cases practicably impossible. . . .

✕ 4

United States v. Aluminum Company of America

U.S. Circuit Court of Appeals,
Second Circuit, 1945. 148 F.2d 416.

This "big" case aimed at a 45-year-old monopoly, which was then the 28th largest U.S. industrial firm. The decision rejected the rule of reason, treating the conscious maintenance of monopoly as critical. Judge Hand's comment about 90, 60, and 30 percent market shares is still the usual rule of thumb. This "landmark" case actually resulted, on remand, in very modest relief: mainly, disposal of World War II aluminum plants to new firms rather than to Alcoa.

Before Learned Hand, Swan, and Augustus N. Hand, Circuit Judges.

L. Hand, J. . . . The action was brought . . . to adjudge that the defendant, Aluminum Company of America, was monopolizing interstate and foreign commerce, particularly in the manufacture and sale of "virgin" aluminum ingot, and that it be dissolved; and further to adjudge that that company and the defendant, Aluminum Limited, had entered into a conspiracy in restraint of such commerce. It also asked incidental relief. . . . The action came to trial on June 1, 1938, and proceeded without much interruption until August 14, 1940, when the case was closed after more than 40,000 pages of testimony had been taken. The judge took time to consider the evidence and delivered an oral opinion which occupied him from September 30 to October 9, 1941. Again he took time to prepare findings of fact and conclusions of law which he filed on July 14, 1942; and he entered final judgment dismissing the complaint on July 23 of that year. The petition for an appeal and assignments of error were filed on September 14, 1942, and the petition was allowed on the next day. On June 12, 1944, the Supreme Court, declaring that a quorum of six justices qualified to hear the case was wanting, referred the appeal to this court. . . .

There are various ways of computing Alcoa's control of the aluminum market—as distinct from its production—depending upon what one regards as competing in that market. The judge figured its share—during the years 1929–1938, inclusive—as only about 33 percent; to do so he included "secondary" and excluded that part of Alcoa's own production which it fabricated and did not therefore sell as ingot. If, on the other hand, Alcoa's total production, fabricated and sold, be included and balanced against the sum of imported virgin and secondary, its share of the market was in the neighborhood of 64 percent for that period. The percentage we have already mentioned—over 90—results only if we both include all Alcoa's production and exclude secondary. That percentage is enough to constitute a monopoly; it is doubtful whether 60 or 64 percent would be enough; and certainly 33 percent is not. Hence it is necessary to settle what he shall treat as competing in the ingot market.

. . . Thus, in the case at bar Alcoa always knew that the future supply of ingot would be made up in part of what it produced at the time, and if it was as far-sighted as it proclaims itself, that consideration must have had its share in determining how much to produce. How accurately it could forecast the effect of present production upon the future market is another matter. Experience, no doubt, would help; but it makes no difference that it had to guess; it is enough that it had an inducement to make the best guess it could and that it would regulate that part of the future supply so far as it should turn out to have guessed right. The competition of secondary must therefore be disregarded as soon as we consider the position of Alcoa over a period of years; it was as much within Alcoa's control as was the production of the virgin from which it had been derived. This can be well illustrated by the case of a lawful monopoly: e.g., a patent or a copyright. The monopolist cannot prevent those to whom he sells from reselling at whatever prices they please. . . .

We conclude therefore that Alcoa's control over the ingot market must be reckoned at over 90 percent; that being the proportion which its production bears to imported virgin ingot. If the fraction which it did not supply were the produce of domestic manufacture, there could be no doubt that this percentage gave it a monopoly—lawful or unlawful, as the case might be. The producer of so large a proportion of the supply has complete control within certain limits. . . .

. . . But the whole issue is irrelevant anyway, for it is no excuse for "monopolizing" a market that the monopoly has not been used to extract from the consumer more than a "fair" profit. The Act has wider purposes. Indeed, even though we disregarded all but economic considerations, it would by no means follow that such concentration of producing power is to be desired, when it has not been used extortionately. Many people believe that possession of unchallenged economic power deadens initiative, discourages thrift, and depresses energy; that immunity from competition is a narcotic, and rivalry is a stimulant to industrial progress; that the spur of constant stress is necessary to counteract an inevitable disposition to let well enough alone. Such people believe that competitors, versed in the craft as no consumer can be, will be quick to detect opportunities for saving and new shifts in production and be eager to profit by them. In any event the mere fact that a producer, having command of the domestic market has not been able to make more than a "fair" profit, is no evidence that a "fair" profit could not have been made at lower prices.

. . . True, it might have been thought adequate to condemn only those monopolies which could not show that they had exercised the highest possible ingenuity, had adopted every possible economy, had anticipated every conceivable improvement, stimulated every possible demand. No doubt, that would be one way of dealing with the matter, although it would imply constant scrutiny and constant supervision, such as courts are unable to provide. Be that as it may, that was not the way that Congress chose; it did not condone "good trusts" and condemn "bad" ones; it forbad all. Moreover, in so doing it was not necessarily actuated by economic motives alone. It is possible, because of its indirect social or moral effect, to prefer a system of small producers, each dependent for his success upon his own skill and character, to one in which the great mass of those engaged must accept the direction of a few. These considerations, which we have suggested only as possible purposes of the Act, we think the decisions prove to have been in fact its purposes.

. . . Throughout the history of these statutes it has been constantly assumed that one of their purposes was to perpetuate and preserve, for its own sake and in spite of possible cost, an organization of industry in small units which can effectively compete with each other. We hold that Alcoa's monopoly of ingot was of the kind covered by § 2.

It does not follow because Alcoa had such a monopoly, that it monopolized the ingot market: it may not have achieved monopoly; monopoly may have been thrust upon it. If it had been a combination of existing smelters which united the whole industry and controlled the production of all aluminum ingot, it would certainly have monopolized the market. In several decisions the Supreme Court has decreed the dissolution of such combinations, although they had engaged in no unlawful trade practices. . . .

A market may, for example, be so limited that it is impossible to produce at all and meet the cost of production except by a plant large enough to supply the whole demand. Or there may be changes in taste

or in cost which drive out all but one purveyor. A single producer may
be the survivor out of a group of active competitors merely by virtue of
his superior skill, foresight, and industry. In such cases a strong argument can be made that, although the result may expose the public to the
evils of monopoly, the Act does not mean to condemn the resultant of
those very forces which it is its prime object to foster: finis opus coronat.
The successful competitor, having been urged to compete, must not be
turned upon when he wins. . . .

It would completely misconstrue Alcoa's position in 1940 to hold that
it was the passive beneficiary of a monopoly, following upon an involuntary elimination of competitors by automatically operative economic
forces. Already in 1909, when its last lawful monopoly ended, it sought
to strengthen its position by unlawful practices, and these concededly
continued until 1912.

. . . We need charge it with no moral derelictions after 1912; we may
assume that all it claims for itself is true. The only question is whether it
falls within the exception established in favor of those who do not seek,
but cannot avoid, the control of a market. It seems to us that that question scarcely survives its statement. It was not inevitable that it should
always anticipate increases in the demand for ingot and be prepared to
supply them. Nothing compelled it to keep doubling and redoubling its
capacity before others entered the field. It insists that it never excluded
competitors; but we can think of no more effective exclusion than progressively to embrace each new opportunity as it opened and to face
each newcomer with new capacity already geared into a great organization, having the advantage of experience, trade connections, and the
elite of personnel. Only in case we interpret "exclusion" as limited to
maneuvers not honestly industrial, but actuated solely by a desire to
prevent competition, can such a course, indefatigably pursued, be
deemed not "exclusionary." So to limit it would in our judgment
emasculate the Act; would permit just such consolidations as it was
designed to prevent. . . .

In order to fall within § 2, the monopolist must have both the power
to monopolize and the intent to monopolize. To read the passage as
demanding any "specific" intent makes nonsense of it, for no monopolist monopolizes unconscious of what he is doing. So here, Alcoa
meant to keep, and did keep, that complete and exclusive hold upon the
ingot market with which it started. That was to monopolize that market,
however innocently it otherwise proceeded. So far as the judgment held
that it was not within § 2, it must be reversed.

✺ 5

United States v. *United Shoe Machinery Corp.*

U.S. District Court, District of
Massachusetts, 1953. 110 F.Supp. 205,
affirmed per curiam 347 U.S. 521 (1954)

This case refined the reasons by which even a "good" monopolist could be convicted, if it had (1) high market share plus (2) some specific actions to get or keep the share. USM's extensive price discrimination was one such action. Judge Wyzanski, a leading jurist on antitrust matters, retained Carl Kaysen as an expert economic assistant. The remedy was modest, and USM was, in any case, small. In 1969 further steps had to be negotiated to end USM's now-tiny quasi-monopoly.

Wyzanski, J.   December 15, 1947, the Government filed a complaint against United Shoe Machinery Corporation . . . in order to restrain alleged violations of §§ 1 and 2 of [the Sherman Act].

Stripped to its essentials, the 52-page complaint charged, *first*, that since 1912 United had been "monopolizing interstate trade and commerce in the shoe machinery industry of the United States."

. . . The facts show that (1) defendant has, and exercises, such overwhelming strength in the shoe machinery market that it controls that market, (2) this strength excludes some potential, and limits some actual, competition, and (3) this strength is not attributable solely to defendant's ability, economies of scale, research, natural advantages, and adaptation to inevitable economic laws.

In estimating defendant's strength, this Court gives some weight to the 75 plus percentage of the shoe machinery market which United serves. But the Court considers other factors as well. In the relatively static shoe machinery market where there are no sudden changes in the style of machines or in the volume of demand, United has a network of long-term, complicated leases with over 90 percent of the shoe factories. These leases assure closer and more frequent contacts between United and its customers than would exist if United were a seller and its customers were buyers. Beyond this general quality, these leases are so drawn and so applied as to strengthen United's power to exclude competitors. Moreover, United offers a long line of machine types, while no competitor offers more than a short line. Since in some parts of its line United faces no important competition, United has the power to discriminate by wide differentials and over long periods of time in the rate of return it procures from different machine types. Furthermore, being by far the largest company in the field with by far the largest resources in dollars, in patents, in facilities, and in knowledge, United has a marked capacity to attract offers of inventions, inventors' services, and shoe machinery businesses. And, finally, there is no substantial substitute competition from a vigorous secondhand market in shoe machinery.

To combat United's market control, a competitor must be prepared with knowledge of shoemaking, engineering skill, capacity to invent around patents, and financial resources sufficient to bear the expense of long developmental and experimental processes. The competitor must be prepared for consumers' resistance founded on their long-term satisfactory relations with United and on the cost to them of surrendering United's leases. Also, the competitor must be prepared to give, or point to the source of, repair and other services, and to the source of supplies for machine parts, expendable parts, and the like. Indeed, perhaps a competitor who aims at any large-scale success must also be prepared to lease his machines. These considerations would all affect *potential* competition and have not been without their effect on *actual* competition.

Not only does the evidence show United has control of the market, but also the evidence does not show that the control is due entirely to excusable causes. The three principal sources of United's power have been the original constitution of the company, the superiority of United's products and services, and the leasing system. The first two of these are plainly beyond reproach. . . .

But United's control does not rest solely on its original constitution, its ability, its research, or its economies of scale. There are other barriers to competition, and these barriers were erected by United's own business policies. Much of United's market power is traceable to the magnetic ties inherent in its system of leasing, and not selling, its more important machines. The lease-only system of distributing complicated machines has many "partnership" aspects, and it has exclusionary features such as the ten-year term, the full capacity clause, the return charges, and the failure to segregate service charges from machine charges. Moreover, the leasing system has aided United in maintaining a pricing system which discriminates between machine types. . . .

They are contracts, arrangements, and policies which, instead of encouraging competition based on pure merit, further the dominance of a particular firm. In this sense, they are unnatural barriers; they unnecessarily exclude actual and potential competition; they restrict a free market. While the law allows many enterprises to use such practices, the Sherman Act is now construed by superior courts to forbid the continuance of effective market control based in part upon such practices. Those courts hold that market control is inherently evil and constitutes a violation of § 2 unless economically inevitable or specifically authorized and regulated by law. . . .

Although leasing should not now be abolished by judicial decree, the Court agrees with the Government that the leases should be purged of their restrictive features. In the decree filed herewith, the term of the lease is shortened, the full capacity clause is eliminated, the discriminatory commutative charges are removed, and United is required to segregate its charges for machines from its charges for repair service.

. . . Some price discrimination, if not too rigid, is inevitable. Some may be justified as resting on patent monopolies. Some price discrimination is economically desirable, if it promotes competition in a market where several multiproduct firms compete. And while price discrimination has been an evidence of United's monopoly power, a buttress to it, and a cause of its perpetuation, its eradication cannot be accomplished without turning United into a public utility and the Court into a public utility commission, or requiring United to observe a general injunction of nondiscrimination between different products—an injunction which would be contrary to sound theory, which would require the use of practices not followed in any business known to the Court, and which could not be enforced. . . .

✕ 6

United States v. *E. I. du Pont de Nemours & Co.*

U.S. Supreme Court
351 U.S. 377 (1956)

DuPont's virtual monopoly of cellophane did display clear intent and high profits, but the majority chose to define the market broadly. The Court was soon defining markets much more closely (see Grinnell *and the merger cases below). What was the "correct" market boundary here?*

Reed, J.   The United States brought this civil action under § 4 of the Sherman Act against E. I. du Pont de Nemours and Company. The complaint . . . charged du Pont with monopolizing, attempting to monopolize, and conspiracy to monopolize interstate commerce in cellophane and cellulosic caps and bands in violation of § 2 of the Sherman Act. . . . After a lengthy trial, judgment was entered for du Pont on all issues. . . . The appeal, as specifically stated by the Government, "attacks only the ruling that du Pont has not monopolized trade in cellophane." At issue for determination is only this alleged violation by du Pont of § 2 of the Sherman Act.

During the period that is relevant to this action, du Pont produced almost 75 percent of the cellophane sold in the United States, and cellophane constituted less than 20 percent of all "flexible packaging material" sales.

. . . In considering what is the relevant market for determining the control of price and competition, no more definite rule can be declared than that commodities reasonably interchangeable by consumers for the same purposes make up that "part of the trade or commerce," monopolization of which may be illegal. As respects flexible packaging materials, the market geographically is nationwide.

. . . Cellophane costs more than many competing products and less than a few. But whatever the price, there are various flexible wrapping materials that are bought by manufacturers for packaging their goods in their own plants or are sold to converters who shape and print them for use in the packaging of the commodities to be wrapped.

Cellophane differs from other flexible packaging materials. From some it differs more than from others. The basic materials from which the wrappings are made and the advantages and disadvantages of the products to the packaging industry are summarized in Findings 62 and 63. They are aluminum, cellulose acetate, chlorides, wood pulp, rubber hydrochloride, and ethylene gas. It will adequately illustrate the similarity in characteristics of the various products by noting here Finding 62 as to glassine. Its use is almost as extensive as cellophane and many of its characteristics equally or more satisfactory to users.

It may be admitted that cellophane combines the desirable elements of transparency, strength, and cheapness more definitely than any of the others. . . .

But, despite cellophane's advantages, it has to meet competition from other materials in every one of its uses. . . . Food products are the chief outlet, with cigarettes next. The Government makes no challenge to Finding 283 that cellophane furnishes less than 7 percent of wrappings for bakery products, 25 percent for candy, 32 percent for snacks, 35 percent for meats and poultry, 27 percent for crackers and biscuits, 47 percent for fresh produce, and 34 percent for frozen foods. Seventy-five to 80 percent of cigarettes are wrapped in cellophane. Thus, cellophane shares the packaging market with others. The overall result is that cellophane accounts for 17.9 percent of flexible wrapping materials, measured by the wrapping surface. . . .

The facts above considered dispose also of any contention that competitors have been excluded by du Pont from the packaging material market. That market has many producers and there is no proof du Pont ever has possessed power to exclude any of them from the rapidly expanding flexible packaging market. . . . Nor can we say that du Pont's profits, while liberal (according to the Government 15.9 percent net after taxes on the 1937–47 average), demonstrate the existence of a monopoly without proof of lack of comparable profits during those years in other prosperous industries. Cellophane was a leader, over 17 percent, in the flexible packaging materials market. There is no showing that du Pont's rate of return was greater or less than that of other producers of flexible packaging materials. . . .

The "market" which one must study to determine when a producer has monopoly power will vary with the part of commerce under consideration. The tests are constant. That market is composed of products that have reasonable interchangeability for the purposes for which they are produced—price, use, and qualities considered. While the application of the tests remains uncertain, it seems to us that du Pont should not be found to monopolize cellophane when that product has the competition and interchangeability with other wrappings that this record shows.

On the findings of the District Court, its judgment is affirmed.

Warren, C.J., with whom Black and Douglas, JJ., join, dissenting:

. . . We cannot agree that cellophane, in the language of *Times-Picayune Publishing Co.* v. *United States*, 345 U.S. 594, 613, 73 S.Ct. 872, 883, 97 L.Ed. 1277, is "the self-same product" as glassine, grease-proof and vegetable parchment papers, waxed papers, sulphite papers, aluminum foil, cellulose acetate, and Pliofilm and other films.

If the conduct of buyers indicated that glassine, waxed and sulphite papers, and aluminum foil were actually "the self-same products" as cellophane, the qualitative differences demonstrated by the comparison of physical properties in Finding 59 would not be conclusive. But the record provides convincing proof that businessmen did not so regard these products. During the period covered by the complaint (1923–47) cellophane enjoyed phenomenal growth. Du Pont's 1924 production was 361,249 pounds, which sold for $1,306,662. Its 1947 production was 133,502,858 pounds, which sold for $55,339,626. Findings 297 and 337. Yet throughout this period the price of cellophane was far greater than that of glassine, waxed paper, or sulphite paper. Finding 136 states that in 1929 cellophane's price was seven times that of glassine; in 1934, four times, and in 1949 still more than twice glassine's price. Reference to DX–994, the graph upon which Finding 136 is based, shows that cellophane had a similar price relation to waxed paper and that sulphite paper sold at even less than glassine and waxed paper. We cannot believe that buyers, practical businessmen, would have bought cellophane in increasing amounts over a quarter of a century if close substitutes were available at from one seventh to one half cellophane's price. That they did so is testimony to cellophane's distinctiveness.

The inference yielded by the conduct by cellophane buyers is reinforced by the conduct of sellers other than du Pont. Finding 587 states that Sylvania, the only other cellophane producer, absolutely and immediately followed every du Pont price change, even dating back its price list to the effective date of du Pont's change. Producers of glassine and waxed paper, on the other hand, displayed apparent indifference to du Pont's repeated and substantial price cuts. DX–994 shows that from 1924 to 1932 du Pont dropped the price of plain cellophane 84 percent, while the price of glassine remained constant. And during the period 1933–46 the prices for glassine and waxed paper actually increased in the face of a further 21-percent decline in the price of cellophane. If "shifts of business" due to "price sensitivity" had been substantial, glassine and waxed paper producers who wanted to stay in business would have been compelled by market forces to meet du Pont's price challenge just as Sylvania was. . . .

Certainly du Pont itself shared our view. From the first, du Pont recognized that it need not concern itself with competition from other packaging materials. For example, when du Pont was contemplating entry into cellophane production, its development department reported that glassine "is so inferior that it belongs in an entirely different class and has hardly to be considered as a competitor of cellophane." This was still du Pont's view in 1950 when its survey of competitive prospects wholly omitted reference to glassine, waxed paper, or sulphite paper and stated that "Competition for du Pont cellophane will come from competitive cellophane and from noncellophane films made by us or by others."

. . . A confidential du Pont report shows that during the period 1937–47, despite great expansion of sales, du Pont's "operative return" (before taxes) averaged 31 percent, while its average "net return" (after deduction of taxes, bonuses, and fundamental research expenditures) was 15.9 percent. Such profits provide a powerful incentive for the entry of competitors.

Yet from 1924 to 1951 only one new firm, Sylvania, was able to begin cellophane production. And Sylvania could not have entered if La Cellophane's secret process had not been stolen. . . .

The foregoing analysis of the record shows conclusively that cellophane is the relevant market. Since du Pont has the lion's share of that market, it must have monopoly power, as the majority concede. This being so, we think it clear that, in the circumstances of this case, du Pont is guilty of "monopolization." The briefest sketch of du Pont's business history precludes it from falling within the "exception to the Sherman Act prohibitions of monopoly power" (majority opinion, 76 S.Ct. 1004) by successfully asserting that monopoly was "thrust upon" it. Du Pont was not "the passive beneficiary of a monopoly" within the meaning of

United States v. *Aluminum Co. of America, supra,* 148 F.2d at pages 429–30. It sought and maintained dominance through illegal agreements dividing the world market, concealing and suppressing technological information, and restricting its licensee's production by prohibitive royalties and through numerous maneuvers which might have been "honestly industrial" but whose necessary effect was nevertheless exclusionary. . . .

✳ 7

United States v. *Grinnell Corp.*

U.S. Supreme Court
384 U.S. 563 (1966)

> Grinnell *contrasts with* Cellophane: *The Warren Court grew more sensitive to the existence of significant market power.* Grinnell *was next acquired by ITT and then divested into genuinely competitive conditions in 1971. Its performance is reported to be sharply improved. But was the majority decision correct in defining the true market?*

Douglas, J.   This case presents an important question under § 2 of the Sherman Act, which makes it an offense for any person to "monopolize . . . any part of the trade or commerce among the several States." This is a civil suit brought by the United States against Grinnell Corporation (Grinnell), American District Telegraph Co. (ADT), Holmes Electric Protective Co. (Holmes) and Automatic Fire Alarm Co. of Delaware (AFA). . . .

Grinnell manufactures plumbing supplies and fire sprinkler systems. It also owns 76 percent of the stock of ADT, 89 percent of the stock of AFA, and 100 percent of the stock of Holmes. ADT provides both burglary and fire protection services; Holmes provides burglary services alone; AFA supplies only fire protection service. Each offers a central station service under which hazard-detecting devices installed on the protected premises automatically transmit an electric signal to a central station. The central station is manned 24 hours a day. Upon receipt of a signal, the central station, where appropriate, dispatches guards to the protected premises and notifies the police or fire department direct. There are other forms of protective services. But the record shows that subscribers to accredited central station service (i.e., that approved by the insurance underwriters) receive reductions in their insurance premiums that are substantially greater than the reduction received by the users of other kinds of protection service. In 1961 accredited companies in the central station service business grossed $65,000,000. ADT, Holmes, and AFA are the three largest companies in the business in terms of revenue: ADT (with 121 central stations in 115 cities) has 73 percent of the business; Holmes (with 12 central stations in three large cities) has 12.5 percent; AFA (with three central stations in three large cities) has 2 percent. Thus the three companies that Grinnell controls have over 87 percent of the business. . . .

ADT over the years reduced its minimum basic rates to meet competition and renewed contracts at substantially increased rates in cities where it had a monopoly of accredited central station service. ADT threatened retaliation against firms that contemplated inaugurating central station service. And the record indicates that, in contemplating opening a new central station, ADT officials frequently stressed that such action would deter their competitors from opening a new station in that area.

The offense of monopoly under § 2 of the Sherman Act has two elements: (1) the possession of monopoly power in the relevant market and (2) the willful acquisition or maintenance of that power as distinguished from growth or development as a consequence of a superior product, business acumen, or historic accident. We shall see that this second ingredient presents no major problem here, as what was done in building the empire was done plainly and explicitly for a single purpose. . . . In the present case, 87 percent of the accredited central station service business leaves no doubt that the congeries of these defendants have monopoly power—power which, as our discussion of the record indicates, they did not hesitate to wield—if that business is the relevant market. The only remaining question therefore is, what is the relevant market? . . .

The District Court treated the entire accredited central station service business as a single market, and we think it was justified in so doing. Defendants argue that the different central station services offered are so diverse that they cannot under *du Pont* be lumped together to make up the relevant market. For example, burglar alarm services are not interchangeable with fire alarm services. They further urge that *du Pont* requires that protective services other than those of the central station variety be included in the market definition.

But there is here a single use, i.e., the protection of property, through a central station that receives signals. It is that service, accredited, that is unique and that competes with all the other forms of property protection. We see no barrier to combining in a single market a number of different products or services where that combination reflects commercial realities. To repeat, there is here a single basic service—the protection of property through use of a central service station—that must be compared with all other forms of property protection. . . .

Burglar alarm service is in a sense different from fire alarm service; from waterflow alarms; and so on. But it would be unrealistic on this record to break down the market into the various kinds of central station protective services that are available. Central station companies recognize that to compete effectively they must offer all or nearly all types of service. The different forms of accredited central station service are provided from a single office and customers utilize different services in combination.

Fortas, J., with whom Stewart, J., joins, dissenting:

The trial court's definition of the "product" market even more dramatically demonstrates that its action has been Procrustean—that it has tailored the market to the dimensions of the defendants. It recognizes that a person seeking protective services has many alternative sources. It lists "watchmen, watchdogs, automatic proprietary systems confined to one site (often, but not always), alarm systems connected with some local police or fire station, often unaccredited CSPS [central station protective services], and often accredited CSPS." The court finds that even in the same city a single customer seeking protection for several premises may "exercise its option" differently for different locations. It may choose accredited CSPS for one of its locations and a different type of service for another.

But the court isolates from all of these alternatives only those services in which defendants engage. It eliminates all of the alternative sources despite its conscientious enumeration of them. Its definition of the "relevant market" is not merely confined to "central station" protective services, but to those central station protective services which are "accredited" by insurance companies.

There is no pretense that these furnish peculiar services for which there is no alternative in the market place, on either a price or a functional basis. The court relies solely upon its finding that the services offered by accredited central stations are of better quality, and upon its conclusion that the insurance companies tend to give "noticeably larger" discounts to policyholders who are accredited central station protective services. This Court now approves this strange red-haired, bearded, one-eyed man-with-a-limp classification.

I do not suggest that wide disparities in quality, price, and customer appeal could never affect the definition of the market. But this follows only where the disparities are so great that they create separate and distinct categories of buyers and sellers. The record here and the findings do not approach this standard. They fall far short of justifying the narrowing of the market as practiced here. I need refer only to the exclusion of nonaccredited central stations, which the court seeks to justify by reference to differentials in insurance discounts. This differential may indeed affect the relative cost to the consumer of the competing modes of protection. But, in the absence of proof that it results in eliminating the competing services from the category of those to which the purchaser "can practicably turn" for supplies, it does not justify their total exclusion. This sort of exclusion of the supposedly not-quite-so-attractive service from the basic definition of the kinds of business and service against which defendants' activity will be measured, is entirely unjustified on this record.

✳ 8

United States v. International Business Machines Corporation

U.S. District Court
for the Southern District of New York
Civil Action No. 69 CIV. 200

Filed on January 17, 1969, this briefly worded suit climaxed a three-year investigation and set up what may be the big Section 2 case of the 1970s. The alleged market share is about 70 percent: the plus is pervasive price discrimination. Trial finally began in 1975 and, in 1978, was only about half completed. If the case ran the full course, any remedy could take at least ten years more to be applied.

. . . IBM was originally organized as the Computer-Tabulating-Recording Co. and from 1911 to 1933 it owned a majority of the capital stock of, and controlled, The Tabulating Machine Company, a corporation organized in 1905 under the laws of the State of New Jersey. During this period IBM operated in the tabulating field through The Tabulating Machine Company, which was merged with IBM in 1933. The tabulating business continued to represent the major product line of IBM until the advent of the electronic computer in the 1950s.

11. In 1932 the United States filed a civil antitrust suit against IBM and Remington Rand, Inc., charging that they had unreasonably re-

strained and monopolized interstate trade and commerce in tabulating machines and tabulating cards by entering into agreements in which they agreed:

a. To lease only and not sell tabulating machines.
b. To adhere to minimum prices for the rental of tabulating machines as fixed by IBM.
c. To require customers to purchase their cards and requirements from the lessor or pay a higher price for the rental of machines.

The agreements between IBM and Remington Rand, Inc., were cancelled in 1934 prior to the trial of that suit, and the issues presented by the agreements were withdrawn from the case. The lease provision requiring the lessees to purchase cards from the lessor was adjudged to be illegal by this Court.

12. On January 21, 1952, the United States filed another civil antitrust suit against IBM charging that it had violated Sections 1 and 2 of the Sherman Act by attempting to monopolize and monopolizing interstate trade and commerce in the tabulating industry. The complaint alleged that IBM owned more than 90 percent of all the tabulating machines in the United States and manufactured and sold about 90 percent of all tabulating cards sold in the United States. This suit was terminated by the entry of a consent judgment by this Court on January 25, 1956. . . .

16. IBM's total revenues from the sale or lease of general purpose digital computers in the United States increased from $506,668,000 in 1961 to $2,311,353,000 in 1967. During this period of time IBM's share of total industry revenues of these products varied from approximately 69 percent to approximately 80 percent. In 1967 IBM's share of such revenues was approximately 74 percent. Its nearest competitor in 1967 had revenues of approximately $156,000,000 or 5 percent of the total.

17. Approximately 76 percent of the value of all general purpose digital computers shipped in the United States in 1967 were shipped by IBM while its two nearest competitors together accounted for about 8 percent of such shipments. At the end of the same year, approximately 67 percent of the value of all installed general purpose digital computers in the United States was represented by machines that had been manufactured by IBM.

18. IBM manufactures general purpose digital computers at its plants located in Poughkeepsie and Endicott, New York, and manufactures parts, components, and subassemblies at numerous other plants in the United States. Such computers and related products are shipped to customers located throughout the United States. . . .

20. Pursuant to and in furtherance of the aforesaid attempt to monopolize and the monopolization, the defendant has pursued a manufacturing and marketing policy that has prevented competing manufac-

turers of general purpose digital computers from having an adequate opportunity effectively to compete for business in the general purpose digital computer market and has done, among other acts, the following:

a.   Maintained a pricing policy whereby it quotes a single price for hardware, software, and related support and thereunder, (i) discriminated among customers by providing certain customers with extensive software and related support in a manner that unreasonably inhibited the entry or growth of competitors; and (ii) limited the development and scope of activities of an independent software and computer support industry as a result of which the ability of its competitors to compete effectively was unreasonably impaired.

b.   Used its accumulated software and related support to preclude its competitors from effectively competing for various customer accounts.

c.   Restrained and attempted to restrain competitors from entering or remaining in the general purpose digital computer market by introducing selected computers, with unusually low profit expectations, in those segments of the market where competitors had or appeared likely to have unusual competitive success, and by announcing future production of new models for such markets when it knew that it was unlikely to be able to complete production within the announced time.

d.   Dominated the educational market for general purpose digital computers, which was of unusual importance to the growth of competitors both by reason of this market's substantiality and by reason of its ultimate impact on the purchasing decisions in the commercial market, by granting exceptional discriminatory allowances in favor of universities and other educational institutions. . . .

✖ 9

Federal Trade Commission, In the matter of Xerox Corporation

Docket No. 8909
(Complaint, January 16, 1973[m] Decision, July 29, 1975)
Final Consent Order

The FTC's complaint against Xerox was issued in January 1973 and settled with remarkable speed in July 1975. A first proposed settlement was withdrawn after widespread criticism for being too weak. The final compromise sought to open up access to Xerox's patents, and it restricted certain forms of price discrimination. Should the FTC have been stricter, persevering for divestiture? Did the compromise help Savin and Canon to enter in 1976?

COMPLAINT

The Federal Trade Commission, having reason to believe that Xerox Corporation, hereinafter referred to as Xerox or respondent, has violated and is violating Section 5 of the Federal Trade Commission Act and that a proceeding in respect thereof would be in the public interest, issues this complaint, stating its charges as follows:

*   *   *   *   *

II. Respondent

Paragraph 2. Xerox is a corporation organized and existing under and by virtue of the laws of the State of New York, with its executive office located at Stamford, Conn. Respondent was incorporated in 1906 as the Haloid Company, and its name was changed to Haloid Xerox, Inc., in 1958 and to Xerox Corporation in 1961.

*   *   *   *   *

IV. Nature of Trade and Commerce

Par. 8. The relevant market is the sale and lease of office copiers in the United States, hereinafter referred to as the office copier market. This market includes as a relevant submarket the sale and lease of plain paper office copiers in the United States, hereinafter referred to as the plain paper submarket. The office copier market is dominated by the plain paper submarket, and Xerox dominates the plain paper submarket.

Par. 9. *(a)* In 1971, revenues from the sale and lease of office copiers were approximately $1.1 billion and total revenues from the sale and lease of office copiers and supplies were approximately $1.7 billion; Xerox accounted for approximately 86 percent of the former and 60 percent of the latter. In 1971, revenues from the sale and lease of plain paper copiers and supplies were approximately $1.0 billion; Xerox accounted for approximately 95 percent of said revenues.

*   *   *   *   *

VI. Violations

Par. 12. *(a)* Xerox has monopoly power in the relevant market and submarket.

(b) Xerox has the power to inhibit, frustrate, and hinder effective competition among firms participating in the relevant market and submarket.

Par. 13. Xerox has engaged in marketing acts, practices, and methods of competition including, but not limited to,

(a) Following a lease only policy pursuant to which Xerox refuses to sell and discourages the sale of its office copiers,

(b) Using package leasing plans and quantity discount rental price plans,

(c) Discriminating in price among customers,

(d) Maintaining a stock of depreciated copiers and planning to use or using such copiers to inhibit, frustrate, or hinder price competition,

(e) Announcing new copier models and taking orders thereon before availability of such copiers in response to introduction of competing copiers by actual or potential competitors,

(f) Requiring that it be the exclusive source of maintenance and repair service for leased Xerox office copiers,

(g) Falsely disparaging competitive supplies,

(h) Tying supplies to the lease of office copiers.

Par. 14. Xerox has engaged in acts, practices, and methods of competition relating to patents including, but not limited to,

(a) Monopolizing and attempting to monopolize patents applicable to office copiers,

(b) Maintaining a patent barrier to competition by attempting to re-create a patent structure which would be equivalent in scope to expired patents,

(c) Developing and maintaining a patent structure of great size, complexity, and obscurity of boundaries,

(d) Using its patent position to obtain access to technology owned by actual or potential competitors,

(e) Entering into cross-license arrangements with actual or potential competitors,

(f) Including in licenses under United States Patent Number 3,121,006 provisions having the effect of limiting licensees to the manufacture and sale of only coated paper copiers,

(g) Offering patent licenses applicable to plain paper copiers with provisions which, in effect, limit the licensee to the manufacture or sale of low speed copiers,

(h) Including in patent licenses provisions having the effect of precluding the licensee from utilizing Xerox patents in the office copier market,

(i) Entering into and maintaining agreements with Battelle Memorial Institute, Inc., and Battelle Development Corporation, Delaware corporations with principal offices at Columbus, Ohio, hereinafter referred to collectively as Battelle, pursuant to which Battelle is required to convey to Xerox all patents, patent applications, and know-how coming into its possession relative to xerography,

(j) Preventing actual and potential competitors from developing plain paper copiers while permitting them to develop coated paper copiers.

Par. 15. *(a)* For many years, and at least as of 1969, Rank Xerox was a substantial, viable, separate corporation capable of competing in the office copier market and plain paper submarket.

(b) Xerox has entered into and maintained agreements with Rank and Rank Xerox which have effectively divided up the world market for plain paper copiers among Xerox, Rank Xerox, and Fuji Xerox.

(c) In December 1969, Xerox acquired a 51-percent interest in Rank Xerox voting stock and continues to maintain such interest.

Par. 16. Xerox has engaged and is engaging in acts, practices, and methods of competition as hereinabove alleged for the purpose and with effect of

(a) Monopolizing the office copier market and the plain paper submarket,

(b) Preserving, maintaining, and furthering a highly concentrated market structure with high barriers to entry,

(c) Hindering, restraining, foreclosing, and frustrating competition in the office copier market and plain paper submarket and the entry of new competitors into said markets,

(d) Materially reducing the independence of Rank Xerox, the influence of Rank Xerox as a potential competitor and the probability that Rank Xerox would enter competition in the office copier market or plain paper submarket,

(e) Foreclosing Rank, Fuji, Rank Xerox, and Fuji Xerox from competing with Xerox in the Western Hemisphere, including the United States, and foreclosing Xerox from competing in export trade from the United States,

(f) Depriving consumers of the benefits of competition.

Par. 17. The aforesaid acts, practices, and methods of competition in commerce are unfair and constitute violations of Section 5 *(a)* of the Federal Trade Commission Act.

Decision and Order

*   *   *   *   *

Now in conformity with the procedure prescribed in Section 3.25(d) of its rules, the Commission hereby makes the following jurisdictional findings and enters the following order: . . .

That Xerox shall forthwith grant or cause to be granted to any person making written application to Xerox at any time under this order a nonexclusive license for the full unexpired term under any, some or all *order patents* to make, have made, use, or vend any, some, or all of the following:

(1) *Office copiers* (including the right to have made parts, components and raw materials for use therein), (2) toner, developer, paper, and similar consumable supplies, (3) toner, developer, paper, and similar consumable supplies which may be used in future office copiers, (4) containers (such as toner cartridges) for consumable supplies, and (5) photosensitive elements. However, at Xerox's option exercised on a nondiscriminatory basis, the effective date of licenses pertaining to *polychromatic color office copier products* may be up to three years from the date of issuance of this order for *present patents* and three years from the date the *patent* is *issued* for *future patents*. Nothing in any license granted pursuant to the terms of this order shall be deemed to prohibit a *licensee* from using a licensed *office copier* in conjunction with any other device for use in addition to the convenient reproduction of an original document.

III

Xerox, Rank Xerox, and Fuji Xerox shall agree not to sue any *licensee*, or customers or suppliers of the *licensee*, for *patent* infringement or royalties with respect to any *office copier*, photosensitive element, toner, developer, paper, or container (such as toner cartridges) for consumable supplies manufactured by or for the *licensee* prior to the date of issuance of this order, or to maintain any such suit.

IV

It is further ordered, That no license of an *order patent* granted pursuant to the terms of this order shall contain or be conditioned upon any restriction, except as hereinafter provided:

A. The *licensee* may, at his option, designate up to a total of three *order patents* which shall be licensed or sublicensed royalty-free; *Provided, however,* That in each country the *licensee* may substitute another *order patent* as royalty-free for any *order patent* previously designated as royalty-free which the *licensee* has discontinued using in that country. On *order patents* other than the three designated as royalty-free by the *licensee*, Xerox may, in its sole discretion, charge a royalty not to exceed ½ percent per patent up to a maximum accumulated royalty of 1½ percent of the *licensee's net revenues* for each *royalty-bearing product* which is manufactured, leased, or sold by or for the *licensee*. With respect to any *royalty-bearing product* of the *licensee* which the *licensee* uses or consumes himself, the royalty shall be computed on the basis of the *net revenues* that would have been received by the *licensee* in an ordinary commercial transaction. The royalty shall be computed separately for each *royalty-bearing product* on the basis of *order patents* subject to royalty which are used in such *royalty-bearing product*. In no event shall more than three royalty-free *patents* apply to any one *royalty-bearing product* at any one time irrespective of the number of licenses granted by Xerox with respect to such *royalty-bearing product*. For the purpose of this Paragraph IV A, a *patent* and all *Corresponding Patents* in all countries shall count as one *patent*. The *licensee* need not take a license under any *corresponding patent*.

B. Xerox may require that a *licensee* agree not to sue Xerox, Rank Xerox, or Fuji Xerox, or their customers or suppliers, for patent infringement or royalties with respect to any *office copier*, photosensitive element, toner, developer, paper, or container (such as toner cartridges) for consumable supplies manufactured by or for them prior to the date of issuance of this order, or to maintain any such suit.

C. To the extent the *licensee* has the power to grant licenses or sublicenses, Xerox may require the grant to Xerox, Rank Xerox, and Fuji Xerox of a nonexclusive license for the full unexpired term under any, some, or all *patents* of the *licensee* to make, have made, use, or vend any, some, or all of the following: *(a) office copiers* (including the right to have made parts, components, and raw materials for use therein), *(b)* toner, developer, paper, and similar consumable supplies, *(c)* toner, developer, paper, and similar consumable supplies which may be used in future *office copiers, (d)* containers (such as toner cartridges) for consumable supplies, and *(e)* photosensitive elements, as hereinafter provided in this Paragraph IV C.

(1) Xerox may (at any time) require the license of one *patent of the licensee* to Xerox, Rank Xerox, and Fuji Xerox for each Xerox *patent* licensed to the *licensee* in excess of the first three *order patents* licensed to the *licensee* but in so doing Xerox may not require the license of *(a)* a greater number of *present patents of the licensee* than the number of Xerox *present patents* licensed to the *licensee*, or *(b)* a greater number of *future*

patents of the *licensee* than the number of Xerox *future patents* licensed to the *licensee*. . . .

(2) The license of *present patents of the licensee* shall not become effective until four years after the date of issuance of this order or four years after an *office copier product* (of the *licensee* or its licensee) using an invention covered by the *patent* first becomes *commercially available*, whichever is later. The license of *future patents of the licensee* shall not become effective until four years after the date the *future patent of the licensee* is *issued* or four years after an *office copier product* (of the *licensee* or its licensee) using an invention covered by the *patent* first becomes *commercially available*, whichever is later. . . .

(4) Xerox may require a *licensee* to grant to Xerox, Rank Xerox, and Fuji Xerox a nonexclusive license under all *improvement patents* on Xerox *patents* licensed to the *licensee*. . . .

(5) Xerox shall grant to the *licensee* a nonexclusive license under all Xerox *improvement patents* on *patents* licensed to Xerox. . . .

(6) The *licensee* may charge Xerox, Rank Xerox, and Fuji Xerox a reasonable royalty for *patents* licensed to any or all of them pursuant to this order, computed on the basis of the *net revenues* of Xerox, Rank Xerox, and Fuji Xerox for each *royalty-bearing product* which they manufactured, leased or sold. . . .

(7) Xerox, Rank Xerox, and Fuji Xerox may require that they be permitted to sublicense any person in which they own, directly or indirectly, 50 percent or less, but not less than 20 percent of the voting stock if such *person* makes its *present* and *future patents* available for licensing pursuant to Paragraph II of this order. . . .

*   *   *   *   *

VII

It is further ordered, That:

A. During the period ending five years after the date of issuance of this order, Xerox shall make available to *licensees* of United States *order patents* under a license pursuant to the terms of this order who make written application therefor all *know-how* (1) in existence on the date of issuance of this order or (2) made available to any other *United States* manufacturer (except a supplier to Xerox) or *United States* marketer of *office copier products* for use in connection with such products during the five-year period. The delivery of the *know-how* requested shall begin within 30 days and shall be completed within 120 days after the initial application therefor is received by Xerox; the response to subsequent requests shall be completed within a reasonable period of time. Such *know-how* shall be of such a nature as to enable one skilled in manufacturing electromechanical office machinery and in the technologies embodied in *office copier products* or comparable technologies to manufacture, refurbish, recondition, and service Xerox Corporation's *office copier products*. . . .

* * * * *

X

It is further ordered, That for the period ending ten years after the date of issuance of this order, Xerox shall not, directly or indirectly, acquire from any *person* (including The Rank Organisation Limited and Fuji Photo Film Co., Ltd.) any exclusive rights, whether by license or otherwise to any *patents* or know-how for use in *office copier products* except those *(a)* resulting from the work of Xerox, Rank Xerox or Fuji Xerox employees, Xerox, Rank Xerox, or Fuji Xerox consultants, or research organizations doing sponsored research for Xerox, Rank Xerox, or Fuji Xerox, or *(b)* under which Xerox grants or causes to be granted to any *person* making written application a nonexclusive, royalty-free, unrestricted license to make, have made, use, or vend *office copier products* under such *patent* or know-how. . . .

XII

It is further ordered, That for the period ending ten years after the date of issuance of this order Xerox shall not, directly or indirectly, acquire any interest in a *person* (including The Rank Organisation Limited and Fuji Photo Film Co., Ltd.) engaged in the manufacture, sale, lease, or development of *office copiers*, or toner, developer, paper, or photosensitive elements used in *office copiers* or form a joint venture involving any such products with any such *person* (except The Rank Organisation Limited or Fuji Photo Film Co., Ltd. so long as either is a party to a joint venture with Xerox or Rank Xerox relating to *office copier products*). . . .

XIII

It is further ordered, That during the period ending ten years after the date of issuance of this order, Xerox shall not, directly or indirectly, make contracts in the *United States* restricting employees working in its *office copier products* business from in the future working for any other *person*, provided that Xerox may make contracts which prohibit the use or disclosure of trade secrets and confidential information as prohibited by Xerox's present form of "Proprietary Information and Conflict of Interest Agreement" which has been submitted to the Commission.

XIV

It is further ordered, That during the period commencing on a date not later than nine months after the date of issuance of this order and ending five years after said commencement date, Xerox shall not, directly or indirectly, utilize in the *United States* any price plan for the sale or lease of an *officer copier* which depends upon the customer purchasing or leasing one or more additional *office copiers* of a different model. Any minimum qualifying level for a pricing plan or price schedule respecting any *office copier* shall be based solely on volume, revenues, number of *office copiers,* or the like of the same model.

XV

It is further ordered, That:

A. During the period ending ten years after the date of issuance of this order, Xerox shall, in addition to instructing its employees in the *United States* not to comment on the quality of competitive toner or developer, place a notice in a location conspicuous to the key operator on each *office copier* sold or leased by it in the *United States* stating the following: "Xerox Corporation manufactures and distributes toner and developer for use in this machine. Other suppliers may also provide toner and developer for this machine. It may be necessary to adjust the machine to accommodate toner or developer which is provided by either Xerox or any other supplier."

B. In the event that Xerox shall publish reasonable specifications for the toner and developer used in a particular machine, Xerox (1) may include the following additional statement in the aforementioned notice: "The toner and developer used in this machine must comply with specifications published by Xerox Corporation," (2) shall promptly notify all suppliers of toner and developer who request such notification of any changes in such specifications and shall promptly notify a supplier when his toner or developer does not comply with such specifications in a letter signed by an officer of Xerox, and (3) may not require suppliers of toner or developer for Xerox's *office copiers* to provide to Xerox's customers a certification that the toner or developer supplied by them meets such specifications.

C. Xerox shall promptly notify all suppliers of toner and developer, who request such notification, of changes in Xerox *office copiers* which may affect the useability of the toner and developer in such *office copiers.*

D. Nothing herein contained shall prevent Xerox from advising a customer, in a letter signed by an officer of Xerox, that a non–Xerox toner or developer is not useable in a particular Xerox *office copier,* provided that Xerox simultaneously advises the supplier of such toner or developer in a letter signed by an officer of Xerox, that (1) in the opinion of Xerox, the supplier's toner or developer is not useable in a particular *office copier* model, and (2) disputes regarding the useability of the toner and developer are subject to arbitration pursuant to this order. Disputes regarding the useability of non–Xerox toner and developer or the reasonableness of Xerox specifications shall be subject to arbitration in accordance with Paragraph VIII *(b)* and *(c)* of this order.

E. Xerox may not, directly or indirectly, require in the *United States* that it be the sole supplier of toner or developer for leased or sold *office copiers;* however, it may impose such a requirement with respect to a new model during the six months from the date such model first becomes *commercially available.* For purposes of this Paragraph XV, "new model" includes collectively the basic *office copier* model and all subsequent models not embodying material variations in the xerographic processor thereof.

* * * * *

✳ 10

United States v. *American Telephone and Telegraph Company*

U.S. District Court for the
District of Columbia
Civil Action No. 74–1698 (1974)

This is probably the major Section 2 suit to be filed in the 1970s. It challenges a variety of structural forms and restrictive practices in the telecommunications sector, which is dominated by the Bell System. Though much of the sector is "regulated" as a "natural monopoly," many experts now urge that large parts are potentially quite competitive (only local-service switching is universally agreed to be a natural monopoly). The suit aims mainly at Western Electric's monopoly of equipment supply and at the Long Lines Departments' role. If carried through, it would breed competition both in (1) the supply of equipment to Bell companies and to customers, and in (2) the transmission of bulk message and data traffic among cities. Unless it is settled by compromise, the case is likely to come to trial after 1980 and take perhaps another decade or more to run its full course. It is reproduced in full here as a fine example of a brief complaint which—whatever its ultimate merit may be—casts a long shadow.

COMPLAINT

The United States of America, plaintiff, by its attorneys, acting under the direction of the Attorney General of the United States, brings this civil action to obtain equitable relief against the defendants named herein, and complains and alleges as follows:

I. Jurisdiction and Venue

1. This complaint is filed and this action is instituted under Section 4 of the Act of Congress of July 2, 1890, as amended (15 U.S.C. § 4), commonly known as the Sherman Act, in order to prevent and restrain the continuing violations by the defendants, as hereinafter alleged, of Section 2 of the Sherman Act (15 U.S.C. § 2).

2. Defendants American Telephone and Telegraph Company and Western Electric Company, Inc., transact business and are found within the District of Columbia.

II. The Defendants

3. American Telephone and Telegraph Company (hereinafter referred to as "AT&T") is made a defendant herein. AT&T is a corporation organized and existing under the laws of the State of New York, with its principal place of business in New York, New York. AT&T, directly and through subsidiaries, is engaged in providing telecommunications service and in the manufacture of telecommunications equipment.

4. Western Electric Company, Inc. (hereinafter referred to as "Western Electric"), is made a defendant herein. Western Electric is a corporation organized and existing under the laws of the State of New York with its principal place of business in New York, New York. Western Electric is engaged, directly and through subsidiaries, in the manufacture and supply of telecommunications equipment. Western Electric is a wholly-owned subsidiary of AT&T.

5. Bell Telephone Laboratories, Inc. (hereinafter referred to as "Bell Labs"), is made a defendant herein. Bell Labs is a corporation organized and existing under the laws of the State of New York, with its principal place of business in Murray Hill, New Jersey. Bell Labs is engaged in telecommunications research, development, and design work. Bell Labs is owned jointly by AT&T and Western Electric.

III. Co-Conspirators

6. Various other persons, firms and corporations not made defendants herein have participated as co-conspirators with the defendants in

the violations hereinafter alleged and have performed acts and made statements in furtherance thereof. Said co-conspirators include, but are not limited to, the following telephone companies:

Name of Corporation	Percentage of Voting Shares Owned by AT&T	Area Served
New England Telephone & Telegraph Company	85.4	Maine, Massachusetts, New Hampshire, Rhode Island, Vermont
The Southern New England Telephone Company	17.1	Connecticut
New York Telephone Company	100.0	New York, Connecticut
New Jersey Bell Telephone Company	100.0	New Jersey
The Bell Telephone Company of Pennsylvania	100.0	Pennsylvania
The Diamond State Telephone Company	100.0	Delaware
The Chesapeake and Potomac Telephone Company	100.0	Washington, D.C.
The Chesapeake and Potomac Telephone Company of Maryland	100.0	Maryland
The Chesapeake and Potomac Telephone Company of Virginia	100.0	Virginia
The Chesapeake and Potomac Telephone Company of West Virginia	100.0	West Virginia
Southern Bell Telephone and Telegraph Company	100.0	Florida, Georgia, North Carolina, South Carolina
South Central Bell Telephone Company	100.0	Alabama, Kentucky, Louisiana, Mississippi, Tennessee
The Ohio Bell Telephone Company	100.0	Ohio
Cincinnati, Bell, Incorporated	25.7	Ohio, Kentucky, Indiana
Michigan Bell Telephone Company	100.0	Michigan
Indiana Bell Telephone Company, Incorporated	100.0	Indiana

(continued on following page)

(continued)

Name of Corporation	Percentage of Voting Shares Owned by AT&T	Area Served
Wisconsin Telephone Company	100.0	Wisconsin
Illinois Bell Telephone Company	100.0	Illinois, Indiana
Northwestern Bell Telephone Company	100.0	Iowa, Minnesota, Nebraska, North Dakota, South Dakota
Southwestern Bell Telephone Company	100.0	Arkansas, Kansas, Missouri, Oklahoma, Texas, Illinois
The Mountain States Telephone and Telegraph Company	87.8	Arizona, Colorado, Idaho, Montana, New Mexico, Utah, Wyoming, Texas
Pacific Northwest Bell Telephone Company	89.2	Oregon, Washington, Idaho
The Pacific Telephone & Telegraph Company	89.7	California, Nevada

IV. Definitions

7. As used herein:

a. "Bell Operating Companies" shall mean the companies listed in paragraph 6 above and their subsidiaries.
b. "Bell System" shall mean AT&T and the Bell Operating Companies.
c. "Independent telephone companies" shall mean all telephone operating companies in the United States except the Bell Operating Companies.

V. Trade and Commerce

8. Telecommunications consists of the electronic and electromagnetic transmission of voice, data, and other communications by wire, cable, microwave radio, and communications satellite.

9. Telephone communication is the most common form of telecommunications service. Telephone service permits voice telephone communication between subscribers and includes among other services local exchange service for telephone calls between subscribers located within the same local telephone exchange area and long distance or "message toll service" for telephone calls between subscribers located in different exchange areas.

10. Local exchange service is provided by connecting all subscribers

in the same local exchange area through one or more central offices. Typically, wire pairs connect each subscriber to telephone company central office switching facilities in that exchange area.

11. Message toll service is provided by connecting central offices in different local exchange areas. The connection of these local exchange areas, through trunk lines and toll switching offices, permits long distance telephone service throughout the United States. Message toll service typically involves the transmission of telecommunications via microwave radio or coaxial cable between local telephone exchanges, with central office switching equipment in each local exchange area providing each subscriber access to the long distance toll network. The long distance toll network is a nationwide web of trunk lines and toll offices linking all of the telephone operating companies in the United States.

12. Telephone service in the United States is provided by the Bell System and by approximately 1,705 independent telephone companies. Telephone operating companies typically contract with subscribers for local exchange service, connecting the subscriber with the telephone company central office. Subscribers typically are charged installation fees and a monthly charge for service. The telephone companies retain title to the equipment installed and retain control over the equipment after service is terminated.

13. The Bell Operating Companies provide local telephone service in the 48 contiguous states. As of December 31, 1973, the Bell Operating Companies served approximately 113.2 million telephones, or approximately 82 percent of the nation's telephones. Approximately 1,705 independent telephone companies account for the remaining 18 percent of the nation's telephones. The AT&T's Long Lines Department provides interstate telephone service. For the year ending December 31, 1973, more than 90 percent of all interstate telephone calls in the United States were routed in whole or in part over Bell System facilities. In 1973 the Bell System's total revenue from telephone service was approximately $22 billion. The Bell System is by far the largest supplier of telephone service in the United States.

14. In addition to telephone service, telecommunications includes the transmission of data, facsimile, audio and video programming, and other specialized forms of telecommunications. Transmission of these specialized telecommunications may be accomplished over the same nationwide switched network which accommodates telephone service or over private lines.

15. Private line service involves the leasing of telecommunications circuits to subscribers with a high volume of communications requirements between specific locations. Private lines may be used for the transmission of voice, data, audio and video programming, and other specialized forms of telecommunications. Private line service may sim-

ply connect two points or may be switched between and among multiple points. A private line may be connected with the switched telephone network.

16. The Bell System provides intercity private line service for the transmission of voice, data, facsimile, audio and video programming, and other telecommunications. Private line services are also provided by Specialized Common Carriers, Miscellaneous Common Carriers and Domestic Satellite Carriers. Specialized Common Carriers, Miscellaneous Common Carriers and Domestic Satellite Carriers compete with the Bell System in providing private line service. Total revenue from private line service in 1973 was approximately $1.1 billion. In 1973 Bell System revenue from private line service was approximately $1 billion, or approximately 90 percent of total private line revenue. The Bell System is by far the largest supplier of private line service in the United States.

17. Although many organizations with substantial needs for long distance voice and data telecommunications purchase such services on a private line basis, some organizations construct and maintain private systems for the long distance transmission of voice, data, and other telecommunications.

18. Land mobile telecommunications consist of paging, dispatch, and mobile telephone service provided by radio communication. These services may be interconnected with the nationwide switched telephone system, permitting communication with telephone subscribers on both a local exchange and a message toll basis. Land mobile telecommunications are provided by Radio Common Carriers, independent telephone companies and the Bell Operating Companies.

19. Telecommunications equipment is used to provide telephone service and other telecommunications and includes terminal equipment, switching equipment, and transmission equipment. Terminal equipment is equipment used principally in telecommunications and installed at the premises of the subscriber. Switching equipment is equipment in local exchange central offices and toll offices used to route and switch telecommunications between subscribers. Transmission equipment is used to transmit telecommunications.

20. Until about 1968, telephone operating companies typically prohibited the interconnection of customer provided terminal equipment with telephone company facilities and, with limited exceptions, provided all the terminal equipment located on subscribers' premises. Telephone operating companies were thus the only significant purchasers of telecommunications terminal equipment.

21. Telephone subscribers and other telecommunications customers may provide their own terminal equipment and need not rely solely on the offerings of telephone operating companies. Customers may obtain terminal equipment from numerous manufacturers and suppliers, known collectively as the "interconnect industry."

22. Western Electric manufactures and supplies telecommunications equipment for the Bell System and is the largest manufacturer of telecommunications equipment in the United States. Western Electric's subsidiary, Teletype Corporation, manufactures teletypewriters and data transmission equipment. A substantial majority of the telecommunications transmission, switching and terminal equipment used by the Bell System is supplied by Western Electric. Although Western Electric also sells telecommunications equipment to government agencies, it typically does not sell equipment to independent telephone companies or other users of telecommunications equipment. In 1973, Western Electric's sales to the Bell System were $6.2 billion. Western Electric's total sales in 1973 were $7.0 billion. Western Electric is by far the largest supplier, and the Bell System is by far the largest purchaser, of telecommunications equipment in the United States.

23. AT&T provides services to each Bell Operating Company pursuant to agreements known as "License Contracts." Under these agreements AT&T undertakes to maintain arrangements whereby telephones and related equipment may be manufactured under patents owned or controlled by AT&T and may be purchased by each Operating Company for use within a specified territory; to prosecute research in telephony continuously and to make available to the Operating Company benefits derived therefrom; and to furnish advice and assistance with respect to virtually all phases of the Operating Company's business. The License Contracts, or supplementary agreements in the case of four Operating Companies, provide that AT&T will maintain connections between each licensee's telephone system and the systems of the other Bell Operating Companies, and provide for joint use of certain rights-of-way and facilities. Supplementary agreements cover the sharing of revenues derived by AT&T and the Bell Operating Companies from interstate and foreign services.

24. Western Electric manufactures and supplies equipment to AT&T and each Bell Operating Company pursuant to agreements known as "Standard Supply Contracts." Under these agreements as supplemented, Western Electric agrees, upon the order of each Operating Company and to the extent reasonably required for the latter's business, to manufacture materials or to purchase and inspect materials manufactured by others and to sell these materials to the Operating Company. Western Electric also agrees to maintain stocks at distribution points, to prepare equipment specifications, to perform installations of materials, and to repair, sell, or otherwise dispose of used materials. Under each agreement Western Electric's prices and terms are to be as low as to its most favored customers for like materials and services under comparable conditions.

25. Bell Labs conducts telecommunications research and development for Western Electric and the Bell System. Owned jointly by AT&T

and Western Electric, Bell Labs' 1974 budget for telecommunications research and development exceeded $500 million. Bell Labs maintains its principal laboratories in Murray Hill, Holmdel, and Whippany, New Jersey, and Naperville, Illinois, and additional facilities in seven other states. Bell Labs is by far the largest telecommunications research and development facility in the United States.

26. AT&T, directly and through subsidiaries, regularly transmits voice, data, and other telecommunications across state lines to customers located throughout the United States. Western Electric, directly and through subsidiaries, manufactures telecommunications equipment at locations in many states and regularly sells and ships such equipment across state lines to customers located throughout the United States. Bell Labs conducts telecommunications research and development at locations in many states and regularly disseminates the results of such research and development to consumers thereof throughout the United States. AT&T, Western Electric, and Bell Labs have been and are engaged in interstate commerce.

VI. Violations Alleged

27. For many years past and continuing up to and including the date of the filing of this complaint, the defendants and co-conspirators have been engaged in an unlawful combination and conspiracy to monopolize, and the defendants have attempted to monopolize and have monopolized the aforesaid interstate trade and commerce in telecommunications service and submarkets thereof and telecommunications equipment and submarkets thereof in violation of Section 2 of the Sherman Act. Defendants are continuing and will continue these violations unless the relief hereinafter prayed for is granted.

28. The aforesaid combination and conspiracy to monopolize has consisted of a continuing agreement and concert of action among the defendants and co-conspirators, the substantial terms of which have been and are:

a.   That AT&T shall achieve and maintain control over the operations and policies of Western Electric, Bell Labs, and the Bell Operating Companies;

b.   That the defendants and co-conspirators shall attempt to prevent, restrict, and eliminate competition from other telecommunications common carriers;

c.   That the defendants and co-conspirators shall attempt to prevent, restrict, and eliminate competition from private telecommunications systems;

d.   That Western Electric shall supply the telecommunications equipment requirements of the Bell System;

e. That defendants and co-conspirators shall attempt to prevent, restrict, and eliminate competition from other manufacturers and suppliers of telecommunications equipment.

29. Pursuant to and in effectuation of the aforesaid combination and conspiracy to monopolize, attempt to monopolize, and monopolization, the defendants, among other things, have done the following:

a. Attempted to obstruct and obstructed the interconnection of Specialized Common Carriers with the Bell System.
b. Attempted to obstruct and obstructed the interconnection of Miscellaneous Common Carriers with the Bell System.
c. Attempted to obstruct and obstructed the interconnection of Radio Common Carriers with the Bell System.
d. Attempted to obstruct and obstructed the interconnection of Domestic Satellite Carriers with the Bell System.
e. Attempted to obstruct and obstructed the interconnection of customer provided terminal equipment with the Bell System.
f. Refused to sell terminal equipment to subscribers of Bell System telecommunications service.
g. Caused Western Electric to manufacture substantially all of the telecommunications equipment requirements of the Bell System.
h. Caused the Bell System to purchase substantially all of its telecommunications equipment requirements from Western Electric.

VII. Effects

30. The aforesaid violations have had the following effects, among others:
a. Defendants have achieved and maintained a monopoly of telecommunications service and submarkets thereof and telecommunications equipment and submarkets thereof in the United States.
b. Actual and potential competition in telecommunications service and submarkets thereof and telecommunications equipment and submarkets thereof has been restrained and eliminated.
c. Purchasers of telecommunications service and telecommunications equipment have been denied the benefits of a free and competitive market.

PRAYER

Wherefore, plaintiff prays:

1. That the Court adjudge and decree that defendants have combined and conspired to monopolize, have attempted to monopolize, and have monopolized interstate trade and commerce in telecommunications ser-

vice and submarkets thereof and telecommunications equipment and submarkets thereof in violation of Section 2 of the Sherman Act.

2. That each of the defendants, their officers, directors, agents, employees, and all persons, firms, or corporations acting on behalf of defendants or any one of them be perpetually enjoined from continuing to carry out, directly or indirectly, the aforesaid combination and conspiracy to monopolize, attempt to monopolize, and monopolization of the aforesaid interstate trade and commerce in telecommunications service and equipment and that they be perpetually enjoined from engaging in or participating in practices, contracts, agreements, or understandings, or claiming any rights thereunder, having the purpose or effect of continuing, reviving, or renewing any of the aforesaid violations or any violations similar thereto.

3. That defendant AT&T be required to divest all of its capital stock interest in Western Electric.

4. That defendant Western Electric be required to divest manufacturing and other assets sufficient to insure competition in the manufacture and sale of telecommunications equipment.

5. That defendant AT&T be required, through divestiture of capital stock interests or other assets, to separate some or all of the Long Lines Department of AT&T from some or all of the Bell Operating Companies, as may be necessary to insure competition in telecommunications service and telecommunications equipment.

6. That pursuant to Section 5 of the Sherman Act the Court order summons to be issued to Bell Telephone Laboratories, Inc., commanding it to appear and answer the allegations contained in this Complaint and to abide and perform such orders and decrees as the Court may make in the premises.

7. That the plaintiff have such other and further relief as the nature of the case may require and as the Court may deem just and proper.

8. That the plaintiff recover the costs of this action.

Bro Uttal

✒ 11
If Ma Bell Is Broken Up*

Breaking up AT&T has become something of a preoccupation in Washington. The Justice Department is pushing the idea in an antitrust suit, FCC officials keep bringing it up from time to time, and last month members of the House communications subcommittee came out for splitting up the company too. The Bell System vigorously opposes the notion, but in light of its current marketing problems, divestiture may be just what the company needs.

Ever since the FCC allowed competitors into the telecommunications markets in the 60s, AT&T has been learning how hard it is to operate simultaneously in monopoly and competitive markets. The state regulatory process, which once protected the company against competition, now hinders its marketing efforts. When Bell files tariffs for new products, competitors howl that the rates are subsidized by profits from the monopoly business. Though Bell can continue to sell in most states while the question is being debated, potential customers may hesitate to order the product because they don't know what the final rates will be. Meanwhile, competitors who have pored over the tariff filing's elaborate description of the product's price and performance have plenty of opportunity to respond.

Two years ago, for example, Bell filed tariffs for its Dimension switchboard in 48 states. Hearings were ordered in 33 of them. By the time final decisions came down from most regulators, competitors had already launched superior switchboards at lower prices.

AT&T could reduce its regulatory troubles by divesting itself of Western Electric, say, by spinning off the $8-billion manufacturing arm to shareholders. If Western Electric were independent and therefore unregulated, it would not only be relieved of regulatory delays but also have more freedom to experiment with pricing schemes. The company might even start selling equipment to users, which makes little sense as long as it is owned by AT&T and its equipment goes into the parent's rate base. And it could start offering computer equipment, which as a part of AT&T it is now forbidden to do by a 1956 consent decree.

Fortune magazine, July 17, 1978, p. 104. Bro Uttal is a staff writer for *Fortune*.

Federal regulation of interstate transmission is a more tangled subject. It is almost impossible to determine a fair price for competitive private line services because they share facilities and personnel with monopoly services and the costs attributable to each are hard to separate. Incredible as it may seem, the FCC has been trying to determine a fair price for private line service for 18 years, without success, meanwhile limiting the extent to which AT&T could market some of its offerings. Every private line tariff the company has filed has run into trouble at the commission or in the courts.

Bell hopes to solve the problem by the 1980s, when it finishes putting in a $70-million computerized accounting system that will make routine cost allocations to different services. But since many allocations must be arbitrary, competitors can still have a field day at the FCC. If AT&T were to split off its competitive transmission services by putting them into an independently managed subsidiary, it could avoid those interminable cost-allocation hassles. John Eger, former director of the Office of Telecommunications Policy in the White House, says that idea "should be so appealing to AT&T that it would voluntarily restructure itself."

✻ 12

Berkey Photo, Inc. v. *Eastman Kodak Co.*
U.S. District Court, So. Dist. of N.Y.
No. 73 Civ. 424 (MEF)
Trade Reg. Reporter, June 26, 1978, 62.092.
Memorandum on Post-Trial Motions

This is an important example of a private antitrust suit against a dominant firm. Berkey sued Kodak in 1973, charging that it had been severely damaged by a number of anticompetitive actions by Kodak. In a jury trial, Berkey won in 1978, primarily on the count that Kodak had introduced certain new products in ways which deliberately excluded competition and increased its monopoly power. The judge clarified the issues and set the damages in a June 1978 opinion, which is briefly excerpted here. Berkey was to receive $81 million (27 million, tripled), but divestiture and other severe actions were ruled out. Was Kodak guilty in your opinion? Do the remedies make economic sense?

Frankel, D. J.   Defendant has moved under F. R. Civ. P. 50(b) for judgment notwithstanding the jury's verdicts. Plaintiff has moved for numerous and detailed kinds of injunctive relief, including some divestitures, provisions for predisclosure, and various restrictions on Kodak's business procedures and practices. It is convenient to treat both motions together and to record some pertinent observations on both in this single memorandum.

I. DEFENDANT'S MOTION FOR JUDGMENT N. O. V.

Many of the issues canvassed in the briefs on this motion were considered at length during the trial, in conversations on the record, and the resolutions reached by the court are largely reflected in the charges to the jury. . . . [T]he court will limit its observations herein to a relatively few matters of possible further interest. On the claims with respect to which the motion is being granted, the result of which will be to reduce the total award from $37,620,130 to $27,154,700, the court will of course state the reasons why the jury's verdict is found now to be vulnerable to this extent.

110 Cameras

The largest single item of damages awarded by the jury was for Berkey's lost profits, $15,250,000, resulting from Kodak's unlawful monopolization and attempt to monopolize the amateur camera market. The predominant part of the evidence supporting this claim dealt with the introduction of the 110 camera line as part of a interdependent photographic products, without prior disclosure to competing camera manufacturers of the information about the new Kodacolor II film format that would have enabled these other manufacturers to enter the market at about the same time as, and compete on the merits with, Kodak's initial line of 110 cameras.

. . . [T]he jury undoubtedly found that defendant resolved some years before the 110 introduction to introduce the new camera and film, made to work with each other and designed to displace with overwhelming suddenness huge segments of the market for 126 cameras. Defendant's responsible executives determined that the simultaneity of these introductions was to be the key weapon against competitors, brushing aside technical objections that the new film was unsatisfactory, inferior to the predecessor Kodacolor X in vital respects, and requiring further research and development to become a satisfactory product. The paramount strategy and goal were thus to use the film monopoly—Kodak's power in a field where its market share consistently exceeded 80%—as a lever for suddenly swelling defendant's power in the camera market, achieving there at least a temporary total monopoly of a vital new segment to be created by the system introduction. Some "responsible persons" within Kodak urged unsuccessfully that predisclosure concerning the new film format be given to camera competitors (as well as photofinishers and photofinishing equipment makers) so that they would not suffer in one blow the instant obsolescence of inventories and work in progress and the inability to compete at all with their cameras in the terrain of the newly announced system. The 110 announcement came substantially as a surprise, following some minimal predisclosures, for a price, two or three months earlier. And these events, it is worth mentioning, followed hard after a magicube coup in June of 1970, when Kodak gained a similar advantage of surprise and temporary exclusivity from what the jury found, and the court entirely agrees, was an unlawful combination in restraint of trade with Sylvania.

Without dwelling further on the facts of a huge record leading to the jury's award, the court refers briefly to some recurrent arguments defendant has pressed on this subject and sketches the reasons why they have been and are once again rejected.

1. The claim of immunity per se for product introductions

Throughout the case, defendant has urged, and it urges once more, that a company's introduction of a new product—though the company be a huge one like Kodak with monopoly power in a mosaic of interconnected markets and though the introduction be designed deliberately to employ monopoly power in one market to create or enhance such power in another—must "as a matter of law" be immune from attack under the antitrust laws. If this is sound law, defendant should indeed be relieved of the verdict with respect to 110 camera damages. The court remains persuaded, however, that there is no such enclave for "product introductions" and that the mode, purpose, and impact of product introductions may, as in this case, play central parts in findings of unlawful monopolization and attempts to monopolize, no less than other, ordinarily lawful and "normal" business activities like leasing rather than selling machinery, *United States* v. *United Shoe Machinery Co.* [1953 Trade Cases ¶ 67,436], 110 F. Supp. 295, 344 (D. Mass. 1953), aff'd per curiam [1954 Trade Cases ¶ 67,755], 347 U.S. 521 (1954), the creation of useful resources for added productive capacity, *United States* v. *Aluminum Co. of America* [1944–1945 Trade Cases ¶ 57,342], 148 F. 2d 416, 430–31 (2d Cir. 1945), or the discount offered on used equipment and the adoption of separate charges for separate services condemned as exclusionary in *Greyhound Computer Corp.* v. *International Business Machines Corp.* [1977–2 Trade Cases ¶ 61,603], 559 F. 2d 488, 499–503 (9th Cir. 1977), cert. denied, 46 U. S. L. W. 3453 (1978).

*   *   *   *   *

. . . [T]he evidence reveals a monopolist in one market (film) engineering that power to thrust itself into a monopoly position in a second market (cameras). The result was a world away from being "economically inevitable," *United Shoe*, 110 F. Supp. at 345; it was plainly avoidable, and the means Kodak chose to employ were plainly to be shunned.

Kodak's complaint at root is that it faces liability for conduct which other business firms, lacking monopoly power, engage in regularly with impunity. Even if the factual premise were to be credited, the short answer is that the antitrust laws do not permit willful maintenance of monopoly power by conduct that might for a company without such power be deemed "honestly industrial." *Alcoa, supra*, 148 F. 2d at 431; *United Shoe, supra*, 110 F. Supp. at 344. The present case illustrates the now settled rule that "[t]here are kinds of acts which would be lawful in the absence of monopoly but because of their tendency to foreclose competitors from access to markets or customers or some other inherently anticompetitive tendency are unlawful under § 2 if done by a monopolist. . . ." *Sargent-Welch Scientific Co.* v. *Ventron Corp.* (1977–2 Trade Cases ¶ 61,761], 567 F. 2d 701, 711–12 (7th Cir. 1977).

2. Predisclosure

Plaintiff's theory on the camera monopoly claim included the contention that if defendant had given them advance information about the size and other pertinent qualities of the new Kodacolor II film, other camera manufacturers, including plaintiff, could have geared up to be ready to compete on the merits with Kodak in offering cameras suitable for use with the new film. . . .

Without disputing the foregoing facts and others from which the jury could have found the 110 introduction a scheme contrived almost wholly to crush competitors, and scarcely or not at all to compete by serving consumers better, defendant preserves its position that failure to predisclose could not as a matter of law go before the jury as a possibly material factor. The argument, characteristically robust and uncompromising, is that "the law," according to Kodak, "leaves to Kodak, acting in its own commercial interest, the decision when and how to bring its products to market."

That extends the line Kodak has sought to have drawn throughout the case. The court adheres to the view that defendant is in error. Again, the court perceives the principles of the Sherman Act and the pertinent precedents as demanding a frequently subtle, inevitably comprehensive appraisal of actions by a company like Kodak wielding enormous monopoly power. Given such power, we were reminded not long ago, it becomes an essential question whether the evidence shows "the willful acquisition or maintenance of that power as distinguished from growth or development as a consequence of a superior product, business acumen, or historic accident" *United States* v. *Grinnell Corp.* [1966 Trade Cases ¶ 71,789], 384 U. S. 563, 570–71 (1966). . . .

*   *   *   *   *

Kodacolor II photofinishing damages

The jury found on unquestionably sufficient evidence that defendant had used its film monopoly—itself unlawfully maintained, as the jury also found—to injure plaintiff as a photofinisher. Under the court's charge, it was essential to this finding that the jury condemned "Kodak's mode of introducing the 110 system without predisclosure to photofinishers . . . [as] exclusionary or anticompetitive conduct unlawful affecting Berkey and other competing photofinishers. . . ." That determination emerged from circumstances that included a pattern of dealing with photofinishers by which Kodak kept these enterprises relatively small, numerous, dependent upon Kodak, subject to shocks and shifts of their business resulting from sudden changes in Kodak's film operations and almost inevitably inferior to, and less informed than, Kodak's own Color Print and Processing organization ("CP&P").

Without disputing the factual basis for this finding of liability and the award of $55,700 in damages for this, defendant argues two grounds of law for setting aside this portion of the verdict:

(1) That the failure to predisclose, notwithstanding the circumstances in which it was shown, could not in law be a basis for liability.

(2) That the finding of illegality cannot stand in the face of the jury's findings that Kodak had neither monopolized nor attempted to monopolize the photofinishing market.

The legal issue as to predisclosure, though its factual cast is different, is largely the same in this connection as in the dispute about 110 cameras. Like the camera manufacturers, photofinishers lived under the shadow and at the mercy of Kodak's omnipotent film monopoly. Like defendant's camera manufacturing division, its processing organization was secretly informed, and specially prepared, to process the new film promptly after its arrival on the market. Other finishers were left to scramble to catch up; were offered only equipment markedly inferior to CP&P's; continued to be kept ignorant of technical facts and developments needed for maximally effective performance of the finishing service, were barred from competing while CP&P enjoyed a temporary monopoly; and had to watch helplessly as CP&P's reputation for preeminence was enhanced, not only by being first and best informed, but also by being needed for some time to process the other finishers' Kodacolor II orders and by being enabled to employ this opportunity to stuff these competitors' return envelopes to customers with Kodak CP&P advertising literature. Once more, the general proposition that predisclosure of new products is not required is subject to modification, as the jury found, when it is tested by circumstances of market power like Kodak's capable of paralyzing impacts upon adjoining sectors of the economy.

*   *   *   *   *

Film Overcharges

Two substantial contentions by defendant concerning the film over-charge award of $11,500,000 merit attention here. First, defendant says that conceding *arguendo* the evidence showed use of its monopoly power in film to extend its power over *other* markets (cameras, photofinishing, etc.), there was not evidence of anticompetitive conduct to maintain or employ the film monopoly itself, and this precludes any recovery for allegedly excessive film prices. The court assumes for present purposes that a showing of anticompetitive conduct *affecting the film market* was essential to Berkey's case. Accepting this assumption, Kodak's argument does not prevail.

Defendant correctly describes as a central theme in Berkey's case the attacks on the use of Kodak film power for leveraging in other markets. There was also ample evidence, however, of anticompetitive actions serving to maintain the steadily huge share Kodak enjoyed of the film market. Without exploring or necessarily accepting all the kinds of conduct plaintiff would characterize in this way, the court notes two solidly proved items as sufficient. Probably the more important one was the carefully contrived introduction and promotion of the 110 system, already treated in considering the camera monopoly. . . .

The remaining course of conduct to be noted here was the persistent and continued practice of CP&P to offer processing services only for Kodak films. While the CP&P monopoly in color film processing was ended by the consent decree of 1954, this Kodak organization was shown to remain the "prestige" photofinisher. The residual advantages of its extended past monopoly, its special access to the film monopolist's secrets, and its possession of the preeminent name in the industry place it at a strategic gateway affecting the acceptance and salability of any competitor's, or potential competitor's, amateur film. The network of retailers employing CP&P and otherwise wedded to Kodak were surely discouraged from stocking others' films when the esteemed and powerful CP&P organization would not handle it. The urge to compete by effective service and increased sales is so characteristic a pressure in American business that CP&P personnel requested the freedom to process non–Kodak film.

Tests conducted by Kodak's Photographic Technology Division showed that non–Kodak film could be processed through the same solutions with good results and without adverse effects on the Kodak film. But Kodak's management unswervingly rejected the pleas. And the record supports plaintiff's thesis that the purpose and effect were to impede the efforts of competitors in film manufacturing.

*   *   *   *   *

Stated more fully, the rule on which the verdict rests in this respect is that where a defendant

a.   Has monopoly power in a relevant market,
b.   Has acquired or maintained this power by anticompetitive conduct, and
c.   Has employed its monopoly power to charge a price higher than what a competitive market price was or would have been,

a purchaser required to pay the monopoly price may recover the excess.

*   *   *   *   *

Color Print Paper Overcharges

The jury awarded $8,803,000 for color print paper overcharges. The court is compelled to conclude that this award must be set aside in its entirety because the evidence upon further study is found to be insufficient to sustain either the finding of liability or the award of damages.

The finding that Kodak monopolized the market in color paper would seem to be amply supported so far as the element of market power is concerned. Defendant's share of this market ranged during the years in question from a high of 91 percent in 1969 down to a low of 60 percent in 1976. It also appeared that the disappearance of a substantial competitor, GAF, in 1977 foretold a reversal of the downward trend. While the rather steep decline in the period 1969–76 may be some reflection of a market no longer monopolized, the 60 percent figure would remain sufficient to uphold the jury's verdict in this respect.

The fatal void in the evidentiary foundation is the required proof of exclusionary or anticompetitive conduct. Plaintiff has struggled with characteristic vigor and imagination to show that the necessary demonstration was made. But the court's restudy of the arguments and the evidence invoked to support them leads to the adverse conclusion stated at the outset. A single item of anticompetitive behavior seems sustainable, namely, the insistence by defendant that its backprint appear on paper sold to photofinishers. But this is insufficient, the court concludes, to sustain the verdicts on liability and damages, or either of them. . . .

II. APPLICATION FOR EQUITABLE RELIEF

Plaintiff has applied for a broad array of equitable remedies, from divestiture through the publication of notice of the judgment. The subject has been thoroughly argued. The issues have been studied with care. For reasons hereinafter outlined, the court has concluded that all but two of the items of proposed equitable relief should be denied.

Divestiture

The most drastic form of equitable relief sought by plaintiff is an order of divestiture. Specifically, plaintiff asks that Kodak be stripped of (1) its facilities for manufacturing cameras, projectors, photofinishing equipment, and "related items of equipment," (2) its facilities for the commercial processing and printing of film, and (3) such trademarks as "Kodak," "Kodacolor," and other scarcely less powerful names.

Whether divestiture may be ordered as a species of the "injunctive relief" authorized by section 16 of the Clayton Act, 15 U. S. C. § 26, is a vexed question. Even in a case of unlawful acquisitions, the Ninth Circuit has said no, *Int'l Tel. & Tel. Corp.* v. *Gen. Tel. & Elec. Corp.* [1975–1 Trade Cases ¶ 60,291], 518 F. 2d 913, 920 et seq. (1975), and the Third Circuit, more favorably disposed, has indicated that it would require a strong case to make that remedy seem appropriate, *NBO Industries Treadway Cos.* v. *Brunswick Corp.* [1975–2 Trade Cases ¶ 60,479], 523 F. 2d 262, 278–279 (1975), rev'd on other grounds *sub nom. Brunswick Corp.* v. *Pueblo Bowl-O-Mat, Inc.* [1977–1 Trade Cases ¶ 61,255], 429 U. S. 477 (1977). A thoughtful opinion by Judge Ward of this Court has also indicated that divestiture might be available to undo acquisitions in violation of Clayton Act § 7. *Fuchs Sugars & Syrups, Inc.* v. *Amstar Corporation* [1975–2 Trade Cases ¶ 60,568], 402 F. Supp. 636 (1975). There is a spread of other opinions on the subject. See *NBO Industries, supra,* 523 F. 2d at 278 n. 17.

In the instant case, however, the case against divestiture seems too clear to require a firm choice among the divergent precedents. Accepting, as the court does, all the pertinent findings upon which the jury proceeded, this is not a case of unlawful acquisitions. The facilities plaintiff seeks to have stripped from Kodak are long established and integral parts of the organization unquestionably devoted in large measure for many years to constructive and lawful ends. The trademarks are likewise valuable, longstanding, and lawfully usable in diverse ways far transcending the boundaries of this particular lawsuit. The pertinent injuries to plaintiff, assuming they were not amply remedied by the award of substantial damages, and their recurrence not deterred by the effect of the award, *Brunswick Corp.* v. *Pueblo Bowl-O-Mat, Inc.* [1977–1 Trade Cases ¶ 61,255], 429 U. S. 477, 485 (1977), could not justify the devastating remedy of divestiture, which would, in all the circumstances, be punitive rather than appropriately curative. See *Hartford-Empire Co.* v. *United States* [1944–1945 Trade Cases ¶ 57,319], 323 U. S. 386, 409 (1945).

Concerning CP&P

As an alternative to divestiture of CP&P, Berkey seeks requirements that Kodak disclose to photofinishers information that has heretofore been given first, or only, to CP&P, thus giving the latter temporary or permanent advantages over other photofinishers.

The prayer rests upon a verdict embodying findings, *inter alia*, that defendant has used its film monopoly unlawfully "to foreclose competition, to gain a competitive advantage, or to destroy a competitor" in the market for photofinishing services. . . .

*   *   *   *   *

All of these are items which reflect the use of Kodak's monopoly power in film or color print paper to handicap competitors and discourage competition in photofinishing. It is plain that Berkey has a very real stake in the future conduct of Kodak's film and paper operations which have been used in the past to give unfair and improper advantages over competitors to CP&P. The record supports the conclusion that Kodak will, unless enjoined, continue to engage in conduct of this sort. The problem is rooted in the structure of Kodak, where the film, paper, and processing operations are ultimately part of a single corporation. Believing divestiture to be uncalled for here, but convinced that a remedial scheme with lasting impact is needed, the court has given serious consideration to Berkey's proposals for elaborate disclosure requirements.

The details of Berkey's proposals reflect the complexities of relationships in an area of complex technology. They also lead to instant awareness of how troublesome it would be for Kodak to share its developmental secrets in this fashion with 600 or more photofinishers spread across the length and breadth of the land. A problem of balancing seems to emerge.

Having employed its spectrum of monopoly powers to keep photofinishers subservient, frequently uninformed of vital things known to CP&P, and subject to the disruptive shocks of sudden change followed by belated clues for adaptation, Kodak is properly called upon to remedy this course of conduct affecting Berkey and other photofinishers in the future. The demand is specially compelling in light of the 1954 decree, which appears to have been frustrated, at least in spirit, by Kodak's practice of favoring CP&P. If the remedy can be achieved, however, without undue injury to Kodak, that course should be pursued.

The court concludes that the simplest and most readily manageable technique will be for Kodak to treat all photofinishers, including CP&P, alike in relevant respects. This will leave to Kodak power to disclose or not, but deprive it of the power to confer unfair and anticompetitive advantages upon CP&P. While it might seem superficially unrealistic, the record of this case contains persuasive evidence that Kodak is able, when this is desired, to maintain walls of secrecy between its various components. Accordingly, the decree will contain a requirement that defendant make no disclosures to CP&P concerning new or modified films, color print paper, processing chemistry, cameras, projectors, or photofinishing equipment without making identical disclosures to all other photofinishers with which it does business. Though this is simply stated here, the precise details of the decretal language, and any appropriate qualifiers will, of course, be the subject of further consultations with counsel. . . .

B. MERGERS

The three kinds of mergers—horizontal, vertical, and conglomerate—are often mixed in actual mergers. They are under the same policy test: Will the merger tend substantially to reduce competition in any significant market? If any "significant" market can be defined in which the merger will reduce competition, the merger is illegal.

Yet this clear test has been diluted by two provisos. One is an insistence that "the" relevant market be conclusively decided. The other is an injection of economies as a defense. A "trade-off" is to be drawn between the possible costs and benefits of a merger. That is: How much will competition be reduced (if at all) and with what bad effects on performance? *versus* What true economies, if any, (of scale, integration, "synergy," or other type) will be achieved by the merger? Therefore, the second proviso requires a comparison between the monopoly losses and *net* economies (beyond internal growth) from the merger. (The correct *legal* treatment ignores economies, because the Celler-Kefauver Act makes no mention of them.)

Merger cases mostly date from 1958, when the 1950 Celler-Kefauver Act was first applied in the *Bethlehem-Youngstown* case. Horizontal, vertical, and conglomerate issues have been kept pretty distinct both in the economic literature and the series of court decisions. Horizontal limits were drawn very tightly by 1962 in the *Brown Shoe* case. Few vertical mergers were tested, and the policy lines are still vague. Conglomerate mergers have been tested against a series of criteria (such as "deep pocket," potential competition and "toe-holds"). Yet they, too, have not yet been given clear guidelines by the Court.

Horizontal Mergers

The full evaluation is rarely done. Rather, courts have focused on the merger's effect on market structure: What is the relevant market? Is it concentrated? Increasingly so? What would the merged firms' market share be? If the share would be over 10 percent, the merger will probably be prevented. The firms often urge that economies would result, but the

Supreme Court usually gives them little weight. (Is this good, if rough, economics implicitly treating the *net* economies [beyond internal growth] as if they were small?)

Brown Shoe in 1962 was the first clear horizontal merger decision by the Supreme Court. It had both horizontal and vertical aspects. The relevant markets were said by the Court to include separate types of shoes, as sold in various cities. The combined share in the national industry was low, but the merger would continue a trend toward concentration. Hence, it was forbidden. The *Philadelphia National Bank* decision in 1963 spread the coverage beyond industry and trade to banking. *Continental Can* in 1964 involved a debatable market definition (What *was* the correct scope of the market in this case?). The *Von's Grocery* decision in 1966 stretched to cover an 8-percent share in a fragmented local grocery market: The Court wanted to halt a "threatening trend toward concentration." Then in 1973 the Court in *General Dynamics* shifted back toward a broader view of market definition and asked for more proof that monopoly losses would occur. Yet in practice that decision has not markedly loosened the policy lines.

Notice that in marginal cases one can look to one set of conditions in the market (rising concentration, market shares) and find a threat. Or one can look instead at other conditions (low level of concentration, turnover among firms, lack of proven harms) and find no ill effect from the same merger. This exactly parallels the debate in general research about market structure and its effects.

✖ 13

Brown Shoe Co., Inc. v. *United States*

U.S. Supreme Court
370 U.S. 294 (1962)

Brown Shoe seemed to involve only marginal effects on competition in both the vertical and horizontal planes. Yet the Court firmly prohibited the merger in what is the landmark merger case. Was the Court too strict? Could economies of scale or integration have offset the monopoly effects?

Mr. Chief Justice Warren.   This suit was initiated in November 1955 when the Government filed a civil action in the United States District Court for the Eastern District of Missouri alleging that a contemplated merger between the G. R. Kinney Company, Inc. (Kinney), and the

Brown Shoe Company, Inc. (Brown), through an exchange of Kinney for Brown stock, would violate Section 7 of the Clayton Act. . . .

The Industry

The District Court found that although domestic shoe production was scattered among a large number of manufacturers, a small number of large companies occupied a commanding position. Thus, while the 24 largest manufacturers produced about 35 percent of the Nation's shoes, the top 4—International, Endicott-Johnson, Brown (including Kinney) and General Shoe—alone produced approximately 23 percent of the Nation's shoes or 65 percent of the production of the top 24. . . .

The District Court found a "definite trend" among shoe manufacturers to acquire retail outlets. . . . Brown, itself, with no retail outlets of its own prior to 1951, had acquired 845 such outlets by 1956. Moreover, between 1950 and 1956 nine independent shoe store chains, operating 1,114 retail shoe stores, were found to have become subsidiaries of these large firms and to have ceased their independent operations.

And once the manufacturers acquired retail outlets, the District Court found there was a "definite trend" for the parent-manufacturers to supply an ever-increasing percentage of the retail outlets' needs, thereby foreclosing other manufacturers from effectively competing for the retail accounts. Manufacturer-dominated stores were found to be "drying up" the available outlets for independent producers. . . .

Brown Shoe

Brown Shoe was found not only to have been a participant, but also a moving factor, in these industry trends. Although Brown had experimented several times with operating its own retail outlets, by 1945 it had disposed of them all. However, in 1951, Brown again began to seek retail outlets by acquiring the Nation's largest operator of leased shoe departments, Wohl Shoe Company (Wohl), which operated 250 shoe departments in department stores throughout the United States. Between 1952 and 1955 Brown made a number of smaller acquisitions. . . . In 1954, Brown made another major acquisition: Regal Shoe Corporation which, at the time, operated one manufacturing plant producing men's shoes and 110 retail outlets.

The acquisition of these corporations was found to lead to increased sales by Brown to the acquired companies. . . .

During the same period of time, Brown also acquired the stock or assets of seven companies engaged solely in shoe manufacturing. As a result, in 1955 Brown was the fourth largest shoe manufacturer in the country, producing about 25.6 million pairs of shoes or about 4 percent of the Nation's total footwear production.

Kinney

Kinney is principally engaged in operating the largest family-style shoe store chain in the United States. At the time of trial, Kinney was found to be operating over 400 such stores in more than 270 cities. These stores were found to make about 1.2 percent of all national retail shoe sales by dollar volume. Moreover, in 1955 the Kinney stores sold approximately 8 million pairs of nonrubber shoes or about 1.6 percent of the national pairage sales of such shoes. . . .

In addition to this extensive retail activity, Kinney owned and operated four plants which manufactured men's, women's, and children's shoes and whose combined output was 0.5 percent of the national shoe production in 1955, making Kinney the twelfth largest shoe manufacturer in the United States.

Kinney stores were found to obtain about 20 percent of their shoes from Kinney's own manufacturing plants. At the time of the merger, Kinney bought no shoes from Brown; however, in line with Brown's conceded reasons for acquiring Kinney, Brown had, by 1957, become the largest outside supplier of Kinney's shoes, supplying 7.9 percent of all Kinney's needs. . . .

THE VERTICAL ASPECTS OF THE MERGER

Economic arrangements between companies standing in a supplier-customer relationship are characterized as "vertical." The primary vice of a vertical merger or other arrangement tying a customer to a supplier is that, by foreclosing the competitors of either party from a segment of the market otherwise open to them, the arrangement may act as a "clog on competition." . . .

The Product Market

The outer boundaries of a product market are determined by the reasonable interchangeability of use or the cross-elasticity of demand between the product itself and substitutes for it. . . .

Applying these considerations to the present case, we conclude that the record supports the District Court's finding that the relevant lines of commerce are men's, women's, and children's shoes. These product lines are recognized by the public; each line is manufactured in separate plants; each has characteristics peculiar to itself rendering it generally noncompetitive with the others; and each is, of course, directed toward a distinct class of customers. . . .

The Geographic Market

We agree with the parties and the District Court that insofar as the vertical aspect of this merger is concerned the relevant geographic market is the entire Nation. The relationships of product value, bulk, weight, and consumer demand enable manufacturers to distribute their shoes on a nationwide basis, as Brown and Kinney, in fact, do. The anticompetitive effects of the merger are to be measured within this range of distribution.

The Probable Effect of the Merger

Once the area of effective competition affected by a vertical arrangement has been defined, an analysis must be made to determine if the effect of the arrangement "may be substantially to lessen competition or to tend to create a monopoly" in this market.

Since the diminution of the vigor of competition which may stem from a vertical arrangement results primarily from a foreclosure of a share of the market otherwise open to competitors, an important consideration in determining whether the effect of a vertical arrangement "may be substantially to lessen competition or to tend to create a monopoly" is the size of the share of the market foreclosed. However, this factor will seldom be determinative. . . .

Between these extremes, in cases such as the one before us in which the foreclosure is neither of monopoly nor *de minimis* proportions, the percentage of the market foreclosed by the vertical arrangement cannot itself be decisive. In such cases, it becomes necessary to undertake an examination of various economic and historical factors in order to determine whether the arrangement under review is of the type Congress sought to proscribe.

The present merger involved neither small companies nor failing companies. In 1955, the date of this merger, Brown was the fourth largest manufacturer in the shoe industry with sales of approximately 25 million pairs of shoes and assets of over $72,000,000 while Kinney had sales of about 8 million pairs of shoes and assets of about $18,000,000. Not only was Brown one of the leading manufacturers of men's, women's, and children's shoes, but Kinney, with over 350 retail outlets, owned and operated the largest independent chain of family shoe stores in the Nation. Thus, in this industry, no merger between a manufacturer and an independent retailer could involve a larger potential market foreclosure. Moreover, it is apparent both from past behavior of Brown and from the testimony of Brown's President, that Brown would use its ownership of Kinney to force Brown shoes into Kinney stores. Thus, in operation this vertical arrangement would be quite analogous to one involving a tying clause.

Another important factor to consider is the trend toward concentration in the industry. It is true, of course, that the statute prohibits a given merger only if the effect of *that* merger may be substantially to lessen competition. But the very wording of Section 7 requires a prognosis of the probable *future* effect of the merger.

The existence of a trend toward vertical integration, which the District Court found, is well substantiated by the record. Moreover, the court found a tendency of the acquiring manufacturers to become increasingly important sources of supply for their acquired outlets. The necessary corollary of these trends is the foreclosure of independent manufacturers from markets otherwise open to them. And because these trends are not the product of accident but are rather the result of deliberate policies of Brown and other leading shoe manufacturers, account must be taken of these facts in order to predict the probable future consequences of this merger. It is against this background of continuing concentration that the present merger must be viewed.

Brown argues, however, that the shoe industry is at present composed of a large number of manufacturers and retailers and that the industry is dynamically competitive. But remaining vigor cannot immunize a merger if the trend in that industry is toward oligopoly. . . . It is the probable effect of the merger upon the future as well as the present which the Clayton Act commands the courts and the Commission to examine.

Moreover, as we have remarked above, not only must we consider the probable effects of the merger upon the economics of the particular markets affected but also we must consider its probable effects upon the economic way of life sought to be preserved by Congress. Congress was desirous of preventing the formation of further oligopolies with their attendant adverse effects upon local control of industry and upon small business. Where an industry was composed of numerous independent units, Congress appeared anxious to preserve this structure. . . .

THE HORIZONTAL ASPECTS OF THE MERGER

An economic arrangement between companies performing similar functions in the production or sale of comparable goods or services is characterized as "horizontal." The effect on competition of such an arrangement depends, of course, upon its character and scope.

The Product Market

Shoes are sold in the United States in retail shoe stores and in shoe departments of general stores. These outlets sell: (1) men's shoes, (2) women's shoes, (3) women's or children's shoes, or (4) men's, women's or children's shoes. Prior to the merger, both Brown and Kinney sold their shoes in competition with one another through the enumerated kinds of outlets characteristic of the industry. . . .

We therefore agree that the District Court properly defined the relevant geographic markets in which to analyze this merger as those cities with a population exceeding 10,000 and their environs in which both Brown and Kinney retailed shoes through their own outlets. Such markets are large enough to include the downtown shops and suburban shopping centers in areas contiguous to the city, which are the important competitive factors, and yet are small enough to exclude stores beyond the immediate environs of the city which are of little competitive significance.

The Probable Effect of the Merger

. . . Although Brown objects to some details in the Government's computations used in drafting these exhibits, appellant cannot deny the correctness of the more general picture they reveal. . . . They show, for example, that during 1955 in 32 separate cities, ranging in size and location from Topeka, Kansas, to Batavia, New York, and Hobbs, New Mexico, the combined share of Brown and Kinney sales of women's shoes (by unit volume) exceeded 20 percent. In 31 cities—some the same as those used in measuring the effect of the merger in the women's line—the combined share of children's shoes sales exceeded 20 percent; in 6 cities their share exceeded 40 percent. In Dodge City, Kansas, their combined share of the market for women's shoes was over 57 percent; their share of the children's shoe market in that city was 49 percent. In the 7 cities in which Brown's and Kinney's combined shares of the market for women's shoes were greatest (ranging from 33 percent to 57 percent), each of the parties alone, prior to the merger, had captured substantial portions of those markets (ranging from 13 percent to 34 percent); the merger intensified this existing concentration. In 118 separate cities the combined shares of the market of Brown and Kinney in the sale of one of the relevant lines of commerce exceeded 5 percent. In 47 cities, their share exceeded 5 percent in all three lines.

The market share which companies may control by merging is one of the most important factors to be considered when determining the probable effects of the combination on effective competition in the relevant market. In an industry as fragmented as shoe retailing, the control of substantial shares of the trade in a city may have important effects on competition. If a merger achieving 5 percent control were now approved, we might be required to approve future merger efforts by Brown's competitors seeking similar market shares. The oligopoly Congress sought to avoid would then be furthered, and it would be difficult to dissolve the combinations previously approved. Furthermore, in this fragmented industry, even if the combination controls but a small share of a particular market, the fact that this share is held by a large national chain can adversely affect competition. . . .

Of course, some of the results of large integrated or chain operations are beneficial to consumers. Their expansion is not rendered unlawful by the mere fact that small independent stores may be adversely affected. It is competition, not competitors, which the Act protects. But we cannot fail to recognize Congress's desire to promote competition through the protection of viable, small, locally owned businesses. Congress appreciated that occasional higher costs and prices might result from the maintenance of fragmented industries and markets. It resolved these competing considerations in favor of decentralization. We must give effect to that decision.

Other factors to be considered in evaluating the probable effects of a merger in the relevant market lend additional support to the District Court's conclusion that this merger may substantially lessen competition. One such factor is the history of tendency toward concentration in the industry. As we have previously pointed out, the shoe industry has in recent years been a prime example of such a trend. . . .

By the merger in this case, the largest single group of retail stores still independent of one of the large manufacturers was absorbed into an already substantial aggregation of more or less controlled retail outlets. As a result of this merger, Brown moved into second place nationally in terms of retail stores directly owned. Including the stores on its franchise plan, the merger placed under Brown's control almost 1,600 shoe outlets, or about 7.2 percent of the Nation's retail "shoe stores" as defined by the Census Bureau, and 2.3 percent of the Nation's total retail shoe outlets. We cannot avoid the mandate of Congress that tendencies toward concentration in industry are to be curbed in their incipiency, particularly when those tendencies are being accelerated through giant steps striding across a hundred cities at a time. In the light of the trends in this industry we agree with the Government and the court below that this is an appropriate place at which to call a halt.

. . . On the basis of the record before us, we believe the Government sustained its burden of proof. We hold that the District Court was correct in concluding that this merger may tend to lessen competition substantially in the retail sale of men's, women's, and children's shoes in the overwhelming majority of those cities and their environs in which both Brown and Kinney sell through owned or controlled outlets.

The judgment is *Affirmed.*

✺ 14

United States v. *Philadelphia National Bank*
U.S. Supreme Court 374 U.S. 321 (1963)

After a wave of major bank mergers, the Court finally drew the line in this landmark case. Though some banking markets are national, the Court held that the local banking market is real and important enough to govern the decision. After this case, banking mergers came under much the same limits as others (see Von's *below).*

Mr. Justice Brennan. The United States, appellant here, brought this civil action . . . to enjoin a proposed merger of The Philadelphia National Bank (PNB) and Girard Trust Corn Exchange Bank (Girard), appellees here. The complaint charged violations of Section 1 of the Sherman Act, . . . and Section 7 of the Clayton Act. . . . From a judgment for appellees after trial . . . the United States appealed to this Court. . . . We reverse the judgment of the District Court. We hold that the merger of appellees is forbidden by Section 7 of the Clayton Act and so must be enjoined; we need not, and therefore do not, reach the further question of alleged violation of Section 1 of the Sherman Act. . . .

The Proposed Merger of PNB and Girard

The Philadelphia National Bank and Girard Trust Corn Exchange Bank are, respectively, the second and third largest of the 42 commercial banks with head offices in the Philadelphia metropolitan area, which consists of the City of Philadelphia and its three contiguous counties in Pennsylvania. The home county of both banks is the city itself; Pennsylvania law, however, permits branching into the counties contiguous to the home country, . . . and both banks have offices throughout the four-county area. PNB, a national bank, has assets of over

$1,000,000,000, making it (as of 1959) the twenty-first largest bank in the Nation. Girard, a state bank, is a member of the FRS and is insured by the FDIC; it has assets of about $750,000,000. Were the proposed merger to be consummated, the resulting bank would be the largest in the four-county area, with (approximately) 36 percent of the area banks' total assets, 36 percent of deposits, and 34 percent of net loans. It and the second largest (First Pennsylvania Bank and Trust Company, now the largest) would have between them 59 percent of the total assets, 58 percent of deposits, and 58 percent of the net loans, while after the merger the four largest banks in the area would have 78 percent of total assets, 77 percent of deposits, and 78 percent of net loans.

The present size of both PNB and Girard is in part the result of mergers. Indeed, the trend toward concentration is noticeable in the Philadelphia area generally, in which the number of commercial banks has declined from 108 in 1947 to the present 42. Since 1950, PNB has acquired nine formerly independent banks and Girard six; and these acquisitions have accounted for 59 percent and 85 percent of the respective banks' asset growth during the period, 63 percent and 91 percent of their deposit growth, and 12 percent and 37 percent of their loan growth. During this period, the seven largest banks in the area increased their combined share of the area's total commercial bank resources from about 61 percent to about 90 percent. . . .

THE LAWFULNESS OF THE PROPOSED MERGER
UNDER SECTION 7

. . . We agree with the District Court that the cluster of products (various kinds of credit) and services (such as checking accounts and trust administration) denoted by the term "commercial banking" . . . composes a distinct line of commerce. Some commercial banking products or services are so distinctive that they are entirely free of effective competition from products or services of other financial institutions; the checking account is in this category. Others enjoy such cost advantages as to be insulated within a broad range from substitutes furnished by other institutions. For example, commercial banks compete with small-loan companies in the personal-loan market; but the small-loan companies' rates are invariably much higher than the banks', in part, it seems, because the companies' working capital consists in substantial part of bank loans. Finally, there are banking facilities which, although in terms of cost and price they are freely competitive with the facilities provided by other financial institutions, nevertheless enjoy a settled consumer preference, insulating them to a marked degree from competition; this seems to be the case with savings deposits. In sum, it is clear that commercial banking is a market "sufficiently inclusive to be meaningful in terms of trade realities." *Crown Zellerbach Corp.* v. *Federal Trade Comm'n,* 296 F. 2d 800, 811 (C.A. 9th Cir. 1961).

We part company with the District Court on the determination of the appropriate "section of the country." The proper question to be asked in this case is not where the parties to the merger do business or even where they compete, but where, within the area of competitive overlap, the effect of the merger on competition will be direct and immediate. See Bock, *Mergers and Markets* (1960), 42. This depends upon "the geographic structure of supplier-consumer relations." Kaysen and Turner, *Antitrust Policy* (1959), 102. In banking, as in most service industries, convenience of location is essential to effective competition. Individuals and corporations typically confer the bulk of their patronage on banks in their local community; they find it impractical to conduct their banking business at a distance. . . . The factor of inconvenience localizes banking competition as effectively as high transportation costs in other industries. . . . Therefore, since, as we recently said in a related context, the "area of effective competition in the known line of commerce must be charted by careful selection of the market area in which the seller operates, *and to which the purchaser can practicably turn for supplies,*" *Tampa Elec. Co.* v. *Nashville Coal Co.,* 365 U.S. 320, 327 (emphasis supplied); see *Standard Oil Co.* v. *United States,* 337 U.S. 293, 299 and 300, n. 5, the four-county area in which appellees' offices are located would seem to be the relevant geographical market. Cf. *Brown Shoe Co., supra,* at 338–39. In fact, the vast bulk of appellees' business originates in the four-county area. Theoretically, we should be concerned with the possibility that bank offices on the perimeter of the area may be in effective competition with bank offices within; actually, this seems to be a factor of little significance.

We recognize that the area in which appellees have their offices does not delineate with perfect accuracy an appropriate "section of the country" in which to appraise the effect of the merger upon competition. Large borrowers and large depositors, the record shows, may find it practical to do a large part of their banking business outside their home community; very small borrowers and depositors may, as a practical matter, be confined to bank offices in their immediate neighborhood; and customers of intermediate size, it would appear, deal with banks within an area intermediate between these extremes. . . . So also, some banking services are evidently more local in nature than others. But that in banking the relevant geographical market is a function of each separate customer's economic scale means simply that a workable compromise must be found: some fair intermediate delineation which avoids the indefensible extremes of drawing the market either so expansively as to make the effect of the merger upon competition seem insignificant, because only the very largest bank customers are taken into account in defining the market, or so narrowly as to place appellees in different markets, because only the smallest customers are considered. We think that the four-county Philadelphia metropolitan area, which state law apparently recognizes as a meaningful banking community in allowing Philadelphia banks to branch within it and which would seem roughly to delineate the area in which bank customers that are neither very large nor very small find it practical to do their banking business, is a more appropriate "section of the country" in which to appraise the instant merger than any larger or smaller or different area. We are helped to this conclusion by the fact that the three federal banking agencies regard the area in which banks have their offices as an "area of effective competition." . . .

. . . There is no reason to think that concentration is less inimical to the free play of competition in banking than in other service industries. On the contrary, it is in all probability more inimical. For example, banks compete to fill the credit needs of businessmen. Small businessmen especially are, as a practical matter, confined to their locality for the satisfaction of their credit needs. . . . If the number of banks in the locality is reduced, the vigor of competition for filling the marginal small business borrower's needs is likely to diminish. At the same time, his concomitantly greater difficulty in obtaining credit is likely to put him at a disadvantage *vis-à-vis* larger businesses with which he competes. In this fashion, concentration in banking accelerates concentration generally.

. . . Section 7 does not mandate cutthroat competition in the banking industry and does not exclude defenses based on dangers to liquidity or solvency, if to avert them a merger is necessary. It does require, however, that the forces of competition be allowed to operate within the broad framework of governmental regulation of the industry. The fact that banking is a highly regulated industry critical to the Nation's welfare makes the play of competition not less important but more so. At the price of some repetition, we note that if the businessman is denied credit because his banking alternatives have been eliminated by mergers, the whole edifice of an entrepreneurial system is threatened; if the costs of banking services and credit are allowed to become excessive by the absence of competitive pressures, virtually all costs, in our credit economy, will be affected; and unless competition is allowed to fulfill its role as an economic regulator in the banking industry, the result may well be even more governmental regulation. . . .

The judgment of the District Court is reversed and the case remanded with direction to enter judgment enjoining the proposed merger.

It is so ordered.

✳ 15

United States v. *Von's Grocery Co.*

U.S. Supreme Court
384 U.S. 270 (1966)

> *Von's drew the line against horizontal mergers roughly as it stands today: no more than 10 percent combined, if concentration has been rising, even if competition might still be vigorous. The dissent urged instead that the market was competitive and that the merger's effect would be trivial.*

Black, J.   On March 25, 1960, the United States brought this action charging that the acquisition by Von's Grocery Company of its direct competitor Shopping Bag Food Stores, both large retail grocery companies in Los Angeles, California, violated § 7 of the Clayton Act. . . .

The record shows the following facts relevant to our decision. The market involved here is the retail grocery market in the Los Angeles area. In 1958 Von's retail sales ranked third in the area and Shopping Bag's ranked sixth. In 1960 their sales together were 7.5 percent of the total two and one-half billion dollars of retail groceries sold in the Los Angeles market each year. For many years before the merger both companies had enjoyed great success as rapidly growing companies. From 1948 to 1958 the number of Von's stores in the Los Angeles area practically doubled from 14 to 27, while at the same time the number of Shopping Bag's stores jumped from 15 to 34. During that same decade, Von's sales increased fourfold and its share of the market almost doubled while Shopping Bag's sales multiplied seven times and its share of the market tripled. The merger of these two highly successful, expanding and aggressive competitors created the second largest grocery chain in Los Angeles with sales of almost $172,488,000 annually. In addition the findings of the District Court show that the number of owners operating a single store in the Los Angeles retail grocery market decreased from 5,365 in 1950 to 3,818 in 1961. By 1963, three years after the merger, the number of single-store owners had dropped still further to 3,590. During roughly the same period from 1953 to 1962 the number of chains with two or more grocery stores increased from 96 to 150. While the grocery business was being concentrated into the hands of fewer and fewer owners, the small companies were continually being absorbed by the larger firms through mergers. According to an exhibit prepared by one of the Government's expert witnesses, in the period from 1949 to 1958 nine of the top 20 chains acquired 126 stores from their smaller competitors. Figures of a principal defense witness, set out below, illustrate the many acquisitions and mergers in the Los Angeles grocery industry from 1953 through 1961 including acquisitions made by Food Giant, Alpha Beta, Fox, and Mayfair, all among the ten leading chains in the area. Moreover, a table prepared by the Federal Trade Commission appearing in the Government's reply brief, but not a part of the record here, shows that acquisitions and mergers in the Los Angeles retail grocery market have continued at a rapid rate since the merger. These facts alone are enough to cause us to conclude contrary to the District Court that the Von's-Shopping Bag merger did violate § 7. Accordingly, we reverse.

. . . By using these terms in § 7 which look not merely to the actual present effect of a merger but instead to its effect upon future competition, Congress sought to preserve competition among many small businesses by arresting a trend toward concentration in its incipiency before that trend developed to the point that a market was left in the grip of a few big companies. Thus, where concentration is gaining momentum in a market, we must be alert to carry out Congress's intent to protect competition against ever increasing concentration through mergers.

The facts of this case present exactly the threatening trend toward concentration which Congress wanted to halt. The number of small grocery companies in the Los Angeles retail grocery market had been declining rapidly before the merger and continued to decline rapidly afterwards. This rapid decline in the number of grocery store owners moved hand in hand with a large number of significant absorptions of the small companies by the larger ones. In the midst of this steadfast trend toward concentration, Von's and Shopping Bag, two of the most successful and largest companies in the area, jointly owning 66 grocery stores merged to become the second largest chain in Los Angeles. This merger cannot be defended on the ground that one of the companies was about to fail or that the two had to merge to save themselves from destruction by some larger and more powerful competitor. What we have on the contrary is simply the case of two already powerful companies merging in a way which makes them even more powerful than they were before. If ever such a merger would not violate § 7, certainly it does when it takes place in a market characterized by a long and continuous trend toward fewer and fewer owner-competitors which is exactly the sort of trend which Congress, with power to do so, declared must be arrested.

Appellees' primary argument is that the merger between Von's and Shopping Bag is not prohibited by § 7 because the Los Angeles grocery market was competitive before the merger, has been since, and may continue to be in the future. Even so, § 7 "requires not merely an appraisal of the immediate impact of the merger upon competition, but a prediction of its impact upon competitive conditions in the future; this is what is meant when it is said that the amended § 7 was intended to arrest anticompetitive tendencies in their 'incipiency.'" *United States* v. *Philadelphia Nat. Bank,* 374 U.S. at p. 362, 83 S.Ct., at 1741, 10 L.Ed.2d 915. It is enough for us that Congress feared that a market marked at the same time by both a continuous decline in the number of small businesses and a large number of mergers would, slowly but inevitably, gravitate from a market of many small competitors to one dominated by one or a few giants, and competition would thereby be destroyed. Congress passed the Celler-Kefauver Act to prevent such a destruction of competition. Our cases since the passage of that Act have faithfully endeavored to enforce this congressional command. We adhere to them now.

Mr. Justice Stewart, with whom Mr. Justice Harlan joins, dissenting.

We first gave consideration to the 1950 amendment of § 7 of the Clayton Act in *Brown Shoe Co.* v. *United States.* . . . The thorough opinion The Chief Justice wrote for the Court in that case made two things plain: First, the standards of § 7 require that every corporate acquisition be judged in the light of the contemporary economic context of its industry. Second, the purpose of § 7 is to protect competition, not to protect competitors, and every § 7 case must be decided in the light of that clear statutory purpose. Today the Court turns its back on these two basic principles and on all the decisions that have followed them.

*   *   *   *   *

The Court rests its conclusion on the "crucial point" that in the 11-year period between 1950 and 1961 the number of single-store grocery firms in Los Angeles decreased 29 percent from 5,365 to 3,818. Such a decline should, of course, be no more than a fact calling for further investigation of the competitive trend in the industry. For the Court, however, that decline is made the end, not the beginning, of the analysis. . . .

I believe that even the most superficial analysis of the record makes plain the fallacy of the Court's syllogism that competition is necessarily reduced when the bare number of competitors has declined. In any meaningful sense, the structure of the Los Angeles grocery market remains unthreatened by concentration. Local competition is vigorous to a fault, not only among chain stores themselves but also between chain stores and single-store operators. The continuing population explosion of the Los Angeles area, which has outrun the expansion plans of even the largest chains, offers a surfeit of business opportunity for stores of all sizes. Affiliated with co-operatives that give the smallest store the buying strength of its largest competitors, new stores have taken full advantage of the remarkable ease of entry into the market. And most important of all, the record simply cries out that the numerical decline in the number of single-store owners is the result of transcending social and technological changes that positively preclude the inference that competition has suffered because of the attrition of competitors.

. . . Between 1948 and 1958, the market share of Safeway, the leading grocery chain in Los Angeles, declined from 14 percent to 8 percent. The combined market shares of the top two chains declined from 21 percent to 14 percent over the same period; for the period 1952–58, the combined shares of the three, four, and five largest firms also declined. It is true that between 1948 and 1958, the combined shares of the top 20 firms in the market increased from 44 percent to 57 percent. The crucial fact here, however, is that 7 of these top 20 firms in 1958 were not even in existence as chains in 1948. Because of the substantial turnover in the membership of the top 20 firms, the increase in market share of the top 20 as a group is hardly a reliable indicator of any tendency toward market concentration.

In addition, statistics in the record for the period 1953–62 strongly suggest that the retail grocery industry in Los Angeles is less concentrated today than it was a decade ago. During this period, the number of chain store firms in the area rose from 96 to 150, or 56 percent. That increase occurred overwhelmingly among chains of the very smallest size, those composed of two or three grocery stores. Between 1953 and 1962, the number of such "chains" increased from 56 to 104, or 86 percent. Although chains of 10 or more stores increased from 10 to 24 during the period, 7 of these 24 chains were not even in existence as chains in Los Angeles in 1953.

Yet even these dramatic statistics do not fully reveal the dynamism and vitality of competition in the retail grocery business in Los Angeles during the period. The record shows that . . . during the period 1953–62 . . . 173 new chains made their appearance in the market area and 119 chains went out of existence as chain stores. The vast majority of this market turbulence represented turnover in chains of two or three stores. . . . [A]lmost without exception, these new chains were the outgrowth of successful one-store operations. There is no indication that comparable turmoil did not equally permeate single-store operations in the area. In fashioning its *per se* rule, based on the net arithmetical decline in the number of single-store operators, the Court completely disregards the obvious procreative vigor of competition in the market as reflected in the turbulent history of entry and exit of competing small chains.

* * * * *

Moreover, contrary to the assumption on which the Court proceeds, the record establishes that the present merger itself has substantial, even predominant, market-extension overtones. The District Court found that the Von's stores were located in the southern and western portions of the Los Angeles metropolitan area and that the Shopping Bag stores were located in the northern and eastern portions. In each of the areas in which Von's and Shopping Bag stores competed directly, there were also at least six other chain stores and several smaller stores competing for the patronage of customers. . . . Even among those stores which competed at least partially with one another, the overlap in sales represented only approximately 25 percent of the combined sales of the two chains in the overall Los Angeles area. The present merger was thus three parts market-extension and only one part horizontal, but the Court nowhere recognizes this market-extension aspect that exists within the local market itself. The actual market share foreclosed by the elimination of Shopping Bag as an independent competitor was thus slightly less than 1 percent of the total grocery store sales in the area. The share of the market preempted by the present merger was therefore practically identical with the 0.77 percent market foreclosure accepted as "quite insubstantial" by the Court in *Tampa Electric Co.* v. *Nashville Coal Co.*, 365 U.S. 320, 331–33.

*   *   *   *   *

Moreover, it is clear that there are no substantial barriers to market entry. The record contains references to numerous highly successful instances of entry with modest initial investments. . . . Enhancing free access to the market is the absence of any such restrictive factors as patented technology, trade secrets, or substantial product differentiation.

*   *   *   *   *

✣ 16

United States v. *General Dynamics Corp. et al.*
U.S. Supreme Court
415 U.S. 486 (1974)

The Brown Shoe *and* Von's Grocery *cases narrowed the problem to market share and related data. Then in the* General Dynamics *decision of 1974, the Court widened the issues again to permit many other aspects to be decisive. Behavior after the merger or likely future changes could also be used to exonerate a merger. Though this seemed likely at first to loosen and complicate merger policy markedly, in fact the shift has been slight. What data should be decisive in merger cases? Market shares, behavior, trends, performance . . . ? Which side had sounder economics, the majority or Justice Douglas in his dissent?*

Mr. Justice Stewart delivered the opinion of the Court.

I

At the time of the acquisition involved here, Material Service Corp. was a large midwest producer and supplier of building materials, concrete, limestone, and coal. All of its coal production was from deep-shaft mines operated by it or its affiliate, appellee Freeman Coal Mining Corp., and production from these operations amounted to 6.9 million tons of coal in 1959 and 8.4 million tons in 1967. In 1954, Material Service began to acquire the stock of United Electric Coal Companies. United Electric at all relevant times operated only strip or open-pit mines in Illinois and Kentucky; at the time of trial in 1970 a number of its mines had closed and its operations had been reduced to four mines in Illinois and none in Kentucky. In 1959, it produced 3.6 million tons of coal, and by 1967, it had increased this output to 5.7 million tons. Material Service's purchase of United Electric stock continued until 1959. At this point Material's holdings amounted to more than 34 percent of United Electric's outstanding shares and—all parties are now agreed on this point—Material had effective control of United Electric. The president of Freeman was elected chairman of United Electric's executive committee, and other changes in the corporate structure of United Electric were made at the behest of Material Service.

Some months after this takeover, Material Service was itself acquired by the appellee General Dynamics Corp. General Dynamics is a large diversified corporation, much of its revenues coming from sales of aircraft, communications, and marine products to Government agencies. The trial court found that its purchase of Material Service was part of a broad diversification program aimed at expanding General Dynamics into commercial nondefense business. As a result of the purchase of Material Service, and through it, of Freeman and United Electric, General Dynamics became the Nation's fifth largest commercial coal producer. During the early 1960s General Dynamics increased its equity in United Electric by direct purchases of United Electric stock, and by 1966 it held or controlled 66.15 percent of United Electric's outstanding shares. In September 1966 the board of directors of General Dynamics authorized a tender offer to holders of the remaining United Electric stock. This offer was successful, and United Electric shortly thereafter became a wholly-owned subsidiary of General Dynamics.

The thrust of the Government's complaint was that the acquisition of United Electric by Material Service in 1959 violated § 7 of the Clayton Act because the takeover substantially lessened competition in the production and sale of coal in either or both of two geographic markets. It contended that a relevant "section of the country" within the meaning of § 7 was, alternatively, the State of Illinois or the Eastern Interior Coal Province Sales Area, the latter being one of four major coal distribution areas recognized by the coal industry and comprising Illinois and Indiana, and parts of Kentucky, Tennessee, Iowa, Minnesota, Wisconsin, and Missouri.

At trial controversy focused on three basic issues: the propriety of coal as a "line of commerce," the definition of Illinois or the Eastern Interior Coal Province Sales Area as a relevant "section of the country," and the probability of a lessening of competition within these or any other product and geographic markets resulting from the acquisition. The District Court decided against the Government on each of these issues. . . .

*   *   *   *   *

II

The Government sought to prove a violation of § 7 of the Clayton Act principally through statistics showing that within certain geographic markets the coal industry was concentrated among a small number of large producers; that this concentration was increasing; and that the acquisition of United Electric would materially enlarge the market share of the acquiring company and thereby contribute to the trend toward concentration.

The concentration of the coal market in Illinois and, alternatively, in the Eastern Interior Coal Province was demonstrated by a table of the shares of the largest two, four, and ten coal-producing firms in each of these areas for both 1957 and 1967 that revealed the following:[1]

	Eastern Interior Coal Province		Illinois	
	1957	1967	1957	1967
Top two firms	29.6	48.6	37.8	52.9
Top four firms	43.0	62.9	54.5	75.2
Top ten firms	65.5	91.4	84.0	98.0

These statistics, the Government argued, showed not only that the coal industry was concentrated among a small number of leading producers,

---

[1]The figures for 1967 reflect the impact on market concentration of the acquisition involved here.

but that the trend had been toward increasing concentration.[2] Further-more, the undisputed fact that the number of coal-producing firms in Illinois decreased almost 73 percent during the period of 1957 to 1967 from 144 to 39 was claimed to be indicative of the same trend. The acquisition of United Electric by Material Service resulted in increased concentration of coal sales among the leading producers in the areas chosen by the Government, as shown by the following table:

	1959			1967		
	Share of Top Two but for Merger	Share of Top Two Given Merger	Percent Increase	Share of Top Two but for Merger	Share of Top Two Given Merger	Percent Increase
Province ...	33.1	37.9	14.5	45.0	48.6	8.0
Illinois	36.6	44.3	22.4	44.0	52.9	20.2

Finally, the Government's statistics indicated that the acquisition in-creased the share of the merged company in the Illinois and Eastern Interior Coal Province coal markets by significant degrees:

	Province		Illinois	
	Rank	Share (percent)	Rank	Share (percent)
1959				
Freeman	2	7.6	2	15.1
United Electric	6	4.8	5	8.1
Combined	2	12.4	1	23.2
1967				
Freeman	5	6.5	2	12.9
United Electric	9	4.4	6	8.9
Combined	2	10.9	2	21.8

* * * * *

The effect of adopting this approach to a determination of a "substan-tial" lessening of competition is to allow the Government to rest its case on a showing of even small increases of market share or market concen-tration in those industries or markets where concentration is already great or has been recently increasing, since "if concentration is already great, the importance of preventing even slight increases in concentra-

---

[2]The figures demonstrating the degree of concentration in the two coal markets chosen by the Government were roughly comparable to those in *United States* v. *Von's Grocery Co.*, 384 U.S. 270, where the top four firms in the market controlled 24.4 percent of the sales, the top eight 40.9 percent, and the top twelve 48.8 percent. See Id., at 281 (White, J., concurring).

tion and so preserving the possibility of eventual deconcentration is correspondingly great." *United States* v. *Aluminum Co. of America,* 377 U.S. 271, 279, citing *United States* v. *Philadelphia National Bank, supra,* at 365 n. 42.

While the statistical showing proffered by the Government in this case, the accuracy of which was not discredited by the District Court or contested by the appellees, would under this approach have sufficed to support a finding of "undue concentration" in the absence of other considerations, the question before us is whether the District Court was justified in finding that other pertinent factors affecting the coal industry and the business of the appellees mandated a conclusion that no substantial lessening of competition occurred or was threatened by the acquisition of United Electric. We are satisfied that the court's ultimate finding was not in error.

In *Brown Shoe* v. *United States, supra,* we cautioned that statistics concerning market share and concentration, while of great significance, were not conclusive indicators of anticompetitive effects:

> Congress indicated plainly that a merger had to be functionally viewed, in the context of its particular industry." 370 U.S., at 321–22.
>
> Statistics reflecting the shares of the market controlled by the industry leaders and the parties to the merger are, of course, the primary index of market power: But only a further examination of the particular market—its structure, history, and probable future—can provide the appropriate setting for judging the probable anticompetitive effect of the merger. Id., at 322 n. 38.

See also *United States* v. *Continental Can Co., supra,* at 458. In this case, the District Court assessed the evidence of the "structure, history, and probable future" of the coal industry, and on the basis of this assessment found no substantial probability of anticompetitive effects from the merger.

Much of the District Court's opinion was devoted to a description of the changes that have affected the coal industry since World War II. On the basis of more than three weeks of testimony and a voluminous record, the court discerned a number of clear and significant developments in the industry. First, it found that coal had become increasingly less able to compete with other sources of energy in many segments of the energy market. Following the war the industry entirely lost its largest single purchaser of coal—the railroads—and faced increasingly stiffer competition from oil and natural gas as sources of energy for industrial and residential uses. Because of these changes in consumption patterns, coal's share of the energy resources consumed in this country fell from 78.4 percent in 1920 to 21.4 percent in 1968. The court reviewed evidence attributing this decline not only to the changing relative economies of alternative fuels and to new distribution and consumption patterns, but also to more recent concern with the effect of coal use on the environment and consequent regulation of the extent and means of such coal consumption.

Second, the court found that to a growing extent since 1954, the electric utility industry has become the mainstay of coal consumption. While electric utilities consumed only 15.76 percent of the coal produced nationally in 1947, their share of total consumption increased every year thereafter, and in 1968 amounted to more than 59 percent of all the coal consumed throughout the Nation.

Third, and most significantly, the court found that to an increasing degree, nearly all coal sold to utilities is transferred under long-term requirements contracts, under which coal producers promise to meet utilities' coal consumption requirements for a fixed period of time and at predetermined prices. . . .

*   *   *   *   *

These developments in the patterns of coal distribution and consumption, the District Court found, have limited the amounts of coal immediately available for "spot" purchases on the open market, since "[t]he growing practice by coal producers of expanding mine capacity only to meet long-term contractual commitments and the gradual disappearance of the small truck mines has tended to limit the production capacity available for spot sales."

Because of these fundamental changes in the structure of the market for coal, the District Court was justified in viewing the statistics relied on by the Government as insufficient to sustain its case. Evidence of past production does not as a matter of logic necessarily give a proper picture of a company's future ability to compete. In most situations, of course, the unstated assumption is that a company that has maintained a certain share of a market in the recent past will be in a position to do so in the immediate future. Thus, companies that have controlled sufficiently large shares of a concentrated market are barred from merger by § 7, not because of their past acts, but because their past performances imply an ability to continue to dominate with at least equal vigor. In markets involving groceries or beer, as in *Von's Grocery, supra,* and *Pabst, supra,* statistics involving annual sales naturally indicate the power of each company to compete in the future. Evidence of the amount of annual sales is relevant as a prediction of future competitive strength, since in most markets distribution systems and brand recognition are such significant factors that one may reasonably suppose that a company which has attracted a given number of sales will retain that competitive strength.

In the coal market, as analyzed by the District Court, however, statistical evidence of coal *production* was of considerably less significance. The bulk of the coal produced is delivered under long-term requirements contracts, and such sales thus do not represent the exercise of competitive power but rather the obligation to fulfill previously negotiated contracts at a previously fixed price. The focus of competition in a given time frame is not on the disposition of coal already produced but on the procurement of new long-term supply contracts. In this situation a company's past ability to produce is of limited significance, since it is in a position to offer for sale neither its past production nor the bulk of the coal it is presently capable of producing, which is typically already committed under a long-term supply contract. A more significant indicator of a company's power effectively to compete with other companies lies in the state of a company's uncommitted reserves of recoverable coal. A company with relatively large supplies of coal which are not already under contract to a consumer will have a more important influence upon competition in the contemporaneous negotiation of supply contracts than a firm with small reserves, even though the latter may presently produce a greater tonnage of coal. In a market where the availability and price of coal are set by long-term contracts rather than immediate or short-term purchases and sales, reserves rather than past production are the best measure of a company's ability to compete.

The testimony and exhibits in the District Court revealed that United Electric's coal reserve prospects were "unpromising." 341 F. Supp., at 559. United's relative position of strength in reserves was considerably weaker than its past and current ability to produce. While United ranked fifth among Illinois coal producers in terms of annual production, it was tenth in reserve holdings, and controlled less than 1 percent of the reserves held by coal producers in Illinois, Indiana, and western Kentucky. Id., at 538. Many of the reserves held by United had already been depleted at the time of trial, forcing the closing of some of United's midwest mines. Even more significantly, the District Court found that of the 52,033,304 tons of currently mineable reserves in Illinois, Indiana, and Kentucky controlled by United, only 4 million tons had not already been committed under long-term contracts. United was found to be facing the future with relatively depleted resources at its disposal and with the vast majority of those resources already committed under contracts allowing no further adjustment in price. In addition, the District Court found that "United Electric has neither the possibility of acquiring more [reserves] nor the ability to develop deep coal reserves," and thus was not in a position to increase its reserves to replace those already depleted or committed. Id., at 560.

Viewed in terms of present and future reserve prospects—and thus in terms of probable future ability to compete—rather than in terms of past production, the District Court held that United Electric was a far less significant factor in the coal market than the Government contended or the production statistics seemed to indicate. . . .

The Government . . . asserts that the paucity of United Electric's coal reserves could not have the significance perceived by the District Court, since all companies engaged in extracting minerals at some point deplete their reserves and then acquire new reserves or the new technology required to extract more minerals from their existing holdings. United Electric, the Government suggests, could at any point either purchase new strip reserves or acquire the expertise to recover currently held deep reserves.

But the District Court specifically found new strip reserves not to be available: "Evidence was presented at trial by experts, by state officials, by industry witnesses, and by the Government itself indicating that economically mineable strip reserves that would permit United Electric to continue operations beyond the life of its present mines are not available. The Government failed to come forward with any evidence that such reserves are *presently* available." 341 F. Supp., at 559. In addition, there was considerable testimony at trial, apparently credited by the District Court, indicating that United Electric and others had tried to find additional strip reserves not already held for coal production and had been largely unable to do so. . . .

The judgment of the District Court is affirmed.

It is so ordered.

Mr. Justice Douglas, with whom Mr. Justice Brennan, Mr. Justice White, and Mr. Justice Marshall concur, dissenting.

I

The combination here challenged is the union of two major Illinois coal producers—Freeman Coal Mining Corp. and United Electric Coal Companies—under the ultimate corporate control of General Dynamics Corp. Material Service Corp. acquired all the stock of Freeman Coal in 1942 and began to acquire United Electric stock in 1954. By 1959, holdings in United reached 34 percent, and Material Service requested and received representation on United's board of directors. As a result, Freeman's president was elected chairman of United's executive committee. "With the affiliation of Freeman and United Electric thus formalized in 1959, common control of the two coal companies was achieved." 341 F. Supp. 534, 537 (1972).

General Dynamics acquired Material Service Corp. in 1959 and moved to solidify the union of Freeman and United by engaging in continued purchases of United's stock throughout the early 1960s. By 1966 it held nearly two thirds of United's outstanding shares, and a successful tender offer increased the holdings to over 90 percent. In early 1967 United became a wholly-owned subsidiary of General Dynamics. With the 1959 union of Freeman and United Electric thus completed, the Government filed this action challenging the legality of the combination which produced in General Dynamics the Nation's fifth largest coal producer with total annual production of over 14 million tons.

II

. . . The court below concluded that "the energy market is the appropriate line of commerce for testing the competitive effect of the United Electric-Freeman combination." 341 F. Supp., at 555. The court rejected the Government's hypothesis of coal as a submarket for antitrust purposes as "untenable," finding that *United States* v. *Continental Can Co.*, 378 U.S. 441 (1964), "compel[s] this court to conclude that since coal competes with gas, oil, uranium, and other forms of energy, the relevant line of commerce must encompass interfuel competition." 341 F. Supp., at 556.

I read *Continental Can* to import no such compulsion. . . .

*   *   *   *   *

Coal has both price advantages and operational disadvantages which combine to delineate within the energy market "economically significant submarket[s]." The consumers for whom price is determinative mark out a submarket in which coal is the overwhelming choice; the boundaries of this submarket are strengthened by coal's virtual inability to compete in other significant sectors of the energy market. Energy-use technology in highway and air transportation necessitates the use of liquid fuels. The relative operational ease of dieselized power plants has worked virtually to foreclose coal from the rail transportation market. Despite their higher cost, gas and oil enjoy a competitive edge in the space-heating market because of simple consumer preference for these sources of energy over coal.

The market for coal is therefore effectively limited to large industrial energy consumers such as electric utilities and certain manufacturers with the ability and economic incentive to consider coal as an energy source. The court below noted that the "utility market has become the mainstay of coal production," 341 F. Supp., at 539. Within this sector coal's economic advantage yields it an overwhelming share of the market. In each year from 1960 to 1967 (the period during which the Freeman-United Electric union solidified) coal accounted for over 90 percent of the B.t.u.'s consumed by steam electric utility plants in the EICP sales area; it also provided 74 percent of the B.t.u.'s consumed by cement plants in the same area and 94 percent of the B.t.u.'s consumed by such plants in Illinois.

The coal market is therefore viewed by energy consumers as a separate economic entity confined to those users with the technological capability to allow the use of coal and the incentive for economy to mandate it. Within that market coal experiences little competition from other fuels since coal's delivered price per B.t.u. in the areas served by Freeman and United Electric is significantly lower than that for any other combustible fuel except interruptible natural gas which is available only on a seasonal basis. Central Illinois Light Co., for example, purchases coal at 27 cents per million B.t.u.'s, firm natural gas at 45 cents, and oil (for ignition purposes) at 70 cents. Since coal consumption facilities are unique and not readily adaptable to alternative energy sources, there is little interfuel price sensitivity. . . .

* * * * *

IV

While finding no violation of § 7 in the Freeman-United Electric combination, the District Court did not make clear the standard used in reaching that ultimate conclusion. The court did not mention what it thought to be the relevant market shares nor did it discuss the effect of the combination on industry concentration. The court merely found that Freeman and United Electric do not compete because they are located in different FRD geographic markets and because they sell different types of coal. As already discussed, nearly all the mines of both companies are located in southern Illinois, and as demonstrated by past distribution patterns with an ability to compete effectively at distances up to 500 miles, their presence in different minute FRD's within southern Illinois has simply *not* rendered them noncompetitive. . . .

* * * * *

The Court urges that United's weak reserve position, rather than establishing a failing-company defense, "went to the heart of the Government's statistical prima facie case based on production figures." Under this view United's weak reserve position at the time of trial constitutes postacquisition evidence which diminishes the possibility of anticompetitive impact and thus directly affects the strength of time-of-acquisition findings. The problem with this analysis is that the District Court made no time-of-acquisition findings which such postacquisition evidence could affect. The majority concedes the obvious need for a limitation on the weight given postacquisition evidence and notes that we have reversed cases where "too much weight" has been given. Here the postacquisition events were given *all* the weight because *all* the District Court's findings were made as of the time of the trial. While findings made as of the time of the merger could concededly be tempered to a limited degree by postacquisition events, no such findings were ever made. . . .

V

Thus, from product and geographic markets to market-share and industry-concentration analysis to the failing-company defense, the findings below are based on legal standards which are either incorrect or not disclosed. While the court did gratuitously state that no § 7 violation would be found "even were this court to accept the Government's unrealistic product and market definitions," this conclusory statement is supported by no analysis sufficient to allow review in this Court. The majority notes that production figures are of limited significance because they include deliveries under long-term contracts entered into in prior years. It is true that uncommitted reserves or sales of previously uncommitted coal would be preferable indicia of competitive strength, but the District Court made *no* findings as to United's or Freeman's respective market shares at the time of the acquisition under either of these standards.

On the basis of a record so devoid of findings based on correct legal standards, the judgment may not be affirmed except on a deep-seated judicial bias against § 7 of the Clayton Act. . . .

Vertical Mergers

Here the literature is mixed. Some writers urge that vertical mergers cannot raise market power. Others note that in real markets, there can be a reduction of entry and a triggering of vertical mergers among all firms, which eliminates the open market. Bork summarizes the one view, while Adams and Dirlam suggest that vertical integration in the steel industry has indeed affected market power.

Apart from *Brown Shoe,* which had vertical aspects, the leading vertical case is *duPont-General Motors.* The vertical tie (du Pont held 23 percent of GM stock since 1917–19) was old but the issues were fresh. The market shares were significant, and there was evidence that the tie did exclude others from a fair chance at selling to GM.

Robert H. Bork (1929–   )

✕ 17

Vertical Integration and the Sherman Act: The Legal History of an Economic Misconception*

Bork here assembles the case that vertical mergers do not—cannot—reduce competition. Since they may also yield large economies, Bork maintains that antitrust should keep hands off all vertical mergers. Only horizontal factors or imperfect capital markets create monopoly; vertical integration cannot extend it.

The utility of the vertical-integration concept for antitrust law seems a much easier subject than is the law that has been built around that concept. Yet there is hardly more agreement about the one than the other. It is the thesis here that the concept is almost entirely lacking in significance as an analytical tool for differentiating between competition and monopoly, and that, with one exception, its only proper use is as a term descriptive of corporate structure. . . .

Monopoly power is usually defined as the ability to alter the market price for a product or service. A firm effects the alteration of market price through changes in its own output that significantly change the total output of the industry. Thus monopoly power depends upon the percentage of the market occupied by the firm, and the ease of entry into that market. Vertical integration does not increase the percentage of the market controlled by a firm. It should be equally apparent that such integration does not impede entry into a market. Even though almost all of the myths concerning the ways in which vertical integration confers market power upon a firm or facilitates the exploitation of such power have been discredited, the theory that vertical integration prolongs monopoly by imposing greater capital requirements upon potential entrants is still confidently advanced in the literature as though it, too, had

*Robert H. Bork, "Vertical Integration and the Sherman Act: The Legal History of an Economic Misconception," *The University of Chicago Law Review,* vol. 22, 1954, excerpted from pp. 194–200. Bork has extended this classical-style analysis to other antitrust issues as a law professor at Yale.

not been badly shaken. Of course, vertical integration could affect entry only if two levels or stages of operation were monopolized by the integrated firm or cartel, so that entrants would have to come in on both levels at once. This would indeed require greater capital than would entrance upon one level. If there are greater-than-competitive profits being made in the industry, however, there seems no reason why the increased capital necessary for entry would not be forthcoming, unless there are impediments in the capital market that prevent capital from flowing to areas where it can most profitably be employed. Until such impediments have been shown to exist, the fact that increased capital is required for vertical integration must be assumed to have no adverse effect upon entry into monopolized markets. Therefore, since vertical integration does not increase the percentage of a market supplied by a firm and cannot be shown to impede entry into that market, such integration can be said to add nothing to monopoly power.

Nor does vertical integration affect a firm's pricing policy. If, for example, a firm operates at both the manufacturing and retail levels, it maximizes overall profit by setting the output at each level as though the levels were independent. Where both levels are competitive, the firm maximizes by equating marginal cost and price at each level; each level makes the competitive return. Where the firm has a monopoly at the manufacturing level but is competitive in retailing, it will, of course, exact a monopoly profit at the first level. And the manufacturing level will sell to the retail level at the same price as it sells to outside retailers. If the integrated firm has monopolies at both the manufacturing and retail levels, however, the levels will not maximize independently. It has already been explained that vertically integrated monopolies can take but one monopoly profit. Therefore, if the manufacturing level charged a monopoly price, the retail level would not act independently and further restrict output but would attempt to sell all of the manufacturing level's output at a competitive margin.

The above analysis supports the thesis that it is always horizontal market power and not integration into other levels which is important. This thesis has recently been attacked with the argument that, since the horizontal monopoly power may be impregnable (because it arises from a patent, natural monopoly in a basic supply, etc.), there may be no alternative but to dissolve the vertical integration which transmits the monopoly power from one level to another. The answer to this argument is clear from what has gone before. Suppose a monopolist at one level does not integrate vertically. He will charge the monopoly price to his customers, and that toll will be passed on to the ultimate consumers. What has already been said shows that the gaining of a second monopoly vertically related to the first would not alter price, output, or the allocation of productive resources on the second level monopolized.

Therefore, dissolving the vertical integration accomplishes precisely nothing.

There is, however, one advantage a monopolist might not otherwise enjoy which he may obtain by vertical integration: the ability to discriminate in price between different classes of customers. A monopolist may have two classes of customers making different products, one of which is willing to pay more than the other and yet, because of reselling between the classes, be unable to take advantage of the situation by discrimination. If, however, the monopolist should integrate with one of the classes, leakage would stop and discrimination become possible. It is not at all clear that this result is socially undesirable. One result of the discrimination is an increased profit for the monopolist. But the objection to monopoly is not that some people make too much money. It is that monopoly leads to a misallocation of society's resources through a restriction of output. In many cases when a monopolist price-discriminates, he tends to increase his output, and the resultant output is more like that dictated by competition than if he had not discriminated. In some cases this result may not occur, but on balance it seems more likely. Therefore, if the horizontal monopoly is legal, there should be no objection to price discrimination, and hence none to vertical integration employed to effect discrimination. The real problem, once more, is horizontal, not vertical.

This brief statement makes clear the position from which the use of the vertical-integration concept is criticized. With this analysis in mind we turn to an examination of some of the more common judicial notions concerning vertical integration. (The italicized statements are abstracted from the cases.)

Vertical integration may be used to gain a monopoly at one level. This notion appears in the cases, but the mechanism by which it operates is rarely mentioned. There is no such mechanism unless a monopoly at another level is already held. In that case the important issue is the first monopoly, not the vertical integration. In any event, the second monopoly adds no power the first did not confer.

Vertical integration makes possible, or lends itself to, the price "squeeze" by which a monopolist at one level drives out competitors at another. The "squeeze" does not automatically result from any internal efficiencies of integration, for the competitive unit does not maximize profit by reflecting cost savings in its selling price but by selling at the price established by its competitors. Nor does vertical integration confer any unique ability to "squeeze" as a monopolizing technique. A "squeeze" is nothing more than a price-cutting campaign at one level. A nonintegrated firm can just as easily wage this sort of warfare by selling its goods at the cost of the raw materials as can the second level of a vertically integrated firm. The use of the term "squeeze" serves only to make the practice seem peculiar to vertical integration and thus lend an undeserved sinister coloration to that form of organization.

The vertically integrated firm can monopolize one level by cutting prices there because it can offset its losses by advancing prices at another level. The theory of recoupment has been exploded many times. If both levels are competitive, prices can be advanced at neither; if either level is monopolistic, prices would already have been advanced there to make the maximum profit. In either case, recoupment of losses incurred in price-cutting is impossible. Leaving out the notion of recoupment, it is possible to say that predation in one market may be continued longer if money is being made elsewhere. But this applies to horizontal and diversified, as well as to vertical, integration.

By eliminating profit at one level the vertically integrated firm can undersell competition at the next. This myth has been as thoroughly discredited as recoupment. The firm can do this only if it is willing to forgo the return on part of its invested capital. Any firm, integrated or not, may do the same thing.

A variation of the above, which appears in the District Court *A & P* opinion, is particularly interesting. *Profit is eliminated at the retail level, and, consequently, increased volume is achieved. The increased volume raises the profits of the manufacturing level. The firm, therefore, not only undersells its competitors at the retail level, but it sacrifices no profits in doing so.* This argument must assume that the manufacturing level had been operating at an inefficient scale so that the increase in volume made up for the loss of retail profits. Of course the firm could have made more money by allowing its manufacturing units to sell to outsiders, thus obtaining increased volume at that level without sacrificing any of its retail profits. When this is seen, it becomes apparent that the mechanism described by the court is merely the sacrifice of profit in order to cut prices. Vertical integration is not relevant.

Money earned at one level gives a vertically integrated firm an advantage over its nonintegrated competitors at another level. This is especially true where the money is paid by the nonintegrated competitors. The advantage is said to be derived from the fact that the money paid in raises the costs of the competitors and lowers the costs of the integrated company. Of course, money received can never lower costs. The competitors' costs are not raised since they would have to pay for essential goods or services at that level in any event. Since output is determined by marginal cost and price (or marginal revenue where there is monopoly power) and since neither is altered by the situation described, the vertically integrated firm derives no competitive advantage.

One level of a vertically integrated firm may harm another of its own levels by charging it too high prices. The higher-than-market price to the second level would cause that level to decrease its output. So long as the market is competitive (or regulated), no one is damaged by this except the integrated firm which finds itself failing to maximize profits. If the market in which the second level sells is monopolistic, a restriction of output would occur anyway. The problem is then the monopoly and not the bookkeeping transactions between the two levels.

Walter Adams (1922–   )
Joel B. Dirlam (1915–   )

✕ 18

Steel Imports and Vertical Oligopoly Power*

In real markets, vertical integration does cause monopoly behavior and results, according to Adams and Dirlam. The steel industry is important in itself. Also, its conditions are found in many others. If Adams's and Dirlam's reasoning is correct, it does away with much of Bork's case, which, they say, holds only in a "hermetically sealed world." Where does the truth lie?

It is our contention that a vertically integrated oligopoly must maintain its administered price structure with all the economic and political weapons at its disposal. It must defend *à outrance* the vertical succession of keystone prices on which the entire price system rests. It must, therefore, contain, insulate, neutralize, and sterilize imports, especially when they threaten the vertically interwoven strategic prices. It cannot allow imports to have more than a sporadic, peripheral, nonstructural impact. Conversely, if the entire noncompetitive price structure is to be eroded, this must be done through an attack on strategic prices. Only if imports are pinpointed at the focus of vertical price policy (i.e., strategic prices) can they trigger price competition in the unconcentrated segments of the industry. . . .

Some of the prices in the vertical steel price structure are of more importance than others. These are what we have earlier called strategic prices. They are the keystone on which a portion of the price edifice rests. If they change, it will be necessary to shift the entire structure. Like the Gulf Coast or Group 3 spot prices for gasoline, they serve as a "peg to hang the price structure on." Thus the price for wire rods is strategic because it is the base on which the superstructure of wire and wire-products prices is built.

*Walter Adams and Joel B. Dirlam, "Steel Imports and Vertical Oligopoly Power," *American Economic Review*, June 1964, excerpted from pp. 626–27, 628–29, 639–40, 645–46, and 651–53. Both authors have been leading specialists on industrial conditions and critics of wayward policies since 1950. Adams is at Michigan State University and Dirlam at the University of Rhode Island.

If the steel oligopoly lived in a hermetically sealed world, it could maintain what it regards as the appropriate relations among prices in the vertical sequences with little difficulty. But no such world exists. The oligopoly has to permit the price structure to respond to outside stimuli, which constantly threaten it at various points. Some of the exogenous forces can be ignored as temporary aberrations. Others may be "contained" by minor adjustments. When a strategic price is threatened, however, the threat must be dealt with at almost any cost, not simply because of the necessity for reevaluating the specific price, but because of the danger to the market structure depending upon it.

The vertically organized giants in the steel industry, therefore, seldom consider a price in isolation. A change in any price introduces uncertainties up and down the line. If a product price is reduced, sales of semifinished steel may fall off because fabricators' margins have been compressed. The same consequence can result from an increase in prices of semifinished materials while product prices remain unchanged. The vertically integrated firms must consider these aspects of policy because they sell varying proportions of their products to nonintegrated firms at different stages of production. Their own customers may compete directly or indirectly with them on the finished product. Yet, for a variety of reasons associated with the individuality of customers and vagaries of location and technology, it does not ordinarily pay to eliminate all outside sales. For all these reasons, a decision to meet or not meet the lower price of a semifinished steel product cannot be made by integrated giants simply on the facts about direct costs and extent of unutilized capacity for that product alone.

The nonintegrated fabricator, on the other hand, lives in an entirely different world. He is aware of the vertical structure of prices only insofar as it affects his margin. When the margin is disturbed—increasing or decreasing—he will respond. But in normal times he lives within the margins permitted by the structure and cooperates with its preservation by not undercutting the prices of fabricated products published by his suppliers of raw or semifinished materials.

. . . Given the tapered integration and dual distribution in the wire segment of the steel industry, the majors had to compete with their nonintegrated customers. Before reducing rod prices, therefore, they had to consider not only the implications for rod revenues, but also the impact of this "cost" reduction on the independent fabricators and the indirect impact on the level of product prices. As long as the independent fabricators continued to buy domestic rod—and most of them used a 50/50 mix of imported and domestic rods in order not to cut themselves off from domestic supply sources—the majors felt that price cutting in the products markets would not get out of hand. On the other hand, if the majors had matched the lower price of imported rods, this would have lowered costs for the nonintegrated fabricators and served as a carte blanche invitation to cut product prices further than they had already been cut. In short, if the integrated steel companies were at all rational, we must presume that they concluded during the 1957–62 period that their losses from cuts in wire-rod prices, including the effect on products prices, would exceed the losses they suffered from relinquishing part of the noncaptive wire-rod market to imports. And this had to be a decision in which vertical considerations were paramount.

*   *   *   *   *

The Spengler-Adelman-Bork position is not in accord with the facts of life in the steel industry. To be sure, the nonintegrated fabricators responded to lower import prices on the individual products they produced because failure to do so would have meant extinction. As producers of a single product—or, at most, a handful of products—they had no alternative than to meet the price reductions precipitated by imports. In addition, they responded to the compression of their fabricating margins by turning in ever-increasing numbers to imported wire rods—that is, to lower-priced supplies of their basic raw material. Their reaction in both the product and raw-material markets, therefore, was roughly in accord with the profit-maximizing calculus applied in a horizontal context.

The integrated firms, by contrast, in a calculated effort to protect the industry's price structure, refused to meet the import prices either of products or rods. On some products, the integrated giants lowered prices to meet price cuts of their domestic nonintegrated competitors. Elsewhere, they preferred to abandon the field to imports altogether rather than to reduce their product prices. . . .

At the wire-rod level, the integrated firms seemed to react perversely to the import threat. They first raised prices (1955–58) and then maintained them with catatonic insensitivity (1958–63.)[1] They did so, not only because of their addiction to cost-plus, target-rate-of-return pricing, but more importantly in an attempt to maintain the vertical relationship between wire-rod and wire-product prices.

---

[1]According to the Spengler theory on vertical integration, rational monopolists or oligopolists would transfer semifinished products from one stage to another at prices free from monopolistic profits, thereby permitting the final price to be set at a lower figure than a price resulting from a series of transactions between independent bilateral oligopolists. If the steel industry conformed to Spengler's hypothesis, the transfer price for wire rods should have been affected by, if not identical with, the cost of imported rods of commensurate quality. The consequent reduction in the cost of wire-rod inputs to the wire divisions should have depressed the price of wire and, ultimately, wire-products prices.

That prices did not behave as the hypothesis suggests is obvious. It is instructive to inquire why. First, the structure of the industry was not that envisaged by Spengler. Integration is not complete, but is tapered forward, so that prices for wire rod and wire are not merely accounting transfer prices, but have a function vis-a-vis independent customers. Second, these prices are fixed by an administrative process in the course of which a

❧ 19

United States v. *E. I. du Pont de Nemours & Co.*

U.S. Supreme Court
353 U.S. 586 (1957)

> *This spectacular case involved an old vertical tie between two very big firms. It foreshadowed the new stricter policy toward mergers and placed even very old mergers within possible reach.*

Brennan, J.   This is a direct appeal . . . from a judgment of the District Court for the Northern District of Illinois, dismissing the Government's action brought in 1949 under § 15 of the Clayton Act. The complaint alleged a violation of § 7 of the Act resulting from the purchase by E. I. du Pont de Nemours and Company in 1917–19 of a 23-percent stock interest in General Motors Corporation. This appeal is from the dismissal of the action as to du Pont, General Motors, and the corporate holders of large amounts of du Pont stock, Christiana Securities Corporation, and Delaware Realty & Investment Company.

The primary issue is whether du Pont's commanding position as General Motors' supplier of automotive finishes and fabrics was achieved on competitive merit alone or because its acquisition of the General Motors' stock, and the consequent close intercompany relationship, led to the insulation of most of the General Motors' market from free competition, with the resultant likelihood at the time of suit of the creation of a monopoly of a line of commerce. . . .

We hold that any acquisition by one corporation of all or any part of the stock of another corporation, competitor or not, is within the reach

---

number of forces are brought to bear on price determination. Not only do the industry leaders take into account target return, but also the possible interactions of prices of wire rod, wire, and wire products, and the attitudes of customers to changes in accustomed differentials. Third, we may doubt whether, in any event, Spengler's optimism is warranted. There is little to show that transfer prices within a vertically integrated firm would, in actuality, be set at lower levels than market prices. In most U.S. industries, oligopolistic pricing policies, which might be expected to set prices in the market, would be regarded as proper procedures by managers responsible for transfer pricing within a vertically integrated firm. Hence, we would not anticipate that a shift to vertical integration in an industry already characterized by horizontal oligopoly would be reflected in appreciable price reductions because of elimination of interstitial profits. In fact, the probabilities would seem to lie in the opposite direction. While a horizontal oligopoly might be immediately affected by import competition and forced to modify its pricing procedures and standards, a partially vertically integrated industry could continue to resist such pressures at one level, maintaining "cost" constituents that a horizontal oligopoly would have been forced to abandon.

of the section whenever the reasonable likelihood appears that the acquisition will result in a restraint of commerce or in the creation of a monopoly of any line of commerce. Thus, although du Pont and General Motors are not competitors, a violation of the section has occurred if, as a result of the acquisition, there was at the time of suit a reasonable likelihood of a monopoly of any line of commerce.

. . . In 1947 General Motors' total purchases of all products from du Pont were $26,628,274, of which $18,938,229 (71 percent) represented purchases from du Pont's Finishes Division. Of the latter amount purchases of "Duco" and the thinner used to apply "Duco" totaled $12,224,798 (65 percent), and "Dulux" purchases totaled $3,179,225. Purchases by General Motors of du Pont fabrics in 1948 amounted to $3,700,000, making it the largest account of du Pont's Fabrics Division. Expressed in percentages, du Pont supplied 67 percent of General Motors' requirements for finishes in 1946 and 68 percent in 1947. In fabrics du Pont supplied 52.3 percent of requirements in 1946 and 38.5 percent in 1947. Because General Motors accounts for almost one half of the automobile industry's annual sales, its requirements for automotive finishes and fabrics must represent approximately one half of the relevant market for these materials. Because the record clearly shows that quantitatively and percentagewise du Pont supplies the largest part of General Motors' requirements, we must conclude that du Pont has a substantial share of the relevant market.

The du Pont Company's commanding position as a General Motors supplier was not achieved until shortly after its purchase of a sizeable block of General Motors stock in 1917. At that time its production for the automobile industry and its sales to General Motors were relatively insignificant. General Motors then produced only about 11 percent of the total automobile production, and its requirements, while relatively substantial, were far short of the proportions they assumed as it forged ahead to its present place in the industry. . . .

This background of the acquisition, particularly the plain implications of the contemporaneous documents, destroys any basis for a conclusion that the purchase was made "solely for investment." Moreover, immediately after the acquisition, du Pont's influence growing out of it was brought to bear within General Motors to achieve primacy for du Pont as General Motors' supplier of automotive fabrics and finishes. . . .

The fact that sticks out in this voluminous record is that the bulk of du Pont's production has always supplied the largest part of the requirements of the one customer in the automobile industry connected to du Pont by a stock interest. The inference is overwhelming that du Pont's commanding position was promoted by its stock interest and was not gained solely on competitive merit. . . .

Conglomerate Mergers

As a catch-all category, conglomerate mergers do not easily fit a single theory or guideline. Neither the monopoly effects nor any possible economies are directly obvious. Cases have tested out several possible effects. In *Procter & Gamble-Clorox* (1967), the FTC and the Supreme Court decided that P&G's advertising strength would entrench Clorox's dominant position (a 50-percent market share) more deeply if a merger were permitted. A "toe-hold" merger with a small firm would have been procompetitive and acceptable. In *Bendix-Fram*, too, the potential entrant would have been permitted to make a "toe-hold" merger. The *Budd-Gindy* decision in 1975 reflected a definite rule that a market share below 10 percent was a "toe-hold." The *ITT-Grinnell* case in 1971 involved the claim that the merged parts would practice reciprocity and entrench the leading firms in their markets. The district court did not agree, and then the cases were settled before reaching a clear answer before the Supreme Court.

✖ 20

Federal Trade Commission v. *Procter & Gamble Co.*

U.S. Supreme Court
386 U.S. 568 (1967)

> *This major case embraced several alternative doctrines for stopping conglomerate mergers. Procter & Gamble was a potential entrant. It could not acquire the largest firm (Clorox), but a toehold acquisition of a smaller bleach firm might have been permitted. Massive advertising advantages were involved, and Procter & Gamble was a very large firm.*

Mr. Justice Douglas.   This is a proceeding initiated by the Federal Trade Commission charging that respondent, Procter & Gamble Co., had acquired the assets of Clorox Chemical Co. in violation of § 7 of the Clayton Act, . . . as amended by the Celler-Kefauver Act. . . . The charge was that Procter's acquisition of Clorox might substantially lessen competition or tend to create a monopoly in the production and sale of household liquid bleaches. . . .

At the time of the merger in 1957, Clorox was the leading manufacturer in the heavily concentrated household liquid bleach industry. It is agreed that household liquid bleach is the relevant line of commerce. The product is used in the home as a germicide and disinfectant and, more importantly, as a whitening agent in washing clothes and fabrics. It is a distinctive product with no close substitutes. Liquid bleach is a low-price high-turnover consumer product sold mainly through grocery stores and supermarkets. The relevant geographical market is the Nation and a series of regional markets. Because of high shipping costs and low sales price, it is not feasible to ship the product more than 300 miles from its point of manufacture. Most manufacturers are limited to competition within a single region since they have but one plant. Clorox is the only firm selling nationally; it has 13 plants distributed throughout the Nation. Purex, Clorox's closest competitor in size, does not distribute its bleach in the northeast or mid-Atlantic States; in 1957, Purex's bleach was available in less than 50 percent of the national market.

At the time of the acquisition, Clorox was the leading manufacturer of household liquid bleach, with 48.8 percent of the national sales—annual sales of slightly less than $40,000,000. Its market share had been steadily increasing for the five years prior to the merger. Its nearest rival was Purex, which manufactures a number of products other than household liquid bleaches, including abrasive cleaners, toilet soap, and detergents. Purex accounted for 15.7 percent of the household liquid bleach market.

Since all liquid bleach is chemically identical, advertising and sales promotion are vital. In 1957 Clorox spent almost $3,700,000 on advertising, imprinting the value of its bleach in the mind of the consumer. In addition, it spent $1,700,000 for other promotional activities. The Commission found that these heavy expenditures went far to explain why Clorox maintained so high a market share despite the fact that its brand, though chemically indistinguishable from rival brands, retailed for a price equal to or, in many instances, higher than its competitors.

Procter is a large, diversified manufacturer of low-price high-turnover household products sold through grocery, drug, and department stores. Prior to its acquisition of Clorox, it did not produce household liquid bleach. Its 1957 sales were in excess of $1,100,000,000 from which it realized profits of more than $67,000,000; its assets were over $500,000,000. Procter has been marked by rapid growth and diversification. It has successfully developed and introduced a number of new products. Its primary activity is in the general area of soaps, detergents, and cleansers; in 1957, of total domestic sales, more than one half (over $500,000,000) were in this field. Procter was the dominant factor in this area. It accounted for 54.4 percent of all packaged detergent sales. The industry is heavily concentrated—Procter and its nearest competitors, Colgate-Palmolive and Lever Brothers, account for 80 percent of the market.

In the marketing of soaps, detergents, and cleansers, as in the marketing of household liquid bleach, advertising and sales promotion are vital. In 1957, Procter was the Nation's largest advertiser, spending more than $80,000,000 on advertising and an additional $47,000,000 on sales promotion. Due to its tremendous volume, Procter receives substantial discounts from the media. As a multiproduct producer Procter enjoys substantial advantages in advertising and sales promotion. Thus, it can and does feature several products in its promotions, reducing the printing, mailing, and other costs for each product. It also purchases network programs on behalf of several products, enabling it to give each product network exposure at a fraction of the cost per product that a firm with only one product to advertise would incur.

Prior to the acquisition, Procter was in the course of diversifying into product lines related to its basic detergent-soap-cleanser business. Liquid bleach was a distinct possibility since packaged detergents—Procter's primary product line—and liquid bleach are used complementarily in washing clothes and fabrics and in general household cleaning. . . .

The anticompetitive effects with which this product-extension merger is fraught can easily be seen: (1) the substitution of the powerful acquiring firm for the smaller, but already dominant, firm may substantially reduce the competitive structure of the industry by raising entry barriers and by dissuading the smaller firms from aggressively competing; (2) the acquisition eliminates the potential competition of the acquiring firm.

. . . There is every reason to assume that the smaller firms would become more cautious in competing due to their fear of retaliation by Procter. It is probable that Procter would become the price leader and that oligopoly would become more rigid.

The acquisition may also have the tendency of raising the barriers to new entry. The major competitive weapon in the successful marketing of bleach is advertising. Clorox was limited in this area by its relatively small budget and its inability to obtain substantial discounts. By contrast, Procter's budget was much larger; and although it would not devote its entire budget to advertising Clorox, it could divert a large portion to meet the short-term threat of a new entrant. Procter would be able to use its volume discounts to advantage in advertising Clorox. Thus, a new entrant would be much more reluctant to face the giant Procter than it would have been to face the smaller Clorox.

Possible economies cannot be used as a defense to illegality. Congress was aware that some mergers which lessen competition may also result in economies, but it struck the balance in favor of protecting competition. . . .

The Commission also found that the acquisition of Clorox by Procter eliminated Procter as a potential competitor. The Court of Appeals declared that this finding was not supported by evidence because there was no evidence that Procter's management had ever intended to enter the industry independently and that Procter had never attempted to enter. The evidence, however, clearly shows that Procter was the most likely entrant. Procter had recently launched a new abrasive cleaner in an industry similar to the liquid bleach industry and had wrested leadership from a brand that had enjoyed even a larger market share than had Clorox. Procter was engaged in a vigorous program of diversifying into product lines closely related to its basic products. Liquid bleach was a natural avenue of diversification since it is complementary to Procter's products, is sold to the same customers through the same channels, and is advertised and merchandised in the same manner. Procter had substantial advantages in advertising and sales promotion which, as we have seen, are vital to the success of liquid bleach. No manufacturer had a patent on the product or its manufacture, necessary information relating to manufacturing methods and processes was readily available, there was no shortage of raw material, and the machinery and equipment required for a plant of efficient capacity were available at reasonable costs. Procter's management was experienced in producing and marketing goods similar to liquid bleach. Procter had considered the possibility of independently entering but decided against it because the acquisition of Clorox would enable Procter to capture a more commanding share of the market. . . .

The judgment of the Court of Appeals is reversed and remanded with instructions to affirm and enforce the Commission's order.

It is so ordered.

Justice Harlan, concurring:

. . . The Commission—in my opinion quite correctly—seemed to accept the idea that economies could be used to defend a merger, noting that "[a] merger that results in increased efficiency of production, distribution, or marketing may, in certain cases, increase the vigor of competition in the relevant market." . . . But advertising economies were placed in a different classification since they were said "only to increase the barriers to new entry" and to be "offensive to at least the spirit, if not the letter, of the antitrust laws." . . . Advertising was thought to benefit only the seller by entrenching his market position and to be of no use to the consumer.

I think the Commission's view overstated and oversimplified. Proper advertising serves a legitimate and important purpose in the market by educating the consumer as to available alternatives. This process contributes to consumer demand being developed to the point at which economies of scale can be realized in production. The advertiser's brand name may also be an assurance of quality, and the value of this benefit is demonstrated by the general willingness of consumers to pay a premium for the advertised brands. Undeniably advertising may sometimes be used to create irrational brand preferences and mislead consumers as to the actual differences between products, but it is very difficult to discover at what point advertising ceases to be an aspect of healthy competition. . . . It is not the Commission's function to decide which lawful elements of the "product" offered the consumer should be considered useful and which should be considered the symptoms of industrial "sickness." It is the consumer who must make that election through the exercise of his purchasing power. In my view, true efficiencies in the use of advertising must be considered in assessing economies in the marketing process, which as has been noted are factors in the sort of § 7 proceeding involved here.

I do not think, however, that on the record presented Procter has shown any true efficiencies in advertising. Procter has merely shown that it is able to command equivalent resources at a lower dollar cost than other bleach producers. No peculiarly efficient marketing techniques have been demonstrated, nor does the record show that a smaller net advertising expenditure could be expected. Economies cannot be premised solely on dollar figures, lest accounting controversies dominate § 7 proceedings. Economies employed in defense of a merger must be shown in what economists label "real" terms, that is in terms of resources applied to the accomplishment of the objective. For this reason, the Commission, I think, was justified in discounting Procter's efficiency defense.

✖ 21

Federal Trade Commission v. *The Bendix Corp.*

Docket No. 8739 (1970)
Trade Cases ¶19,288 (1970)

The Bendix-Fram *decision extended and clarified the toehold and potential-entrant criteria. But was* Bendix *really a major potential entrant?*

OPINION OF THE COMMISSION

I. Introduction

By Commissioner Elman. On June 29, 1967, one day before consummation of a merger between Fram Corporation (Fram) and the Bendix Corporation (Bendix), the Commission issued its complaint herein charging that the merger violated Section 7 of the Clayton Act . . . and Section 5 of the Federal Trade Commission Act. . . . Although the merger was thereafter consummated, Fram has been operated as a separate subsidiary of Bendix by agreement between the parties. . . .

There are over 30 manufacturers of automotive filters, including the giant auto makers, General Motors and Ford. Nevertheless, the market is a relatively concentrated one. In 1966, in the broad overall market, the top three companies accounted for 62.9 percent of industry sales, and the top six companies accounted for 79.6 percent. . . .

B. The Respondents

1. *Fram* is a leading United States producer of various kinds of filters, including automotive filters, aerospace filters, and filter water separators. . . . Its sales, earnings, and assets in 1966 were the highest in its history, and it was a financially sound, profitable, and growing company. . . .

Approximately 55 percent of Fram's 1966 sales were in automotive filters. In that field, Fram was not only the third-ranking producer with 12.4 percent of the market, but a pioneer in technology and promotion. . . . Although Fram sold filters in all the distributional channels in the industry, about 90 percent of Fram's filter sales were in the passenger car filter aftermarket, where Fram ranked third in sales with 17.2 percent of the market.

2. *Bendix* is a diversified manufacturer of components and assemblies for aerospace, automotive, automation, scientific, oceanic, and other uses. . . . Bendix sells, through eight separate divisions, a wide variety of automotive parts: fuel pumps, starter drives, ignition components, brakes, brake drums, power steerings, universal joints, carburetors, radios, speed controls, temperature controls, and filters. While the predominant portion of these automotive sales is made to automobile manufacturers and other original equipment makers, Bendix makes substantial sales to the automotive aftermarket, both as proprietary and private brands. . . . Indeed, in 1961, Bendix formed an Automotive Services Division to facilitate the distribution of all Bendix automotive parts in the aftermarket. . . .

In the automotive filter industry, Bendix focused upon the production and sale of heavy duty oil and fuel filters for original equipment makers. The Bendix Filter Division was one of the company's smallest and in the early 1960s was losing money. . . . The only filter product manufactured by Bendix specifically for passenger car application was an air filter element made in the late 1950s for Ford and American Motors. After losing money on the venture, Bendix in 1960 began subcontracting these filters, until 1963 when its Ford contract was terminated.

Thus, the principal remaining issue in this case is whether the merger may substantially lessen competition by eliminating Bendix as a potential entrant and competitor in the automotive filter market. . . .

B. Bendix as a Likely Entrant and Competitor

The evidence in the record and the hearing examiner's relevant findings overwhelmingly establish that Bendix was likely and able to enter the passenger car filter aftermarket, one way or another. The probability of its entry into this market was clear: The only question was the form that such entry would take.

Bendix was a major participant in the automotive parts business, with 1966 sales well over $200 million. Bendix also made substantial sales in the automotive parts replacement market, with 1966 sales of $40.6 million; and half of these sales were under Bendix's proprietary label. . . .

Furthermore, Bendix was already a minor participant in the automotive filter industry. In 1966, Bendix's automotive filter sales allowed Bendix to control 0.35 percent of the market—a share equal to or larger than almost one third of the firms in that market. . . .

In sum, from the objective evidence only one conclusion is possible: The whole logic of Bendix's corporate development, its size, resources, and direct proximity to the passenger car filter aftermarket, and the unambiguous direction of its business growth, all pointed to expansion into the passenger car filter aftermarket.

The record also establishes that this was recognized by Bendix's management. . . .

. . . [I]t . . . was convinced that Bendix should make a substantial entry into the passenger car filter aftermarket in an attempt to salvage the current Bendix investment in filters and to bring greater profits and stability to the corporation as a whole. . . .

Thus, all likely routes for potential entry into the relevant market must be considered in determining the legality of the merger route which was in fact chosen. A potential entrant may enter not only by internal expansion; he may enter the market by acquiring a failing company, or a small company in difficulty, or by making a toehold acquisition of a small member of the industry. These methods of entry, no less than internal expansion, and in some cases perhaps more than entry by internal expansion, may inject a new competitive element of vigor and strength into an otherwise stagnant market. Indeed, where entry into some markets by internal expansion is foreclosed and/or restricted, entry by toehold acquisition may be the most feasible route for developing new competition. Furthermore, in an age of mergers and acquisitions, the threat of a toehold merger by a powerful firm may often serve as a much greater incentive to competitive performance in the affected market than does the prospect of more costly and slower internal *de novo* expansion.

In short, it is offensive to the merger law to eliminate the potential competition offered by likely entrants at a market's edge that may come into it through a toehold or other procompetitive acquisition, especially where the market is a concentrated one in need of new competition. . . .

The record leaves no doubt that, if Bendix had based its expansion decisions on a correct legal premise, namely, that Section 7 firmly closed the door to entry into the aftermarket by a leading firm acquisition but left the door wide open to a toehold acquisition, Bendix would long ago have entered the market by the latter route.

The evidence as to the likelihood of such an acquisition entry is substantial. . . . [I]n the 1960s, Bendix management decided to diversify into nongovernment, nonmilitary business. One area seen as not only lucrative but compatible with Bendix's other business was the automotive filter market—particularly the profitable and growing aftermarket.

As a result, between 1961 and 1966, Bendix considered the acquisition of numerous filter makers. . . .

Bendix possessed the resources and size necessary to engage in any prolonged battle against the major filter makers, which included the nation's industrial giants—Ford and General Motors. Bendix also had the experience and necessary technology for making filters. This could be advantageous in expanding a small filter maker that might not have the experience in producing a full line of filters. . . .

If any barrier to entry by this acquisition route existed for Bendix, it was, as respondents contend, due to the mass marketing and promotional techniques necessary to sell filters in the aftermarket. But this was precisely the barrier that Bendix could have surmounted by a toehold acquisition of a firm with substantial promotional facilities. . . .

The only question was the form that new entry would take. Bendix had three choices: (1) to expand internally; (2) to make a toehold acquisition looking toward expansion on that base; and (3) to merge with a leading firm. If Bendix had taken either of the first two routes of entry, it would have become an actual competitor of Fram and would have provided a beneficial new element in the market. Either of those two routes would have promoted competition; neither violated Section 7; indeed, either was the sort of entry into a new market which Congress intended to encourage. Instead, Bendix chose the third route—acquisition of Fram, a leading firm—and thus the likelihood of substantial competition between these two firms was forever eliminated. By the same token, the competitive input that Bendix could have brought to the entire market, had it entered by a toehold acquisition, was also lost. . . .

The competitively lethargic state of the industry is reflected in the stabilized pricing patterns found by the hearing examiner. Whatever competition there is seems to be in terms of promotion, selling, and distribution. Manufacturers build up sales by brand differentiation, advertising, by large numbers of salesmen and promotional men, and by such promotional gimmicks as bonus stamps, coupons, contests, and prizes. All these various forms of nonprice competition seem to have contributed to a continued dominance by the leaders in the industry and the comfortable profits prevalent among all sellers. . . .

✳ 22

Federal Trade Commission, In the matter of *The Budd Co.*

FTC Docket 8848
TRR No. 731, September 1975

Here the FTC firmly applies the toe-hold doctrine, letting a firm below 10 percent of the market be merged even with a clear potential entrant. Was its market definition correct? Would preventing the merger have been a more prudent action?

OPINION OF THE COMMISSION

By Engman, Commissioner: The Budd Company appeals from the Initial Decision in this matter in which the Administrative Law Judge found that its acquisition of the Gindy Manufacturing Corporation ("Gindy") in 1968 violated Section 7 of the Clayton Act.

According to the Fortune Directory of the 500 largest United States Industrial Corporations, in 1967 Budd was the 250th largest industrial corporation in the nation in terms of sales ($469.5 million) and was one of the largest independent automotive suppliers in the nation and the largest independent supplier of body parts to the automotive industry. Budd principally manufactured automotive bodies, wheels, rims, hubs, drums, brakes, jigs and dies used in the manufacture of automotive body parts. In addition it was a leading manufacturer of railroad and mass transit cars.

Prior to its acquisition by Budd on October 22, 1968, Gindy was a Pennsylvania corporation engaged in the manufacture and sale of van trailers, containers, and container chassis. For fiscal year 1968, Gindy sales were approximately $32 million, and its assets amounted to about $44 million.

On October 22, 1968, through an exchange of Budd stock valued at $29.7 million, Budd acquired the outstanding capital stock of Gindy.

The complaint alleges that prior to the acquisition Budd was one of the most likely potential entrants into the manufacture and sale of van trailers, closed-top dry freight van trailers, open-top van trailers, and containers and container chassis, and that by acquiring Gindy, Budd eliminated itself as a substantial potential competitor in these markets. The complaint further alleges that these markets and segments thereof are highly concentrated and characterized by high entry barriers.

After extensive hearings, the Administrative Law Judge sustained these allegations and entered an order requiring divestiture of the acquired firm.

I. RELEVANT PRODUCT MARKETS

. . . We are satisfied that the "van trailer" and "containers and chassis" each constitute appropriate markets for purposes of the case. It is not disputed that van trailers are produced on fairly unique production lines which cannot be quickly utilized to produce other types of nonvan trailers such as tank, platform, logging, or dump trailers. Also, because of their special design, there is little or no substitution in end use between van trailers and these other types of truck trailers. Likewise, containers and chassis serve a distinct function that separate them from van trailers, and they are usually constructed on different assembly lines than those used to build van trailers. . . .

We agree with respondent and its expert witness that "closed-top dry freight van trailers" and "open-top van trailers" do not constitute meaningful economic markets. The market for open-top trailers is limited as they are used mainly to carry freight, such as steel lengths which must be loaded from the top by cranes. Census reported a total of $19.8 million in open-top van trailer production for 1968 as compared to $246.1 million for closed-top dry freight van trailers.[1] Although it is true that a buyer may not find these types substitutable for particular end uses, the record nevertheless establishes that production and distribution facilities for each are identical and are essentially identical among other types of vans. Both "closed" and "open" top vans are commonly made by all van trailer manufacturers, including Gindy, and do not require separate assembly lines.

No doubt the reason that complaint counsel urge the existence of separate "closed-top" and "open-top" van markets is that Gindy's

---

[1]Total production of all vans in 1968 amounted to $381.7 million. It should be noted that "open-top vans" and "closed-top dry freight vans" do not account for all vans. In addition to these subcategories, Census lists under "vans" the following: insulated vans ($84 million), drop frame (furniture-type) vans ($22 million), and livestock vans ($9 million).

"market share" is much higher if these product lines are used. Although Gindy's share of all van trailer shipments in 1968 was 8.4 percent (giving it an industry rank of number 4), its production of open-top trailers happened to represent nearly 16 percent of all open-top van trailer shipments in that year (giving it a rank of number 2 in the production of open-top vans). Its share of U.S. production of "closed-top dry freight vans" in 1968 and 1969 also exceeded 10 percent.

III. MARKET CONCENTRATION

Universe figures for the various lines of commerce described above were taken from Census Bureau publications. Shipments of individual firms were obtained directly from the manufacturers. The table (p. 112) shows relevant data for the years 1966 through 1968 for Gindy and the leading three firms in each of the markets.

Before the loss of a potential entrant can be viewed as violating Section 7, it must be established that the market is concentrated or threatens to become so, that entry barriers are high, and that the acquired firm is a leading factor in the market. *Kennecott Copper Corp.*, 78 F.T.C. 744, 921–22 (1971), aff'd, 467 F. 2d 67 (10th Cir. 1972); *The Bendix Corp.*, 77 F.T.C. 731 (1970), remanded for further proceedings, 450 F. 2d 534 (6th Cir. 1971). If the market is not concentrated, there is usually little opportunity for the sellers to maintain collectively prices above competitive levels and any diminution of potential competition will not be material. On the other hand, if the market is concentrated but entry barriers are low, potential competition will be important, but since there will be a large number of firms able to come into the market under approximately the same conditions, the merger of one of those firms with an existing seller will make no difference because the threat of new entry will remain approximately the same. *Beatrice Foods Company*, 81 F.T.C. 481, 530 (1972); *General Mills, Inc.*, Dkt. 8836. Slip Opinion October 5, 1973, p. 5 n. 2.

As the following table (p. 112) shows, four-firm concentration ratios are approximately 60 percent or more, with the largest firm, Fruehauf, usually representing about 25 percent of output. The top three firms (Fruehauf, Trailmobile, and Strick) collectively shared more than 50 percent of the output in each of the markets during the three years leading up to the year of acquisition. Although the record indicates that the balance of the markets are shared by nearly 100 firms, clearly these markets are substantially concentrated. *The Stanley Works*, 78 F.T.C. 1023, 1065 n. 12 (1971), aff'd, 469 F. 2d 498 (2d Cir. 1972); *Beatrice Foods Company*, Dkt. 8864 (July 1, 1975).

In addition, the ALJ found that there were substantial barriers to entry insofar as entering on a substantial level of production is con-

Table 1

	All Trailer Production Less Tanks and Bulk Commodity Trailers		1968 Van Trailers		Containers and Chassis	
	Dollars (000)	Percent	Dollars (000)	Percent	Dollars (000)	Percent
Industry	$593,387		$381,665		$81,956	
Fruehauf	171,377	28.08	105,148	27.61	28,868	35.35
Trailmobile	73,238	12.34	47,465	12.35	19,094	23.38
Strick	65,781	11.25	40,441	10.60	21,029	25.75
Gindy	35,661	6.01	32,176	8.48	3,128	3.83
Top 4		58.49		58.99		90.23
Top 8		75.83		80.69		99.48
Gindy's Rank		4		4		6

cerned. Respondent argues that no barriers exist as the manufacture of trailers and containers requires no extensive know-how or expensive equipment, patent licenses are not required, only a small amount of capital is needed to start manufacturing, and there appear to be no significant economies of scale in manufacturing. However, we think the record bears out the ALJ's finding, although the term "barriers to effective competition" might convey a more accurate picture than "barriers to entry," see *Fruehauf Trailer Co.*, 67 F.T.C. 878, 930–31 (1965).

*   *   *   *   *

IV. BUDD AS A POTENTIAL ENTRANT

The Administrative Law Judge found that since at least 1956 Budd has been a potential entrant into the manufacture and sale of van trailers and containers and chassis and that by acquiring Gindy, Budd removed itself as an actual future entrant in these markets either by entry de novo or by acquisition of a small company. In addition he found that Budd was perceived by firms in the market as a potential entrant and loss of its presence at the edge of the market removed any disciplining effects that would have ensued from its continued presence as a perceived potential entrant.

Respondent takes strong issues with all of these findings, arguing that Budd was not interested in entering the trailer industry except by acquisition of a firm having an operation of the scale and profitability that Gindy possessed. Respondent argues that the Gindy acquisition was in fact procompetitive because Gindy's advancement in the market had reached a plateau and without access to capital for expansion and financing of sales on a mere competitive basis it could not hope to make inroads on the market position of Fruehauf and Trailmobile.

On the question of whether Budd was a perceived potential entrant, we disagree with the ALJ. A large number of industry witnesses testified in this proceeding and when asked whether they had viewed Budd as a potential entrant before the Gindy acquisition, the response was uniformly "no." Notwithstanding such testimony the ALJ reasoned:

> In the spring of 1968, Gindy suspended [merger] negotiations with Budd. At that time Budd's executives contacted Miller and Dorsey, both van trailer manufacturers, concerning possible acquisition. A third party consultant approached Theurer, another van trailer manufacturer. Budd also contacted Utility twice during the period 1963 to 1968. Thus, at least four van trailer manufacturers were aware of Budd's interest shortly before the acquisition of Gindy. (Initial Decision p. 55.)

However, executives from Miller, Dorsey, Theurer, and Utility testified they did not perceive Budd as a potential entrant (Tr. 714, 1660, 1831, 1852, 1917). Prior to the time Budd acquired Gindy, these and the other trailer companies who appeared at the hearing did not take Budd into account in formulating competitive practices and prices (Tr. 524, 714, 753–54, 1304, 1439, 1510–11, 1646, 1738–39, 1776, 1904, 1917, 2216–17). Nor is there any reason to believe that had the Gindy acquisition not taken place Budd's continued presence outside the market would have influenced industry prices. Numerous industry witnesses, including representatives from the market leaders, identified other firms and types of firms they considered more likely to enter the truck trailer industry than Budd. These included automobile manufacturers (Tr. 1362–63), truck tractor manufacturers (Tr. 1362–63, 1511–14, 1591, 1628–29, 1633, 1740–42, 1777–78, 1868) and truck body manufacturers (Tr. 1588–91, 1753–54). No witness testified that their prices or practices were affected by these firms. The only conclusion that can be reasonably drawn from the evidence is that there is no basis upon which to believe that *Budd's* continued presence at the edge of the market would have any greater effect on market performance.

We are left then with the argument that Budd was a likely actual entrant which would have entered the market at some time in the future by means other than the Gindy acquisition. This finding is also strongly disputed by the respondent. We find it unnecessary, however, to review the lengthy arguments that have been presented on this issue.

Although the ALJ found that Budd was an actual potential entrant into the van and container markets, we think he jumped too quickly to the conclusion that entry by way of acquiring Gindy was anticompetitive. Insufficient attention was paid to whether Gindy should be viewed as a "toehold or foothold firm," acquisition of which would lead to improved competition against dominant market leaders. As the Commission observed in *Bendix Corporation, supra* 77 F.T.C. at 818–19 (1970); "[I]n a highly concentrated, sluggish market, the acquisition of a small industry member by a powerful, innovative firm which, by building upon the base of the smaller firm can pose a more effective competitive challenge to the industry giants [may promote competition]. Such pro-competitive mergers are not only not forbidden by Section 7, they are positively encouraged." "[T]he threat of a toehold merger by a powerful firm may often serve as a much greater incentive to competitive performance in the affected market than the prospect of more costly and slower internal *de novo* expansion." id. at 819.

In the *Bendix* case the Commission struck down the acquisition by Bendix of the third-ranking firm (Fram) which had 17.2 percent of the market. However, it characterized as a toehold firm that could lawfully have been acquired by Bendix, fourth-ranking Wix Manufacturing Company which had 9.5 percent of the market and was not shown to be technologically inferior. Similarly, the Ajax Company, recognized as a permissible toehold or foothold candidate in *Stanley Works*, 78 F.T.C. 1023, 1072 (1971) aff'd on other grounds, 469 F. 2d 498, 508–09 n. 24 (2d Cir. 1972), ranked third in the market with a share of about 8 percent. As we recently noted, the Commission has generally considered "firms having market shares below 10 percent as toehold companies, acquisition of which would have been procompetitive" *Beatrice Foods Company*, Dkt. 8864 (July 1, 1975, slip opinion p. 17 n. 8).

V. GINDY'S POSITION IN THE INDUSTRY

Market share data set forth, *supra*, show that Gindy ranked considerably below Fruehauf, Trailmobile, and Strick. In the overall trailer market Gindy's share fluctuated between 4.9 percent and 6.5 percent during the three years prior to the merger. In the van trailer market, where Gindy's share was highest, it never rose appreciably above 7–8 percent as compared to Fruehauf's 27 percent and Trailmobile's 17 percent. Gindy's market position in 1968 was much closer to firms ranking below it, such as Brown Trailer (6.6 percent of the van trailer market in 1968), Highway (5.5 percent), and Great Dane (5.1 percent). Complaint counsel in fact characterize Highway and Great Dane as available "toehold" firms. In the container-and-chassis market, Gindy ranked number 6 with only 3.8 percent of the market. . . .

The Administrative Law Judge, holding that Gindy could not be viewed as a toehold or foothold acquisition candidate, relied on the fact that Gindy's shares in the alleged submarket "closed-top freight vans" exceeded 10 percent in 1968 and 1969 (Findings 151–54). However, as we have held, this is not a meaningful economic market or submarket, and Gindy's shares varied from 3 to 8 percent in the relevant markets during the years immediately prior to the merger.

We believe it to be desirable to observe a general rule in potential competition cases that firms possessing no more than 10 percent in a target market (where, as here, the 4-firm concentration is approximately 60 percent or more) should ordinarily be presumed to be toehold or foothold firms. This presumption by no means is conclusive and the inference of lack of anticompetitive effects flowing from acquisition of such a firm can be rebutted in particular cases. The 10-percent demarcation is supported by the prior Commission cases, as noted, and is not inconsistent with the Department of Justice Merger Guidelines.

In this case, the presumption is supported by the record which shows that the acquisition of Gindy by Budd engendered increased capacity and other procompetitive forces, the very effects the toehold doctrine was designed to elicit. . . .

In view of our finding that the acquisition did not lessen competition, the initial decision will be vacated and the complaint dismissed.

DISSENTING STATEMENT OF COMMISSIONER HANFORD

By Commissioner Hanford.   I agree with Commissioner Dixon that open-top van trailers and closed-top dry freight vans are distinct product submarkets and that the submarket which the majority has defined as encompassing both types of trailers fails to reflect economic reality. Accordingly, I find I am unable to agree with the majority's conclusion that Budd's purchase of Gindy constitutes entry by toehold acquisition.

What we have here is a situation in which Budd was, prior to the acquisition, an actual potential entrant into markets which are characterized by high concentration and substantial barriers to effective competition. Moreover, it was one of the few most likely potential entrants into these markets. Budd could have entered these markets by toehold acquisition or de novo through internal expansion. It had the capacity to do so. Had it entered in either of these two ways, it would have been a direct competitor of Gindy, which at the time of the acquisition was ranked number two in the production of open-top van trailers. In addition, the other leading firms in this market would have had to contend with aggressive new competition from Budd as well as the existing competition from Gindy. Thus, the acquisition results in the loss of one of the few firms which could have and was likely to be, had it entered de novo or by a toehold acquisition, an important additional competitor in this highly concentrated market.

C. BEHAVIOR

First we consider three types of *collective* action, in which separate firms act directly or indirectly to suppress competition among themselves. Then follow three categories of *unilateral* actions by individual firms to improve their own positions at the expense of others.

Price Fixing and Related Restraints

The line against price fixing has been strictly enforced since 1897, even where the conspirators have only part of the market. The government need prove only that price fixing occurred, not that it had large effects on price or economic performance. *Addyston, Trenton Potteries,* and *Socony-Vacuum* are the landmark cases in this line. This *"per se"* rule makes economic sense, for if positive proof of harm were required, cases would become mired in endless claims and counterclaims. As it is, in few cases if any does price fixing yield true social gains.

The electrical equipment cases were very large. In 1975, action was extended to professional price fixing in the professions, by the *Goldfarb* and *Bates & O'Stein* decisions dealing with lawyers. Actions toward other professional groups (architects, doctors, engineers, and the like) were also under way.

✺ 23

United States v. *Addyston Pipe & Steel Co.*

United States Circuit Court of Appeals,
Sixth Circuit, 1898. 85 F. 271, 29 C.C.A. 141,
affirmed 175 U.S. 211 (1899)

William Howard Taft, then a District Judge, early set a firm line against price-fixing in Addyston. *The Supreme Court affirmed fully.*

The defendants, being manufacturers and vendors of cast-iron pipe, entered into a combination to raise the prices for pipe for all the states west and south of New York, Pennsylvania, and Virginia, constituting considerably more than three quarters of the territory of the United States, and significantly called by the associates "pay territory."
. . . Much evidence is adduced upon affidavit to prove that defendants had no power arbitrarily to fix prices and that they were always obliged to meet competition. To the extent that they could not impose prices on the public in excess of the cost price of pipe with freight from the Atlantic seaboard added, this is true; but within that limit, they could fix prices as they chose. The most cogent evidence that they had this power is the fact, everywhere apparent in the record, that they exercised it. . . . The defendants were, by their combination, therefore able to deprive the public in a large territory of the advantages otherwise accruing to them from the proximity of defendants' pipe factories and, by keeping prices just low enough to prevent competition by Eastern manufacturers, to compel the public to pay an increase over what the price would have been if fixed by competition between defendants, nearly equal to the advantage in freight rates enjoyed by defendants over Eastern competitors. The defendants acquired this power by voluntarily agreeing to sell only at prices fixed by their committee and by allowing the highest bidder at the secret "auction pool" to become the lowest bidder of them at the public letting. Now, the restraint thus imposed on themselves was only partial. It did not cover the United States. There was not a complete monopoly. It was tempered by the fear of competition, and it affected only a part of the price. But this certainly does not take the contract of association out of the annulling effect of the rule against monopolies.
It has been earnestly pressed upon us that the prices at which the castiron pipe was sold in pay territory were reasonable. A great many affidavits of purchasers of pipe in pay territory, all drawn by the same hand or from the same model, are produced, in which the affiants say

that in their opinion the prices at which pipe has been sold by defendants have been reasonable. We do not think the issue an important one because, as already stated, we do not think that at common law there is any question of reasonableness open to the courts with reference to such a contract. Its tendency was certainly to give defendants the power to charge unreasonable prices had they chosen to do so. But if it were important, we should unhesitatingly find that the prices charged in the instances which were in evidence were unreasonable. The letters from the manager of the Chattanooga foundry written to the other defendants and discussing the prices fixed by the association do not leave the slightest doubt upon this point and outweigh the perfunctory affidavits produced by the defendants. The cost of producing pipe at Chattanooga, together with a reasonable profit, did not exceed $15 a ton. It could have been delivered at Atlanta at $17 to $18 a ton, and yet the lowest price which that foundry was permitted by the rules of the association to bid was $24.25. The same thing was true all through pay territory to a greater or less degree and especially at "reserved cities."

* * * * *

✎ 24

United States v. *Trenton Potteries Co.*
U.S. Supreme Court
273 U.S. 392 (1927)

A "rule of reason" about price fixing was again rejected by the Court in Trenton Potteries.

Chief Justice Harlan F. Stone.   Respondents, engaged in the manufacture or distribution of 82 percent of the vitreous pottery fixtures produced in the United States for use in bathrooms and lavatories, were members of a trade organization known as the Sanitary Potters' Association. Twelve of the corporate respondents had their factories and chief places of business in New Jersey, one was located in California, and the others were situated in Illinois, Michigan, West Virginia, Indiana, Ohio, and Pennsylvania. Many of them sold and delivered their product within the southern district of New York, and some maintained sales offices and agents there.

There is no contention here that the verdict was not supported by sufficient evidence that respondents, controlling some 82 percent of the business of manufacturing and distributing in the United States vitreous pottery of the type described, combined to fix prices and to limit sales in interstate commerce to jobbers.

The issues raised here by the government's specification of errors relate only to the decision of the Circuit Court of Appeals upon its review of certain rulings of the District Court made in the course of the trial. It is urged that the court below erred in holding in effect that the trial court should have submitted to the jury the question whether the price agreement complained of constituted an unreasonable restraint of trade.

. . . The question therefore to be considered here is whether the trial judge correctly withdrew from the jury the consideration of the reasonableness of the particular restraints charged.

That only those restraints upon interstate commerce which are unreasonable are prohibited by the Sherman Law was the rule laid down by the opinions of this Court in the Standard Oil and Tobacco Cases. But it does not follow that agreements to fix or maintain prices are reasonable restraints and therefore permitted by the statute, merely because the prices themselves are reasonable. Reasonableness is not a concept of definite and unchanging content. Its meaning necessarily varies in the different fields of the law because it is used as a convenient summary of the dominant considerations which control in the application of legal doctrines. Our view of what is a reasonable restraint of commerce is controlled by the recognized purpose of the Sherman Law itself. Whether this type of restraint is reasonable or not must be judged in part at least, in the light of its effect on competition, for whatever difference of opinion there may be among economists as to the social and economic desirability of an unrestrained competitive system, it cannot be doubted that the Sherman Law and the judicial decisions interpreting it are based upon the assumption that the public interest is best protected from the evils of monopoly and price control by the maintenance of competition.

The aim and result of every price-fixing agreement, if effective, is the elimination of one form of competition. The power to fix prices, whether reasonably exercised or not, involves power to control the market and to fix arbitrary and unreasonable prices. The reasonable price fixed today may through economic and business changes become the unreasonable price of tomorrow. Once established, it may be maintained unchanged because of the absence of competition secured by the agreement for a price reasonable when fixed. Agreements which create such potential power may well be held to be in themselves unreasonable or unlawful restraints, without the necessity of minute inquiry whether a particular price is reasonable or unreasonable as fixed and without placing on the government in enforcing the Sherman Law the burden of ascertaining from day to day whether it has become unreasonable through the mere variation of economic conditions. Moreover, in the absence of express legislation requiring it, we should hesitate to adopt a construction making the difference between legal and illegal conduct in the field of business relations depend upon so uncertain a test as whether prices are reasonable—a determination which can be satisfactorily made only after a complete survey of our economic organization and a choice between rival philosophies. . . .

✺ 25

United States v. *Socony-Vacuum Oil Co., Inc.*
U.S. Supreme Court
310 U.S. 150 (1940)

In Appalachian Coals in 1933, the Court let by a plan for stabilizing coal prices under Depression conditions. This small loophole was closed by Socony-Vacuum, which dealt with an extensive industry system to protect gasoline prices from competition. That price fixing is illegal per se *was flatly reaffirmed.*

*   *   *   *   *

Justice Douglas.   Therefore the sole remaining question on this phase of the case is the applicability of the rule of the *Trenton Potteries* case to these facts.

Respondents seek to distinguish the *Trenton Potteries* case from the instant one. They assert that in that case the parties substituted an agreed-on price for one determined by competition; that the defendants there had the power and purpose to suppress the play of competition in the determination of the market price; and therefore that the controlling factor in that decision was the destruction of market competition, not whether prices were higher or lower, reasonable or unreasonable. Respondents contend that in the instant case there was no elimination in the spot tank car market of competition which prevented the prices in that market from being made by the play of competition in sales between independent refiners and their jobber and consumer customers; that during the buying programs those prices were in fact determined by such competition; that the purchases under those programs were closely related to or dependent on the spot market prices; that there was no evidence that the purchases of distress gasoline under those programs had any effect on the competitive market price beyond that flowing from the removal of a competitive evil; and that if respondents had tried to do more than free competition from the effect of distress gasoline and to set an arbitrary noncompetitive price through their purchases, they would have been without power to do so.

But we do not deem those distinctions material.

In the first place, there was abundant evidence that the combination had the purpose to raise prices. And likewise, there was ample evidence that the buying programs at least contributed to the price rise and the stability of the spot markets and to increases in the price of gasoline sold in the midwestern area during the indictment period. That other factors also may have contributed to that rise and stability of the markets is immaterial. For in any such market movement, forces other than the purchasing power of the buyers normally would contribute to the price rise and the market stability. So far as cause and effect are concerned, it is sufficient in this type of case if the buying programs of the combination resulted in a price rise and market stability which but for them would not have happened. For this reason the charge to the jury that the buying programs must have "caused" the price rise and its continuance was more favorable to respondents than they could have required. Proof that there was a conspiracy, that its purpose was to raise prices, and that it caused or contributed to a price rise is proof of the actual consummation or execution of a conspiracy under § 1 of the Sherman Act.

Secondly, the fact that sales on the spot markets were still governed by some competition is of no consequence. For it is indisputable that that competition was restricted through the removal by respondents of a part of the supply which but for the buying programs would have been a factor in determining the going prices on those markets. But the vice of the conspiracy was not merely the restriction of supply of gasoline by removal of a surplus. As we have said, this was a well-organized program. The timing and strategic placement of the buying orders for distress gasoline played an important and significant role. Buying orders were carefully placed so as to remove the distress gasoline from weak hands. Purchases were timed. Sellers were assigned to the buyers so that regular outlets for distress gasoline would be available. The whole scheme was carefully planned and executed to the end that distress gasoline would not overhang the markets and depress them at any time. And as a result of the payment of fair going market prices a floor was placed and kept under the spot markets. Prices rose and jobbers and consumers in the midwestern area paid more for their gasoline than they would have paid but for the conspiracy. Competition was not eliminated from the markets; but it was clearly curtailed since restriction of the supply of gasoline, the timing and placement of the purchases under the buying programs, and the placing of a floor under the spot markets obviously reduced the play of the forces of supply and demand.

The elimination of so-called competitive evils is no legal justification for such buying programs. The elimination of such conditions was sought primarily for its effect on the price structures. Fairer competitive prices, it is claimed, resulted when distress gasoline was removed from the market. But such defense is typical of the protestations usually made in price-fixing cases. Ruinous competition, financial disaster, evils of price cutting, and the like appear throughout our history as ostensible justifications for price-fixing. If the so-called competitive abuses were to be appraised here, the reasonableness of prices would necessarily become an issue in every price-fixing case. In that event the Sherman Act would soon be emasculated; its philosophy would be supplanted by one which is wholly alien to a system of free competition; it would not be the charter of freedom which its framers intended.

The reasonableness of prices has no constancy due to the dynamic quality of the business facts underlying price structures. Those who fixed reasonable prices today would perpetuate unreasonable prices tomorrow, since those prices would not be subject to continuous administrative supervision and readjustment in light of changed conditions. Those who controlled the prices would control or effectively dominate the market. And those who were in that strategic position would have it in their power to destroy or drastically impair the competitive system. But the thrust of the rule is deeper and reaches more than monopoly power. Any combination which tampers with price structures is engaged in an unlawful activity. Even though the members of the price-fixing group were in no position to control the market, to the extent that they raised, lowered, or stabilized prices they would be directly interfering with the free play of market forces. The Act places all such schemes beyond the pale and protects that vital part of our economy against any degree of interference. Congress has not left with us the determination of whether or not particular price-fixing schemes are wise or unwise, healthy or destructive. It has not permitted the age-old cry of ruinous competition and competitive evils to be a defense to price-fixing conspiracies. It has no more allowed genuine or fancied competitive abuses as a legal justification for such schemes than it has the good intentions of the members of the combination. If such a shift is to be made, it must be done by the Congress.

As we have indicated, the machinery employed by a combination for price-fixing is immaterial.

Under the Sherman Act a combination formed for the purpose and with the effect of raising, depressing, fixing, pegging, or stabilizing the price of a commodity in interstate or foreign commerce is illegal per se. Where the machinery for price-fixing is an agreement on the prices to be charged or paid for the commodity in the interstate or foreign channels of trade, the power to fix prices exists if the combination has control of a substantial part of the commerce in that commodity. Where the means for price-fixing are purchases or sales of the commodity in a market operation or, as here, purchases of a part of the supply of the commodity for the purpose of keeping it from having a depressive effect on the markets, such power may be found to exist though the combination does not control a substantial part of the commodity. In such case that power may be established if, as a result of market conditions, the resources available to the combinations, the timing and the strategic placement of orders and the like, effective means are at hand to accomplish the desired objective. But there may be effective influence over the market though the group in question does not control it. Price-fixing agreements may have utility to members of the group though the power possessed or exerted falls far short of domination and control. Monopoly power . . . is not the only power which the Act strikes down, as we have said. Proof that a combination was formed for the purpose of fixing prices and that it caused them to be fixed or contributed to that result is proof of the completion of a price-fixing conspiracy under § 1 of the Act. The indictment in this case charged that this combination had that purpose and effect. And there was abundant evidence to support it. Hence the existence of power on the part of members of the combination to fix prices was but a conclusion from the finding that the buying programs caused or contributed to the rise and stability of prices.

. . . As we have seen, price-fixing combinations which lack Congressional sanction are illegal per se; they are not evaluated in terms of their purpose, aim, or effect in the elimination of so-called competitive evils. Only in the event that they were would such considerations have been relevant.

Richard A. Smith (1911–   )

✳ 26

*General Electric: A Crisis of Antitrust**

> *The biggest price-fixing case in U.S. history embraced some eight con-spiracies among electrical equipment companies, which had become "a way of life" well before 1950. Smith conveys the flavor and form of these hotel-room connivances. There were fines, jail sentences, and large damage claims. Has price collusion in this industry disappeared? How widely do these shenanigans occur in other industries?*

Roughly $650 million in sales was involved, according to Justice De-partment estimates, from 1951 through 1958. The annual total amounted to about $75 million and was broken down into two categories, sealed bids and open bids. The sealed-bid business (between $15 million and $18 million per year) was done with public agencies, city, state, and federal. The private-sector business was conducted with private utilities and totaled $55 million to $60 million per annum.

The object of the conspiracy, in so far as the sealed-bid business was concerned, was to rotate that business on a fixed-percentage basis among four participating companies, then the only circuit-breaker man-ufacturers in the United States. G.E. got 45 percent, Westinghouse 35, Allis-Chalmers 10, Federal Pacific 10. Every ten days to two weeks working-level meetings were called in order to decide whose turn was next. Turns were determined by the "ledger list," a table of who had got what in recent weeks, and after that the only thing left to decide was the price that the company picked to "win" would submit as the lowest bid.

Above this working-level group was a second tier of conspirators who dealt generally with the overall scheme of rigging the sealed bids but whose prime purpose was maintenance of book prices (quoted prices) and market shares in the yearly $55 million to $60 million worth of private-sector business. Once each week, the top executives (general managers and vice presidents) responsible for carrying out the conspir-

———————
*Richard A. Smith, "General Electric: A Crisis of Antitrust," excerpted from *Corpora-tions in Crisis* (New York: Doubleday, 1962), pp. 125–27, 134, and 148–51. Smith is a *Fortune* staff writer.

acy would get the word to each other via intercompany memo. A different executive would have the "duty" over each 30-day period. That involved initiating the memos, which all dealt with the same subject matter; the jobs coming up that week, the book price each company was setting, comments on the general level of equipment prices.

The conspiracies had their own lingo and their own standard operating procedures. The attendance list was known as the "Christmas-card list," meetings as "choir practices." Companies had code numbers —G.E. 1, Westinghouse 2, Allis-Chalmers 3, Federal Pacific 7—which were used in conjunction with first names when calling a conspirator at home for price information ("This is Bob, what is 7's bid?"). At the hotel meetings it was S.O.P. not to list one's employer when registering and not to have breakfast with fellow conspirators in the dining room. The G.E. men observed two additional precautions: never to be the ones who kept the records and never to tell G.E.'s lawyers anything.

But things were not always smooth even inside this well-oiled machine, for the conspirators actually had no more compunction at breaking the rules of the conspiracy than at breaching the Sherman Act. "Everyone accused the others of not living up to the agreement," Clarence Burke recalled, "and the ones they complained about tried to shift the blame onto someone else." The most constant source of irritation occurred in the sealed-bid business, where chiseling was difficult to detect. But breaks in book price to the utilities in the open-bid business also generated ill will and vituperation. Indeed, one of the many ironies of the whole affair is that the conspiracy couldn't entirely suppress the competitive instinct. Every so often some company would decide that cutthroat competition outside was preferable to the throat-cutting that went on in the cartel; they would break contact and sit out the conspiracy for a couple of years.

*   *   *   *   *

G.E. was involved in at least seven other conspiracies during the time the circuit-breaker cartel was inoperative. The one in power transformers (G.E. Vice President Raymond W. Smith) was going, for G.E. had yet to develop the "black box" (a design breakthrough using standard components to produce tailor-made transformers), which two years later would enable it to take price leadership away from Westinghouse. The one in turbine generators (G.E. Vice President William S. Ginn) was functioning too. In the fall of 1957 it was agreed at the Barclay Hotel to give G.E. "position" in bidding on a 500,000-kilowatt TVA unit.

The question that naturally arises, the cartels being so numerous, is why didn't G.E.'s top management stop them? Cordiner has been criticized within the company, and rightly so, for sitting aloofly in New York and sending out "pieces of paper"—his 20.5 antitrust directive—

rather than having 20.5 personally handed to the local staff by the local boss. But there was also a failure in human relations. . . .

The first grand jury was looking into conspiracies in insulators, switchgear, circuit breakers, and several other products. The second grand jury was hearing four transformer cases and one on industrial controls. With a score of Justice men working on them, cases proliferated, and from December on lawyers began popping up trying to get immunity for their clients in return for testimony. Scarcely a week went by that Bicks and company didn't get information on at least two new cases. But what they still needed was decisive data that would break a case wide open. In January 1960, at just about the time Ralph Cordiner was making an important speech to G.E.'s management corps ("every company and every industry—yes, and every country—that is operated on a basis of cartel systems is liquidating its present strength and future opportunities"), the trust busters hit the jackpot in switchgear.

"The Phases of the Moon."   Switchgear had been particularly baffling to the Antitrust Division, so much that in trying to establish a cartel pattern in the jumble of switchgear prices the trust busters got the bright idea they might be in code. A cryptographer was brought in to puzzle over the figures and try to crack the secret of how a conspirator could tell what to bid and when he'd win. But the cryptographer was soon as flummoxed as everyone else. One of the government attorneys in the case, however, had made a point of dropping in on a college classmate who was the president of a small midwestern electrical-equipment company. This executive didn't have chapter and verse on the switchgear cartel, but what he did have was enough for Justice to throw a scare into a bigger company, I-T-E Circuit Breaker. Indicating that subpoenas would follow, antitrust investigators asked I-T-E's general counsel, Franklyn Judson, to supply the names of sales managers in specific product lines. Judson decided to conduct an investigation of his own. When the subpoenas did come, a pink-cheeked blond young man named Nye Spencer, the company's sales manager for switchgear, was resolutely waiting—his arms loaded with data. He had decided he wasn't about to commit another crime by destroying the records so carefully laid away in his cellar.

There were pages on pages of notes taken during sessions of the switchgear conspiracy—incriminating entries like "Potomac Light & Power, O.K. for G.E." and "Before bidding on this, check with G.E."; neat copies of the ground rules for meetings of the conspirators: no breakfasting together, no registering at the hotel with company names, no calls to the office, no papers to be left in hotel-room wastebaskets. Spencer, it seems, had been instructed to handle some of the secretarial work of the cartel and believed in doing it right; he'd hung onto the documents to help in training an assistant. But the most valuable windfall from the meticulous recordkeeper was a pile of copies of the "phases of the moon" pricing formula for as far back as May 1958.

Not much to look at—just sheets of paper, each containing a half-dozen columns of figures—they immediately solved the enigma of switchgear prices in commercial contracts. One group of columns established the bidding order of the seven switchgear manufacturers—a different company, each with its own code number, phasing into the priority position every two weeks (hence "phases of the moon"). A second group of columns, keyed into the company code numbers, established how much each company was to knock off the agreed-upon book price. For example, if it were No. 1's (G.E.'s) turn to be low bidder at a certain number of dollars off book, then all Westinghouse (No. 2) or Allis-Chalmers (No. 3) had to do was look for their code number in the second group of columns to find how many dollars they were to bid *above* No. 1. These bids would then be fuzzed up by having a little added to them or taken away by companies 2, 3, etc. Thus there was not even a hint that the winning bid had been collusively arrived at.

With this little device in hand, the trust busters found they could light up the whole conspiracy like a switchboard. The new evidence made an equally profound impression on the grand juries. On February 16 and 17, 1960, they handed down the first seven indictments. Forty companies and eighteen individuals were charged with fixing prices or dividing the market on seven electrical products. Switchgear led the list.

*   *   *   *   *

27

John R. Bates and Van O'Steen v. State Bar of Arizona

U.S. Supreme Court
S.C. 76–346 (1977)

This decision, with the Goldfarb decision of 1975, placed most restrictions upon competition and advertising in "the professions"—such as law, medicine, architecture, veterinarians, accountants, and so on—under antitrust attack. There has been resistance to this new enforcement, and change has come gradually. Can you find many advertisements by lawyers in newspapers or on television? Do they inform? Is deception likely? Is competition probably lowering "professional quality?"

Mr. Justice Blackmun delivered the opinion of the Court.

As part of its regulation of the Arizona Bar, the Supreme Court of that State has imposed and enforces a disciplinary rule that restricts advertising by attorneys. This case presents two issues: whether § § 1 and 2 of the Sherman Act, 15 U.S.C. § § 1 and 2, forbid such state regulation, and whether the operation of the rule violates the First Amendment, made applicable to the States through the Fourteenth.[1]

I

Appellants John R. Bates and Van O'Steen are attorneys licensed to practice law in the State of Arizona.[2] As such, they are members of the appellee, the State Bar of Arizona. After admission to the bar in 1972, appellants worked as attorneys with the Maricopa County Legal Aid Society. App. 221.

In March 1974, appellants left the Society and opened a law office which they call a "legal clinic" in Phoenix. Their aim was to provide legal services at modest fees to persons of moderate income who did not qualify for governmental legal aid. Id., at 75. In order to achieve this end, they would accept only routine matters, such as uncontested divorces, uncontested adoptions, simple personal bankruptcies, and changes of name, for which costs could be kept down by extensive use of paralegals, automatic typewriting equipment, and standardized forms and office procedures. More complicated cases, such as contested divorces, would not be accepted. Id., at 97. Because appellants set their prices so as to have a relatively low return on each case they handled, they depended on substantial volume. Id., at 122–23.

After conducting their practice in this manner for two years, appellants concluded that their practice and clinical concept could not survive unless the availability of legal services at low cost was advertised and, in particular, fees were advertised. Id., at 120–23. Consequently, in order to generate the necessary flow of business, that is, "to attract clients," Id., at 121; Tr. of Oral Arg. 4, appellants on February 22, 1976, placed an advertisement . . . in the *Arizona Republic*, a daily newspaper of general circulation in the Phoenix metropolitan area. As may be seen, the advertisement stated that appellants were offering "legal services at very reasonable fees" and listed their fees for certain services.[3] . . .

---

[1]See *Bigelow* v. *Virginia*, 421 U.S. 809, 811 (1975); *Schneider* v. *State*, 308 U.S. 147, 160 (1939).

[2]Each appellant is a 1972 graduate of Arizona State University College of Law. Mr. Bates was named by the faculty of that law school as the outstanding student of his class; Mr. O'Steen graduated *cum laude*. App. 220–21.

[3]The office benefited from an increase in business after the appearance of the adver-

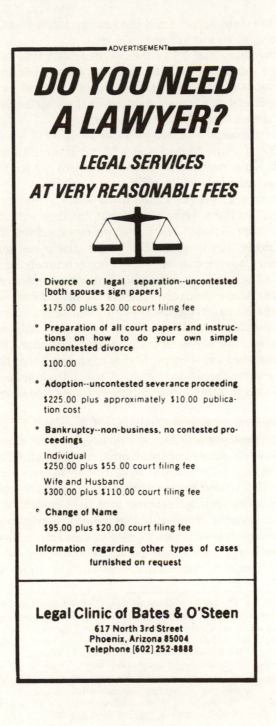

[The State Bar Association acted to penalize Bates and O'Steen, who then appealed it up to the Supreme Court.]

In *Goldfarb* we held that § 1 of the Sherman Act was violated by the publication of a minimum-fee schedule by a county bar association and by its enforcement by the State Bar. The schedule and its enforcement mechanism operated to create a rigid price floor for services and thus constituted a classic example of price fixing. . . .

The heart of the dispute before us today is whether lawyers also may constitutionally advertise the *prices* at which certain routine services will be performed. Numerous justifications are proffered for the restriction of such price advertising. We consider each in turn:

1. The Adverse Effect on Professionalism. Appellee places particular emphasis on the adverse effects that it feels price advertising will have on the legal profession. The key to professionalism, it is argued, is the sense of pride that involvement in the discipline generates. It is claimed that price advertising will bring about commercialization, which will undermine the attorney's sense of dignity and self-worth. The hustle of the marketplace will adversely affect the profession's service orientation and irreparably damage the delicate balance between the lawyer's need to earn and his obligation selflessly to serve. Advertising is also said to erode the client's trust in his attorney: Once the client perceives that the lawyer is motivated by profit, his confidence that the attorney is acting out of a commitment to the client's welfare is jeopardized. And advertising is said to tarnish the dignified public image of the profession.

We recognize, of course, and commend the spirit of public service with which the profession of law is practiced and to which it is dedicated. The present Members of this Court, licensed attorneys all, could not feel otherwise. And we would have reason to pause if we felt that our decision today would undercut that spirit. But we find the postulated connection between advertising and the erosion of true professionalism to be severely strained. At its core, the argument presumes that attorneys must conceal from themselves and from their clients the real-life fact that lawyers earn their livelihood at the bar. We suspect that few attorneys engage in such self-deception.[4] And rare is the client,

---

tisement. App. 235–36, 479–80. It is doubtful, however, whether the increase was due solely to the advertisement, for the advertising itself prompted several news stories. App. 229. It might be expected, nonetheless, that advertising will increase business. See Hobbs, "Lawyer Advertising: A Good Beginning but Not Enough," 62 *A. B. A. J.* 735, 736 (1976) (lawyer referral service that advertised referred more than 11 times as many clients as one that did not advertise in another city of comparable size).

[4]Counsel for the appellee at oral argument readily stated: "We all know that law offices are big businesses, that they may have billion-dollar or million-dollar clients, they're run with computers, and all the rest. And so the argument may be made that to term them noncommercial is sanctimonious humbug." Tr. of Oral Arg. 64.

moreover, even one of modest means, who enlists the aid of an attorney with the expectation that his services will be rendered free of charge. See B. Christensen, "Lawyers for People of Moderate Means," 152–53 (1970). In fact, the American Bar Association advises that an attorney should reach "a clear agreement with his client as to the basis of the fee charges to be made," and that this is to be done "[a]s soon as feasible after a lawyer has been employed." *Code of Professional Responsibility*, EC 2–19 (1976). If the commercial basis of the relationship is to be promptly disclosed on ethical grounds, once the client is in the office, it seems inconsistent to condemn the candid revelation of the same information before he arrives at that office.

Moreover, the assertion that advertising will diminish the attorney's reputation in the community is open to question. Bankers and engineers advertise,[5] and yet these professions are not regarded as undignified. In fact, it has been suggested that the failure of lawyers to advertise creates public disillusionment with the profession.[6] The absence of advertising may be seen to reflect the profession's failure to reach out and serve the community: Studies reveal that many persons do not obtain counsel even when they perceive a need because of the feared price of services or because of an inability to locate a competent attorney. Indeed, cynicism with regard to the profession may be created by the fact that it long has publicly eschewed advertising, while condoning the actions of the attorney who structures his social or civic associations so as to provide contacts with potential clients.

---

[5]See B. Christensen, "Lawyers for People of Moderate Means," 151–52 (1970); "Note, Advertising, Solicitation and the Profession's Duty to Make Legal Counsel Available," 81 *Yale L. J.* 1181, 1190 (1972). Indeed, it appears that even the medical profession now views the alleged adverse effect of advertising in a somewhat different light from the appellee. A Statement of the Judicial Council of the American Medical Association provides in part:

"Advertising—The *Principles* [*of Medical Ethics*] do not proscribe advertising; they proscribe the solicitation of patients. . . . The public is entitled to know the names of physicians, the location of their offices, their office hours, and other useful information that will enable people to make a more informed choice of physician.

"The physician may furnish this information through the accepted local media of advertising or communication, which are open to all physicians on like conditions. Office signs, professional cards, dignified announcements, telephone directory listings, and reputable directories are examples of acceptable media for making information available to the public.

"A physician may give biographical and other relevant data for listing in a reputable directory. . . . If the physician, at his option, chooses to supply fee information, the published data may include his charge for a standard office visit or his fee or range of fees for specific types of services, provided disclosure is made of the variable and other pertinent factors affecting the amount of the fee specified. The published data may include other relevant facts about the physician, but false, misleading, or deceptive statements of claims should be avoided." 235 *J. A. M. A.* 2328 (1976).

[6]See M. Freedman, "Lawyers' Ethics in an Adversary System" 115–16 (1975); Branca & Steinberg, "Attorney Fee Schedules and Legal Advertising: the Implications of *Goldfarb*," 24 *U. C. L. A. L. Rev.* 475, 516–17 (1977).

It appears that the ban on advertising originated as a rule of etiquette and not as a rule of ethics. Early lawyers in Britain viewed the law as a form of public service, rather than as a means of earning a living, and they looked down on "trade" as unseemly. See H. Drinker, "Legal Ethics 5, 210–11 (1953). Eventually, the attitude toward advertising fostered by this view evolved into an aspect of the ethics of the profession. Id., at 211. But habit and tradition are not in themselves an adequate answer to a constitutional challenge. In this day, we do not belittle the person who earns his living by the strength of his arm or the force of his mind. Since the belief that lawyers are somehow "above" trade has become an anachronism, the historical foundation for the advertising restraint has crumbled.

2. The Inherently Misleading Nature of Attorney Advertising.   It is argued that advertising of legal services inevitably will be misleading (a) because such services are so individualized with regard to content and quality as to prevent informed comparison on the basis of an advertisement, (b) because the consumer of legal services is unable to determine in advance just what services he needs, and (c) because advertising by attorneys will highlight irrelevant factors and fail to show the relevant factor of skill.

We are not persuaded that restrained professional advertising by lawyers inevitably will be misleading. Although many services performed by attorneys are indeed unique, it is doubtful that any attorney would or could advertise fixed prices for services of that type.[7] The only services that lend themselves to advertising are the routine ones: the uncontested divorce, the simple adoption, the uncontested personal bankruptcy, the change of name, and the like—the very services advertised by appellants. Although the precise service demanded in each task may vary slightly and although legal services are not fungible, these facts do not make advertising misleading so long as the attorney does the necessary work at the advertised price. The argument that legal services are so unique that fixed rates cannot meaningfully be established is refuted by the record in this case: The appellee State Bar itself sponsors a Legal Services Program in which the participating attorneys agree to perform services like those advertised by the appellants at standardized rates. App. 459–78. Indeed, until the decision of this Court in *Goldfarb* v. *Virginia State Bar*, 421 U. S. 773 (1975), the Maricopa County Bar Association apparently had a schedule of suggested minimum fees

---

[7]See Morgan, "The Evolving Concept of Professional Responsibility," 90 *Harv. L. Rev.* 702, 741 (1977); "Note, Advertising, Solicitation and the Profession's Duty to Make Legal Counsel Available," 81 *Yale L. J.* 1181, 1203 (1972). Economic considerations suggest that advertising is a more significant force in the marketing of inexpensive and frequently used goods and services with mass markets than in the marketing of unique products or services.

for standard legal tasks. App. 355. We thus find of little force the assertion that advertising is misleading because of an inherent lack of stan-
dardization in legal services.

The second component of the argument—that advertising ignores the
diagnostic role—fares little better. It is unlikely that many people go to
an attorney merely to ascertain if they have a clean bill of legal health.
Rather, attorneys are likely to be employed to perform specific tasks.
Although the client may not know the detail involved in performing the
task, he no doubt is able to identify the service he desires at the level of
generality to which advertising lends itself.

The third component is not without merit: Advertising does not provide a complete foundation on which to select an attorney. But it seems
peculiar to deny the consumer, on the ground that the information is
incomplete, at least some of the relevant information needed to reach an
informed decision. The alternative—the prohibition of advertising—
serves only to restrict the information that flows to consumers.
Moreover, the argument assumes that the public is not sophisticated
enough to realize the limitations of advertising and that the public is
better kept in ignorance than trusted with correct but incomplete information. We suspect the argument rests on an underestimation of the
public. In any event, we view as dubious any justification that is based
on the benefits of public ignorance. See *Virginia Pharmacy Board* v. *Virginia Consumer Council*, 425 U.S., at 769–70. Although, of course, the bar
retains the power to correct omissions that have the effect of presenting
an inaccurate picture, the preferred remedy is more disclosure, rather
than less. If the naiveté of the public will cause advertising by attorneys
to be misleading, then it is the bar's role to assure that the populace is
sufficiently informed as to enable it to place advertising in its proper
perspective.

3. The Adverse Effect on the Administration of Justice. Advertising is said to have the undesirable effect of stirring up litigation. The
judicial machinery is designed to serve those who feel sufficiently ag-
grieved to bring forward their claims. Advertising, it is argued, serves to
encourage the assertion of legal rights in the courts, thereby undesirably
unsettling societal repose. There is even a suggestion of barratry. See,
e.g., "Comment, A Critical Analysis of Rules against Solicitation by
Lawyers," 25 *U. Chi. L. Rev.* 674, 675–76 (1958).

But advertising by attorneys is not an unmitigated source of harm to
the administration of justice. It may offer great benefits. Although advertising might increase the use of the judicial machinery, we cannot
accept the notion that it is always better for a person to suffer a wrong
silently than to redress it by legal action. As the bar acknowledges, "the
middle 70 percent of our population is not being reached or served
adequately by the legal profession." American Bar Association, *Revised*

Handbook on Prepaid Legal Services: Papers and Documents Assembled by the Special Committee on Prepaid Legal Services 2 (1972). Among the reasons for this underutilization is fear of the cost and an inability to locate a suitable lawyer. See nn. 22 and 23, *supra.* Advertising can help to solve this acknowledged problem: Advertising is the traditional mechanism in a free-market economy for a supplier to inform a potential purchaser of the availability and terms of exchange. The disciplinary rule at issue likely has served to burden access to legal services, particularly for the not-quite-poor and the unknowledgable. A rule allowing restrained advertising would be in accord with the bar's obligation to "facilitate the process of intelligent selection of lawyers and to assist in making legal services fully available." American Bar Association, *Code of Professional Responsibility*, EC 2–1 (1976).

4. The Undesirable Economic Effects of Advertising. It is claimed that advertising will increase the overhead costs of the profession and that these costs then will be passed along to consumers in the form of increased fees. Moreover, it is claimed that the additional cost of practice will create a substantial entry barrier, deterring or preventing young attorneys from penetrating the market and entrenching the position of the bar's established members.

These two arguments seem dubious at best. Neither distinguishes lawyers from others, see *Virginia Pharmacy Board* v. *Virginia Consumer Council*, 425 U.S., at 768, and neither appears relevant to the First Amendment. The ban on advertising serves to increase the difficulty of discovering the lowest-cost seller of acceptable ability. As a result, to this extent attorneys are isolated from competition, and the incentive to price competitively is reduced. Although it is true that the effect of advertising on the price of services has not been demonstrated, there is revealing evidence with regard to products; where consumers have the benefit of price advertising, retail prices often are dramatically lower than they would be without advertising. It is entirely possible that advertising will serve to reduce, not advance, the cost of legal services to the consumer.

The entry barrier argument is equally unpersuasive. In the absence of advertising, an attorney must rely on his contacts with the community to generate a flow of business. In view of the time necessary to develop such contacts, the ban in fact serves to perpetuate the market position of established attorneys. Consideration of entry-barrier problems would urge that advertising be allowed so as to aid the new competitor in penetrating the market.

5. The Adverse Effect of Advertising on the Quality of Service. It is argued that the attorney may advertise a given "package" of service at a set price and will be inclined to provide, by indiscriminate use, the standard package regardless of whether it fits the client's needs.

Restraints on advertising, however, are an ineffective way of deterring shoddy work. An attorney who is inclined to cut quality will do so regardless of the rule on advertising. And the advertisement of a standardized fee does not necessarily mean that the services offered are undesirably standardized. Indeed, the assertion that an attorney who advertises a standard fee will cut quality is substantially undermined by the fixed fee schedule of appellee's own prepaid Legal Services Program. Even if advertising leads to the creation of "legal clinics" like that of appellants'—clinics that emphasize standardized procedures for routine problems—it is possible that such clinics will improve service by reducing the likelihood of error.

6. The Difficulties of Enforcement. Finally, it is argued that the wholesale restriction is justified by the problems of enforcement if any other course is taken. Because the public lacks sophistication in legal matters, it may be particularly susceptible to misleading or deceptive advertising by lawyers. After-the-fact action by the consumer lured by such advertising may not provide a realistic restraint because of the inability of the layman to assess whether the service he has received meets professional standards. Thus, the vigilance of a regulatory agency will be required. But because of the numerous purveyors of services, the overseeing of advertising will be burdensome.

It is at least somewhat incongruous for the opponents of advertising to extol the virtues and altruism of the legal profession at one point and, at another, to assert that its members will seize the opportunity to mislead and distort. We suspect that, with advertising, most lawyers will behave as they always have: They will abide by their solemn oaths to uphold the integrity and honor of their profession and of the legal system. For every attorney who overreaches through advertising, there will be thousands of others who will be candid and honest and straightforward. And, of course, it will be in the latters' interest, as in other cases of misconduct at the bar, to assist in weeding out those few who abuse their trust.

In sum, we are not persuaded that any of the proffered justifications rises to the level of an acceptable reason for the suppression of all advertising by attorneys. . . .

Tacit Collusion

When collusion is indirect, the effects are often less definite. Such "parallel pricing" (or "shared monopoly," or "implicit coordination") lacks hard legal evidence, and it can be hard to evaluate. Yet varying degrees of tacit collusion do occur in many (perhaps most) concentrated markets, and so it has become a leading unsolved problem of antitrust policy. It falls between Sections 1 and 2 of the Sherman Act.

In the 1940s, the courts were quick to try to apply the new doctrines of oligopoly pricing. The *American Tobacco* decision of 1946 convicted the oligopolists even though explicit collusion was quite absent. Yet no remedy was applied. Strictness ceased with the *Theater Enterprises* decision of 1954. An important recent case involved General Electric Company and Westinghouse Electric Corp. After the 1960 price-fixing convictions, the two firms established a system of indirect collusion, in which they followed set pricing formulas and renounced all price cutting. The settlement excerpted here headed off a formal suit by the Antitrust Division. Still, tacit collusion in a broad range of markets remains a vexing antitrust riddle.

✖ 28

American Tobacco Company v. *United States*
U.S. Supreme Court
328 U.S. 781 (1946)

Is oligopoly liable to antitrust treatment, even though there is no tangible collusion (Sherman Act, Section 1) nor single dominant firm (Section 2)? This landmark decision said yes. But the legal conclusion was not followed by significant remedy. What could the remedy have been?

Mr. Justice Burton. The petitioners are The American Tobacco Company, Liggett & Myers Tobacco Company, R. J. Reynolds Tobacco Company, American Suppliers, Inc., a subsidiary of American, and certain officials of the respective companies who were convicted by a jury in the District Court of the United States for the Eastern District of Kentucky of violating § § 1 and 2 of the Sherman Antitrust Act. . . .

The requirement stated to the jury and contained in the statute was only that the offenders shall "monopolize any part of the trade or commerce among the several States or with foreign nations." This particular conspiracy may well have derived special vitality in the eyes of the jury from the fact that its existence was established, not through the presentation of a formal written agreement, but through the evidence of widespread and effective conduct on the part of petitioners in relation to their existing or potential competitors. . . .

First of all, the monopoly found by the jury to exist in the present cases appears to have been completely separable from the old American

Tobacco Trust which was dissolved in 1911. The conspiracy to monopolize and the monopolization charged here do not depend upon proof
relating to the old tobacco trust but upon a dominance and control by
petitioners in recent years over purchases of the raw material and over
the sale of the finished product in the form of cigarettes. The fact, however, that the purchases of leaf tobacco and the sales of so many products of the tobacco industry have remained largely within the same
general group of business organizations for over a generation, inevitably
has contributed to the ease with which control over competition within
the industry and the mobilization of power to resist new competition can
be exercised. . . . The verdicts indicate that practices of an informal and
flexible nature were adopted and that the results were so uniformly
beneficial to the petitioners in protecting their common interests as
against those of competitors that, entirely from circumstantial evidence,
the jury found that a combination or conspiracy existed among the
petitioners from 1937 to 1940, with power and intent to exclude competitors to such a substantial extent as to violate the Sherman Act as
interpreted by the trial court. . . .

The Government introduced evidence showing . . . that petitioners
refused to purchase tobacco on these [auction] markets unless the other
petitioners were also represented thereon. There were attempts made by
others to open new tobacco markets, but none of the petitioners would
participate in them unless the other petitioners were present. Consequently, such markets were failures due to the absence of buyers.
. . . In this way the new tobacco markets and their locations were determined by the unanimous consent of the petitioners, and in arriving at
their determination, the petitioners consulted with each other as to
whether or not a community deserved a market.

The Government presented evidence to support its claim that before
the markets opened the petitioners placed limitations and restrictions on
the prices which their buyers were permitted to pay for tobacco. None of
the buyers exceeded these price ceilings. Grades of tobacco were formulated in such a way as to result in the absence of competition between
the petitioners. There was manipulation of the price of lower grade
tobaccos in order to restrict competition from manufacturers of the lower
priced cigarettes. Methods used included the practice of the petitioners
of calling their respective buyers in prior to the opening of the annual
markets and giving them instructions as to the prices to be paid for leaf
tobacco in each of the markets. These instructions were in terms of top
prices or price ranges. The price ceilings thus established for the buyers
were the same for each of them. . . .

Where one or two of the petitioners secured their percentage of the
crop on a certain market or were not interested in the purchase of certain
offerings of tobacco, their buyers, nevertheless, would enter the bidding

in order to force the other petitioners to bid up to the maximum price. The petitioners were not so much concerned with the prices they paid for the leaf tobacco as that each should pay the same price for the same grade and that none would secure any advantage in purchasing tobacco. . . .

The verdicts show also that the jury found that the petitioners conspired to fix prices and to exclude undesired competition in the distribution and sale of their principal products. The petitioners sold and distributed their products to jobbers and to selected dealers who bought at list prices, less discounts. . . . The list prices charged and the discounts allowed by petitioners have been practically identical since 1923 and absolutely identical since 1928. Since the latter date, only seven changes have been made by the three companies, and those have been identical in amount. The increases were first announced by Reynolds. American and Liggett thereupon increased their list prices in identical amounts.

It is not the form of the combination or the particular means used but the result to be achieved that the statute condemns. It is not of importance whether the means used to accomplish the unlawful objectives are in themselves lawful or unlawful. Acts done to give effect to the conspiracy may be in themselves wholly innocent acts. Yet, if they are part of the sum of the acts which are relied upon to effectuate the conspiracy which the statute forbids, they come within its prohibition. No formal agreement is necessary to constitute an unlawful conspiracy. Often crimes are a matter of inference deduced from the acts of the person accused and done in pursuance of a criminal purpose. Where the conspiracy is proved, as here, from the evidence of the action taken in concert by the parties to it, it is all the more convincing proof of an intent to exercise the power of exclusion acquired through that conspiracy. The essential combination or conspiracy in violation of the Sherman Act may be found in a course of dealing or other circumstances as well as in an exchange of words. . . . Where the circumstances are such as to warrant a jury in finding that the conspirators had a unity of purpose, or a common design and understanding, or a meeting of minds in an unlawful arrangement, the conclusion that a conspiracy is established is justified. Neither proof of exertion of the power to exclude nor proof of actual exclusion of existing or potential competitors is essential to sustain a charge of monopolization under the Sherman Act. . . .

In the present cases, the petitioners have been found to have conspired to establish a monopoly and also to have the power and intent to establish and maintain the monopoly. To hold that they do not come within the prohibition of the Sherman Act would destroy the force of that Act. Accordingly, the instructions of the trial court under § 2 of the Act are approved and the judgment of the Circuit Court of Appeals is *Affirmed.*

29

Theatre Enterprises, Inc. v. *Paramount Film Distributing Corp. et al.*

U.S. Supreme Court
346 U.S. 537 (1954)

After several years of finding tacit collusion to approximate explicit price fixing, the Court in 1954 reversed course and refused to rely on "speculative" evidence of collusion. This was one of the key cases in that reversal. Was there collusion, nonetheless? How firm does the evidence need to be in order to reflect a real economic result?

Mr. Justice Clark. Petitioner brought this suit for treble damages and an injunction under § § 4 and 16 of the Clayton Act, alleging that respondent motion picture producers and distributors had violated the antitrust laws by conspiring to restrict "first-run"[1] pictures to downtown Baltimore theatres, thus confining its suburban theatre to subsequent runs and unreasonable "clearances."[2] After hearing the evidence a jury returned a general verdict for respondents. The Court of Appeals for the Fourth Circuit affirmed the judgment based on the verdict. . . .

Petitioner now urges, as it did in the Court of Appeals, that the trial judge should have directed a verdict in its favor and submitted to the jury only the question of the amount of damages. Alternatively, petitioner claims that the trial judge erred by inadequately instructing the jury as to the scope and effect of the decrees in *United States* v. *Paramount Pictures, Inc.*, the Government's prior equity suit against respondents. We think both contentions are untenable.

The opinion of the Court of Appeals contains a complete summary of the evidence presented to the jury. We need not recite that evidence again. It is sufficient to note that petitioner owns and operates the Crest Theatre, located in a neighborhood shopping district some six miles from the downtown shopping center in Baltimore, Maryland. The Crest, possessing the most modern improvements and appointments, opened

---

[1]"Runs are successive exhibitions of a feature in a given area, first-run being the first exhibition in that area, second-run being the next subsequent, and so on. . . ." *United States* v. *Paramount Pictures, Inc.*, 334 U.S. 131, 144–45, n. 6 (1948).

[2]"A clearance is the period of time, usually stipulated in license contracts, which must elapse between runs of the same feature within a particular area or in specified theatres." *United States* v. *Paramount Pictures, Inc.*, 334 U.S. 131, 144, n. 6 (1948).

on February 26, 1949. Before and after the opening, petitioner, through its president, repeatedly sought to obtain first-run features for the theatre. Petitioner approached each respondent separately, initially requesting exclusive first-runs, later asking for first-runs on a "day and date" basis.[3] But respondents uniformly rebuffed petitioner's efforts and adhered to an established policy of restricting first-runs in Baltimore to the eight downtown theatres. Admittedly there is no direct evidence of illegal agreement between the respondents, and no conspiracy is charged as to the independent exhibitors in Baltimore who account for 63 percent of first-run exhibitions. The various respondents advanced much the same reasons for denying petitioner's offers. Among other reasons, they asserted that day-and-date first-runs are normally granted only to noncompeting theatres. Since the Crest is in "substantial competition" with the downtown theatres, a day-and-date arrangement would be economically unfeasible. And even if respondents wished to grant petitioner such a license, no downtown exhibitor would waive his clearance rights over the Crest and agree to a simultaneous showing. As a result, if petitioner were to receive first-runs, the license would have to be an exclusive one. However, an exclusive license would be economically unsound because the Crest is a suburban theatre, located in a small shopping center, and served by limited public transportation facilities; and with a drawing area of less than one tenth that of a downtown theatre, it cannot compare with those easily accessible theatres in the power to draw patrons. Hence the downtown theatres offer far greater opportunities for the widespread advertisement and exploitation of newly released features, which is thought necessary to maximize the overall return from subsequent runs as well as first-runs. The respondents, in the light of these conditions, attacked the guaranteed offers of petitioner, one of which occurred during the trial, as not being made in good faith. Respondents Loew's and Warner refused petitioner an exclusive license because they owned the three downtown theatres receiving their first-run product.

The crucial question is whether respondents' conduct toward petitioner stemmed from independent decision or from an agreement, tacit or express. To be sure, business behavior is admissible circumstantial evidence from which the fact finder may infer agreement. *Interstate Circuit, Inc.* v. *United States*, 306 U.S. 208 (1939); *United States* v. *Masonite Corp.*, 316 U.S. 265 (1942); *United States* v. *Bausch & Lomb Optical Co.*, 321 U.S. 707 (1944); *American Tobacco Co.* v. *United States*, 328 U.S. 781 (1946); *United States* v. *Paramount Pictures, Inc.*, 334 U.S. 131 (1948). But this

---

[3]A first-run "day and date" means that two theatres exhibit a first-run at the same time. Had petitioner's request for a day-and-date first-run been granted, the Crest and a downtown theatre would have exhibited the same features simultaneously.

Court has never held that proof of parallel business behavior conclusively establishes agreement or, phrased differently, that such behavior itself constitutes a Sherman Act offense. Circumstantial evidence of consciously parallel behavior may have made heavy inroads into the traditional judicial attitude toward conspiracy; but "conscious parallelism" has not yet read conspiracy out of the Sherman Act entirely. Realizing this, petitioner attempts to bolster its argument for a directed verdict by urging that the conscious unanimity of action by respondents should be "measured against the background and findings in the *Paramount* case." In other words, since the same respondents had conspired in the *Paramount* case to impose a uniform system of runs and clearances without adequate explanation to sustain them as reasonable restraints of trade, use of the same device in the present case should be legally equated to conspiracy. But the *Paramount* decrees, even if admissible, were only prima facie evidence of a conspiracy covering the area and existing during the period there involved. Alone or in conjunction with the other proof of the petitioner, they would form no basis for a directed verdict. Here each of the respondents had denied the existence of any collaboration and in addition had introduced evidence of the local conditions surrounding the Crest operation which, they contended, precluded it from being a successful first-run house. They also attacked the good faith of the guaranteed offers of the petitioner for first-run pictures and attributed uniform action to individual business judgment motivated by the desire for maximum revenue. This evidence, together with other testimony of an explanatory nature, raised fact issues requiring the trial judge to submit the issue of conspiracy to the jury. . . .

Affirmed.

*   *   *   *   *

✺ 30

United States v. General Electric Co. and Westinghouse Electric Corp.

United States District Court,
Eastern District of Pennsylvania
Civil No. 28228 (1976)
Plaintiff's Memorandum in Support of a Proposed Modification
to the Final Judgment Entered on October 1, 1962, against Each
Defendant

> *The "tacit collusion" here rested upon a variety of definite actions by
> the duopolists. The Antitrust Division's action was triggered by a private
> suit filed by American Electric Power Co. (a utility firm) against GE and
> Westinghouse in 1971.*

The United States, by the undersigned, files this memorandum in
support of its joint proposals with the General Electric Company and the
Westinghouse Electric Corporation to modify the final judgment against
each company in this action. The modification is designed to prohibit
certain pricing practices which have occurred in the turbine-generator
industry since 1963. . . .

I. Nature and Purpose of the Proceeding

On June 29, 1960, the Government obtained an indictment charging
GE, Westinghouse, and Allis-Chalmers Manufacturing Corporation,
and four individuals with fixing the prices of large turbine-generators.
Contemporaneous with the indictment, the Government filed a civil
action against the corporations in which it sought an injunction against
further violations of Section 1 of the Sherman Act. Both the indictment
and the civil complaint charged, among other things, that representatives of the defendants held meetings at which they agreed upon adjustments in the prices of certain turbine-generators, coordinated price
increases, and determined which defendant would submit the winning
bid to a given utility. The criminal case ultimately resulted in the entry of
guilty pleas by the three corporate defendants and pleas of nolo-con-
tendere by the four individual defendants. All defendants were fined
and one individual received a prison sentence. The civil action ended
with the entry of consent decrees against the corporate defendants.

Filed on October 1, 1962, the consent decrees were designed to deal
with the pricing situation that had developed during the 1950s. The

decrees enjoined the defendants from fixing prices, allocating product and geographic markets, bid-rigging, and refusing to deal with certain customers. It ordered the defendants not to communicate pricing information to one another until after the information had been released generally to the trade. The decrees also required that each defendant independently and individually review, determine, and announce its book prices for turbine-generators unless the defendant certified to the court that it had taken such action after June 29, 1960, but before the effective date of the decree. In essence, the goal of the 1962 decrees was to uproot the unlawful pricing behavior and replace it with pricing behavior founded on legitimate competitive considerations.

Price competition prevailed in the turbine-generator industry from 1960 to 1963. In the opinion of the Department, however, prices since then have stabilized, and there has been little or no discounting or negotiation regarding price. The Department of Justice has uncovered no evidence that, to achieve the present price stability, GE and Westinghouse reached an agreement through direct, covert communication. Instead, the Department's investigation has revealed that the elimination of price competition has been the result of identical policies deliberately adopted and published in 1963–64 and adhered to since.

The 1962 consent decrees allowed the publication of price books and the public exchange of competitive information. On the other hand, the decrees prohibited all price-fixing agreements regardless of where or how they were formed. Since 1963, the nature and content of the public communication of pricing intentions and the mechanics of the pricing system have been such that GE and Westinghouse have succeeded in assuring one another that they will not deviate from published price levels. In the opinion of the Department, this public exchange of assurances, with such intent, did constitute an agreement to stabilize prices which warranted the filing of a civil action by it alleging a violation of the Sherman Act or of the 1962 consent decrees.

To obtain an injunction against further use of these pricing policies, the Department was prepared to file a civil suit against GE and Westinghouse. When, as is customary, the Department notified counsel for the prospective defendants of its intention, the companies vigorously asserted their innocence. To avoid suit, however, they offered to accept, without admitting liability, a modification of the 1962 decrees which would prohibit the practices that the Department deemed objectionable. They also agreed that the modification would be effected in a manner consistent with the disclosure requirements of the Antitrust Procedures and Penalties Act, 15 U.S.C. § 16.

The Department responded favorably to the modification offer primarily because it presented the opportunity immediately to secure substantially the same remedial relief that it would have sought in a civil action that probably would have taken years to complete and whose outcome could not be predicted. . . .

II. Description of Events and Practices Giving Rise to the Alleged Violation

Turbine-generator prices, which began a precipitous decline in 1958, continued to decline following the indictment of GE, Westinghouse, and Allis-Chalmers for price fixing in 1960. By December, 1962 Allis-Chalmers had withdrawn from the market, but the industry continued to be plagued by overcapacity, and prices continued to decline. Relatively few sales are made in any year, and the pressure to obtain any given order was substantial. Moreover, the product is not homogeneous, and although the companies utilized price books, there was little adherence to published prices, and considerable discounting occurred on particular projects.

In May 1963, GE announced a new pricing policy. The principal purpose of this policy was to end the discounting by establishing a new price level that would not be eroded in the market. GE published several documents on or about May 20, 1963, that communicated to its utility customers and to Westinghouse the purpose and the mechanics of the new pricing policy. In each of these publications, GE stated its intention to adhere to the new published price level by quoting only book prices on all transactions.

The new pricing strategy included a revised book which contained simplified procedures for pricing turbine-generators; the use of a published multiplier to be applied to book prices; the introduction of a price protection policy designed to implement the equal treatment philosophy; and the publication of outstanding orders and price quotations. Each of these features of the new pricing policy will be briefly outlined below to indicate what the Department believes their respective roles were in GE's effort to stabilize prices.

The 1963 price book was an essential feature of GE's new pricing policy. The book employed various formulas which greatly simplified the pricing of these highly complex and customized machines. The book also contained a series of pricing examples which explained the use of the formulas. Virtually all of the pricing information necessary to calculate the book price of any large turbine-generator (and other terms and conditions of sale including the level of various performance guarantees) was included.

Moreover, the price book set forth the so-called exhaust end loading limits for different types of turbine-generator blades. The publication of these limits made it possible to determine the specific size and type of turbine-generator that GE would bid in response to specifications provided by a utility customer.

To compute the actual published price in effect at any given time, GE employed a published multiplier—another key aspect of the 1963 strategy. The multiplier was expressed in terms of a percentage figure and was applied to book prices. For example, the price quoted to a customer in May 1963 was computed by multiplying the book price by the multiplier of .76. The use of the multiplier permitted GE to make swift changes in price without the complexity—and possible source of misinterpretation by Westinghouse—inherent in printing an entirely new book.

The end result of the information contained in the 1963 price book combined with GE's public announcement that it would not deviate from published prices was that Westinghouse could ascertain the price that GE would employ in any given sales situation. This effectively removed a major source of uncertainty and a major stumbling block in the industry's attempt to stabilize prices for such a highly complex product. Moreover, GE's internal documents reveal, in the opinion of the Department, that such was the intent of GE in issuing the price book and the actual effect perceived by GE after the book was issued. Also, again in the opinion of the Department, internal documents of Westinghouse reveal that it perceived this to be the purpose and the effect of the GE pricing policy.

In any attempt to stabilize prices, there is always the risk that one firm will seek to gain an advantage by employing selective secret discounts to win individual customers. Such behavior is often the source of the breakup of a price agreement. More to the point, the fear by one firm that another will seek to gain an advantage may lead the first to initiate the very strategy it fears from the other.

To deal with the problem of secret discounts, a third element in the pricing strategy announced by GE was the "price protection clause." This clause appeared in the price book and was to be included in all GE contracts for the sale of large turbine-generators. The clause was also described in GE's letter to utility presidents.

The price protection clause operated in such a way that in the event price was lowered by GE for a particular customer any buyer within the previous six-month period would be given an identical discount retroactively upon request.[1] Hence selective price cuts could not be employed by GE without imposing a substantial penalty upon itself. The result of the price protection policy was to provide assurance to Westinghouse

---

[1] The problem of secrecy was overcome by permitting buyers in any period to audit GE's books with respect to sales made in the subsequent six months.

that GE would not give selective discounts. Westinghouse adopted a price protection clause in 1964.

The Department believes that internal documents of both GE and Westinghouse could have led a trier of fact to conclude that price protection was intended to and did provide the firms with assurance that each would avoid price competition.

The Marketing Information Letter issued in May 1963 contained a fourth element of the pricing strategy. This was the publication by GE of all of the orders it had received and the quotations it had made before May 20 at the preexisting price levels. Unless Westinghouse knew that a quote at the lower price level had been made prior to the price increase, it would not be able to know for certain whether GE had "cheated" on the new price level. Since discounting had been prevalent prior to May 1963, this information was necessary to assure Westinghouse that GE had followed through on its intention to stick to published price levels. Westinghouse adopted this practice in 1964, and both firms have used it over the years when price increases were announced. The Department believes that a court could have concluded from internal documents of both firms that the purpose and perceived effect of publishing outstanding orders and price quotations was to eliminate a potential source of disruption at the time of price changes.

Westinghouse learned of the new GE policy very soon after it was announced. Within days, it withdrew its own price book and began to use the new GE book and the .76 multiplier to compute its prices. As noted above, Westinghouse's next book, published ten months later, in March 1964 was similar in many significant respects to GE's and enabled GE to predict the offering Westinghouse would make in a given situation.

In June 1964, GE reduced its multiplier in response to what it believed was secret price-cutting by Westinghouse but which evidently was a misinterpretation by Westinghouse of the GE book. Then, in July, Westinghouse announced a price increase, published for the first time a list of outstanding orders and quotations and, also for the first time, announced it would offer a price protection clause. Two months later, Westinghouse and GE were both back at the pre–June price level. Since then, both companies have used the same multiplier applied to identical book price levels.

The Department believes that internal Westinghouse documents reveal that Westinghouse perceived GE's actions as an invitation to stabilize prices. Moreover, these documents, in the opinion of the Department, reveal the extraordinary steps Westinghouse took to insure that the strategy was not upset intentionally or inadvertently.

Since the summer of 1964, GE and Westinghouse have applied the prevailing multiplier to book prices, resulting in a pattern of equal pricing in the sale of turbine-generators for fossil fuel power plants. The same pattern emerged in the pricing of turbine-generators for nuclear plants when, in October 1964, GE applied this pricing policy to the marketing of those units.

Representatives of GE and Westinghouse in meetings with the Antitrust Division have disputed the government's factual and legal conclusions. They have argued that this conduct cannot form the basis of any unlawful agreement or understanding. They have denied that their behavior had the intent or the effect to stabilize prices. Instead they have emphasized that, for most of the time since 1963, they have been the only two domestic manufacturers of large turbine-generators and that demand has climbed steadily. They have claimed that identical price levels have been the result of conscious parallelism or the exercise of price leadership by GE. Such "interdependent" pricing, they say, has to be expected in a duopoly because each company's pricing decisions must take into account likely decisions of the other. Thus, it is argued, any identical pricing pattern has been the inevitable consequence of industry structure.

The Department believes that the differences between the behavior here and classic price leadership are extensive and important. The complexity of the product and the secretive and uncertain nature of the bidding process made it necessary for GE to go beyond the simple announcement of an intention to discontinue discounting if Westinghouse were to have the information concerning and confidence in GE's intentions to follow. Prior to May 1963, there was no body of public data that would identify the "appropriate" price of a given turbine-generator or provide the assurance that such price would, in fact, be quoted by its seller. GE's 1963 policy and its subsequent adoption by Westinghouse neutralized competitive pressures resulting from these uncertainties.

The Department believes that Westinghouse's activities went beyond mere passive following of GE's lead. In addition to adopting the price increases, it published a book with the same format and formulas as GE's. It adopted the multiplier system, published lists of outstanding orders, and offered price protection. These acts reflect the painstaking effort of Westinghouse to manifest its acceptance of GE's strategy to stabilize turbine-generator prices.

In this context, the Department believes that if it filed a civil action a trial on the merits could lead a court to conclude that the public exchange of information and assurances by GE and Westinghouse that neither would cut prices violated Section 1 of the Sherman Act as well as the consent decrees entered in 1962. Such a case would, however, be quite complex and novel in the sense that the court would be asked to find a violation in the absence of proof of direct, covert communications between GE and Westinghouse.

III. The Proposed Modification

. . . The injunctive provisions of the proposed modification take four approaches designed to limit direct and indirect communication by each manufacturer to the other.

The first approach is designed to prohibit the kind of public statement of pricing policy that is actually intended to signal or communicate an invitation from one manufacturer to the other to eliminate various elements of competition.

The second enjoins certain specific practices that served to police or reinforce the manufacturers' agreement, such as the price protection policy and the publication of outstanding quotations.

The third is to prohibit the nature and quantity of price and price-related information publicly disseminated by each manufacturer from which a general pricing policy or strategy can be inferred.

The fourth is to prohibit the examination by each manufacturer of price-related documents that the other manufacturer may legitimately distribute to individual customers from which the one manufacturer might infer the pricing policy or strategy of the other.

The effect of the injunctive provisions of the proposed modification will be to create uncertainty on the part of each manufacturer regarding the prices, terms, and conditions of sale, and performance guarantees offered by the other. This uncertainty is designed to foster competitive responses by the manufacturers to invitations to bid on turbine generators. . . .

Other Collective Activities

Firms have also done a wide range of other cooperative activities, such as mutually adopting a single system of delivered pricing, exchanging price information, and pooling patents. Each of these is illustrated by a selection below. Some are neutral or trivial in their effects, while others reduce competition without providing any compensating social gains.

Delivered pricing was a vehicle for reducing competition in the steel, cement, and other industries from 1890 to the 1940s. It was finally outlawed by the FTC (with the Supreme Court's backing) in the 1948 *Cement Institute* decision. The opinion states the economic issues.

Price information was made instantly available to competitors in the system covered by the *Container Corporation et al* case in 1969. Since buyers were not given equal access to information, the system—marginal though its effects were—was held likely to "chill" price competition.

The *Hartford-Empire* case remains a leading example of thorough patent pooling which suppresses competition.

✺ 31

Federal Trade Commission v. *Cement Institute et al.*

U.S. Supreme Court
333 U.S. 685 (1948)

> *This decision put an end to tightly collusive basing-point systems with only one or several basing points. If delivered pricing persists with many basing points, does it cause inefficiency? Is the opinion here good economics?*

Mr. Justice Black.   We granted certiorari to review the decree of the Circuit Court of Appeals which, with one judge dissenting, vacated and set aside a cease and desist order issued by the Federal Trade Commission against the respondents. 157 F. 2d 533. Those respondents are: The Cement Institute, an unincorporated trade association composed of 74 corporations which manufacture, sell, and distribute cement; the 74 corporate members of the Institute; and 21 individuals who are associated with the Institute. It took three years for a trial examiner to hear the evidence which consists of about 49,000 pages of oral testimony and 50,000 pages of exhibits. Even the findings and conclusions of the Commission cover 176 pages. The briefs with accompanying appendixes submitted by the parties contain more than 4,000 pages. The legal questions raised by the Commission and by the different respondents are many and varied. . . .

The proceedings were begun by a Commission complaint of two counts. The first charged that certain alleged conduct set out at length constituted an unfair method of competition in violation of § 5 of the Federal Trade Commission Act. 38 Stat. 719, 15 U.S. C. § 45. The core of the charge was that the respondents had restrained and hindered competition in the sale and distribution of cement by means of a combination among themselves made effective through mutual understanding or agreement to employ a multiple basing point system of pricing. It was alleged that this system resulted in the quotation of identical terms of sale and identical prices for cement by the respondents at any given point in the United States. This system had worked so successfully, it was further charged, that for many years prior to the filing of the complaint all cement buyers throughout the nation, with rare exceptions, had been unable to purchase cement for delivery in any given locality from any one of the respondents at a lower price or on more favorable terms than from any of the other respondents.

The second count of the complaint, resting chiefly on the same allegations of fact set out in Count I, charged that the multiple basing point system of sales resulted in systematic price discriminations between the customers of each respondent. These discriminations were made, it was alleged, with the purpose of destroying competition in price between the various respondents in violation of § 2 of the Clayton Act, 38 Stat. 730, as amended by the Robinson-Patman Act, 49 Stat. 1526. . . .

*   *   *   *   *

The Multiple Basing Point Delivered Price System.   Since the multiple basing point delivered price system of fixing prices and terms of cement sales is the nub of this controversy, it will be helpful at this preliminary stage to point out in general what it is and how it works. A brief reference to the distinctive characteristics of "factory" or "mill prices" and "delivered prices" is of importance to an understanding of the basing point delivered price system here involved.

Goods may be sold and delivered to customers at the seller's mill or warehouse door or may be sold free on board (f. o. b.) trucks or railroad cars immediately adjacent to the seller's mill or warehouse. In either event the actual cost of the goods to the purchaser is, broadly speaking, the seller's "mill price" plus the purchaser's cost of transportation. However, if the seller fixes a price at which he undertakes to deliver goods to the purchaser where they are to be used, the cost to the purchaser is the "delivered price." A seller who makes the "mill price" identical for all purchasers of like amount and quality simply delivers his goods at the same place (his mill) and for the same price (price at the mill). He thus receives for all f. o. b. mill sales an identical net amount of money for like goods from all customers. But a "delivered price" system creates complications which may result in a seller's receiving different net returns from the sale of like goods. The cost of transporting 500 miles is almost always more than the cost of transporting 100 miles. Consequently if customers 100 and 500 miles away pay the same "delivered price," the seller's net return is less from the more distant customer. This difference in the producer's net return from sales to customers in different localities under a "delivered price" system is an important element in the charge under Count I of the complaint and is the crux of Count II.

The best known early example of a basing point price system was called "Pittsburgh plus." It related to the price of steel. The Pittsburgh price was the base price, Pittsburgh being therefore called a price basing point. In order for the system to work, sales had to be made only at delivered prices. Under this system the delivered price of steel from anywhere in the United States to a point of delivery anywhere in the United States was in general the Pittsburgh price plus the railroad freight rate from Pittsburgh to the point of delivery. Take Chicago, Illinois, as an illustration of the operation and consequences of the system. A Chicago steel producer was not free to sell his steel at cost plus a reasonable profit. He must sell it at the Pittsburgh price plus the railroad freight rate from Pittsburgh to the point of delivery. Chicago steel customers were by this pricing plan thus arbitrarily required to pay for Chicago produced steel the Pittsburgh base price plus what it would have cost to ship the steel by rail from Pittsburgh to Chicago had it been shipped. The theoretical cost of this fictitious shipment became known as "phantom freight." But had it been economically possible under this plan for a Chicago producer to ship his steel to Pittsburgh, his "delivered price" would have been merely the Pittsburgh price, although he actually would have been required to pay the freight from Chicago to Pittsburgh. Thus the "delivered price" under these latter circumstances required a Chicago (nonbasing point) producer to "absorb" freight costs. That is, such a seller's net returns became smaller and smaller as his deliveries approached closer and closer to the basing point.

Several results obviously flow from use of a single basing point system such as "Pittsburgh plus" originally was. One is that the "delivered prices" of all producers in every locality where deliveries are made are always the same regardless of the producers' different freight costs. Another is that sales made by a nonbase mill for delivery at different localities result in net receipts to the seller which vary in amounts equivalent to the "phantom freight" included in or the "freight absorption" taken from the "delivered price."

As commonly employed by respondents, the basing point system is not single but multiple. That is, instead of one basing point, like that in "Pittsburgh plus," a number of basing point localities are used. In the multiple basing point system, just as in the single basing point system, freight absorption or phantom freight is an element of the delivered price on all sales not governed by a basing point actually located at the seller's mill. And all sellers quote identical delivered prices in any given locality regardless of their different costs of production and their different freight expenses. Thus the multiple and single systems function in the same general manner and produce the same consequences—identity of prices and diversity of net returns. Such differences as there are in matters here pertinent are therefore differences of degree only.

*   *   *   *   *

The Commission's findings of fact set out at great length and with painstaking detail numerous concerted activities carried on in order to make the multiple basing point system work in such a way that competition in quality, price, and terms of sale of cement would be nonexistent and that uniform prices, job contracts, discounts, and terms of sale would be continuously maintained. The Commission found that many of these activities were carried on by the Cement Institute, the industry's unincorporated trade association, and that in other instances the activities were under the immediate control of groups of respondents. Among the collective methods used to accomplish these purposes, according to the findings, were boycotts; discharge of uncooperative employees; organized opposition to the erection of new cement plants; selling cement in a recalcitrant price cutter's sales territory at a price so low that the recalcitrant was forced to adhere to the established basing point prices; discouraging the shipment of cement by truck or barge; and preparing and distributing freight rate books which provided respondents with similar figures to use as actual or "phantom" freight factors, thus guaranteeing that their delivered prices (base prices plus freight factors) would be identical on all sales whether made to individual purchasers under open bids or to governmental agencies under sealed bids. These are but a few of the many activities of respondents which the Commission found to have been done in combination to reduce or destroy price competition in cement. . . .

*   *   *   *   *

Although there is much more evidence to which reference could be made, we think that the following facts shown by evidence in the record, some of which are in dispute, are sufficient to warrant the Commission's finding of concerted action.

When the Commission rendered its decision, there were about 80 cement manufacturing companies in the United States operating about 150 mills. Ten companies controlled more than half of the mills, and there were substantial corporate affiliations among many of the others. This concentration of productive capacity made concerted action far less difficult than it would otherwise have been. The belief is prevalent in the industry that because of the standardized nature of cement, among other reasons, price competition is wholly unsuited to it. That belief is historic. It has resulted in concerted activities to devise means and measures to do away with competition in the industry. Out of those activities came the multiple basing point delivered price system. Evidence shows it to be a handy instrument to bring about elimination of any kind of price competition. The use of the multiple basing point delivered price system by the cement producers has been coincident with a situation whereby for many years, with rare exceptions, cement has been offered for sale in every given locality at identical prices and terms by all producers. Thousands of secret sealed bids have been received by public agencies which corresponded in prices of cement down to a fractional part of a penny.

Occasionally foreign cement has been imported, and cement dealers have sold it below the delivered price of the domestic product. Dealers who persisted in selling foreign cement were boycotted by the domestic producers. Officers of the Institute took the lead in securing pledges by producers not to permit sales f. o. b. mill to purchasers who furnished their own trucks, a practice regarded as seriously disruptive of the entire delivered price structure of the industry.

During the Depression in the 1930s, slow business prompted some producers to deviate from the prices fixed by the delivered price system. Meetings were held by other producers; an effective plan was devised to punish the recalcitrants and bring them into line. The plan was simple but successful. Other producers made the recalcitrant's plant an involuntary base point. The base price was driven down with relatively insignificant losses to the producers who imposed the punitive basing point but with heavy losses to the recalcitrant who had to make all its sales on this basis. In one instance, where a producer had made a low public bid, a punitive base point price was put on its plant, and cement was reduced 10¢ per barrel; further reductions quickly followed until the base price at which this recalcitrant had to sell its cement dropped to 75¢ per barrel, scarcely one half of its former base price of $1.45. Within six weeks after the base price hit 75¢ capitulation occurred, and the recalcitrant joined a Portland cement association. Cement in that locality then bounced back to $1.15, later to $1.35, and finally to $1.75.

The foregoing are but illustrations of the practices shown to have been utilized to maintain the basing point price system. . . .

*   *   *   *   *

Our conclusion is that there was evidence to support the Commission's findings that all of the respondents, including the California companies, Northwestern Portland and Superior Portland, Huron and Marquette, cooperated in carrying out the objectives of the basing point delivered price system.

Unfair Methods of Competition.   We sustain the Commission's holding that concerted maintenance of the basing point delivered price system is an unfair method of competition prohibited by the Federal Trade Commission Act. In so doing we give great weight to the Commission's conclusion, as this Court has done in other cases. *Federal Trade Comm'n v. R. F. Keppel & Bro.*, 291 U.S. 304, 314; *Federal Trade Comm'n v. Pacific States Paper Trade Assn.*, 273 U.S. 52, 63. In the *Keppel* case the Court called attention to the express intention of Congress to create an agency whose membership would at all times be experienced, so that its conclusions would be the result of an expertness coming from experience. We are persuaded that the Commission's long and close examination of the questions it here decided has provided it with precisely the experience that fits it for performance of its statutory duty. The kind of specialized knowledge Congress wanted its agency to have was an expertness that would fit it to stop at the threshold every unfair trade practice—that kind of practice which, if left alone, "destroys competition and establishes monopoly." *Federal Trade Comm'n* v. *Raladam Co.*, 283 U.S. 643, 647, 650. And see *Federal Trade Comm'n* v. *Raladam Co.*, 316 U.S. 149, 152.

We cannot say that the Commission is wrong in concluding that the delivered-price system as here used provides an effective instrument which if left free for use of the respondents would result in complete destruction of competition and the establishment of monopoly in the cement industry. That the basing point price system may lend itself to industrywide anticompetitive practices is illustrated in the following among other cases: *United States* v. *United States Gypsum Co.*, 333 U.S. 364, *Sugar Institute* v. *United States*, 297 U.S. 553. We uphold the Commission's conclusion that the basing point delivered price system employed by respondents is an unfair trade practice which the Trade Commission may suppress.

The Price Discrimination Charge in Count Two. The Commission found that respondents' combination to use the multiple basing point delivered price system had effected systematic price discrimination in violation of § 2 of the Clayton Act as amended by the Robinson-Patman Act. 49 Stat. 1526, 15 U.S.C. § 13. Section 2 (a) of that Act declares it to "be unlawful for any person engaged in commerce . . . either directly or indirectly, to discriminate in price between different purchasers of commodities of like grade and quality . . . where the effect of such discrimination may be substantially to lessen competition or tend to create a monopoly in any line of commerce, or to injure, destroy, or prevent competition with any person who either grants or knowingly receives the benefit of such discrimination, or with customers of either of them. . . ." Section 2 (b) provides that proof of discrimination in price (selling the same kind of goods cheaper to one purchaser than to another) makes out a prima facie case of violation but permits the seller to rebut "the prima-facie case thus made by showing that his lower price . . . was made in good faith to meet an equally low price of a competitor. . . ."

The Commission held that the varying mill nets received by respondents on sales between customers in different localities constituted a "discrimination in price between different purchasers" within the prohibition of § 2 (a) and that the effect of this discrimination was the substantial lessening of competition between respondents. The Circuit Court of Appeals reversed the Commission on this count. It agreed that respondents' prices were unlawful insofar as they involved the collection of phantom freight, but it held that prices involving only freight absorption came within the "good faith" proviso of § 2 (b).

The respondents contend that the differences in their net returns from sales in different localities which result from use of the multiple basing point delivered price system are not price discriminations within the meaning of § 2 (a). If held that these net return differences are price discriminations prohibited by § 2 (a), they contend that the discriminations were justified under § 2 (b) because "made in good faith to meet an equally low price of a competitor." Practically all the arguments presented by respondents in support of their contentions were considered by this Court and rejected in 1945 in *Corn Products Co.* v. *Federal Trade Comm'n,* 324 U.S. 726, and in the related case of *Federal Trade Comm'n* v. *Staley Co.,* 324 U.S. 746. . . . Consequently, we see no reason for again reviewing the questions that were there decided. . . .

Section 2 (b) permits a single company to sell to one customer at a lower price than it sells to another if the price is "made in good faith to meet an equally low price of a competitor." But this does not mean that § 2 (b) permits a seller to use a sales system which constantly results in his getting more money for like goods from some customers than he does from others. We held to the contrary in the *Staley* case. There we said that the Act "speaks only of the seller's 'lower' price and of that only to the extent that it is made 'in good faith to meet an equally low price of a competitor.' The Act thus places emphasis on individual competitive situations, rather than upon a general system of competition." *Federal Trade Comm'n* v. *Staley, supra* at 753. Each of the respondents, whether all its mills were basing points or not, sold some cement at prices determined by the basing point formula and governed by other base mills. Thus, all respondents to this extent adopted a discriminatory pricing system condemned by § 2. . . .

*   *   *   *   *

Many other arguments have been presented by respondents. All have been examined, but we find them without merit.

*   *   *   *   *

The Commission's order should not have been set aside by the Circuit Court of Appeals. Its judgment is reversed, and the cause is remanded to that court with directions to enforce the order.

It is so ordered.

*   *   *   *   *

✖ 32

United States v. *Container Corp. of America et al.*

U.S. Supreme Court
393 U.S. 333 (1969)

> *This case explored the margin of cooperation among firms in sharing price information. The key: Sellers could routinely demand and get each others' latest sale price, but buyers could not do the same. By reducing sellers' uncertainty about competitive offers, it could reduce the likelihood of price cutting, thereby "chilling" competition. But was this effect strong enough to justify the conviction?*

Mr. Justice Douglas.   This is a civil antitrust action charging a price-fixing agreement in violation of § 1 of the Sherman Act. . . .

The case as proved is unlike any of other price decisions we have rendered. There was here an exchange of price information but no agreement to adhere to a price schedule as in *Sugar Institute* v. *United States*, 297 U.S. 553, or *United States* v. *Socony-Vacuum Oil Co.*, 310 U.S. 150. There was here an exchange of information concerning specific sales to identified customers, not a statistical report on the average cost to all members, without identifying the parties to specific transactions, as in *Maple Flooring Mfrs. Assn.* v. *United States*, 268 U.S. 563. While there was present here, as in *Cement Mfrs. Protective Assn.* v. *United States*, 268 U.S. 588, an exchange of prices to specific customers, there was absent the controlling circumstance, *viz.*, that cement manufacturers, to protect themselves from delivering to contractors more cement than was needed for a specific job and thus receiving a lower price, exchanged price information as a means of protecting their legal rights from fraudulent inducements to deliver more cement than needed for a specific job.

Here all that was present was a request by each defendant of its competitor for information as to the most recent price charged or quoted, whenever it needed such information and whenever it was not available from another source. Each defendant on receiving that request usually furnished the data with the expectation that it would be furnished reciprocal information when it wanted it. That concerted action is, of course, sufficient to establish the combination or conspiracy, the initial ingredient of a violation of § 1 of the Sherman Act.

There was, of course, freedom to withdraw from the agreement. But the fact remains that when a defendant requested and received price information it was affirming its willingness to furnish such information in return.

There was, to be sure, an infrequency and irregularity of price exchanges between the defendants; and often the data were available from the records of the defendants or from the customers themselves. Yet the essence of the agreement was to furnish price information whenever requested.

Moreover, although the most recent price charged or quoted was sometimes fragmentary, each defendant had the manuals with which it could compute the price charged by a competitor on a specific order to a specific customer.

Further, the price quoted was the current price which a customer would need to pay in order to obtain products from the defendant furnishing the data.

The defendants account for about 90 percent of the shipment of corrugated containers from plants in the southeastern United States. While containers vary as to dimensions, weight, color, and so on, they are substantially identical no matter who produces them when made to particular specifications. The prices paid depend on price alternatives. Suppliers when seeking new or additional business or keeping old customers do not exceed a competitor's price. It is common for purchasers to buy from two or more suppliers concurrently. A defendant supplying a customer with containers would usually quote the same price on additional orders, unless costs had changed. Yet where a competitor was charging a particular price, a defendant would normally quote the same price or even a lower price.

The exchange of price information seemed to have the effect of keeping prices within a fairly narrow ambit. Capacity has exceeded the demand from 1955 to 1963, the period covered by the complaint, and the trend of corrugated container prices has been downward. Yet despite this excess capacity and the downward trend of prices, the industry has expanded in the Southeast from 30 manufacturers with 49 plants to 51 manufacturers with 98 plants. An abundance of raw materials and machinery makes entry into the industry easy with an investment of $50,000 to $75,000.

The result of this reciprocal exchange of prices was to stabilize prices though at a downward level. Knowledge of a competitor's price usually meant matching that price. The continuation of some price competition is not fatal to the Government's case. The limitation or reduction of price competition brings the case within the ban, for as we held in *United States* v. *Socony-Vacuum Oil Co., supra,* at 224, n. 59, interference with the setting of price by free market forces is unlawful per se. Price information exchanged in some markets may have no effect on a truly competitive price. But the corrugated container industry is dominated by relatively few sellers. The product is fungible and the competition for sales is price. The demand is inelastic, as buyers place orders only for immediate short-run needs. The exchange of price data tends toward price uniformity. For a lower price does not mean a larger share of the available business but a sharing of the existing business at a lower return. Stabilizing prices as well as raising them is within the ban of § 1 of the Sherman Act. . . . The inferences are irresistible that the exchange of price information has had an anticompetitive effect in the industry, chilling the vigor of price competition. . . .

Price is too critical, too sensitive a control to allow it to be used even in an informal manner to restrain competition.

Reversed.

Mr. Justice Marshall, with whom Mr. Justice Harlan and Mr. Justice Stewart join, dissenting.

. . . Complete market knowledge is certainly not an evil in perfectly competitive markets. This is not, however, such a market, and there is admittedly some danger that price information will be used for anticompetitive purposes, particularly the maintenance of prices at a high level. If the danger that price information will be so used is particularly high in a given situation, then perhaps exchange of information should be condemned.

I do not think the danger is sufficiently high in the present case. Defendants are only 18 of the 51 producers of corrugated containers in the southeastern United States. Together, they do make up 90 percent of the market, and the six largest defendants do control 60 percent of the market. But entry is easy; an investment of $50,000 to $75,000 is ordinarily all that is necessary. In fact, the number of sellers has increased from 30 to the present 51 in the eight-year period covered by the complaint. The size of the market has almost doubled because of increased demand for corrugated containers. Nevertheless, some excess capacity is present. The products produced by defendants are undifferentiated. Industry demand is inelastic, so that price changes will not, up to a certain point, affect the total amount purchased. The only effect of price changes will be to reallocate market shares among sellers. . . .

The Government is ultimately forced to fall back on the theoretical argument that prices would have been more unstable and would have fallen faster without price information. As I said earlier, I cannot make this assumption on the basis of the evidence in this record. The findings of the Court below simply do not indicate that the exchange of information had a significant anticompetitive effect; if we rely on these findings, at worst all we can assume is that the exchange was a neutral factor in the market. . . .

✳ 33

Hartford-Empire Co. et al. v. United States

U.S. Supreme Court
323 U.S. 391 (1945)

This case dealt with one of the most thorough patent pools ever devised. It set a precedent limiting such pooling among leading firms. But was the majority too lenient, as the dissent suggests?

Mr. Justice Roberts.   These are appeals from a decree awarding an injunction against violations of § § 1 and 2 of the Sherman Act, as amended, and § 3 of the Clayton Act. Two questions are presented. Were violations provided? If so, are the provisions of the decree right?

The complaint named as defendants 12 corporations and 101 individuals associated with them as officers or directors. It was dismissed as to 3 corporations and 40 individuals. The corporations are the leaders in automatic glassmaking machinery and in the glassware industry. The charge is that all the defendants agreed, conspired, and combined to monopolize, and did monopolize and restrain interstate and foreign commerce by acquiring patents covering the manufacture of glassmaking machinery, and by excluding others from a fair opportunity freely to engage in commerce in such machinery and in the manufacture and distribution of glass products. The gravamen of the case is that the defendants have cooperated in obtaining and licensing patents covering glassmaking machinery, have limited and restricted the use of the patented machinery by a network of agreements, and have maintained prices for unpatented glassware.

The trial lasted 112 days. The court filed an opinion of 160 pages, 628 findings of fact and 89 conclusions of law, and entered a decree covering 46 printed pages and comprising 60 numbered paragraphs. The printed record contains over 16,500 pages. . . .

*   *   *   *   *

In 1919 the Glass Container Association of America was formed. Prior to 1933 its members produced 82 percent of the glass containers made in the United States and since have produced 92 percent. Since 1931 (except while the National Industrial Recovery Act was in force) the association has had a statistical committee of seven, on which Owens, Hazel, Thatcher, and since 1933, Ball were represented. These appellants also were represented in the Board of Directors. Hartford, though not a member, has closely cooperated with the officers of the association in efforts to discourage outsiders from increasing production of glassware and newcomers from entering the field. The court below, on sufficient evidence, has found that the association, through its statistical committee, assigned production quotas to its members and that they and Hartford were zealous in seeing that these were observed.

In summary, the situation brought about in the glass industry and existing in 1938 was this: Hartford, with the technical and financial aid of others in the conspiracy, had acquired, by issue to it or assignment from the owners, more than 600 patents. These, with over 100 Corning controlled patents, over 60 Owens patents, over 70 Hazel patents, and some 12 Lynch patents, had been, by cross-licensing agreements, merged into a pool which effectually controlled the industry. This control was exercised to allot production in Corning's field to Corning and that in restricted classes within the general container field to Owens, Hazel, Thatcher, Ball, and such other smaller manufacturers as the group agreed should be licensed. The result was that 94 percent of the glass containers manufactured in this country on feeders and formers were made on machinery licensed under the pooled patents.

The District Court found that invention of glassmaking machinery had been discouraged, that competition in the manufacture and sale or licensing of such machinery had been suppressed, and that the system of restricted licensing had been employed to suppress competition in the manufacture of unpatented glassware and to maintain prices of the manufactured product. The findings are full and adequate and are supported by evidence, much of it contemporary writings of corporate defendants or their officers and agents.

*   *   *   *   *

We affirm the District Court's findings and conclusions that the corporate appellants combined in violation of the Sherman Act, that Hartford and Lynch contracted in violation of the Clayton Act, and that the individual appellants with exceptions to be noted participated in the violations in their capacities as officers and directors of the corporations.

*   *   *   *   *

I

. . . It is clear that by cooperative arrangements and binding agreements the appellant corporations, over a period of years, regulated and suppressed competition in the use of glassmaking machinery and employed their joint patent position to allocate fields of manufacture and to maintain prices of unpatented glassware.

The explanations offered by the appellants are unconvincing. It is said on behalf of Hartford that its business in its inception was lawful and within the patent laws; and that in order to protect its legitimate interests as holder of patents for automatic glass machinery it was justified in buying up and fencing off improvement patents, the grant of which, while leaving the fundamental inventions untouched, would hamper their use unless tribute were paid to the owners of the so-called improvements which, of themselves, had only a nuisance value.

The explanation fails to account for the offensive and defensive alliance of patent owners with its concomitant stifling of initiative, invention, and competition. . . .

II

The Government sought the dissolution of Hartford. The court, however, decided that a continuance of certain of Hartford's activities would be of advantage to the glass industry and denied, for the time being, that form of relief. The court was of opinion, however, that the long series of transactions and the persistent manifestations of a purpose to violate the antitrust statutes required the entry of a decree which would preclude the resumption of unlawful practices. It was faced, therefore, with the difficult problem of awarding an injunction which would insure the desired end without imposing punishments or other sanctions for past misconduct, a problem especially difficult in view of the status and relationship of the parties.

At the trial the Government stated that in this suit it was not attacking the validity of any patent or claiming any patent had been awarded an improper priority.

At the time of the District Court's decision, Hartford had reduced the royalties of all its licensees to its then schedule of standard royalties so that all stood on an equal basis so far as license fees were concerned. Government counsel did not assert, or attempt to prove, that these royalties were not reasonable in amount.

Owens, as respects suction invention licenses, had removed all restrictive clauses; Hartford had done the same with respect to all its glass machinery licenses and so had Hartford and Lynch with respect to forming machine licenses. At the moment, therefore, no licensee was restricted either as to kind or quantity of glassware it might manufacture by use of the patented machines, and no patent owner was restricted by formal agreement as to the use or licensing of its patents. . . .

The association had ceased to allot quotas amongst the glass manufacturers or to furnish advance information or make recommendations to its members. The licensing system of Hartford remained that of leasing machinery built for it embodying the patented inventions. Rentals consisted of standard royalties on production. Under this system Hartford rendered a service in the repair, maintenance, and protection of the machines which is valuable, if not essential, to the users. This was the status with which the court had to deal.

The applicable principles are not doubtful. The Sherman Act provides criminal penalties for its violation and authorizes the recovery of a penal sum in addition to damages in a civil suit by one injured by violation. It also authorizes an injunction to prevent continuing violations by those acting contrary to its proscriptions. The present suit is in the last named category, and we may not impose penalties[1] in the guise of preventing future violations. This is not to say that a decree need deal only with the exact type of acts found to have been committed[2] or that the court should not, in framing its decree, resolve all doubts in favor of the Government,[3] or may not prohibit acts which in another setting would be unobjectionable. But even so, the court may not create, as to the defendants, new duties, prescription of which is the function of Congress, or place the defendants for the future "in a different class than other people" as the Government has suggested. The decree must not be "so vague as to put the whole conduct of the defendants' business at the peril of a summons for contempt"; enjoin "all possible breaches of the law"; or cause the defendants hereafter not "to be under the protection of the law of the land." With these principles in mind we proceed to examine the terms of the decree entered. . . .

*   *   *   *   *

That a patent is property, protected against appropriation both by individuals and by government, has long been settled. In recognition of this quality of a patent the courts, in enjoining violations of the Sherman Act arising from the use of patent licenses, agreements, and leases, have abstained from action which amounted to a forfeiture of the patents.

*   *   *   *   *

. . . Hartford and the other corporate defendants mentioned in paragraph 24 should be required to lease or license glassmaking machinery of the classes each now manufactures to any who may desire to take licenses (under patents on such machinery or on improvements, methods, or processes applicable thereto) at standard royalties and without discrimination or restriction, and if at the time of entry of the decree there are any alleged infringers who are willing to take such licenses, they should be released and the patent owner deprived of all damages and profits which it might have claimed for past infringement. The decree should, however, be without prejudice to the future institu-

---

[1]*Standard Oil Co.* v. *United States*, 221 U.S. 1, 77–78.
[2]*Ethyl Gasoline Corp.* v. *United States*, 309 U.S. 436, 461.
[3]*Local 167* v. *United States*, 291 U.S. 293, 299.

tion of any suit or suits for asserted infringements against persons refusing to take licenses under any of the presently licensed inventions
arising out of their use after the date of the decree. The decree should
not forbid any defendant from seeking recovery for infringement, occurring after the date of the final decree, of patents not covering feeders,
formers, stackers, lehrs, or processes or methods applicable to any of
them.

*   *   *   *   *

Paragraph 28 orders cancellation of all Hartford machinery leases now
outstanding and requires that each lessee be offered a new license
(without royalty, pursuant to paragraph 24) and offered the right to
purchase all of the machinery now held under lease (as required by
paragraph 23). In view of what has been said this provision should not
stand. . . .

*   *   *   *   *

The corporate appellants have amended, or agreed to amend, existing
leases and licenses to remove all such restrictions as are enjoined. . . .

*   *   *   *   *

Paragraph 31 requires court approval of "any agreement between any
of the defendants" and "of any license agreement made pursuant to this
judgment." This is too sweeping. The provision is without limit of time
and not terminable upon fulfilment of any condition. . . .

*   *   *   *   *

Paragraph 35 enjoins each individual defendant from holding, at the
same time, an office or directorship in more than one corporation which
manufactures and sells glassware or manufactures or distributes
glassmaking machinery. The injunction is not limited to directorships in
more than one of the defendant corporations. . . . [Yet] . . . There may
be many instances when the normal freedom to act as a director of more
than one company will in no wise conflict with the policies of the antitrust laws or tend to the fostering of practices which those laws forbid. . . .

*   *   *   *   *

Paragraph 52 deals with the problem of suppressed or unworked
patents. Much is said in the opinion below and in the briefs about the
practice of the appellants in applying for patents to "block off" or "fence
in" competing inventions. In the cooperative effort of certain of the
appellants to obtain dominance in the field of patented glassmaking
machinery, many patents were applied for to prevent others from ob-

taining patents on improvements which might, to some extent, limit the return in the way of royalty on original or fundamental inventions. The decree should restrain agreements and combinations with this object. But it is another matter to restrain every defendant for the indefinite future from attempting to patent improvements of machines or processes previously patented and then owned by such defendant. This paragraph is, in our judgment, too broad. In effect it prohibits several of the corporate defendants from applying for patents covering their own inventions in the art of glassmaking. For reasons elsewhere elaborated it cannot be sustained. . . .

* * * * *

Mr. Justice Black, dissenting in part.

I agree with the Court's judgment insofar as it sustains the decree of the District Judge.

I cannot, however, agree to many of the modifications of that decree. These appellants have violated the antitrust laws. The District Court's decree, taken as a whole, is an effective remedy, admirably suited to neutralize the consequences of such violations, to guard against repetition of similar illegal activities, and to dissipate the unlawful aggregate of economic power which arose out of, and fed upon, monopolization and restraints. *United States* v. *Crescent Amusement Co.*, 323 U.S. 173. Many of this Court's modifications seriously impair the decree and frustrate its purposes.

It would probably serve no useful purpose to state at length the reasons which justify the District Court's decree, since they are set forth clearly and well in its opinion. In particular, however, it is my belief that any reasonable assurance that these appellants will not continue to violate the antitrust law requires that we leave intact the District Court's decree insofar as it (1) provides for appointment of a receiver and the impounding of Hartford's royalties (Paragraphs 10–20 of the Decree); (2) requires that glassware machines should be disposed of by outright sale rather than by leases (Paragraphs 21, 22, 23); (3) requires that patents, already owned, be licensed royalty free; (4) prohibits the restrictive licensing practices which the appellants so effectively used to create and maintain their monopoly (Paragraph 29); (5) enjoins the appellants from the practice of obtaining patents for the purpose of "fencing in" and "blocking off" new inventions, (Paragraph 52).

The District Court's opinion in my judgment laid a careful and well-reasoned foundation establishing the necessity for every one of these Paragraphs. It would be difficult to add to what the court there said. It is sufficient for me to say only a few words.

The District Court found that these defendants started out in 1916 to acquire a monopoly on a large segment of the glass industry. Their efforts were rewarded by complete success. They have become absolute masters of that domain of our public economy. They achieved this result largely through the manipulation of patents and licensing agreements. They obtained patents for the express purpose of furthering their monopoly. They utilized various types of restrictions in connection with leasing those patents so as to retain their dominance in that industry. The history of this country has perhaps never witnessed a more completely successful economic tyranny over any field of industry than that accomplished by these appellants. They planned their monopolistic program on the basis of getting and keeping and using patents, which they dedicated to the destruction of free competition in the glass container industry. Their declared object was "To block the development of machines which might be constructed by others . . ." and "To secure patents on possible improvements of competing machines, so as to 'fence in' those and prevent their reaching an improved state." These patents were the major weapons in the campaign to subjugate the industry; they were also the fruits of appellants' victory. The restoration of competition in the glass container industry demands that appellants be deprived of these weapons. The most effective way to accomplish this end is to require, as the District Court did, that these patents be licensed royalty free.

The decree of the court below was well fashioned to prevent a continuation of appellants' monopolistic practices. The decree as modified leaves them free, in a large measure, to continue to follow the competition-destroying methods by which they achieved control of the industry. In fact, they have received much milder treatment from this Court than they anticipated. . . .

Price Discrimination

There are many forms and settings of price discrimination, and its effects vary. Discrimination occurs when the price-cost ratios are not equal to different buyers of the same or related goods. It can help a firm to gain market dominance, to fend off competition by selective price cutting, and/or to maximize its monopoly profits. The harm can be "primary" line (at that level) or "secondary" line (among firms which use the product as an input). Discrimination can be procompetitive when it is done sporadically by firms with small market shares. But done systematically by a dominant firm, it can be a key strategy to reduce competition. In extreme cases, it may be part of a "predatory" action to harm, discipline, or eliminate a competitor.

The first problem is to establish that discrimination occurred: that price-cost ratios did differ. The *Morton Salt* and *Borden* cases helped to set the precedents that apply. Price discounts may be "cost justified," or they may reflect true differences between two goods. But such cost and quality differences must be proven, and the cases show that it may not be easy to do so.

Predatory pricing is an old issue. For example, the old Standard Oil Company used selective pricing and railroad rebates during 1870–90 to create its dominant position. The recent literature offers two main views. One group notes that predatory actions are a large category, of which pricing tactics are only one part. Basil Yamey puts this view lucidly, and the *Berkey-Eastman Kodak* verdict of 1978 (above) reflects it. Another group regards pricing as the only predatory weapon. It says that prices are predatory only if they go below short-run marginal cost or long-run average cost. The Areeda-Turner paper advances such cost criteria. It places a heavy burden of proof upon the injured party to present convincing cost and price data.

Several cases show how such issues can be resolved. IBM and Xerox have practiced extensive price discrimination. Both the agencies and competitors have alleged that the pricing is part of predatory strategies (see the Division's *IBM* suit [above] and the *Telex* and *Greyhound* suits against IBM in the 1970s. The FTC's complaint and SCM's successful suit against Xerox [tried in 1977–78] also contain claims of predatory actions).

The cases included here give more variety in simpler conditions. The *Utah Pie* case involved attempts by large chain bakers to undercut prices by a leading (but small) frozen-pie firm in Utah. Though the decision oddly favored the dominant firm (Utah Pie) against new entrants, does it have a certain validity nonetheless? (Utah Pie went out of business soon after!) *International Air Industries* involved an intent to damage competitors, but the court adopted the Areeda-Turner view and looked only at prices.

✂ 34

Federal Trade Commission v. *Morton Salt Co.*

U.S. Supreme Court
334 U.S. 37 (1948)

Mr. Justice Black.   The Federal Trade Commission, after a hearing, found that the respondent, which manufactures and sells table salt in interstate commerce, had discriminated in price between different purchasers of like grades and qualities and concluded that such discriminations were in violation of Section 2 of the Clayton Act . . . as amended by the Robinson-Patman Act. . . . It accordingly issued a cease and desist order. . . . [The Circuit Court of Appeals reversed, and the FTC appealed.] Since questions of importance in the construction and administration of the Act were presented, we granted certiorari. . . .

Respondent manufactures several different brands of table salt and sells them directly to (1) wholesalers or jobbers, who in turn resell to the retail trade, and (2) large retailers, including chain store retailers. Respondent sells its finest brand of table salt, known as Blue Label, on what it terms a standard quantity discount system available to all customers. Under this system the purchasers pay a delivered price and the cost to both wholesale and retail purchasers of this brand differs according to the quantities bought. These prices are as follows, after making allowance for rebates and discounts:

	Per Case
Less-than-carload purchases	$1.60
Carload purchases	1.50
5,000-case purchases in any consecutive 12 months	1.40
50,000-case purchases in any consecutive 12 months	1.35

Only five companies have ever bought sufficient quantities of respondent's salt to obtain the $1.35 per case price. These companies could buy in such quantities because they operate large chains of retail stores in various parts of the country. As a result of this low price these five companies have been able to sell Blue Label salt at retail cheaper than wholesale purchasers from respondent could reasonably sell the same brand of salt to independently operated retail stores, many of whom competed with the local outlets of the five chain stores. . . .

In addition to these standard quantity discounts, special allowances were granted certain favored customers who competed with other customers to whom they were denied.

First. Respondent's basic contention, whch it argues this case hinges upon, is that its "standard quantity discounts, available to all on equal terms, as contrasted, for example, to hidden or special rebates, allowances, prices or discounts, are not discriminatory within the meaning of the Robinson-Patman Act." Theoretically, these discounts are equally available to all, but functionally they are not. For as the record indicates (if reference to it on this point were necessary), no single independent retail grocery store and probably no single wholesaler bought as many as 50,000 cases or as much as $50,000 worth of table salt in one year. Furthermore, the record shows that while certain purchasers were enjoying one or more of respondent's standard quantity discounts some of their competitors made purchases in such small quantities that they could not qualify for any of respondent's discounts, even those based on carload shipments. The legislative history of the Robinson-Patman Act makes it abundantly clear that Congress considered it to be an evil that a large buyer could secure a competitive advantage over a small buyer solely because of the large buyer's quantity purchasing ability. The Robinson-Patman Act was passed to deprive a large buyer of such advantages except to the extent that a lower price could be justified by reason of a seller's diminished costs due to quantity manufacture, delivery or sale, or by reason of the seller's good faith effort to meet a competitor's equally low price.

*   *   *   *   *

Second.   The Government interprets the opinion of the Circuit Court of Appeals as having held that in order to establish "discrimination in price" under the Act the burden rested on the Commission to prove that respondent's quantity discount differentials were not justified by its cost savings. Respondent does not so understand the Court of Appeals decision and furthermore admits that no such burden rests on the Commission. We agree that it does not. . . .

Third.   It is argued that the findings fail to show that respondent's discriminatory discounts had in fact caused injury to competition. There are specific findings that such injuries had resulted from respondent's discounts, although the statute does not require the Commission to find that injury has actually resulted. The statute requires no more than that the effect of the prohibited price discriminations "may be substantially to lessen competition . . . or to injure, destroy, or prevent competition." . . . Here the Commission found what would appear to be obvious, that the competitive opportunities of certain merchants were injured when they had to pay respondent substantially more for their goods than their competitors had to pay. The findings are adequate.

Fourth.   It is urged that the evidence is inadequate to support the Commission's findings of injury to competition. As we have pointed out, however, the Commission is authorized by the Act to bar discriminatory prices upon the "reasonable possibility" that different prices for like goods to competing purchasers may have the defined effect on competition. That respondent's quantity discounts did result in price differentials between competing purchasers sufficient in amount to influence their resale prices of salt was shown by evidence. This showing in itself is adequate to support the Commission's appropriate findings that the effect of such price discriminations "may be substantially to lessen competition . . . and to injure, destroy, and prevent competition."

*   *   *   *   *

Fifth.   The Circuit Court of Appeals held, and respondent here contends, that the order was too sweeping. . . .

. . . True, the Commission did not merely prohibit future discounts, rebates, and allowances in the exact mathematical percentages previously utilized by respondent. Had the order done no more than that, respondent could have continued substantially the same unlawful practices despite the order by simply altering the discount percentages and the quantities of salt to which the percentages applied. . . .

The judgment of the Circuit Court of Appeals is reversed and the proceedings are remanded to that court to be disposed of in conformity with this opinion.

Reversed.

35

Federal Trade Commission v. *Borden Co.*

U.S. Supreme Court
383 U.S. 637 (1966)

Mr. Justice White. The Borden Company, respondent here, produces and sells evaporated milk under the Borden name, a nationally advertised brand. At the same time Borden packs and markets evaporated milk under various private brands owned by its customers. This milk is physically and chemically identical with the milk it distributes under its own brand but is sold at both the wholesale and retail level at prices regularly below those obtained for the Borden brand milk. The Federal Trade Commission found the milk sold under the Borden and the private labels to be of like grade and quality as required for the applicability of § 2 (a) of the Robinson-Patman Act, held the price differential to be discriminatory within the meaning of the section, ascertained the requisite adverse effect on commerce, rejected Borden's claim of cost justification, and consequently issued a cease-and-desist order. The Court of Appeals set aside the Commission's order on the sole ground that as a matter of law the customer label milk was not of the same grade and quality as the milk sold under the Borden brand. . . . We now reverse the decision of the Court of Appeals and remand the case to that court for the determination of the remaining issues raised by respondent Borden in that court. . . .

The position of Borden and of the Court of Appeals is that the determination of like grade and quality, which is a threshold finding essential to the applicability of § 2 (a), may not be based solely on the physical properties of the products without regard to the brand names they bear and the relative public acceptance these brands enjoy—"consideration should be given to all commercially significant distinctions which affect market value, whether they be physical or promotional." 339 F. 2d, at 137. Here, because the milk bearing the Borden brand regularly sold at a higher price than did the milk with a buyer's label, the court considered the products to be "commercially" different and hence of different "grade" for the purposes of § 2 (a), even though they were physically identical and of equal quality. Although a mere difference in brand would not in itself demonstrate a difference in grade, decided consumer preference for one brand over another, reflected in the willingness to pay a higher price for the well-known brand, was, in the view of the Court of Appeals, sufficient to differentiate chemically identical products and to place the price differential beyond the reach of § 2 (a).

We reject this construction of § 2 (a), as did both the examiner and the Commission in this case. The Commission's view is that labels do not differentiate products for the purpose of determining grade or quality, even though the one label may have more customer appeal and command a higher price in the marketplace from a substantial segment of the public. That this is the Commission's long-standing interpretation of the present Act, as well as of § 2 of the Clayton Act before its amendment by the Robinson-Patman Act, may be gathered from the Commission's decisions dating back to 1936. . . . These views of the agency are entitled to respect . . . and represent a more reasonable construction of the statute than that offered by the Court of Appeals.

Obviously there is nothing in the language of the statute indicating that grade, as distinguished from quality, is not to be determined by the characteristics of the product itself, but by consumer preferences, brand acceptability or what customers think of it and are willing to pay for it. Moreover, what legislative history there is concerning this question supports the Commission's construction of the statute rather than that of the Court of Appeals.

*   *   *   *   *

If two products, physically identical but differently branded, are to be deemed of different grade because the seller regularly and successfully markets some quantity of both at different prices, the seller could, as far as § 2 (a) is concerned, make either product available to some customers and deny it to others, however discriminatory this might be and however damaging to competition. Those who were offered only one of the two products would be barred from competing for those customers who want or might buy the other. The retailer who was permitted to buy and sell only the more expensive brand would have no chance to sell to those who always buy the cheaper product or to convince others, by experience or otherwise, of the fact which he and all other dealers already know—that the cheaper product is actually identical with that carrying the more expensive label.

The seller, to escape the Act, would have only to succeed in selling some unspecified amount of each product to some unspecified portion of his customers, however large or small the price differential might be. The seller's pricing and branding policy, by being successful, would apparently validate itself by creating a difference in "grade" and thus taking itself beyond the purview of the Act.

Our holding neither ignores the economic realities of the marketplace nor denies that some labels will command a higher price than others, at least from some portion of the public. But it does mean that "the economic factors inherent in brand names and national advertising should not be considered in the jurisdictional inquiry under the statutory 'like grade and quality' tests." Report of the Attorney General's National Committee to Study the Antitrust Laws 158 (1955). And it does mean that transactions like those involved in this case may be examined by the Commission under § 2 (a). The Commission will determine, subject to judicial review, whether the differential under attack is discriminatory within the meaning of the Act, whether competition may be injured, and whether the differential is cost-justified or is defensible as a good-faith effort to meet the price of a competitor. "[T]angible consumer preferences as between branded and unbranded commodities should receive due legal recognition in the more flexible 'injury' and 'cost justification' provisions of the statute." Id., at 159. This, we think, is precisely what Congress intended. The arguments for exempting private brand selling from § 2 (a) are, therefore, more appropriately addressed to the Congress than to this Court. . . .

. . . The judgment of the Court of Appeals is reversed and the case is remanded for further proceedings consistent with this opinion.

Basil S. Yamey (1916–   )

36
Predatory Price Cutting: Notes and Comments*†

Yamey notes that predatory actions are strategies which can involve many devices besides prices. Therefore, one must take a broad view in judging whether predation has occurred and competition has been harmed. Price-cost relations alone will not do.

I

In various post-war contributions to the analysis and empirical study of predatory price cutting, the practice has been defined as temporary selling at prices below its costs by a firm (or concerted group of firms) to drive out or crush a competitor. For convenience, the two firms will be called aggressor and rival or predator and victim.

An early contribution by John S. McGee broke new ground by arguing that price cutting of this kind is not a sensible or profitable strategy for an aggressor to adopt since a better alternative is at hand.[1] He concluded: "Whereas it is *conceivable* that some one might embark on a predatory program, I cannot see that it would pay him to do so, since outright purchase [of the rival firm] is both cheaper and more reliable."[2] McGee did not consider specifically a close substitute for acquisition, namely the formation of a cartel between the two firms jointly to exploit the monopoly. In the earlier of two papers on predatory pricing Lester Telser noted this alternative and concluded on lines similar to McGee's:

*Basil S. Yamey, "Predatory Price Cutting: Notes and Comments," *Journal of Law and Economics*, vol. 15 (April 1972), pp. 129–42, excerpted from pp. 129–37. Yamey is Professor of Economics at the London School of Economics and Political Science and a British expert on industrial economics and competition policy (as they are called there). He has been a member of the U.K. Monopolies Commission.

†I am grateful to R. H. Coase and G. R. J. Richardson for valuable comments and suggestions.

[1]John S. McGee, "Predatory Price Cutting: The Standard Oil (N.J.) Case, "1 *J. Law & Econ.*, 137, 138–43 (1958). See also Lester G. Telser, "Abusive Trade Practices: An Economic Analysis," 30 *Law & Contemp. Prob.* 488, 494–96 (1965).

[2]John S. McGee, *supra* note 1, at 143; see also 168. The inclusion of the word "conceivable" seems to have been made to cover cases of error. The word "reliable" refers to the advantage of purchase of assets over their competitive elimination, since the latter course does not sterilise them from further use.

"Either some form of collusion or a merger of the competitors would seem preferable to any possible outcome of economic predation."[3]

The key element in McGee's analysis is that predatory price cutting involves both firms, the predator and its victim, in unnecessary and avoidable loss of profits. In McGee's words: "Since the revenues to be gotten during the predatory price war will always be less than those that could be gotten immediately through purchase and will not be higher after the war is concluded [as compared with the revenues after the merger], present worth [of the aggressor] will be higher in the purchase case."[4] Telser's more striking formulation is similar: "Price warfare between the two [firms] is equivalent to forming a coalition between each firm and the consumers, such that the consumers gain from the conflict between the firms. Since both firms can benefit by agreeing on a merger price, and both stand to lose by sales below cost, one would think that rational men would prefer merger."[5]

McGee's strong conclusion that monopoly achieved by the acquisition of the rival is cheaper than monopoly achieved by the elimination of the rival in economic war was modified by later contributors, including Telser.[6] Considerations omitted or dismissed in McGee's study have been brought into the analysis; and their inclusion serves to mitigate the conclusion that predatory pricing necessarily is economic folly. These considerations concern, *inter alia,* the elements of strategical and tactical manoeuvre which may affect the outcomes, including the long-term implications, of the alternative courses of action open to the aggressor. Some elaboration of these considerations follows.

The price to be agreed upon in the purchase of the rival is not a matter of indifference to the aggressor, can affect its choice of a strategy for dealing with the problem created by the presence of the rival, and may itself be capable of being affected by predatory pricing. Initially it is unlikely that the aggressor and its rival will make the same assessment and valuation of the latter's prospects of profits in the given situation. Two possibilities can be distinguished. First, initially the rival's minimum asking price may exceed the aggressor's maximum offer price (and, *mutatis mutandis,* a similar deadlock may exist when the formation

---

[3]Lester G. Telser, *supra* note 1, at 495.

[4]John S. McGee, *supra* note 1, at 140.

[5]Lester G. Telser, "Cutthroat Competition and the Long Purse," 9 *J. Law & Econ.,* 259, 265 (1966).

[6]For the relevant contributions, see Lester G. Telser, *supra* note 5, at 259–70; Richard Zerbe, "The American Sugar Refinery Company, 1887–1914: The Story of a Monopoly," 12 *J. Law & Econ.* 339, 363 n. 120 (1969); Donald Dewey, *The Theory of Imperfect Competition: A Radical Reconstruction,* ch. 7 (1969); Kenneth G. Elzinga, "Predatory Pricing: The Case of the Gunpowder Trust," 13 *J. Law & Econ.* 223 (1970).

of a cartel is at issue). A bout of price warfare initiated by the aggressor or a threat of such activity might serve to cause the rival to revise its expectations and, hence, to alter its terms of sale to an acceptable level.[7] Second, initially the minimum asking price of the rival may be less than the maximum price the aggressor is willing to pay, so that a mutually satisfactory transaction would be possible. Nevertheless, the use or the threat of predatory pricing may be a useful component in the course of bargaining in which the aggressor tries to beat down the actual price to be paid towards the minimum asking price, as well as to induce the rival to reduce the minimum price.[8]

The aggressor will, moreover, be looking beyond the immediate problem of dealing with its present rival. Alternative strategies for dealing with that rival may have different effects on the flow of future rivals. A policy of preserving monopoly by buying-up rivals may possibly be inferred from the purchase of a particular rival; and the purchase may then have the unfortunate effect of encouraging potential entrants to enter and to offer themselves as willing sellers, thereby progressively diluting the original owners' share of the monopoly profits. A policy of using predatory pricing, either regularly or occasionally, is likely to have a more discouraging effect.[9] It may be noted in passing that the effect of predatory pricing on the calculations of potential entrants makes it yet more difficult for the empirical investigator to determine whether or not a particular attempt at predation succeeded in achieving its purpose.

The preceding considerations apply independently of any assumption that the rival has less easy access to capital than the aggressor. Where access is more restricted for the former, perhaps because it is the smaller firm in the relevant market, the relative advantages of predatory pricing may be increased. However, in assessing the impact of the rela-

---

[7] It is conceivable that even where both the aggressor and the rival have identical expectations about the future profits of the latter, no acquisition price may be acceptable to both parties. This could be the case, for example, where the owners of the independent firm place a high value on their independence and on the ownership and control of their own enterprise. A period of losses induced by predatory pricing may change their attitude.

[8] It is not only the dominant firm or group which can initiate temporary price cutting in an attempt to achieve its anticompetitive ends. The analysis applies symmetrically to a dominant firm and to the independent rival. Provided that the rival has, or can expand its output to secure, a sufficient share of business in that sector of the market in which it wishes to concentrate its pressure—the sector could be a separate region, a particular class of customer, or selected qualities or varieties of the product—it can initiate price cutting with the intention of inducing the dominant firm to agree to a more favourable settlement (that is, a bigger share of the cartel or a higher acquisition price) than it otherwise would have been prepared to grant.

[9] Elzinga has suggested that the response of potential entrants to the driving-out of established independents by predatory pricing "is not easily predicted." The "demonstration effect" may deter some. On the other hand, others "may realize the inability of the dominant firm to continue such a costly practice and promptly enter." Kenneth G. Elzinga, *supra* note 6, at 240. The latter possibility cannot be denied. But a policy of buying up new entrants without a fight is bound to attract new entrants.

tive ease of access to capital, it should be recognized that the drain on resources would be larger for the firm with the larger share of the affected market (assuming the costs of the two firms to be the same). The aggressor may ordinarily be expected to be the larger of the two firms.

The modification of McGee's strong proposition about the folly of predatory pricing makes it difficult to predict the frequency with which the practice is likely to be used and the types of circumstances in which it may be expected to be relatively more or less common. Nevertheless, the opinion has been expressed that predatory pricing will be rare. Thus Telser has written: "Although it does not seem possible a priori to predict the frequency of price warfare, these will be rare if entrepreneurs are reasonable and intelligent."[10] Zerbe's view is "that predatory price wars might occur but would be unlikely."[11] One imagines that these views are not only influenced by the appeal of McGee's analysis but also that they are coloured to some extent by the fact that systematic and searching examinations of the historical record have shown in a number of cases that supposed instances of price predation were nothing of the kind or that the available evidence is incomplete or consistent with different explanations.[12]

It is not suggested in this paper that predatory pricing in the McGee sense has been frequent or is likely to be frequent even in the absence of hostile legislation. Indeed, because reasonably documented examples of the use of the practice are rare—a dearth intensified by the results of the thorough researches of McGee and others—there is some interest in presenting, in section III, a short account of one reasonably clear-cut example of predatory pricing, to augment by one the exiguous stock of recorded cases [omitted in this excerpt—Ed.] Before coming to that section, however, the argument in the next section will suggest that predatory pricing, as it is currently defined, should be considered not as constituting a distinct analytical category but rather as being an extreme variant of a broader class of temporary price cutting practices designed to drive out or crush an independent competitor so that the aggressor can achieve or restore a monopoly position. Although their identification is beset with difficulties, examples of this broader class may not be so hard to find as are examples of predatory pricing in the strict McGee sense.

---

[10]Lester G. Telser, *supra* note 5, at 268.

[11]Richard Zerbe, *supra* note 6, at 363 n. 120. See also Kenneth G. Elzinga, *supra* note 6, at 240.

[12]For studies of real or alleged instances of predation, see John S. McGee, *supra* note 1; Richard Zerbe, *supra* note 6; Kenneth G. Elzinga, *supra* note 6; P. T. Bauer, *West African Trade*, 121–24 (1954); M. A. Adelman, *A & P: A Study in Price-Cost Behavior and Public Policy*, 372–79 (1959); and Gt. Brit., *Monopolies Comm'n, Electrical Wiring, Harnesses for Motor Vehicles: A Report on Whether Uneconomic Prices are Quoted* (1966). See also F. M. Scherer, *Industrial Market Structure and Economic Performance*, 273–78 (1970).

II

The crucial point in McGee's analysis of predatory pricing is that the practice involves predator and victim in unnecessary loss of profits. Such loss or sacrifice of profits is independent, however, of whether the deliberate price cutting by the predator takes the price below cost (say, below its long-run marginal cost or average cost): All that is necessary is that the price is taken to a level lower than that which would otherwise prevail. Any deliberate price cut to achieve some ulterior aim involves a sacrifice of profits of this kind. The only special feature of price cutting below cost is that the loss of profits includes some loss in the absolute sense, that is, that the firm is "losing money." But nothing either in McGee's original analysis or in subsequent elaborations depends upon this feature, which cannot have any distinctive analytical significance.

It is true that in their expositions both McGee and Telser seem to assume that the price ruling before predatory pricing is instigated (or the merger concluded) is at the competitive level,[13] so that any deliberate price cut must be a cut below cost. But this restrictive assumption is not required for their analyses. In the duopolistic market situation which is postulated the initial price could be at any level, from the competitive price at one extreme to the monopoly price at the other. The considerations included in McGee's analysis would be relevant regardless of the level of the initial price[14] and of the extent of the reduction from the price.

Again, the considerations which have led to the withdrawal from McGee's strong proposition do not depend for their relevance on the fact that sales are being made at a price below cost during the period of predatory pricing. The aggressor may be able to achieve its objective of eliminating or disciplining the rival and of discouraging potential entrants by means of price cutting falling short of predatory pricing as this is defined currently. The aggressor has an obvious interest in minimising the extent of its price cutting to achieve a particular result and has a choice of tactics. A smaller cut may in some circumstances be as effective as a larger cut, especially where the rival has reason to suppose that the aggressor will go further if necessary. On the other hand, a sharp initial cut may sometimes convey the intended message more emphatically and achieve the intended result more quickly.[15]

In so far as the aggressor's pricing behaviour may have the desired

---

[13]John S. McGee, *supra* note 1, at 140; Lester G. Telser, *supra* note 5, at 263.

[14] This is seen to be so even where the initial price is the monopoly price. The aggressor has an incentive to remove or neutralise the rival if the prevailing situation does not maximise joint profits because costs are higher than they need be.

[15]Thus one member of a shipping conference expressed the following view in the course of a rate-cutting war with outsiders in the 1890s: "We still think here . . . that it would be better to go at once to an irreducible minimum to show Hendersons [one of the

effect, this will stem from the rival's assessment of the aggressor's de-termination to frustrate its expectations, for example, as to the rate of growth of its sales and its attainable profit margins. It is improbable that the fact that the aggressor has taken price below its own cost rather than, say, to a level somewhat above it would make any difference. It should be remembered, furthermore, that the rival at which the price cutting is being directed cannot know, save in extreme cases, whether prices are in fact being cut below the aggressor's costs, of which it cannot be fully informed. Moreover, in so far as it is the fact that sales are being made at prices below the cutter's costs that is considered to be the crucial element in predatory pricing, the message of the strategy may fail to get through to the victim who may not know which of the various possible concepts of cost—marginal or average, short-run or long-run—it should apply when trying to interpret what course the aggressor is following.[16]

It follows from the foregoing that there can be predatory intent in price cutting whether or not the aggressor sets its prices above or below its costs (in one or other meaning of the latter term). Apart from intent, the common characteristic of predatory price cutting in the broad sense is that it is temporary and that it is in the predator's interest to confine, where possible, the temporary sacrifice of profits to those parts of the market (regions, product varieties, classes of customer) in which the victim is trading.

It follows, further, that an outside observer may often have consider-able difficulty in deciding whether predatory pricing has been practised, even when the category is widened by the removal of the condition that the price must be below cost for the action to qualify as predatory. This is so because a firm may reduce its prices for a variety of reasons and need not change them equally in all submarkets or for all products. It may reduce prices because a new firm has entered the market or an estab-lished firm has increased its output, so adding to total supply. It may reduce its prices because of an actual or expected change in costs or in demand, or in an attempt to induce nonusers of its products to become users. The predatory nature of temporary price cutting, where it is pres-ent, is a reflection of the aggressor's intention, which is to eliminate its rival as an independent competitor, not through the exercise of greater efficiency in the usual sense but through a pricing manoeuvre contain-

---

outsiders] that we are really in earnest. The extra cost would not matter if it shortened the struggle." Quoted in Francis E. Hyde, *Shipping Enterprise and Management 1830–1939: Har-risons of Liverpool*, 76 (1967).

[16]It might seem more relevant to define predatory pricing as pricing below the costs of the rival to be eliminated rather than to regard the predator's costs as the standard by which to appraise the character of the price cutting. But this alternative definition would carry no greater analytical significance. And, save in extreme cases, the predator would not know for certain whether the price he set was below the level of his rival's costs in their relevant specification. . . .

ing an undertone of threat. Such an intention is obviously difficult to establish conclusively and can be inferred with reasonable confidence only when the observer, be he judge or academic, has been able to gain a detailed and thorough understanding of the surrounding circumstances in all their complexity. It would certainly be incorrect to describe an established firm as a predator simply on the basis of a record that it had reduced the price of its product and then raised it when a rival withdrew or came to terms with it. Any attempt to define predation in this way and to brand it as illegal would make it virtually impossible for an established firm with a large share of the market to compete effectively with smaller firms or new entrants. (One may note, parenthetically, that according to McGee's analysis it would be economic folly for such a firm to compete on prices either in a predatory or a nonpredatory way—unless mergers by such firms were ruled out by law.) On the other hand, any attempt to narrow the definition by inserting in it the requirement that the reduced price be lower than cost (in some sense) would be inappropriate, since it has been shown here that selling at reduced prices above cost can serve the same purpose in the context of predatory intent. Moreover, the difficulties or identifying predatory pricing in the McGee sense are certainly no smaller than those noted above.

It is perhaps not surprising that it has been hard to find clear-cut historical examples of the extreme McGee variant of predatory price cutting, even when one is not unduly fussy about the appropriate definition of cost which should be used. But if it is correct to infer from the McGee analysis and its elaboration that predatory pricing (involving sales below cost) is likely to be rare or exceptional, it would also be correct to infer that predatory price cutting activities of a less extreme kind should also be rare or exceptional.

Temporary price cutting by dominant firms or groups has, of course, been practised quite frequently. And although, as has been suggested above, there are severe difficulties in distinguishing between temporary price cutting which is predatory in intent and that which is not, it appears that the predatory variety may not have been uncommon. If this were the case, it would seem to follow that the weight to be given to the factors which weaken McGee's strong conclusion concerning the folly of economic warfare should be greater than that suggested in several of the contributions on the subject which have appeared since McGee's paper was published.

On the information available several of the bouts of price cutting rejected in the recent literature as instances of predatory pricing seem to be eligible as instances of temporary localised price cutting designed to deal predatorily with an independent competitor. Further examples can be suggested. The use of "fighting ships" by shipping cartels (conferences) is well documented, the *Mogul* case discussed in the next section being one example. The essence of the practice is for ships belonging to the conference to be used to cut freight rates when and where independent rivals are active so as to deny them business and profits. The special rates are not offered at other times and places. Both the majority and the minority groups of the Royal Commission on Shipping Rings reported in 1909 in terms suggesting that such temporary price cutting was a standard weapon in the armoury of shipping conferences for dealing with interlopers. The majority reported that the practice (together with other practices) was used "until the opposition line is either driven off or admitted to the Conference," and the minority that "undercutting their competitors" continued "until they have driven them away."

Other examples of temporary price cutting which may be predatory are provided by the use of "fighting brands" by a monopolist to meet the competition of a new entrant in those parts of the market where it is trying to become established or to extend its operations. A special brand is introduced for the purpose. Its sale is confined to the affected areas; the quantities offered are controlled so as not to make unnecessary sacrifices of profit; and it is withdrawn as soon as the objective has been attained, namely the acquisition of the independent by the monopolist, or the withdrawal of the independent, or its abandonment of plans for enlarging its share of the market. Good examples of the use of fighting brands are provided by the activities of the match monopoly in Canada from its creation by merger in 1927 to the outbreak of the Second World War. The dominant firm used the device at various times, and this suggests that the firm was convinced of its efficacy.

The use of temporary localised price cuts probably with predatory intent can also be illustrated from the workings of the basing point system in some industries. The normal operation of the system itself discouraged independent pricing because other sellers, regardless of their location, would match a reduction in a base price initiated by one of their number. The use of punitive basing points and punitive base prices went further. A small seller who was not adhering strictly to the rules of the system could be punished and brought back into line by the expedient of the cartel introducing a deliberately low base price in his principal production centre: All (or most of) his sales would have to be made at this low price because of his competitors' willingness to supply at that price in the affected area. This practice of localised price cutting was used, for example, with some effect in the United States cement industry in the interwar years.

It has sometimes been suggested that alleged examples of predatory pricing in a particular submarket may be nothing other than manifestations of profit-maximising price discrimination. However, the various examples touched upon here cannot reasonably be regarded as instances of the exploitation by a monopolist of a perceived opportunity to discriminate in his prices between submarkets in which demand intrinsically is of materially different price elasticities. The price differentiation is removed as soon as the rival comes to heel. The long arm of coincidence would have had to be in frequent operation for the successful neutralisation of the rival in such cases to have been coincident with changes in underlying demand elasticities.

However, while the explanation of the phenomena as instances of price discrimination may be rejected, it must be stressed that it is not possible on the information available to decide unambiguously whether all our examples of temporary price cutting should be classified as predatory or not. The distinction turns not on form but on intent; and on the latter the available information is incomplete. . . .

Phillip Areeda (1926–   )
Donald F. Turner (1920–   )

✺ 37

Predatory Pricing and Related Practices under Section 2 of the Sherman Act*

Areeda and Turner deal here with price-cost patterns that may be predatory. They define a number of categories and urge that predation be found only when price can be shown to go below marginal cost. Usually, they expect, average variable cost will have to be used as an estimator of marginal cost. Their long article, here only briefly excerpted, mixes logical and practical issues. It was immediately influential in several appeals court opinions which acquitted firms accused of predatory actions. Do you agree with its focus on price as the main predatory device? Is its balancing of logical and practical problems a good one?

Although antitrust law is not usually concerned with setting a limit on price competition, under certain conditions low prices may have anticompetitive effects. A firm which drives out or excludes rivals by selling at unremunerative prices is not competing on the merits, but engaging in behavior that may properly be called predatory. There is, therefore, good reason for including a "predatory pricing" antitrust offense within the proscription of monopolization or attempts to monopolize in section 2 of the Sherman Act.[1]

Treatment of predatory pricing in the cases and the literature, how-

---

*Phillip Areeda and Donald F. Turner, "Predatory Prices and Related Practices under Section 2 of the Sherman Act," *Harvard Law Review*, vol. 88 (June 1975), pp. 697–733, excerpted from pp. 697–99, 704–705, 709–16, 728–29, 732–33. Both authors are leading specialists on antitrust law on the faculty at Harvard Law School. Turner was head of the Antitrust Division during 1965–68.

[1]15 U.S. C. § 2 (1970); see e.g., *United States* v. *American Tobacco Co.*, 221 U.S. 106, 182 (1911); *Standard Oil Co.* v. *United States*, 221 U.S. 1, 43 (1910). The Clayton Act, as amended by the Robinson-Patman Act, also provides a safeguard against predation in its prohibition of price discrimination. 15 U.S. C. § 13 (1970); see e.g., *Moore* v. *Mead's Fine Bread Co.*, 348 U.S. 115 (1954); *Puerto Rican American Tobacco Co.* v. *American Tobacco Co.*, 30 F. 2d 234 (2d Cir.), cert. denied, 279 U.S. 858 (1929). See also 15 U.S. C. § 13a (1970) (unlawful to "sell . . . at unreasonably low prices for the purpose of destroying competition or eliminating a competitor"). Although most of our discussion will be based on the reach of the Sherman Act, § 2, the issues are substantially the same under the Clayton Act insofar as that statute is concerned with predatory pricing. See pp. 724–28 *infra*.

ever, has commonly suffered from two interrelated defects: failure to delineate clearly and correctly what practices should constitute the offense, and exaggerated fears that large firms will be inclined to engage in it.

. . . [P]redation in any meaningful sense cannot exist unless there is a temporary sacrifice of net revenues in the expectation of greater future gains. Indeed, the classically feared case of predation has been the deliberate sacrifice of present revenues for the purpose of driving rivals out of the market and then recouping the losses through higher profits earned in the absence of competition. Thus, predatory pricing would make little economic sense to a potential predator unless he had (1) greater financial staying power than his rivals, and (2) a very substantial prospect that the losses he incurs in the predatory campaign will be exceeded by the profits to be earned after his rivals have been destroyed.

*   *   *   *   *

Losses incurred through predation could be regained in markets with very high barriers to entry. In many markets, however, and especially in those having a number of small rivals, entry barriers may be nonexistent or at least too low to preclude entry. Admittedly, a demonstrated willingness to indulge in predatory pricing might itself deter some smaller potential entrants, but it is unlikely to inhibit firms with resources comparable to those of the predator. Repeated predation in the same market, moreover, is not only costly but is likely to be easily detectable and thus the occasion for severe antitrust sanctions. The prospects of an adequate future payoff, therefore, will seldom be sufficient to motivate predation. Indeed, proven cases of predatory pricing have been extremely rare.

That predatory pricing seems highly unlikely does not necessarily mean that there should be no antitrust rules against it. But it does suggest that extreme care be taken in formulating such rules, lest the threat of litigation, particularly by private parties, materially deter legitimate, competitive pricing. Courts in predatory pricing cases have generally turned to such empty formulae as "below cost" pricing, ruinous competition, or predatory intent in adjudicating liability. These standards provide little, if any, basis for analyzing the predatory pricing offense. In this Article we will attempt to formulate meaningful and workable tests for distinguishing between predatory and competitive pricing by examining the relationship between a firm's costs and its prices. . . .

B. Prices at or above Average Cost

. . . When a monopolist sells at a price at or above average cost but could earn higher short-run profits at a higher price, the necessary ele-

ment of predation is presumably present.[2] Unless acting irrationally or
out of ignorance, the firm is likely to be charging the lower price in order
to preserve or enhance its market share by deterring rivals.[3] Such pricing may take two forms: (1) the firm may permanently charge less than a
profit-maximizing price in order to deter entry or to destroy rivals; or (2)
it may first charge a profit-maximizing price, lower the price when rivals
appear, and then raise the price when the rivals are extinguished. However, in both instances, we conclude that such pricing behavior should
be deemed nonpredatory so long as the prices equal or exceed average
total cost. Our analysis of each variation follows. In each instance we
assume that the price is equal to or greater than both average cost and
marginal cost.

1. Limit Pricing. A monopolist protected by an insurmountable
barrier to the entry of others can charge whatever price will maximize his
profit. The ability of other firms to overcome entry barriers may, however, affect the monopolist's price. . . .

The limit price is intended by the monopolist to impair the opportunities of rivals, and if successful, it does prevent competition from
arising. In the absence of limit pricing, competition might arise and force
the price down to the former limit price or even lower, if the presence of
additional firms induces cost paring, reduction of "slack," and in the
long run, more efficient production. Without limit pricing other benefits
of competition may also arise. More firms in the market might, for
example, lead to more invention and innovation and a quicker disper-
sion of existing innovations throughout the economy.

We do not, however, believe that these arguments justify a prohibition against limit pricing. Superior products or service, successful innovation, or other effective competition on the merits always tends to
exclude rivals. . . .

In sum, a rule forbidding reversal of a price reduction would impose
on enforcement agencies and the courts administrative burdens that are
not justified by the speculative benefits such a rule might bring. Accordingly, we conclude that a price at or above average cost should be

---

[2]When a firm sells at a price *below* average cost, it is incurring a loss. The mere fact that
the firm is not recovering full costs, however, is not grounds for concluding that its price is
predatory. Losses are sometimes inevitable; demand conditions may dictate that a firm
earn its maximum net revenue over variable costs at a price below average cost. . . . The
short-run loss-minimizing price cannot, therefore, be considered predatory or otherwise
objectionable by antitrust law.

This proposition will not resolve many real cases. It will be exceedingly difficult to
know what is or is not a loss-minimizing price. Nevertheless, the proposition is an important one in principle, for it serves to remind us that the defendant's failure to earn profits
or even to recover his full cost is not necessarily objectionable.

[3]The firm may also be keeping price down to reasonable levels during periods of high
demand in order to preserve customer goodwill.

deemed nonpredatory and not in law exclusionary, whether permanent or not.

We are under no illusions that a rule permitting prices at or above average cost is easily applied. Average cost includes a "normal" return on investment, a figure usually not determinable with any precision. But the principle that average-cost pricing is legitimately competitive is an important one and may serve to dispose quickly of cases in which the alleged predator's rate of return is normal by any reasonable test.[4]

C. Marginal-Cost Pricing

In the previous Section we considered the threat to rivals and new entrants posed by a price that is profitable to the monopolist but not to the rival. In some instances, however, the monopolist's price may both generate below-normal returns—that is, it may be below average cost—and be below the loss-minimizing price. Because such a price yields less than the normal return on capital, it can threaten the survival of equally efficient rivals with less staying power than the monopolist enjoys. We will consider these loss-producing prices in two categories: (1) those equal to or greater than marginal cost and (2) those less than marginal cost.

1. Prices at or above Marginal Cost. At the outset we can eliminate from our consideration situations in which the monopolist is producing beyond the output at which his plant functions most efficiently, since at such high levels of production, marginal cost will exceed average cost. In such cases, pricing at or above marginal cost will not eliminate equally efficient rivals or potential entrants who may freely restrict their output to efficient levels and thus make substantial profits at the monopolist's price.

We need consider, then, only instances when marginal cost is below average cost, a situation which will not occur unless the monopolist possesses "excess capacity." Only then will the monopolist's marginal cost price deprive equally efficient rivals, actual or potential, of "normal" returns on their capital.

Although narrowed, the problem remains: The equally efficient rival might be destroyed or dissuaded from entering not because he is less efficient but because he has less capital. Consider two illustrations. First, suppose that the monopolist occupies an entire market by himself and that his plant has excess capacity. Suppose further that the monopolist could maximize profits at a price exceeding average cost but chooses to

---

[4]The district court in *Telex Corp.* v. *IBM*, 367 F. Supp. 258 (N.D. Okla. 1973) apparently failed to recognize this principle. Despite a lack of evidence that IBM reduced prices below cost and a reasonable profit and despite IBM's anticipation of returns "in excess of 20 percent," the court found that IBM had engaged in predatory pricing. Id. at 306.

dissuade entry by pricing at marginal cost, which is now below average cost. Although it may preserve a monopoly, this price seems socially appropriate, because the construction of additional capacity where excess capacity already exists would waste social resources. Indeed, a price higher than marginal cost would yield a smaller output and would waste present resources. Existing capacity that could be used to produce at a cost less than the added value to consumers would be idled.

Second, suppose that (1) a monopolist and his smaller rival have identical cost curves, (2) both have been producing at full capacity and earning significant profits, (3) demand falls during a temporary two-year recession, (4) the monopolist would maximize profits at a price above average cost, (5) the monopolist chooses to price at marginal cost, which is now below average cost, (6) the rival has insufficient liquid resources or access to new capital to cover his losses and service his capital debt, (7) the rival thereby expires, (8) his assets and business are withdrawn from the market, and (9) subsequent new entry is difficult. In this set of circumstances, marginal-cost pricing by the monopolist does not merely discourage the addition of immediately redundant capacity, but has the effect of destroying an equally efficient rival.[5]

Nevertheless, we conclude that prices at or above marginal cost, even though they are not profit-maximizing, should not be considered predatory. If a monopolist produces to a point where price equals marginal cost, only less efficient firms will suffer larger losses per unit of output; more efficient firms will be losing less or even operating profitably. Admittedly, the destruction of an equally efficient rival and the deterrence of entry of firms which are equally efficient pose some threat to competition in the long run; if demand increases to its former level, only the monopolist will occupy the market which he formerly shared with the rival. However, we see no satisfactory method of eliminating this risk. Establishing a price floor above marginal cost would permit survival not only of equally efficient firms, but less efficient ones as well. And in the short run, at least, entry even by equally efficient firms will be undesirable since excess capacity already exists.

Furthermore, to force the firm to charge a higher price would reduce industry output and waste economic resources in the short run. Output that could be produced at a cost lower than its value to consumers would be eliminated. Thus, pricing at marginal cost is the competitive and socially optimal result.

Finally, enforcement of a prohibition against marginal-cost pricing

---

[5]This illustration is not meant to suggest that facts number four and number five will actually occur with any frequency; nor is it inevitable that the rival will fail to ride out the recession, that his assets will in fact be withdrawn from the industry, or that reentry will be difficult. Nevertheless, we are posing a testing case in order to examine the principle that marginal-cost pricing should be considered lawful.

would create serious administrative problems. If the monopolist were prohibited from dropping his price down to marginal cost, then some price floor above marginal cost would be required. Such a floor should be set no higher than a monopolist's loss-minimizing price since a higher price is not predatory and would require the monopolist to incur greater losses. Yet, a floor so defined would be more difficult to administer or comply with than a marginal-cost floor. Difficult as it may be for a firm to calculate marginal cost, it is vastly more difficult to calculate in advance what the loss-minimizing price would be. . . .

Thus, we conclude that a prohibition of marginal-cost pricing cannot be justified either by economic theory or administrative convenience.[6]

2. Prices below Marginal Cost.   By definition, a firm producing at an output where marginal cost exceeds price is selling at least part of that output at an out-of-pocket loss. It could eliminate that loss by reducing its output or, where the highest obtainable price is below average variable cost at all levels of output, by ceasing operations altogether.

We have concluded above that marginal-cost pricing by a monopolist should be tolerated even though losses could be minimized or profits increased at a lower output and higher price for the reasons, among others, that marginal-cost pricing leads to a proper resource allocation and is consistent with competition on the merits. Neither reason obtains when the monopolist prices below marginal cost. The monopolist is not only incurring private losses but wasting social resources when marginal costs exceed the value of what is produced. And pricing below marginal cost greatly increases the possibility that rivalry will be extinguished or prevented for reasons unrelated to the efficiency of the monopolist. Accordingly, a monopolist pricing below marginal cost should be presumed to have engaged in a predatory or exclusionary practice.[7]

---

[6]It is possible that a firm may temporarily reduce its price to marginal cost in order to punish competitors for shading its higher price. If the firm's marginal-cost price merely meets that of its competitors, we see no justification for finding a predatory offense. Meeting a rival's price with a price above marginal cost is competition on the merits and prohibition of that practice would coerce a firm into giving up a portion of its market share whenever rivals choose to cut their prices.

Price reductions below that of a rival are more objectionable, but even here identification of the violation will be difficult in many instances. In an oligopoly situation it would be difficult if not impossible to distinguish "disciplinary" price-cutting from an outbreak of competitive pricing under the pressures of excess capacity. It would be plainly perverse to impose a constraint on competitive pricing and thus reinforce the innate tendencies of oligopolists to maintain noncompetitive prices by cooperation or collusion.

When a monopolist engages in temporary marginal-cost pricing to discipline small rivals, predation is more easily inferred. Nevertheless, because of the difficulties of drawing the lines between monopoly and oligopoly and between "meeting" and "beating" a rival's price, see note 41 *infra,* and because of the administrative problems inherent in setting any price floor above marginal cost, we conclude that disciplinary price cuts to levels above marginal cost should be disregarded.

[7]Because of the substantial problems involved in determining a firm's marginal cost,

. . . This is not justifiable "on principle," since production to the point where marginal cost exceeds price is wasteful whether or not price exceeds average cost. Nevertheless, practical reasons suggest that the case can be disregarded, for it seems unlikely to have any significant anticompetitive consequences. The case could occur, by definition, only when demand exceeds what the firm can produce at minimum average cost. If the excess demand is temporary, there is little need for new entry. If permanent, pricing below marginal cost with its consequent high output may have some deterrent effect on new entry and some adverse effect on existing rivals. . . .

. . . A monopolist may attempt to justify prices below marginal cost by claiming either that the price is being used for promotional purposes or that he is simply meeting an equally low price of a rival. We conclude, however, that these justifications are either so rarely applicable or of such dubious merit for a monopolist that the presumption of illegality for prices below both marginal and average cost should be conclusive.

(a) Promotional Pricing.   A promotional price is a temporary low price designed to induce patronage with the expectation that the customer will continue purchasing the product in the future at a higher price. The promotional price may be below cost and is most easily illustrated by the seller who gives his product away without charge to some or all would-be customers.

Unless continued over a long period of time, in which case it is no longer promotional, promotional pricing by new entrants or small firms without monopoly power threatens little or no harm. Promotional pricing can facilitate new entry or the expansion of small rivals in an industry dominated by one or a few large firms. Entrenched consumer loyalties to established brands constitute barriers to entry and to a small firm's growth. For new or even established firms, promotional pricing serves the purely informational function of advertising by alerting consumers to the existence of new products. The low promotional price is preferable to advertising, for it gives the consumer a better buy during the period of promotion and allows him to judge the product on its merits. Of course, the promotion may on occasion temporarily divert demand from better products or more efficient producers, but the diversion will last only long enough for consumers to judge and reject the inferior promoted product.[8]

The monopolist can make no such case for promotional pricing. His

---

we suggest below that average variable cost be used as a surrogate for marginal cost in distinguishing between predatory and nonpredatory prices. See pp. 716–18 *infra*.

[8]After short-term promotion, a firm might eventually become so dominant as to obtain monopoly power, but it would have obtained its power because of competitive superiority, and the mere fact that the initial promotion got the firm going is no reason for condemning the promotion.

promotion would not usually intensify competition but would only decrease it—existing rivals will be damaged or driven out, and new entry deterred. In contrast to new entrants or small rivals, he has little need to resort to extreme price reductions to acquaint existing consumers with the merits of his brand.

The only other apparent arguments a monopolist could make are (1) that pricing below marginal cost is necessary to raise the overall market demand by attracting new customers who have not heretofore known or been interested in the product or (2) that it is necessary to enable a firm with declining costs to move to a more efficient level of output. The arguments might be held to justify selective reductions to new customers or in new geographical markets, but as a defense to a general price reduction to present as well as new customers, we find these arguments unpersuasive. . . .

*   *   *   *   *

(b) Meeting Competition as a Defense.   We would not permit a monopolist to price below marginal cost in order to meet the lawful price of a rival. . . . The monopolist who goes below marginal cost to meet a rival's promotion is not competing on the merits; the response will destroy or greatly reduce the effects of the rival's promotional effort, a result likely to be particularly serious for the new entrant, whose usual problem is precisely that of obtaining a profitable volume quickly enough to make start-up losses bearable.

The monopolist might attempt to justify a below-marginal-cost price to meet a rival by claiming that he believed he could rapidly reduce his costs to or below those of his rival and that it would cost him less to hold his organization and patronage intact than to recover them in the future. This contention, however, would be made in every case, and it would be difficult for the monopolist to know or the court to determine that the monopolist could achieve cost parity, that it would be less expensive to suffer such interim out-of-pocket losses than to bear the future costs of rebuilding his organization and recovering lost patronage, or indeed, that there would be any such future costs at all. Furthermore, the complex problems of defining meeting-rather-than-beating the rival's price would have to be faced.[9] Courts would have to undertake the difficult task of assessing differences in product quality and thus become involved in speculation about consumer preferences. . . .

---

[9]For a discussion of the difficulties encountered by the courts in applying the "meeting competition" defense of the Robinson-Patman Act, 15 U.S. C. § 13 (b) (1970), see F. Rowe, *Price Discrimination under the Robinson-Patman Act*, 207–64 (1962).

D. Average Variable Cost as a Surrogate for Marginal Cost

In our analysis of predatory pricing we have concluded that marginal-cost pricing is the economically sound division between acceptable, competitive behavior and "below-cost" predation. Thus, we have suggested a prohibition of prices below marginal cost. The primary administrative impediment to enforcing that prohibition is the difficulty of ascertaining a firm's marginal cost. The incremental cost of making and selling the last unit cannot readily be inferred from conventional business accounts, which typically go no further than showing observed average variable cost. Consequently, it may well be necessary to use the latter as an indicator of marginal cost. . . .

There is superficial merit in the argument that effective enforcement of the Robinson-Patman Act requires a more readily determinable test than "marginal cost." We have suggested the use of average variable cost as a surrogate for marginal cost to mitigate the administrative difficulties of enforcement. But even though determinations of cost may remain a substantial problem, it seems clear to us that in this instance it is unavoidable. In the vast majority of situations, discriminatory price-cutting—insofar as primary-line competition is concerned—will be profitable to the firm concerned and procompetitive. Thus any such simple test as "diversion" or "deteriorating price structure" would be wrong most of the time. We should not pay that price for administrative simplicity.

E. "Excessive" Promotional Spending

1. Predatory Spending.   Rather than cutting its price, a firm may undertake advertising campaigns or provide special services and conveniences to consumers with no price increase. These expenditures, of course, increase the firm's costs. The expenditures may impose a burden too great for smaller rivals to maintain and thus result in diminishing their market share or completely driving them out of the market. In theory, the principles we have proposed for defining and dealing with predatory pricing and predatory investment should also apply to "excessive" advertising and other promotional expenditures. If the additional promotional costs raise the firm's average variable cost above its price, then the promotional spending is predatory. There are, however, additional conceptual and practical difficulties in policing excessive promotional spending.

Conceptually, it is extremely difficult to determine whether any given advertising expenditure should be classified as a current expense attributable to current sales or as a capital investment in goodwill designed to maintain or increase the level of sales over some longer period. Usually, it will or was designed to do both. The problem of allocating advertising and promotional expenditures between fixed and variable costs is not peculiar to instances of "excessive" promotional spending. Application of our average variable cost test requires that some allocation be made for all of the firm's advertising expenditures. For the usual and continuing expenditures, however, the firm's past accounting practices should provide an adequate basis for allocation. It is unlikely that over a long period of time a firm will bias its treatment of normal advertising costs in anticipation of defending itself against allegations of predation. . . .

The ambiguous character of short-term promotional expenditures and the uncertainty of their effect prevents relying solely on our variable cost analysis. Accordingly, decisions in cases involving substantial short-run increases in promotional spending would have to incorporate at least one additional consideration, namely timing. The timing of the promotion suggests the possibility of predation if the campaign begins with the appearance of an entrant (or coincides with a rival's promotion) and terminates when the entrant leaves the market (or the rival's efforts cease). In such cases, it seems reasonable to us to consider all the increased expenses as part of variable costs and to conclude presumptively that predation has occurred if average variable costs during the period of the promotion exceed price.[10] Needless to say, predation is negated when the promotion yields a substantial increase in net revenues or even leaves them unaffected.

We are not wholly satisfied with this solution but are reluctant to reach the only other plausible conclusion, which is to impose no legal check on predatory spending.

*   *   *   *   *

IV. CONCLUSIONS

We reach the following conclusions regarding a monopolist's general (nondiscriminatory) pricing in the market in which he has monopoly power:

1. On principle, we conclude that:
    a. A short-run profit-maximizing (or loss-minimizing) price is nonpredatory even though below average cost.
    b. A price at or above average cost should be deemed nonpredatory even though not profit-maximizing in the short run.

---

[10]As in the case of alleged predatory pricing, the presumption would be rebuttable on a showing that average variable costs exceeded what was reasonably anticipated.

      c. A price at or above reasonably anticipated short-run marginal and average variable costs should be deemed nonpredatory even though not loss-minimizing in the short run.

      d. Unless at or above average cost, a price below reasonably anticipated (1) short-run marginal costs or (2) average variable costs should be deemed predatory, and the monopolist may not defend on the grounds that his price was "promotional" or merely met an equally low price of a competitor.

2. Recognizing that marginal cost data are typically unavailable, we conclude that:

      a. A price at or above reasonably anticipated average variable cost should be conclusively presumed lawful.

      b. A price below reasonably anticipated average variable cost should be conclusively presumed unlawful.

As to "predatory" devices other than general price reductions we conclude that:

3. The above conclusions apply to differential returns on different products and to price discrimination, whether between different geographic markets or in the same market, except that a monopolist should have the benefit of any defenses—such as "promotional" pricing or "meeting competition"—available to other sellers in any market in which he lacks monopoly power.

4. There should be no prohibition of investment whether in a new product line or in the monopoly product line.

5. Promotional spending should be deemed predatory when timed to coincide with entry or promotion by a rival and when average variable cost, including the promotional expenditure, exceeds price.

6. There should be no prohibition of nonpredatory spending or of product variation.

[Editor's note: The authors have added the following comments:

"In a revised version of this article included in their treatise, Areeda and Turner modified their position by making average variable cost presumptive evidence of legality only, subject to rebuttal by proof that marginal cost was higher at the output being produced. In addition, after considering what costs should be deemed variable and what fixed, they concluded that advertising costs should be classified as variable costs for testing pricing by a monopolist. On that assumption, 'predatory spending' ceases to be an issue separate from 'predatory pricing.' See P. Areeda and D. Turner, III Antitrust Law ¶¶ 715c, 715d, and 721a (Little Brown, 1978).'']

❧ 38

Utah Pie Co. v. Continental Baking Co.

U.S. Supreme Court
386 U.S. 685 (1967)

This unusual case further limited the range of permissible price dis-
crimination. It could not now be done by large firms even if the "victim"
firm held a dominant market share. This has drawn much criticism from
some economists, as well as from Justices Harlan and Stewart.

Mr. Justice White.   This suit for treble damages and injunction under
§ § 4 and 16 of the Clayton Act . . . was brought by petitioner, Utah Pie
Company, against respondents, Continental Baking Company, Carnation Company, and Pet Milk Company. The complaint charged a conspiracy under § § 1 and 2 of the Sherman Act . . . and violations by each
respondent of § 2 (a) of the Clayton Act as amended by the Robinson-
Patman Act. . . .

The product involved is frozen dessert pies—apple, cherry, boysen-
berry, peach, pumpkin, and mince. The period covered by the suit comprised the years 1958, 1959, and 1960 and the first eight months of 1961.
Petitioner is a Utah corporation which for 30 years has been baking pies
in its plant in Salt Lake City and selling them in Utah and surrounding
States. It entered the frozen pie business in late 1957. It was immediately
successful with its new line and built a new plant in Salt Lake City in
1958. The frozen pie market was a rapidly expanding one: 57,060 dozen
frozen pies were sold in the Salt Lake City market in 1958, 111,729 dozen
in 1959, 184,569 dozen in 1960, and 266,908 dozen in 1961. Utah Pie's
share of this market in those years was 66.5 percent, 34.3 percent, 45.5
percent, and 45.3 percent respectively, its sales volume steadily increasing over the four years. Its financial position also improved.
Petitioner is not, however, a large company. . . .

Each of the respondents is a large company, and each of them is a
major factor in the frozen pie market in one or more regions of the
country. Each entered the Salt Lake City frozen pie market before
petitioner began freezing dessert pies. None of them had a plant in
Utah. . . . The Salt Lake City market was supplied by respondents
chiefly from their California operations. They sold primarily on a delivered price basis. . . .

The major competitive weapon in the Utah market was price. The
location of petitioner's plant gave it natural advantages in the Salt Lake
City marketing area, and it entered the market at a price below the then

going prices for respondents' comparable pies. For most of the period involved here its prices were the lowest in the Salt Lake City market. It was, however, challenged by each of the respondents at one time or another and for varying periods. There was ample evidence to show that each of the respondents contributed to what proved to be a deteriorating price structure over the period covered by this suit, and each of the respondents in the course of the ongoing price competition sold frozen pies in the Salt Lake market at prices lower than it sold pies of like grade and quality in other markets considerably closer to its plants. Utah Pie, which entered the market at a price of $4.15 per dozen at the beginning of the relevant period, was selling "Utah" and "Frost 'N' Flame" pies for $2.75 per dozen when the instant suit was filed some 44 months later. Pet, which was offering pies at $4.92 per dozen in February 1958, was offering "Pet-Ritz" and "Bel-air" pies at $3.56 and $3.46 per dozen respectively in March and April 1961. Carnation's price in early 1958 was $4.82 per dozen, but it was selling at $3.46 per dozen at the conclusion of the period, meanwhile having been down as low as $3.30 per dozen. The price range experienced by Continental during the period covered by this suit ran from a 1958 high of over $5 per dozen to a 1961 low of $2.85 per dozen. . . .

Petitioner's case against Continental is not complicated. Continental was a substantial factor in the market in 1957. But its sales of frozen 22-ounce dessert pies, sold under the "Morton" brand, amounted to only 1.3 percent of the market in 1958, 2.9 percent in 1959, and 1.8 percent in 1960. Its problems were primarily that of cost and in turn that of price, the controlling factor in the market.

. . . In June 1961, it took the steps which are the heart of petitioner's complaint against it. Effective for the last two weeks of June it offered its 22-ounce frozen apple pies in the Utah area at $2.85 per dozen. It was then selling the same pies at substantially higher prices in other markets. The Salt Lake City price was less than its direct cost plus an allocation for overhead. . . Utah's response was immediate. It reduced its price on all of its apple pies to $2.75 per dozen. . . . Continental's total sales of frozen pies increased from 3,350 dozen in 1960 to 18,800 dozen in 1961. Its market share increased from 1.8 percent in 1960 to 8.3 percent in 1961. . . .

Even if the impact on Utah Pie as a competitor was negligible, there remain the consequences to others in the market who had to compete not only with Continental's 22-ounce pie at $2.85 but with Utah's even lower price of $2.75 per dozen for both its proprietary and controlled labels. . . . The evidence was that there were nine other sellers in 1960 who sold 23,473 dozen pies, 12.7 percent of the total market. In 1961 there were eight other sellers who sold less than the year before—18,565 dozen or 8.2 percent of the total—although the total market had ex-

panded from 184,560 dozen to 226,908 dozen. We think there was sufficient evidence from which the jury could find a violation of § 2 (a) by
Continental.

. . . After Carnation's temporary setback in 1959 it instituted a new
pricing policy to regain business in the Salt Lake City market. The new
policy involved a slash in price of 60¢ per dozen pies, which brought
Carnation's price to a level admittedly well below its costs and well
below the other prices prevailing in the market. The impact of the move
was felt immediately, and the two other major sellers in the market
reduced their prices. Carnation's banner year 1960 in the end involved
eight months during which the prices in Salt Lake City were lower than
prices charged in other markets. The trend continued during the eight
months in 1961 that preceded the filing of the complaint in this case. In
each of those months the Salt Lake City prices charged by Carnation
were well below prices charged in other markets, and in all but August
1961 the Salt Lake City delivered price was 20¢ to 50¢ lower than the
prices charged in distant San Francisco.

. . . Sellers may not sell like goods to different purchasers at different
prices if the result may be to injure competition in either the sellers' or
the buyers' market unless such discriminations are justified as permitted
by the Act. This case concerns the sellers' market. In this context, the
Court of Appeals placed heavy emphasis on the fact that Utah Pie constantly increased its sale volume and continued to make a profit. But we
disagree with its apparent view that there is no reasonably possible
injury to competition as long as the volume of sales in a particular
market is expanding and at least some of the competitors in the market
continue to operate at a profit. Nor do we think that the Act only comes
into play to regulate the conduct of price discriminators when their
discriminatory prices consistently undercut other competitors. . . . In
this case there was some evidence of predatory intent with respect to
each of these respondents. There was also other evidence upon which
the jury could rationally find the requisite injury to competition.

Mr. Justice Stewart, with whom Mr. Justice Harlan joins, dissenting.

. . . There is only one issue on this case in its present posture:
. . . [D]id the respondents' actions have the anticompetitive effect required by the statute as an element of a cause of action?

The Court's own description of the Salt Lake City frozen pie market
from 1958 through 1961 shows that the answer to that question must be
no. In 1958 Utah Pie had a quasi-monopolistic 66.5 percent of the market. In 1961—after the alleged predations of the respondents—Utah Pie
still had a commanding 45.3 percent, Pet had 29.4 percent, and the
remainder of the market was divided almost equally between Continen-

tal, Carnation, and other small local bakers. Unless we disregard the lessons so laboriously learned in scores of Sherman and Clayton Act cases, the 1961 situation has to be considered more competitive than that of 1958. Thus, if we assume that the price discrimination proven against the respondents had any effect on competition, that effect must have been beneficial.

That the Court has fallen into the error of reading the Robinson-Patman Act as protecting competitors, instead of competition, can be seen from its unsuccessful attempt to distinguish cases relied upon by the respondents. Those cases are said to be inapposite because they involved "no general decline in price structure," and no "lasting impact upon prices." But lower prices are the hallmark of intensified competition. . . .

I cannot hold that Utah Pie's monopolistic position was protected by the federal antitrust laws from effective price competition, and I therefore respectfully dissent.

✳ 39

International Air Industries Inc. (and Vebco Inc.) v. American Excelsior Co. *

U.S. Court of Appeals, 5th Circuit
517 Fed. Rep. 2d., 714 (1975)

> *In this case, a new entrant was hit by a price war. The firm alleged that the action was predatory, but this claim was rejected at trial and by the appeals court. The very lengthy appeals court opinion is lucidly summarized here. The court used the Areeda-Turner approach explicitly. Was this correct? Would a treatment in Yamey's vein have changed the economic or legal conclusion? (You may want to consult the full opinion.)*

PRICES ABOVE AVERAGE VARIABLE COSTS HELD NEITHER PREDATORY NOR DISCRIMINATORY

A large entrenched firm that in the course of a price war with a fledgling market entrant did not reduce its prices below its average variable production costs engaged in neither predatory nor discriminatory pricing, the U.S. Court of Appeals for the Fifth Circuit decides.

---

*The summary is from *Antitrust and Trade Regulation Report*, no. 730, September 16, 1975, pp. A12–13.

International Air Industries, Inc. v. *American Excelsior Company*, No. 74–1953, CA 5, 8/18/75.

The unsuccessful plaintiff, Vebco, Inc., manufactures and distributes handmade evaporative cooler pads in the southwestern United States and once served as an independent distributor of the defendant Amxco's similar but machine-made pads; however, Amxco terminated Vebco in 1969 upon Vebco's entry into pad manufacturing and consequent "direct competitor" relationship to Amxco in the southwestern U.S. pad market. A subsequent price war between the two rivals during the first months of 1971 brought on this litigation, but after "a lengthy, complex and seemingly disorganized jury trial," Vebco's claims under § 2 (a) of the Robinson-Patman Act and § 2 of the Sherman Act were entirely rejected; Vebco now seeks to overturn that jury verdict.

According to the opinion by Circuit Judge Morgan, Vebco's "primary-line" price discrimination claim (and its "basically identical" monopoly claim) is that Amxco illegally sold cooler pads to El Paso, Texas, customers—where it faced Vebco competition—at prices lower than it sold its pads elsewhere. Evidence of Amxco's predatory intent in offering repeated discounts during the spring of 1971 is, Vebco claims, contained in a March 1971 memo by an Amxco official that states: "If we are committed to a program of stunting the possible growth of Vebco and keeping our foot in this quite sizeable cooler pad market, then the real question we have here is just what price do we need to determine as our lowest price level."

The court notes that the strictures of § 2 (a)—which bar price differentials between different purchasers of commodities of like grade and quality "where the effect of such discrimination may be substantially to lessen competition or tend to create a monopoly in any line of commerce or to injure, destroy, or prevent competition"—are "primarily aimed at national chains that enter a locality and crush a more efficient local concern by cutting prices below cost and subsidizing local losses with excessive profits gleaned in a noncompetitive area." And the opinion continues, "the facts before us indeed reveal a large entrenched firm with a dominant market share confronted by a fledgling company attempting to enter the same market"; however, "encouraging competition while at the same time forbidding anticompetitive behavior calls for considerable care in this case" since "we believe that neither the act nor any social value compels the sheltering of an individual competitor at the expense of the public interest from the competitive process." Thus, the first issue is whether Amxco's price behavior, as evinced by its repeated discounts, was predatory. It was not, the court states, because even the lowest price Amxco charged during the price war was above not only its marginal costs, but also its average costs: "If a monopolist is selling at a price at or above average cost but could earn higher profits at a higher price, it may be attempting to deter entry into the field. Likewise a monopolist may attempt to drive out existing competition by temporarily lowering price to average cost. In either case, we believe that a price above average cost is a fairly competitive price for it is profitable to the monopolist if not to its rivals; in effect, the price excludes only less efficient firms. See Areeda and Turner, 'Predatory Practices Under § 2 of the Sherman Act', 88 *Harv. L. Rev.* 697, 706 (1975)."

In this case, "the entry of Vebco and Southwest created excess manufacturing capacity in the cooler pad market. Therefore, Amxco's marginal cost was almost certainly below its average cost. In such situations we do not believe that the monopolist's pricing behavior could be deemed anticompetitive unless the monopolist set a price below its own marginal cost—since any sale at or above marginal cost does not decrease short-run net returns."

The court then substitutes a firm's average variable cost for its marginal cost in this predatory pricing analysis (because of marginal cost computation difficulties) and decides to depart from that threshold standard, and hold prices above average variable costs nevertheless to be predatory, "only when the barriers to entry are extremely high."

Here, however, "the record indicates that barriers to entry in the cooler pad market were virtually nonexistent." Therefore, since even Amxco's largest discount of 39 percent brought not only a 15-cent per pad profit to Amxco's manufacturing division, but also a gross margin of 33 percent to its sales division, "the price rivalry challenged here "could reasonably be considered procompetitive," and Amxco is not liable for any damages.

Nor can the Amxco official's memo be considered "predatory," the opinion concludes, for it shows merely that "Amxco acted as any legitimately competitive and rational firm would." Indeed, "predatory intent has never been clearly defined," the court points out; and, "any price decrease by even a legitimately competitive firm could be viewed as made with predatory intent, insofar as it will necessarily have a non-remunerative effect upon other firms in the market, if only by decreasing their profit margins." In any event, "quoting out of context the segments of internal company memoranda cannot supply the needed predatory intent" when, as here, Amxco's prices yielded profits.

In addition, despite the claimed discrimination, the opinion notes, with but one exception Vebco's total sales have increased every year since 1968, and its percentage of the El Paso market indeed increased even in 1971 during the assertedly predatory price war. Consequently, the jury verdict is *Affirmed*.

Tie-ins

Making a purchaser buy good A in order to get good B is a "tie-in." It is usually a form of price discrimination, which increases the gain from the especially desired good A. There is debate whether a tie-in applies true leverage, to transfer monopoly power from good A to others. Yet it can reduce competition when done by a firm with a substantial market share. Court decisions have consistently rejected tie-ins by leading firms.

Two uses illustrate the edges of this policy. *Jerrold* permitted a broad tie-in by an infant firm in a new industry, but it stopped such ties once the firm became dominant in a settled industry. *Fortner* went through two landmark decisions. In 1969, the Court seemed to reach nearly a *per se* rule against tie-ins. But in 1977 the Court held instead that a rule of reason must be applied in intermediate situations. Not quite a reversal, the second decision did fit reality and left the main precedent intact.

✖ 40

United States v. *Jerrold Electronics Corporation*
187 F. Supp. 545 (E.D. Pa. 1960);
affirmed per curiam 365 U.S. 567 (1961)

Tie-in sales—to get X you must also buy Y—became virtually per se *illegal in the 1950s, as a device for extending market power. This case explores the further edges of the problem: an "infant industry," involving the innovation of complex new technology. The decision carefully limits any possible exemption to just those temporary, unusual conditions.*

Van Dusen, District Judge.   This action was commenced with the filing of a complaint on February 15, 1957, charging Jerrold Electronics Corporation, its president, Milton Jerrold Shapp, and five of its corporate subsidiaries with being parties to a conspiracy and contracts in unreasonable restraint of trade and commerce in community television antenna equipment in violation of Section 1 of the Sherman Act . . . ; with being parties to a conspiracy and attempting to monopolize trade and commerce in community television antenna equipment in violation of Section 2 of the Sherman Act . . . ; and with contracting to sell and making sales upon unlawful conditions in violation of Section 3 of the Clayton Act. . . .

There are four parts to a community television antenna system. The first is the antenna site, referred to in the trade as the "head end." The second is the apparatus which carries the signal from the antenna into the community, known as the "run to town." The third is the "skeleton system" that is constructed through the town to carry the television signals to the extremities of the area to be covered. Finally, there is the "tap-off" from the skeleton system which carries the signal to the home of each subscriber to the service. . . .

By the spring of 1951, the Jerrold people felt they were prepared to start selling equipment for community television antenna purposes. As a result of their work in Lansford and Mahanoy City, they had developed a new line of equipment for community antenna systems designated "W" equipment. After consulting with his engineers and several of Jerrold's commission salesmen who dealt with the distributors, Shapp decided that the W equipment should only be sold with engineering services to insure that the system would function properly. A general policy, therefore, was established of selling electronic equipment to community antenna companies only on a full system basis and in conjunction with a service contract which provided for technical services with respect to the layout, installation, and operation of the system.

> Since we cannot reasonably be required to perform our obligations as enumerated in this letter if the system contains electronic equipment other than that manufactured by Jerrold Electronics Corporation, you agree not to install, as part of the system, any equipment or attachments which, in our opinion, will impair the quality of television reception and signal distribution capabilities of the system, or which might cause damage to, or impair the efficiency of, any of the equipment comprising the system.

The Government contends that Jerrold's policy and practice of selling on a system basis only and of making sales only in conjunction with a service contract constituted unlawful tie-ins in violation of Section 1 of the Sherman Act . . . and Section 3 of the Clayton Act. . . . It also asserts that the provision in the 103 series contracts for the exclusive use of Jerrold equipment for the addition of extra channels to the system and the provision in all of the contracts not to install unapproved, non–Jerrold equipment violated these sections of the antitrust laws.

III–A. Service Contracts

*   *   *   *   *

The Government concedes that Section 3 of the Clayton Act does not apply to . . . tie-ins involving services. The Government asserts, however, that sales upon the condition that the purchaser subscribe to the services of the vendor constitute an unreasonable restraint of trade in violation of Section 1 of the Sherman Act. Jerrold admits that as to the sale of complete community television antenna systems it was an undoubted leader up until mid-1954, and more than a majority of the new systems from 1950 to mid-1954 were purchased from it. Indeed, Jerrold consistently advertised throughout this period that at least 75 percent of the community systems in the United States were "Jerrold systems." Economic power over a product can be inferred from sales leadership. . . . Another fact from which economic power can be inferred is the desirability of the tying product to the purchaser. *Northern Pacific Railway Co.* v. *United States, supra* . . . (dissent). Mr. Shapp has stated that Jerrold's highly specialized head end equipment was the only equipment available which was designed to meet all of the varying problems arising at the antenna site. It was thus in great demand by system operators. This placed Jerrold in a strategic position and gave it the leverage necessary to persuade customers to agree to its service contracts. This leverage constitutes "economic power" sufficient to invoke the doctrine of *per se* unreasonableness.

When Jerrold was ready to place its W equipment on the market in May 1950, it was confronted with a rather unique situation. In the first place, while it was convinced that its equipment would work, Jerrold recognized that it was sensitive and unstable. Consequently, modifications were still being made. . . . Secondly, as has already been noted, there were hundreds of people anxious to set up community antenna systems. Most of these people had no technical background at all. . . . Finally, Jerrold had directed most of its resources toward the development of its community equipment. It was of utmost importance to it that its investment prove successful.

Shapp, his engineers, and salesmen envisioned widespread chaos if Jerrold simply sold its community equipment to anyone who wanted it. . . . Therefore, it was desirable that the system be installed under the supervision of men whose ability was known to the utility companies through other dealings. For these reasons, it was decided that community equipment should be sold with engineering services in order to foster the orderly growth of the industry on which the future of Jerrold depended.

The Government does not dispute the reasonableness of the contracts for services but objects to the fact that they were compulsory. The crucial question, therefore, is whether Jerrold could have accomplished the ends it sought without requiring the contracts. . . . If Jerrold's equipment was available without a contract, many impatient operators probably would have attempted to install their systems without assistance. . . . Jerrold's supply of equipment was limited. Unrestricted sales would have resulted in much of this equipment going into systems where prospects of success were at best extremely doubtful. Jerrold's short- and long-term well-being depended on the success of these first systems. It could not afford to permit some of its limited equipment to be used in such a way that it would work against its interests. A wave of system failures at the start would have greatly retarded, if not destroyed, this new industry and would have been disastrous for Jerrold. . . . For these reasons, this court concludes that Jerrold's policy and practice of selling its community equipment only in conjunction with a service contract was reasonable and not in violation of Section 1 of the Sherman Act at the time of its inception. . . .

The court's conclusion is based primarily on the fact that the tie-in was instituted in the launching of a new business with a highly uncertain future. As the industry took root and grew, the reasons for the blanket insistence on a service contract disappeared.

. . . [W]hile Jerrold has satisfied this court that its policy was reasonable at its inception, it has failed to satisfy us that it remained reasonable throughout the period of its use, even allowing it a reasonable time to recognize and adjust its policies to changing conditions. Accordingly, the court concludes that the defendants' refusal to sell Jerrold equipment except in conjunction with a service contract violated Section 1 of the Sherman Act during part of the time this policy was in effect.

III–B. Full System Sales

Jerrold also admits that it was its policy and practice from May 1951 to March 1954 not to sell its various items of equipment designed for community antenna systems separately, but only to sell them as components of a complete system. As a result of this program, individual pieces of Jerrold equipment were unavailable for both new systems and existing non–Jerrold systems. The government contends that this too constitutes an unlawful tie-in because Jerrold is driving competitors from the field by using its market power with respect to some of its equipment to induce the purchase of other equipment it manufactures. . . .

There is a further factor, however, which, in the court's opinion, makes Jerrold's decision to sell only full systems reasonable. There was a sound business reason for Jerrold to adopt this policy. Jerrold's decision was intimately associated with its belief that a service contract was essential. This court has already determined that, in view of the condition of Jerrold, the equipment, and the potential customers, the defendants' policy of insisting on a service contract was reasonable at its inception. Jerrold could not render the service it promised and deemed necessary if the customer could purchase any kind of equipment he desired. The limited knowledge and instability of equipment made specifications an impractical, if not impossible, alternative. Furthermore, Jerrold's policy could not have been carried out if separate items of its equipment were made available to existing systems or any other customer because the demand was so great that this equipment would find its way to a new system. Thus, the court concludes that Jerrold's policy of full system sales was a necessary adjunct to its policy of compulsory service and was reasonably regarded as a product as long as the conditions which dictated the use of the service contract continued to exist. As the circumstances changed and the need for compulsory service contracts disappeared, the economic reasons for exclusively selling complete systems were eliminated. Absent these economic reasons, the court feels that a full system was not an appropriate sales unit. . . .

FINAL JUDGMENT

*   *   *   *   *

The defendants are enjoined and restrained from, directly or indirectly:
a. Selling or offering to sell equipment on the condition or understanding that the purchaser thereof purchase services from the defendants;
b. Furnishing or offering to furnish services on the condition or understanding that the recipient thereof purchase any Jerrold equipment;
c. Selling or offering to sell any item of Jerrold equipment on the condition or understanding that the purchaser thereof buy or use any other Jerrold equipment;
d. Selling or offering to sell any equipment on the condition or understanding that the purchaser thereof will not purchase or use equipment manufactured or sold by any other person. . . .

✺ 41

U.S. Steel Corp. et al. v. Fortner Enterprises, Inc.
U.S. Supreme Court
45 LW 4171 (1977)

> *This tiny case had an extraordinarily long and checkered career. In its first decision, in 1969, the Court applied a strict line against tie-ins and ordered a new trial. In the final decision, however, the Court unanimously held that the favorable credit terms given to house builders were not a unique product providing leverage to a dominant firm in the relevant market. Were they correct? What criteria should govern such an economic appraisal? In any event, genuine tie-ins by firms with substantial market shares are still illegal.*

Mr. Justice Stevens delivered the opinion of the Court.

In exchange for respondent's promise to purchase prefabricated houses to be erected on land near Louisville, Ky., petitioners agreed to finance the cost of acquiring and developing the land. Difficulties arose while the development was in progress, and respondent ("Fortner") commenced this treble damage action, claiming that the transaction was a tying arrangement forbidden by the Sherman Act. Fortner alleged that competition for prefabricated houses (the tied product) was restrained by petitioners' abuse of power over credit (the tying product). A summary judgment in favor of petitioners was reversed by this Court. *Fortner Enterprises* v. *U. S. Steel*, 394 U.S. 495 *(Fortner I)*. We held that the agreement affected a "not insubstantial" amount of commerce in the tied product and that Fortner was entitled to an opportunity to prove that petitioners possessed "appreciable economic power" in the market for the tying product. The question now presented is whether the record supports the conclusion that petitioners had such power in the credit market. . . .

I

Only the essential features of the arrangement between the parties need be described. Fortner is a corporation which was activated by an experienced real estate developer for the purpose of buying and improving residential lots. One petitioner, United States Steel Corporation, operates a "Home Division" which manufactures and assembles components of prefabricated houses; the second petitioner, the "Credit Corporation," is a wholly-owned subsidiary which provides financing to customers of the Home Division in order to promote sales. Although their common ownership and control make it appropriate to regard the two as a single seller, they sell two separate products—credit and prefabricated houses. The credit extended to Fortner was not merely for the price of the homes. Petitioners agreed to lend Fortner over $2,000,000 in exchange for Fortner's promise to purchase the components of 210 homes for about $689,000. The additional borrowed funds were intended to cover Fortner's cost of acquiring and developing the vacant real estate and the cost of erecting the houses.

The impact of the agreement on the market for the tied product (prefabricated houses) is not in dispute. On the one hand, there is no claim—nor could there be—that the Home Division had any dominance in the prefabricated housing business. The record indicates that it was only moderately successful and that its sales represented a small fraction of the industry total.[1] On the other hand, we have already held that the dollar value of the sales to respondent was sufficient to meet the "not insubstantial" test described in earlier cases. See 394 U.S., at 501–502. We therefore confine our attention to the source of the tying arrangement—petitioners' "economic power" in the credit market.

II

The evidence supporting the conclusion that the Credit Corporation had appreciable economic power in the credit market relates to four propositions: (1) petitioners were owned by one of the Nation's largest corporations; (2) petitioners entered into tying arrangements with a significant number of customers in addition to Fortner; (3) the Home Division charged respondent a noncompetitive price for its prefabricated homes; and (4) the financing provided to Fortner was "unique," primarily because it covered 100 percent of Fortner's acquisition and development costs.

The Credit Corporation was established in 1954 to provide financing for customers of the Home Division. The United States Steel Corporation not only provided the equity capital, but also allowed the Credit Corporation to use its credit in order to borrow money from banks at the prime rate. Thus, although the Credit Corporation itself was not a particularly large company, it was supported by a corporate parent with great financial strength.

The Credit Corporation's loan policies were primarily intended to

---

[1] In 1960, for example, the Home Division sold a total of 1,793 houses for $6,747,353. There were at least four larger prefabricated home manufacturers, the largest of which sold 16,804 homes in that year. In the following year the Home Division's sales declined while the sales of each of its four principal competitors remained steady or increased.

help the Home Division sell its products.[2] It extended credit only to customers of the Home Division, and over two thirds of the Home Division customers obtained such financing. With few exceptions, all the loan agreements contained a tying clause comparable to the one challenged in this case. Petitioner's home sales in 1960 amounted to $6,747,353. Since over $4,600,000 of these sales were tied to financing provided by the Credit Corporation, it is apparent that the tying arrangement was used with a number of customers in addition to Fortner.

The least expensive house package that Fortner purchased from the Home Division cost about $3,150. One witness testified that petitioner's price was $455 higher than the price of comparable components in a conventional home; another witness, to whom the District Court made no reference in its findings, testified that petitioners' price was $443 higher than a comparable prefabricated product. Whether the price differential was as great as 15 percent is not entirely clear, but the record does support the conclusion that the contract required Fortner to pay a noncompetitive price for petitioners' houses.

The finding that the credit extended to Fortner was unique was based on factors emphasized in the testimony of Fortner's expert witness, Dr. Masten, a professor with special knowledge of lending practices in the Kentucky area. Dr. Masten testified that mortgage loans equal to 100 percent of the acquisition and development cost of real estate were not otherwise available in the Kentucky area; that even though Fortner had a deficit of $16,000, its loan was not guaranteed by a shareholder, officer, or other person interested in its business; and that the interest rate of 6 percent represented a low rate under prevailing economic conditions. Moreover, he explained that the stable price levels at the time made the risk to the lender somewhat higher than would have been the case in a period of rising prices. Dr. Masten concluded that the terms granted to respondent by the Credit Corporation were so distinctly unique that it was almost inconceivable that the funds could have been acquired from any other source. It is a fair summary of his testimony and of the District Court's findings to say that the loan was unique because the lender accepted such a high risk and the borrower assumed such a low cost.

The District Court also found that banks and federally insured savings and loan associations generally were prohibited by law from making 100 percent land acquisition and development loans and "that other conventional lenders would not have made such loans at the time in

---

[2]After reviewing extensive evidence taken from the files of the Credit Corporation, including a memorandum stating that "our only purpose in making the loan . . . is shipping houses," the District Court expressly found "that the Credit Corporation was not so much concerned with the risks involved in loans but whether they would help sell houses." App., at 1588–1589.

question since they were not prudent loans due to the risk involved."
App., at 1596.

Accordingly, the District Court concluded "that all of the required
elements of an illegal tie-in agreement did exist since the tie-in itself was
present, a not insubstantial amount of interstate commerce in the tied
product was restrained, and the Credit Corporation did possess sufficient economic power or leverage to effect such restraint." App., at 1602.

III

Without the finding that the financing provided to Fortner was
"unique," it is clear that the District Court's findings would be insufficient to support the conclusion that the Credit Corporation possessed
any significant economic power in the credit market.

Although the Credit Corporation is owned by one of the Nation's
largest manufacturing corporations, there is nothing in the record to
indicate that this enabled it to borrow funds on terms more favorable
than those available to competing lenders or that it was able to operate
more efficiently than other lending institutions. In short, the affiliation
between the petitioners does not appear to have given the Credit Corporation any cost advantage over its competitors in the credit market.
Instead, the affiliation was significant only because the Credit Corporation provided a source of funds to customers of the Home Division. That
fact tells us nothing about the extent of petitioners' economic power in
the credit market.

The same may be said about the fact that loans from the Credit Corporation were used to obtain house sales from Fortner and others. In some
tying situations a disproportionately large volume of sales of the tied
product resulting from only a few strategic sales of the tying product
may reflect a form of economic "leverage" that is probative of power
in the market for the tying product. If, as some economists have
suggested, the purpose of a tie-in is often to facilitate price discrimination, such evidence would imply the existence of power that a free
market would not tolerate.[3] But in this case Fortner was only required to
purchase houses for the number of lots for which it received financing.
The tying product produced no commitment from Fortner to purchase
varying quantities of the tied product over an extended period of time.
This record, therefore, does not describe the kind of "leverage" found in
some of the Court's prior decisions condemning tying arrangements.[4]

The fact that Fortner—and presumably other Home Division custom-

---

[3]See Bowman, "Tying Arrangements and the Leverage Problem," 67 *Yale L. J.* 19
(1957).

[4]See e. g., *United Shoe Machinery Corp.* v. *United States*, 258 U.S. 451; *International
Business Machines Corp.* v. *United States*, 298 U.S. 131; *International Salt Co.* v. *United States*,

ers as well—paid a noncompetitive price for houses also lends insufficient support to the judgment of the lower court. Proof that Fortner paid a higher price for the tied product is consistent with the possibility that the financing was unusually inexpensive and that the price for the entire package was equal to, or below, a competitive price. And this possibility is equally strong even though a number of Home Division customers made a package purchase of homes and financing.

The most significant finding made by the District Court related to the unique character of the credit extended to Fortner. This finding is particularly important because the unique character of the tying product has provided critical support for the finding of illegality in prior cases. Thus, the statutory grant of a patent monopoly in *International Salt Co. v. United States*, 332 U.S. 392, the copyright monopolies in *United States v. Paramount Pictures, Inc.*, 334 U.S. 131, and *United States v. Loew's Inc.*, 371 U.S. 38, and the extensive land holdings in *Northern Pacific R. Co. v. United States*, 356 U.S. 1, represented tying products that the Court regarded as sufficiently unique to give rise to a presumption of economic power.

As the Court plainly stated in its prior opinion in this case, these decisions do not require that the defendant have a monopoly or even a dominant position throughout the market for a tying product. See 394 U.S., at 502–503. They do, however, focus attention on the question whether the seller has the power within the market for the tying product to raise prices or to require purchasers to accept burdensome terms that could not be exacted in a completely competitive market. In short, the question is whether the seller has some advantage not shared by his competitors in the market for the tying product.

Without any such advantage differentiating his product from that of his competitors, the seller's product does not have the kind of uniqueness considered relevant in prior tying clause cases. The Court made this point explicitly when it remanded this case for trial:

> We do not mean to accept petitioner's apparent argument that market power can be inferred simply because the kind of financing terms offered by a lending company are "unique and unusual." We do mean, however, that uniquely and unusually advantageous terms can reflect a creditor's unique economic advantages over his competitors. 394 U.S., at 505.

An accompanying footnote explained that:

> Uniqueness confers economic power only when other competitors are in some way prevented from offering the distinctive product themselves. Such barriers may be legal, as in the case of patented and copyrighted

---

332 U.S. 392. In his chapter of the 1969 Supreme Court Review, p. 16, Professor Dam suggests that this kind of leverage may also have been present in *Northern Pacific R. Co. v. United States*, 356 U.S. 1.

products, e. g., *International Salt; Loew's,* or physical, as when the product is land, e. g., *Northern Pacific.* It is true that the barriers may also be economic, as when competitors are simply unable to produce the distinctive product profitably, but the uniqueness test in such situations is somewhat confusing since the real source of economic power is not the product itself but rather the seller's cost advantage in producing it. Id., at n. 2.

Quite clearly, if the evidence merely shows that credit terms are unique because the seller is willing to accept a lesser profit—or to incur greater risks—than its competitors, that kind of uniqueness will not give rise to any inference of economic power in the credit market. Yet this is, in substance, all that the record in this case indicates.

The unusual credit bargain offered to Fortner proves nothing more than a willingness to provide cheap financing in order to sell expensive houses. Without any evidence that the Credit Corporation had some cost advantage over its competitors—or could offer a form of financing that was significantly differentiated from that which other lenders could offer if they so elected—the unique character of its financing does not support the conclusion that petitioners had the kind of economic power which Fortner had the burden of proving in order to prevail in this litigation.

The judgment of the Court of Appeals is reversed.

Vertical and Other Restrictions

Here too the action can be anticompetitive if done by a dominant firm but mildly procompetitive if it helps a small firm to strengthen its dealer network. In the 1960s, the Court leaned toward a per se rule against nearly all territorial restrictions on competition (that is, preventing dealers from selling in each other's areas). *White Motor* (1963) was the opening case, and *Schwinn* (1967) seemed to proscribe restraints even when done by a bicycle firm with only 12 percent of the market. *Sealy* continued in this vein. *GTE Sylvania* in 1977 seemed to loosen that rule, but it only involved a firm trying to build up its market share to about 5 percent. Therefore the main line of policy toward leading firms is still in force, and it makes economic sense.

✎ 42

Continental TV, Inc. et al. v. *GTE Sylvania, Inc.*

U.S. Supreme Court
45 LW 4828 (1977)

> *This case was widely seen as replacing a* per se *rule against vertical territorial restrictions with a "rule of reason." Yet the key is the low share which GTE Sylvania held (below 5 percent). Had its share been 20 or 40 percent, its actions probably would have been held to be illegal.*

Mr. Justice Powell.   Franchise agreements between manufacturers and retailers frequently include provisions barring the retailers from selling franchised products from locations other than those specified in the agreements. This case presents important questions concerning the appropriate antitrust analysis of these restrictions under § 1 of the Sherman Act, 15 U.S. C. § 1, and the Court's decision in *United States* v. *Arnold, Schwinn & Co.*, 388 U.S. 365 (1967).

I

Respondent GTE Sylvania, Inc. (Sylvania), manufactures and sells television sets through its Home Entertainment Products Division. Prior to 1962, like most other television manufacturers, Sylvania sold its televisions to independent or company-owned distributors who in turn resold to a large and diverse group of retailers. Prompted by a decline in its market share to a relatively insignificant 1 to 2 percent of national television sales,[1] Sylvania conducted an intensive reassessment of its marketing strategy and in 1962 adopted the franchise plan challenged here. Sylvania phased out its wholesale distributors and began to sell its televisions directly to a smaller and more select group of franchised retailers. An acknowledged purpose of the change was to decrease the number of competing Sylvania retailers in the hope of attracting the more aggressive and competent retailers thought necessary to the improvement of the company's market position.[2] To this end, Sylvania limited the number of franchises granted for any given area and required each franchisee to sell his Sylvania products only from the location or

---

[1]RCA at that time was the dominant firm with as much as 60 to 70 percent of national television sales in an industry with more than 100 manufacturers.

[2]The number of retailers selling Sylvania products declined significantly as a result of the change, but in 1965 there were at least two franchised Sylvania retailers in each metropolitan center of more than 100,000 population.

locations at which he was franchised.[3] A franchise did not constitute an exclusive territory, and Sylvania retained sole discretion to increase the number of retailers in an area in light of the success or failure of existing retailers in developing their market. The revised marketing strategy appears to have been successful during the period at issue here, for by 1965 Sylvania's share of national television sales had increased to approximately 5 percent, and the company ranked as the Nation's eighth largest manufacturer of color television sets.

This suit is the result of the rupture of a franchisor-franchisee relationship that had previously prospered under the revised Sylvania plan. Dissatisfied with its sales in the city of San Francisco,[4] Sylvania decided in the spring of 1965 to franchise Young Brothers, an established San Francisco retailer of televisions, as an additional San Francisco retailer. The proposed location of the new franchise was approximately a mile from a retail outlet operated by petitioner Continental T.V., Inc. (Continental), one of the most successful Sylvania franchisees.[5] Continental protested that the location of the new franchise violated Sylvania's marketing policy, but Sylvania persisted in its plans. Continental then cancelled a large Sylvania order and placed a large order with Phillips, one of Sylvania's competitors.

*   *   *   *   *

[In the following dispute, Sylvania terminated Continental's franchises, and complex cross-claims were filed and litigated. The jury convicted Sylvania under the *Schwinn* rule, and the case was then appealed to the Supreme Court.] . . . Most important for our purposes was the claim that Sylvania had violated § 1 of the Sherman Act by entering into and enforcing franchise agreements that prohibited the sale of Sylvania products other than from specified locations. . . .

III

Sylvania argues that if *Schwinn* cannot be distinguished, it should be reconsidered. Although *Schwinn* is supported by the principle of *stare decisis, Illinois Brick Co.* v. *Illinois,* —— U.S. ——, —— (1977), we are

---

[3]Sylvania imposed no restrictions on the right of the franchisee to sell the products of competing manufacturers.

[4]Sylvania's market share in San Francisco was approximately 2.5 percent—half its national and northern California average.

[5]There are in fact four corporate petitioners: Continental T. V., Inc., A & G Sales; Sylpac, Inc.; and S. A. M. Industries, Inc. All are owned in large part by the same individual, and all conducted business under the trade style of "Continental T. V." We adopt the convention used by the court below of referring to petitioners collectively as "Continental."

convinced that the need for clarification of the law in this area justifies reconsideration. *Schwinn* itself was an abrupt and largely unexplained departure from *White Motor Co.* v. *United States*, 372 U.S. 253 (1963), where only four years earlier the Court had refused to endorse a per se rule for vertical restrictions. Since its announcement, *Schwinn* has been the subject of continuing controversy and confusion, both in the scholarly journals and in the federal courts. The great weight of scholarly opinion has been critical of the decision, and a number of the federal courts confronted with analogous vertical restrictions have sought to limit its reach. In our view, the experience of the past ten years should be brought to bear on this subject of considerable commercial importance.

The traditional framework of analysis under § 1 of the Sherman Act is familiar and does not require extended discussion. Section 1 prohibits "[e]very contract, combination . . . or conspiracy, in restraint of trade or commerce." Since the early years of this century a judicial gloss on this statutory language has established the "rule of reason" as the prevailing standard of analysis. *Standard Oil Co.* v. *United States*, 221 U.S. 1 (1911). Under this rule, the factfinder weighs all of the circumstances of a case in deciding whether a restrictive practice should be prohibited as imposing an unreasonable restraint on competition. Per se rules of illegality are appropriate only when they relate to conduct that is manifestly anticompetitive. As the Court explained in *Northern Pac. R. Co.* v. *United States*, 356 U.S. 1, 5 (1958), "there are certain agreements or practices which because of their pernicious effect on competition and lack of any redeeming virtue are conclusively presumed to be unreasonable and therefore illegal without elaborate inquiry as to the precise harm they have caused or the business excuse for their use."

In essence, the issue before us is whether *Schwinn's* per se rule can be justified under the demanding standards of *Northern Pac. R. Co.* The Court's refusal to endorse a per se rule in *White Motor Co.* was based on its uncertainty as to whether vertical restrictions satisfied those standards. Addressing this question for the first time, the Court stated:

> We need to know more than we do about the actual impact of these arrangements on competition to decide whether they have such a "pernicious effect on competition and lack . . . any redeeming virtue" (*Northern Pac. R. Co.* v. *United States, supra,* p. 5) and therefore should be classified as per se violations of the Sherman Act. 372 U.S., at 263.

Only four years later the Court in *Schwinn* announced its sweeping per se rule without even a reference to *Northern Pac. R. Co.* and with no explanation of its sudden change in position. We turn now to consider *Schwinn* in light of *Northern Pac. R. Co.*

The market impact of vertical restrictions is complex because of their potential for a simultaneous reduction of intrabrand competition and stimulation of interbrand competition. Significantly, the Court in *Schwinn* did not distinguish among the challenged restrictions on the basis of their individual potential for intrabrand harm or interbrand benefit. Restrictions that completely eliminated intrabrand competition among Schwinn distributors were analyzed no differently than those that merely moderated intrabrand competition among retailers. The pivotal factor was the passage of title: All restrictions were held to be *per se* illegal where title had passed, and all were evaluated and sustained under the rule of reason where it had not. The location restriction at issue here would be subject to the same pattern of analysis under *Schwinn*.

It appears that this distinction between sale and nonsale transactions resulted from the Court's effort to accommodate the perceived intrabrand harm and interbrand benefit of vertical restrictions. The per se rule for sale transactions reflected the view that vertical restrictions are "so obviously destructive" of intrabrand competition that their use would "open the door to exclusivity of outlets and limitation of territory further than prudence permits." 388 U.S., at 379, 380. Conversely, the continued adherence to the traditional rule of reason for nonsale transactions reflected the view that the restrictions have too great a potential for the promotion of interbrand competition to justify complete prohibition. The Court's opinion provides no analytical support for these contrasting positions. Nor is there even an assertion in the opinion that the competitive impact of vertical restrictions is significantly affected by the form of the transaction. Nonsale transactions appear to be excluded from the per se rule, not because of a greater danger of intrabrand harm or a greater promise of interbrand benefit, but rather because of the Court's unexplained belief that a complete per se prohibition would be too "inflexible." Id., at 379.

Vertical restrictions reduce intrabrand competition by limiting the number of sellers of a particular product competing for the business of a given group of buyers. Location restrictions have this effect because of practical constraints on the effective marketing area of retail outlets. Although intrabrand competition may be reduced, the ability of retailers to exploit the resulting market may be limited both by the ability of consumers to travel to other franchised locations and, perhaps more importantly, to purchase the competing products of other manufacturers. None of these key variables, however, is affected by the form of the transaction by which a manufacturer conveys his products to the retailers.

Vertical restrictions promote interbrand competition by allowing the manufacturer to achieve certain efficiencies in the distribution of his products. These "redeeming virtues" are implicit in every decision sustaining vertical restrictions under the rule of reason. Economists have identified a number of ways in which manufacturers can use such restrictions to compete more effectively against other manufacturers. See e.g., Preston, "Restrictive Distribution Arrangements: Economic Analysis and Public Policy Standards," 30 *Law & Contemp. Prob.*, 506, 511 (1965). For example, new manufacturers and manufacturers entering new markets can use the restrictions in order to induce competent and aggressive retailers to make the kind of investment of capital and labor that is often required in the distribution of products unknown to the consumer. Established manufacturers can use them to induce retailers to engage in promotional activities or to provide service and repair facilities necessary to the efficient marketing of their products. Service and repair are vital for many products, such as automobiles and major household appliances. The availability and quality of such services affect a manufacturer's good will and the competitiveness of his product. Because of market imperfections such as the so-called free rider effect, these services might not be provided by retailers in a purely competitive situation, despite the fact that each retailer's benefit would be greater if all provided the services than if none did. Posner, *supra*, n. 13, at 285; cf. P. Samuelson, *Economics*, 506–507 (10th ed. 1976).

Economists also have argued that manufacturers have an economic interest in maintaining as much intrabrand competition as is consistent with the efficient distribution of their products. Bork, "The Rule of Reason and the Per Se Concept: Price Fixing and Market Division II," 75 *Yale L. J.* 373, 403 (1966); Posner, *supra*, n. 13, at 283, 287–88. Although the view that the manufacturer's interest necessarily corresponds with that of the public is not universally shared, even the leading critic of vertical restrictions concedes that *Schwinn's* distinction between sale and nonsale transactions is essentially unrelated to any relevant economic impact. Comanor, "Vertical Territorial and Customer Restrictions: White Motor and Its Aftermath," 81 *Harv. L. Rev.* 1419, 1422 (1968). Indeed, to the extent that the form of the transaction is related to intrabrand benefits, the Court's distinction is inconsistent with its articulated concern for the ability of smaller firms to compete effectively with larger ones. Capital requirements and administrative expenses may prevent smaller firms from using the exception for nonsale transactions. See e. g., Baker, *supra*, n. 13, at 538; Phillips, "*Schwinn* Rules and the 'New Economics' of Vertical Relationships." 44 *Antitrust L. J.*, 573, 576 (1975); Pollock, *supra*, n. 13, at 610.

We conclude that the distinction drawn in *Schwinn* between sale and nonsale transactions is not sufficient to justify the application of a per se rule in one situation and a rule of reason in the other. The question remains whether the *per se* rule stated in *Schwinn* should be expanded to include nonsale transactions or abandoned in favor of a return to the rule of reason. We have found no persuasive support for expanding the rule. As noted above, the *Schwinn* Court recognized the undesirability of "prohibit[ing] all vertical restrictions of territory and all franchising. . . ." 388 U.S., at 379–80. And even Continental does not urge us to hold that all such restrictions are per se illegal.

We revert to the standard articulated in *Northern Pac. R. Co.* and reiterated in *White Motor* for determining whether vertical restrictions must be "conclusively presumed to be unreasonable and therefore illegal without elaborate inquiry as to the precise harm they have caused or the business excuse for their use." 356 U.S., at 5. Such restrictions, in varying forms, are widely used in our free market economy. As indicated above, there is substantial scholarly and judicial authority supporting their economic utility. There is relatively little authority to the contrary. Certainly, there has been no showing in this case, either generally or with respect to Sylvania's agreements, that vertical restrictions have or are likely to have a "pernicious effect on competition" or that they "lack . . . any redeeming virtue." Ibid. Accordingly, we conclude that the *per se* rule stated in *Schwinn* must be overruled. In so holding we do not foreclose the possibility that particular applications of vertical restrictions might justify per se prohibition under *Northern Pac. R. Co.* but we do make clear that departure from the rule of reason standard must be based upon demonstrable economic effect rather than—as in *Schwinn*—upon formalistic line drawing.

In sum, we conclude that the appropriate decision is to return to the rule of reason that governed vertical restrictions prior to *Schwinn*. When competitive effects are shown to result from particular vertical restrictions they can be adequately policed under the rule of reason, the standard traditionally applied for the majority of anticompetitive practices challenged under § 1 of the Act. Accordingly, the decision of the Court of Appeals is

Affirmed.

✺ 43

Federal Trade Commission,
In the matter of the *Coca-Cola Co. et al.*

Docket No. 8855
Final Order and Opinion (1978)

> *Long ago, the Coca-Cola Co. and other firms established exclusive*
> *territories as the marketing basis for soda pop. In 1978 the FTC held such*
> *exclusion of intrabrand competition to be illegal (except for pop sold in*
> *returnable bottles). The decision also settled a series of parallel suits*
> *against the other pop companies. (The decision was appealed.) Was the*
> *decision good economics?*

By Dole, Commissioner. The basic question on this appeal is whether territorial restrictions which eliminate competition among the independent bottlers of Coca-Cola and allied soft drink products are unfair within the meaning of Section 5 of the Federal Trade Commission Act.

I. INTRODUCTION

Respondent Coca-Cola requires little introduction. It is a diversified corporation with interests ranging from steam boilers to orange juice. In 1968 it had consolidated net sales in excess of $1.1 billion and consolidated assets exceeding $802 million. Pertinent to the issues raised in the complaint in this proceeding are the operations of its Coca-Cola U.S.A. division. It is this division which manufactures and sells the soft drink syrups and concentrates used in the processing of finished flavored carbonated soft drinks sold under one or more of the trade names licensed by respondents to the bottlers. In 1968 its syrup sales to bottlers exceeded $246 million.

Around the turn of this century, The Coca-Cola Company sold its right to bottle Coca-Cola and licensed the "Coca-Cola" trademark in perpetuity to private investors who, as independent businessmen, operated their own bottling facilities within assigned territories. At the time, The Coca-Cola Company itself produced no bottled soft drinks, and although it does today in certain areas of the country, its entry into the business of bottling the products which bear its trademarks results from the reacquisition of the bottling rights which had been previously granted to local bottlers. Today it operates 27 bottling plants which serve exclusive territories encompassing about 14 percent of the population of the United States. . . . The rest of respondents' bottlers are relatively independent businessmen who conduct their commercial affairs as they see fit, subject to three key limitations:

First, when The Coca-Cola Company decided to sell the rights to bottle its product, it agreed to sell to its bottlers a continuous supply of the necessary soft drink syrups, but it refused to yield the secret Coca-Cola syrup formula which would have enabled the bottlers to produce the syrup themselves. Later, when the allied products were introduced, it adopted a similar policy. As a result, respondent The Coca-Cola Company is the bottlers' only source of vital Coca-Cola and allied product syrups or concentrates used in the preparation of the finished soft drinks.

Second, respondent Coca-Cola has retained the right to establish quality standards for the products which carry its trademarks and to insist that the bottlers maintain those standards. Failure on the part of a bottler to meet the quality standards it has established may trigger one of the few contingencies justifying the forfeiture of a bottler's bottling rights.

Third, respondents have imposed by contract and have enforced in practice the territorial restrictions which prevent these independent soft drink bottlers from competing with one another in the sale of bottled, canned, and premixed Coca-Cola and the allied soft drink products made from the syrups and concentrate ingredients produced by The Coca-Cola Company.[1] It is this latter interference with the bottlers' geographic markets which resulted in the complaint now before us. In essence, this complaint alleges that these territorial restrictions injure competition among the bottlers and deprive retailers and consumers of the benefits of open competition in the sale of Coca-Cola and the allied products packaged in bottles and cans.

After a lengthy trial which delved in detail into the day-to-day business of bottling soft drinks, the administrative law judge issued his initial decision in which he concluded that territorial restrictions are, in the context of the soft drink industry, procompetitive. Accordingly, he entered an order dismissing the complaint, and counsel supporting the complaint have appealed.

*   *   *   *   *

We have carefully reviewed the arguments advanced in briefs and at oral argument in light of the record and the initial decision and have concluded, for the reasons stated below, that the territorial restraints

---

[1]Respondents make no attempt to understate their firmness in enforcing these restrictions. As a consequence, border disputes involving sales of bottled and canned Coca-Cola and allied products by one bottler into the territory of another are rare and usually insignificant.

respondents impose on their independent bottlers are unreasonable and in violation of Section 5 of the Federal Trade Commission Act. Our order will lift the restrictions which place limitations on the sale of Coca-Cola and allied products packaged in premix containers or in nonrefillable, nonreusable bottles and cans. For reasons discussed in detail later in this opinion, we find it unnecessary to disturb the exclusive territorial relationships with respect to the sale of these products packaged in returnable, refillable bottles. . . .

*   *   *   *   *

2. VERTICAL *PER SE* THEORIES

As we mentioned previously, the Supreme Court in overruling *Schwinn* has not entirely rejected the possibility that vertical restrictions may in individual cases be declared per se unlawful, but it has toughened the standard considerably. Only those restraints found to be "pernicious" and without "any redeeming virtue" now justify per se treatment. The types of competitive situations, other than price fixing, which may meet this standard are unclear, but beyond that, the trier of fact and appellate tribunals must be receptive to the fact that situations may exist in which the imposition of a vertical restraint may, under *GTE*, still be per se unlawful.

On the facts before us, we believe the application of a per se rule would be inappropriate. Taking into consideration the competitive dynamics in this industry, there are important unresolved issues in this proceeding concerning whether open intrabrand competition among the bottlers of Coca-Cola and the allied products would adversely affect interbrand competition in the sale of soft drink beverages. The resolution of these issues in this case, we believe, requires a rule of reason analysis. . . .

*   *   *   *   *

B. Suppression of Intrabrand Competition among Respondents' Bottlers

Respondents acknowledge that territorial restrictions prevent intrabrand competition among their bottlers but claim this effect is actually procompetitive and necessary in the interest of promoting the overall efficiency and productivity of its bottler network. Respondents contend, moreover, that the admitted restraint of intrabrand competition is of no concern unless "the restraint is imposed by parties with excessive market power," the "principal indication" of which "is the ability to set the price for a product free from the influence of interbrand competition." On this premise they further contend that the evidence does not show that respondents have "unrestricted market power" with respect to price, packaging, or service, and that evidence concerning market share and profits does not demonstrate that Coca-Cola has "dominant or monopoly power." Implicit in this contention is the idea that absent such market power the asserted efficiency and productivity benefits of restrained intrabrand competition will be passed on to the consumer as a result of interbrand competition.

We do not agree that a showing of "dominant or monopoly power" or "unrestricted market power" is necessary before it may be concluded that suppression of intrabrand competition is unreasonable and in violation of Section 5. Respondents and the ALJ cite the decision in *United States* v. *Columbia Pictures Corp.*, 189 F. Supp. 153 (S.D.N.Y. 1960), where the court made the following summary of the doctrine of ancillary restraints (Id. at 178):

> It permits, as reasonable, a restraint which (1) is reasonably necessary to the legitimate primary purpose of the arrangement and of no broader scope than reasonably necessary; (2) does not unreasonably affect competition in the marketplace; and (3) is not imposed by a party or parties with monopoly power.

Thus, the court did not hold that market power must be demonstrated before a restraint could be held unreasonable under the Sherman Act, but rather held only that the absence of monopoly power was one of several prerequisites before a restraint might be held reasonable. Indeed, in *GTE* the Court indicated that even a less sweeping restraint on intrabrand competition than we have before us here could be found unreasonable without a showing of market power, even though the company imposing the restraint had a small market share and was far removed from the dominant firm in the industry.

While the territories in which Coca-Cola and the allied products are sold are not devoid of interbrand competition, nevertheless Coca-Cola and allied product prices have great competitive significance in the marketplace. Moreover, the record amply demonstrates that respondents' territorial restrictions constitute a serious impediment to free market forces and diminish competition in the manufacture, distribution, and sale of several important soft drink product lines. The record also shows that intrabrand competition would invigorate price competition which would be likely to produce lower wholesale prices for Coca-Cola and the allied products. By suppressing the development of intrabrand competition in the sale of these products packaged in bottles and cans, the restrictions have, over the years, distorted the competitive dynamics of the industry and have disrupted the natural economic forces which would have, in the absence of restraints, caused an evolution in the geographic market boundaries of respondents' bottlers.

2. Territorial Restrictions Prevent Procompetitive Geographic Market Expansion and Eliminate Potential Competition

Complaint counsel contend that respondents' territorial restrictions, rather than fostering greater efficiency, actually deter progress and the efficiency of the bottlers because they prevent the type of production and sales expansion which would enable bottlers to achieve maximum scale economies and further prohibit or discourage the bottlers from taking maximum advantage of improved production, distribution, transportation, and communications systems developed in the last five decades or so. Respondents vigorously dispute each of these contentions. In their view, bottlers large and small have been able to adapt to changing economic conditions, to expand their sales within their territories, and to employ innovative techniques of marketing and packaging.

Respondents are correct in their assertion that many of the adaptable technological breakthroughs of the 20th century have not bypassed the bottling industry. . . .

Originally, the bottlers' territories probably represented a rather close approximation of the geographic boundaries which would have existed in the industry if natural economic forces were left unrestrained. While territories were granted in various sizes and shapes, they probably encompassed an area roughly measured by the distance a turn-of-the-century vehicle could travel in one day. Given the technological and transportation limitations of the late 19th and early 20th centuries under which the original bottlers operated, it seems reasonable to conclude that most territories probably covered an area not significantly smaller than the Coke bottler was capable of servicing efficiently and effectively. As time passed, however, the potential for direct competition among respondents' bottlers grew as automated production of soft drinks replaced manual bottling lines, as new types of packaging were introduced, and as truck transport and road surfaces improved. Despite these advancements, however, respondents' territorial system stands impervious to natural geographic market evolution and procompetitive market extension by independent bottlers.

*   *   *   *   *

4. Territorial Restrictions Deprive Retailers and Consumers of the Benefits of Open Intrabrand Competition

Complaint counsel introduced into the record as part of their case-in-chief evidence which shows that the bottlers are not always able to adapt to changing economic conditions and improved technology in marketing and production to achieve efficiencies, especially if their initiatives are inconsistent with respondents' territorial policy. At the same time, the evidence shows that the restriction prevents any intrabrand competition, including price competition, in the sale of Coca-Cola and allied products in bottles and cans. As a consequence, respondents' restrictions are, as alleged in the complaint, depriving retailers and consumers of the opportunity to purchase Coca-Cola and the allied products in bottles and cans in unrestricted markets at openly competitive prices. Moreover, these restrictions have repressed the freedom of independent bottlers to expand their businesses or to seize opportunities they may perceive to increase their output of Coca-Cola and the allied products by selling these products where and to whom they choose in markets governed by natural economic forces.

*   *   *   *   *

v. Interbrand Competition.   Buttressed by the judge's finding that the "corridor area" exhibits "intense" interbrand soft drink price competition, respondents argue that their restraints on intrabrand competition are reasonable. The judge concluded that the prices which bottlers charge for Coca-Cola and allied products are determined by their costs and interbrand competition and that bottlers cannot price Coca-Cola and allied products above the prices of other brands, such as Pepsi-Cola and 7-Up, without losing sales. He also found that the bottlers of Coca-Cola frequently offer price promotions and that a restriction on intrabrand competition is procompetitive because it allows the bottlers to focus on interbrand rivals, thereby increasing interbrand competition.

The record shows that Coca-Cola and the allied products compete with a wide variety of beverages. Evidence was adduced at the trial from which a list was compiled of the brand or trade names of products which, to one degree or another, compete with Coca-Cola; the list of brands is lengthy and will not be repeated here. In summary, it includes the names of hundreds of national, regional, and local flavored carbonated soft drink brands; private label soft drinks, the bulk of which are produced by contract canners for food chains and other types of chain stores; powdered mixes such as Kool Aid, Funny Face, and Wylers; and noncarbonated drinks, including such brands as Hawaiian Punch, Gatorade, and fruit juices and drinks. The Coca-Cola bottlers who testified in this proceeding agreed that all such products compete, at least to some degree, with Coca-Cola in bottles and cans. However, their testimony clearly demonstrates that flavored carbonated soft drinks generally and the brands, such as Pepsi-Cola, distributed by other bottlers are the Coca-Cola bottlers' primary competitive rivals. As the record in its entirety amply demonstrates, the suppliers of these products exert the greatest influence on their competitive decisions. Consequently, we will focus mainly on the products which the bottlers have identified as their most important interbrand competition. Presumably, this is where the "intensity" of interbrand competition would be most evident.

A. Flavored Carbonated Soft Drink Brand Competition

The judge found that there is intense competition in the sale of flavored carbonated soft drinks "which stems from the fact that there is a large number of brands available to the consumer in local markets." (Id. 36). As impressive as the number of brands on respondents' list may be, however, it is in itself no measure of the intensity of the competitive interaction among the brands or the bottlers or canners which supply them. Indeed, the judge's consideration of interbrand competition at the finished soft drink production and distribution level glosses over the customary practice of major brand bottlers to carry the brands of several different syrup companies, a practice which they refer to as "piggybacking." Nor does the initial decision reflect any analysis of the anticompetitive interbrand effects of geographic market restraints which admittedly permeate the entire industry. We believe that an accurate assessment of the condition of interbrand competition in this industry, that is, its "intensity" or "degree" as reflected in the record, must take these factors into consideration.

*   *   *   *   *

1. Territorial Restrictions as a Method of Protecting Small Business

Respondents' protestations about concentration and the future structure of the industry aside, the thrust of their argument is predicated on the notion that small independent Coca-Cola bottlers would be unfairly disadvantaged by intrabrand competition. Numerous bottlers, particularly the smaller bottlers, testified that they were dependent upon the refuge of their territorial enclaves because intrabrand competition would force them out of business. This assessment was, in turn, based on several assumptions which were adopted in a series of important findings in the initial decision. The judge concluded that without exclusive territories, large bottlers of Coca-Cola would drive smaller bottlers out of business. He further concluded that a Commission order lifting the territorial restrictions:

> . . . would be in direct conflict with the purpose of the Congress in enacting and in agencies administering the antitrust laws "to perpetuate and preserve, for its own sake in spite of possible cost, an organization of industry in small units which can effectively compete with each other." *U.S.* v. *Aluminum Co. of America*, 148 F. 2d 416, 429 (2d Cir. 1945).

We acknowledge this admonition that one of the underlying purposes of the antitrust laws is to protect and preserve small business; indeed, in *American Cyanamid*, the Commission noted that "This agency also has its very roots planted in that philosophy. . . ." Our previous decisions implementing this philosophy clearly indicate, however, that we have never condoned anticompetitive practices solely for the purpose of eliminating competition between large and small firms. We stated in *Procter & Gamble:*

> . . . [I]t may be appropriate . . . to note Congress's concern with the preservation (of small firms) to the extent compatible with social and economic progress of the fundamental benefits of a small-business decentralized economy. The interest of fostering equality of opportunity for small business and in promoting the diffusion of economic power . . . was unquestionably intended by Congress to be relevant in any scheme for the enforcement of Section 7. (63 F.T.C. 1465, 1555–56 1963).

But in effectuating this policy, the Commission made clear that it does not subordinate "the protection of *competition* to the protection of small business *competitors*." "Otherwise," as the Third Circuit has observed in another context, "what is intended as a shield for small competitors becomes a sword against the consumer." *NBO Industries Treadway Cos., Inc.,* v. *Brunswick Corp.,* 523 F. 2d 262, 279 (3rd Cir. 1975), vacated on other grounds and remanded, *Brunswick Corp.* v. *Pueblo Bowl-O-Mat, Inc.,* ____ U.S. ____, 1977–1 Trade Cases, ¶ 61, 255.

Consistent with our prior application of these principles, we conclude that territorial restrictions are not justified as a means of protecting small independent Coca-Cola bottlers from large independent intrabrand rivals, but that ancillary relief is necessary in the public interest to prevent The Coca-Cola Company's integrated bottling operations from exploiting certain advantages which may accrue to it as a dual-distributing trademark licensor.

*   *   *   *   *

D. EFFECTS OF U.S. ANTITRUST POLICIES

Finally, two authors assess the impact of antitrust policy on the market realities. Kenneth G. Elzinga shows that mergers often persist even when rejected by the courts. Donald J. Dewey weighs the several lines of action and explains why the present balance of effort (strict on price fixing and most mergers, moderate on established dominant positions) is likely to continue.

Kenneth G. Elzinga (1941–   )

✳ 44
The Antimerger Law: Pyrrhic Victories?*

After the big decisions and formal victories, what happens? Mergers should be particularly open to good practical remedies. But Elzinga shows, with chapter and verse, that the actual correctives have fallen far short. Can we assume that remedies elsewhere are even less effective?

The relief that has been obtained by the Government in antimerger cases is the object of study in this paper. In short this is an economic study of the "back-side" of the antimerger law—what has happened *after* a merger has been found in violation of the law or the respondents have decided no longer to fight the suit and instead to submit to a consent decree. Its concern will be with the economic effectiveness of relief and the obstacles to the formulation of satisfactory relief. . . .

Whenever an anticompetitive increment in market power is attained by merger, structural relief requires the restoration of the acquired firm through a divestiture order. Only this sort of relief strikes at the very structure of the markets involved. Injunctive relief, that is, some form of order directing the acquiring firm to behave *as if* it did not gain this market power, is clearly unacceptable. Indeed placing such a regulatory role on the Government is repugnant to the whole concept of antitrust. . . .

But disgorging the acquired firm from its acquirer is only a necessary, not a sufficient, condition for enacting effective relief. Along with reestablishing the acquired firm, it is also necessary that this "new" firm be made *viable;* a mere shadow of its former self is not acceptable. Indeed, reestablishing "new" firms that are unable to stand on their own would make any relief efforts farcical.

. . . As long as an anticompetitive acquisition remains consummated, the incremental market power can be used by the acquiring firm. Consequently, effective relief is also a function of the *time* required to reestablish the independent, viable firm. . . .

*Kenneth G. Elzinga, "The Antimerger Law: Pyrrhic Victories?" *Journal of Law and Economics,* 1969, excerpted from pp. 43–52. Elzinga is at the University of Virginia. During 1970–71, he was special Economic Assistant to the Assistant Attorney General for Antitrust.

The Sample

The sample of merger cases to be evaluated is drawn from the universe of all *amended* Section 7 cases filed by the Government since the law's inception through the calendar year 1960, which have been settled either by consent order or decided for the Government by the end of calendar year 1964. The Government had filed 81 antimerger cases by 1960. Forty-two of these were either still pending by 1965, were dropped or settled for the defendant, or were eliminated because of data problems or regulatory aspects. Thirty-nine cases, then, constitute the sample.

IV. THE RESULTS

These thirty-nine cases have been placed on two four-category continuums in Table 1. . . .

For a relief case to qualify for the *successful* category, the acquired firm must be reestablished as an independent firm, or the anticompetitive effects of the acquisition must be stopped in their incipiency so that no restoration is necessary. . . .

. . . In the *sufficient* category a true independent center of initiative has not been restored. Instead the unlawfully acquired firm has been divested in one of four ways:

a. Sold to a "small" horizontal competitor.
b. Sold as a vertical acquisition but with no foreclosure problems.
c. Sold as a market or product extension acquisition with no obvious loss of potential competition.
d. Sold as a conglomerate acquisition to a "very large firm."

* * * * *

[The *deficient*] category essentially includes those cases with one "hole" in the relief decree. The "holes" are:

e. Assets are sold in such manner that an obvious loss of potential competition resulted.
f. Structural relief borders on *sufficient* but a complex marketing order, if enforced, leaves a "hole" in the case condemning it to a lower rung.
g. Government secures only a partial divestiture of the unlawfully acquired firm (or firms).

In short, the *deficient* category is basically for cases where the Government secured structural relief but where it was either incomplete or the assets fell into less than desirable hands. . . .

TABLE 1

Successful Relief	Sufficient Relief	Deficient Relief	Unsuccessful Relief
Bethlehem Steel	Gamble-Skogmo	American Radiator†	American Cyanamid†
Std. Oil of Ohio		Anheuser-Busch*	Automatic Canteen
Union Bag &		National Sugar†	Brillo
Paper		Spalding†	Brown Shoe†
			Continental Baking†
			Continental Can†
			Crown Zellerbach†
			Diamond Crystal
			Diebold
			Farm Journal
			General Shoe
			Gulf Oil
			Hertz
			Hilton
			Hooker Chemical
			International Paper
			Jerrold Electronics
			Leslie Salt†
			Lucky Lager
			Maremont
			MMM†
			National Dairy†
			Owens Illinois†
			Reynolds Metal
			Ryder
			Schenley
			Scott Paper
			Scovill
			Simpson Timber
			Union Carbide†
			Vendo

*Case dropped one rank where structural relief took at least three years, but less than five, from the date of acquisition.

†Case dropped two ranks (where possible) when structural relief was enacted five or more years after the date of acquisition.

The category of *unsuccessful* cases includes the following:

h. No relief whatsoever.

i. No structural relief, only a ban on future acquisitions.

j. Insignificant or *de minimus* divestiture, not striking at the heart of the restraint.

k. Relief takes the form of a marketing order.

l. Relief is a combination of *j* and *k*.

m. Divestiture to a significant horizontal competitor.

n. Vertical divestiture with foreclosure problems.

o. Divestiture of a nonviable firm.

In the *deficient* category, "partial divestiture" was mentioned; in this category the term *"de minimus* divestiture" was used. . . .

A glance at this table provides no gray area. The first three ranks of the continuum have been decimated, now holding less than one quarter of the cases. The last category is full to the brim. Of the four cases remaining in the *successful-sufficient* categories, three involved acquisitions stopped in their incipiency *before* full consummation so that no divestiture was actually necessary; the other was a stock acquisition. This points to the difficulty of unraveling acquisitions after their consummation.

Average Time Spans

The Federal Trade Commission (FTC) cases in the sample had an average time of 19.0 months from the acquisition to the FTC's complaint. For those FTC cases which ended with some form of divestiture, the average duration from acquisition to divestiture was 67.5 months!

The Antitrust Division of the Department of Justice fared somewhat better. For those cases in the sample, the average time span from the acquisition to the complaint was 10.6 months. Where the Antitrust Division secured some form of divestiture in these cases, the average period from the acquisition to the structural relief was 63.8 months! . . .

To find that the Government has been unable to obtain effective relief in many of its antimerger cases is unlikely to surprise those acquainted with the history of the relief obtained in antimonopoly enforcement. In 1955, Dewey stated that "it is a commonplace in antitrust work that the Government wins the opinions and the defendants win the decrees." This position seems well documented. . . .

Donald J. Dewey (1922–   )

✣ 45

The Achievements of Antitrust Policy*

Antitrust has had little clear effect, but there may have been large indirect influences. Dewey's appraisal is lucid, sophisticated, and still valid. How can the effects be tested further scientifically? Or is it inescapably a matter of impressions and guesswork?

1. A Limited Effort

The total amount of money spent to enforce the antitrust laws over 65 years would not buy a medium-size naval vessel, and even if one adds to this figure the costs incurred by private parties in antitrust suits, the resulting sum probably would not finance a modern aircraft carrier. But then where the functions of the State are concerned, money outlay is a poor yardstick of a project's effect on economic welfare. Conceivably the economic consequences of antitrust policy have been, for better or worse, greater than the modest budgets of the enforcement agencies would suggest. We may therefore ask without being naive or cynical, Are there any good reasons for supposing that the structure of the American economy would now be perceptibly different had there been no attempt at an antitrust policy?

2. Cartels and Antitrust Policy

In the domain of cartel regulation, the direct impact of the antitrust laws has been slight. Some considerable fraction of the national income—perhaps as much as one half—originates in firms that are viewed as engaging only in "intrastate commerce" and hence beyond the reach of the federal power. (Not that the Supreme Court has evidenced much concern for States' rights in antitrust matters; the antitrust agencies have never had the funds which would allow them to litigate the boundaries of federal jurisdiction.) The state government effort against cartels has been too cynically frivolous to merit our attention. In industries where

*Donald J. Dewey, "The Achievements of Antitrust Policy," chapter 20 in *Monopoly in Economics and Law* (Chicago: Rand McNally, 1959), excerpted from pp. 302–309. Dewey, one of the most learned and literate scholars of antitrust, is at Columbia University.

the federal government undoubtedly has the authority to act, its challenge to cartel monopoly has been praiseworthy but not much more effective. The poverty of the federal antitrust agencies and the poor political returns to be had from the harassment of cartels have meant that fear of prosecution has not discouraged businessmen from viewing collusion as a normal method of conducting business. But then the amount of federal surveillance needed to ensure that *all* businessmen will think twice before co-operating to restrain competition is staggering to contemplate. The total elimination of collusion should probably be written off as a technical impossibility. At any rate the striving for this goal can only commend itself to one who believes that the biggest government is preferable to the smallest private monopoly.

Antitrust policy, however, has achieved two notable successes in the control of cartels. In the handful of industries that the antitrust agencies elect to police with their limited resources, the threat of prosecution has succeeded in discouraging—and sometimes eliminating—overt collusion. Indeed, in industries that have been visited with the expense and publicity of litigation, notably oil, tobacco, steel, meat packing, and automobiles, officials of rival firms often go to humorous lengths to make sure that they do not have dealings with one another without legal counsel present. Strictly speaking, the whole theory of oligopoly or tacit collusion as manifested in price leadership, market sharing, delivered pricing, etc., is a tribute to the occasional effectiveness of antitrust policy, for these roundabout and inefficient ways of restraining competition are unknown within legal frameworks that permit overt collusion. There is, after all, no point in guessing about the future price policy of a competitor when it is possible to ask him outright for such information.

Second, the development of the doctrine that collusion to restrain competition is illegal per se has rendered the restrictive agreement unenforceable and, thus, has largely eliminated the more elaborate—and profitable—types of co-operation, especially the use of the income-pooling agreement. (The decline of income pooling is perhaps the most striking feature of cartel history in the United States over the last 60 years.) . . .

The victory of the per se doctrine has not been without its costs. When firms lose the right to have their contracts construed in the light of some reasonableness test, their obvious move is agitation to secure statutory exemption from the antitrust laws. Just as any increase in the rate of income taxation (at any rate in the United States) is accompanied by an increase in the number and types of exemptions, so the increasing effectiveness of antitrust policy has led to special treatment for politically powerful or obviously unfortunate industries. At the federal level, the list of industries virtually exempt from the antitrust laws has come to include railroads, trucking, inland waterways, airlines, banking, pipelines, farmer co-operatives, and shipping. At the state level, there is scarcely an important "intrastate" industry that has not somewhere received back from the legislature the rights of collusion taken away by the court.

We should not make too much of the tie between the rise of the per se doctrine and the spread of special-interest legislation. A statute that confers the State's blessing on collusion is always worth having; the refusal of the courts to enforce contracts restraining competition merely gives interested parties a further incentive to seek this boon. When the balance is struck, however, the rule that the courts, unless directed otherwise by the legislature, will not enforce a private agreement that restricts competition is the supreme achievement of antitrust policy in the United States. It is a sobering thought that this result could have been achieved by a brief, explicitly worded statute that required no enforcement machinery, and that even without such legislation, English courts since 1890 have hardly ever enforced contracts restraining competition.

3. Close Combination and Antitrust Policy

The harassing of cartels by antitrust suits, though it may be a worthy thing, does not stir the imagination. The success of antitrust policy, rightly or wrongly, is commonly measured by its consequences for the world of big business, and the enduring importance of the large corporation is often cited as evidence of the inutility of antitrust policy.

We have seen that, so far as corporate concentration is concerned, the antitrust agencies have set two main tasks for themselves. They have sought to check the further progress of concentration by preventing mergers which threaten a reduction of competition, and they have sought to rectify the mistakes of history by dissolving and divesting established corporations that exercise more control over the market than is needed for efficient operation. The success of antitrust policy is generally taken to have been negligible in both ventures, the only serious differences of opinion relating to the reasons for failure. . . .

Actually the main impact of antitrust policy on the structure of the economy has probably resulted from its influence on two industries—oil and steel. In 1948 the Standard Oil Company of New Jersey had an estimated 7.2 percent of the assets of the hundred largest industrial firms, while four other oil companies created by the 1911 decree had a combined total of 8.7 percent of the assets of the hundred largest. (Not that the oil trust had it been left undisturbed in 1911 would necessarily have grown as rapidly as have the modern Standard Oil companies.) The fear that the absorption of major rivals would provoke litigation certainly accounts for some of the decline in the relative importance of the United States Steel Corporation. This company held 22.3 percent of the assets of the hundred largest firms in 1909 and only 5.2 percent in 1948. In fine, antitrust policy has perceptibly reduced concentration in American industries.

*   *   *   *   *

Some authorities have suggested that the limited success of the Sherman Act can be blamed on the inability of the federal government to match the legal talent that the corporate defendants command; that "the people have been represented, in the main, by men of very meagre legal ability." Undoubtedly private attorneys in antitrust cases are paid more than federal attorneys—and there are more of them. (Is there any branch of public business law where this is not true?) Even so, it is difficult to name an important case that the government lost mainly because its attorneys were outclassed in advocacy by the opposition. Nor, at least in recent years, do government briefs appear to have been seriously marred by hasty preparation.

So far as ingenuity in argument goes, the honors in antitrust cases have gone mainly to the government side, but this is because the federal attorneys have faced a more challenging task. Defense lawyers concentrate on cultivating the apprehension, never far below the level of consciousness in the mind of the court, that dissolution and divestiture *might* jeopardize operating efficiency and technological progress. To checkmate this maneuver, the federal attorneys must bear the burden of educating the courts in the intricacies of economic analysis and industrial technology—a task which is often, as in the *Columbia Steel* case, a truly formidable undertaking.

*   *   *   *   *

We may therefore reaffirm the thesis argued in Chapter XVII that the effort at trust busting has had so little success because it seeks a deliberate unsettling of property rights that offends the conservative bias of the courts. Nor, as we have seen, should this failure be taken as evidence that judges have consciously or unconsciously sabotaged congressional intent. The conservative bias is all-pervasive in any legal system worthy of the name. If the courts have been reluctant to order dissolution and divestiture, the moral is only that judges strive to behave in a judicious manner. The road to trust busting on a grand scale must lie through the congressional committee and federal bureau, not through the suit in equity. This is tantamount to saying that trust busting probably has little future as an antimonopoly measure in the United States.

The control of mergers offers a more promising line of action since the courts may reasonably enjoin the consummation of a merger that they would not set aside ten years later. . . . If, as the author believes, technological progress is a centrifugal force making for decentralization, a close check on mergers should ultimately produce lower concentration ratios in important industries.

The tendency of antitrust policy to become a permanent inquisition on the conduct of the country's two or three hundred largest corporations, resulting in endless consent decrees, is understandable given the courts' hostility to dissolution and divestiture. Nevertheless, the tendency is unfortunate. It multiplies uncertainty respecting the law and rests on the doubtful assumption that civil servants are competent to make decisions assessing the welfare consequences of particular business practices, e.g., a patent exchange between two firms. Moreover, it may well be futile. For in the negotiation of a complicated consent decree governing the conduct of a firm, one may presume both that the passage of time will soon make the decree irrelevant and that, since the defendant knows more about his operations than the government, he probably had the best of the compromise in the first place. In any event the ultimate object of policy is not a more detailed surveillance of the business world by the antitrust agencies but rather an economy sufficiently free of monopoly that such surveillance is largely unnecessary.

Questions for Review I: Antitrust

1. "Attempts to apply antitrust are just a misguided application of an extreme theory of perfect competition, which never was valid and certainly has little relation to the real economy now." Is this an accurate statement?

2. Most markets do not have clear boundaries. Yet the definition of the market is critically important to most structural antitrust decisions. Are optimum policy choices therefore impossible?

3. Can vertical integration extend monopoly power from one level of production to another? What public policy would you recommend toward vertical integration?

4. Under what conditions will the extent of vertical integration by existing firms affect the height of the barrier to entry into a market? Explain.

5. If you encountered a "price squeeze," how would you recognize it?

6. What is a per se rule? Does a per se rule on price-fixing fit cost-benefit criteria?

7. Is the economic rationale for a per se prohibition of price-fixing equally valid for internal "price fixing" by firms with large market shares?

8. Significant attempts at price-fixing among competitors occur usually in industries with *moderate* concentration. Why?

9. Explain the significance of *two* of the following for the development of antitrust policy toward price fixing: *(a)* Addyston Pipe, *(b)* Trenton Potteries, *(c)* Socony-Vacuum.

10. In what sense is there a sharp contrast between the American and most European public policies toward collusive business practices?

11. Explain the basic reason why a high-fixed-cost oligopolist is more likely to cut price deeply in a recession than are his low-fixed-cost rivals.

12. Identical prices are often observed, both in atomistic industries and in tight oligopolies. Do identical prices therefore reflect effective competition? What if the three bidders differ sharply in size, location, extent of order backlogs, and current profitability?

13. How would you determine whether pricing behavior in a specific oligopoly market reflected barometric or collusive price leadership?

14. Can price discrimination ever really reduce competition in the long run?

15. Name three industries which have large and systematic price discrimination. Taking one of these, is action against such discrimination warranted? Is it being taken?

16. Why might the common phenomenon of bulk discounts be harmful to competition?

17. Top Dollar, Inc., sells chocolate bananas for $15 to some customers and $12 to others. Is this definitely price discrimination? Is it anticompetitive?

18. Are dominant firms likely to be imitators rather than innovators?

19. Outline the alternative market definitions which Judge Learned Hand considered in his *Alcoa* decision. Which definition did he finally accept? Outline the argument which he employed to support that definition of the relevant market. Is it valid?

20. Despite the strictness of Section 2 of the Sherman Act, actual enforcement has had little effect on U.S. industrial structure. To test this hypothesis, what main categories of information would you need, and how would you analyze it? Illustrate with an actual case.

21. Is it true that most antitrust activity in recent years has come to focus upon conduct (e.g., price-fixing) rather than structure? Would this be futile, since one may have to change the structure in order to change conduct? Cite specific examples where possible.

22. Several new cases have recently touched some of the main firms with high market shares: IBM, Xerox, automobiles (fleet sales), cereals, and so on. Do these correct the Section 2 "gap" since 1952 in action toward dominant firms?

23. Under present law, what prospects are there for reducing the market power of the leading instances in the industrial sector? Discuss three of the "leading instances," from among the following: Western Electric, IBM, General Motors, Xerox, Eastman Kodak, General Electric, Procter & Gamble, Campbell Soup, and Kellogg.

24. Make the best case that you can that there *is* effective competition in either (1) computers, or (2) automobiles.

25. Horizontal mergers are constrained by antitrust policy to 10 percent of the market and below. Section 2 monopoly restructuring cases are confined to 60 percent and above. The gap between 10 and 60 percent is:
    1. A measure of the gross inconsistency in antitrust policy toward structure, or
    2. Fully consistent with reliable evidence about costs and benefits of policy choices, or
    3. _____ (other).

    Pick your ground and explain.

26. "Firms merge only to acquire market power." True?

27. The Justice Department merger guidelines of 1968 have been criticized for rejecting economies of scale as an element in evaluating mergers. Is there a better strategy for reaching full, neutral evaluations?

28. "Some conglomerate mergers are purely financial with few real effects. Others take advantage of genuine economies. Still others are procompetitive. Therefore the Antitrust Division should promote conglomerate mergers or at least not stop them." Do you agree?

29. Are diversified companies more likely to engage in systematic and/or predatory price discrimination than nondiversified companies? In either case, are there serious grounds for antitrust concern?

30. Do the current policies toward horizontal mergers fit good economic analysis (including the possible trade-offs between economics and monopoly effects)?

31. A prohibition of leading-firm conglomerate mergers has both benefits and costs. In light of these, what is an optimum treatment for such mergers?

32. What changes, if any, in the patent laws would be indicated by economic analysis?

33. An antitrust task force in 1968 proposed a drastic program of restructuring major industries. Another task force in 1969 urged instead that resources be used primarily against price-fixing. You now head another task force. What will you recommend on this issue, and why?

34. Antitrust is regularly condemned for being ineffective and praised for maintaining a competitive economy. Choose one of these positions and explain what antitrust has done, or has not done, that makes the case.

35. Problem industries often need joint treatment by two or more public policy tools. Pick such an industry and explain the package of policies you would provisionally recommend for it.

Part II

REGULATION

REGULATION IS A distinctively American experiment, which has had some real content for 20–50 years in various sectors. An independent, "expert" tribunal is created with powers to control prices and profits in "natural monopoly" sectors. Ideally, such regulation of utilities by commissions can apply strict, thorough controls, which keep prices close to minimum costs and set an efficient and fair price structure.

Practice has often worked out differently, as these readings explore. Agencies usually have modest funds, unsure powers, and heavy tasks. The issues can grow complex and confusing. Frequently, the agency first promotes, then negotiates with, then defends its utilities. The 1960s brought new skepticism about regulation, plus after 1965 a convergence of intense new problems: environmental issues, inflationary pressures, high interest rates, in general the end of the age of utility abundance. Calls for abolition or drastic changes in regulation have become frequent and more plausible. The 1970s have brought some marked changes, which are still in process.

Because regulation has been only partly tried, under diverse conditions, no one can sort out its effects and lessons precisely. These readings do pose the main issues about control, induced waste, and social yields. They also face the thorny problems of permitting the "optimal" degree of competition against utility firms who have only a core of "natural monopoly" operations but are keen to monopolize adjacent markets too. With these issues in hand, the student can perhaps begin devising a more effective and adjustable regulatory approach.

The format here has five sections, in this order: first the authority and effectiveness of regulation; then the economic criteria and effects of regulation; and then the three main sectors under regulation (power, telecommunications, and transport).

235

A. AUTHORITY AND EFFECTIVENESS

❊ 46

Munn v. *Illinois*
U.S. Supreme Court
94 U.S. 113 (1877)

> *This was the first assertion of the public's right to regulate private business which is "affected with a public interest."*

Mr. Chief Justice Waite.   The question to be determined in this case is whether the general assembly of Illinois can, under the limitations upon the legislative power of the States imposed by the Constitution of the United States, fix by law the maximum of charges for the storage of grain in warehouses at Chicago and other places in the State having not less than 100,000 inhabitants, "in which grain is stored in bulk, and in which the grain of different owners is mixed together, or in which grain is stored in such a manner that the identity of different lots or parcels cannot be accurately preserved."

It is claimed that such a law is repugnant.

This brings us to inquire as to the principles upon which this power of regulation rests, in order that we may determine what is within and what is without its operative effect. Looking, then, to the common law from whence came the right which the Constitution protects, we find that when private property is "affected with a public interest it ceases to be *juris privati* only."

. . . Property does become clothed with a public interest when used in a manner to make it a public consequence and affect the community at large. When, therefore, one devotes his property to a use in which the public has an interest, he, in effect, grants to the public an interest in that use and must submit to be controlled by the public for the common good to the extent of the interest he has thus created. He may withdraw

236

his grant by discontinuing the use; but, so long as he maintains the use, he must submit to the control. . . .

✻ 47

Nebbia v. New York
U.S. Supreme Court
291 U.S. 502 (1934)

> *Nebbia affirmed the public's right to regulate virtually anything which the Legislature chose to regulate. Any other narrow criteria (e.g., a "utility") were not binding.*

Mr. Justice Roberts.   The Legislature of New York established by Chapter 158 of the Laws of 1933 a Milk Control Board with power, among other things, to "fix minimum and maximum . . . retail prices to be charged by . . . stores to consumers for consumption off the premises. . . ." The Board fixed nine cents as the price to be charged by a store for a quart of milk. Nebbia, the proprietor of a grocery store in Rochester, sold two quarts and a five-cent loaf of bread for eighteen cents; and was convicted for violating the Board's order. At his trial he asserted the statute and order contravene the equal protection clause and the due process clause of the Fourteenth Amendment and renewed the contention in successive appeals to the county court and the Court of Appeals. Both overruled his claim and affirmed the conviction.

The question for decision is whether the Federal Constitution prohibits a state from so fixing the selling price of milk.

The Fifth Amendment, in the field of federal activity, and the Fourteenth, as respects state action, do not prohibit governmental regulation for the public welfare. They merely condition the exertion of the admitted power, by securing that the end shall be accomplished by methods consistent with due process. . . .

But we are told that because the law essays to control prices it denies due process. . . . The argument runs that the public control of rates or prices is per se unreasonable and unconstitutional, save as applied to businesses affected with a public interest; that a business so affected is one in which property undertakes, or one whose owner relies on a public grant or franchise for the right to conduct the business, or in which he is bound to serve all who apply; in short, such as is commonly called a public utility; or a business in its nature a monopoly. The milk industry, it is said, possesses none of these characteristics, and, therefore, not being affected with a public interest, its charges may not be controlled by the state. Upon the soundness of this contention the appellant's case against the statute depends.

The statement that one has dedicated his property to a public use is, therefore, merely another way of saying that if one embarks in a business which public interest demands shall be regulated, he must know regulation will ensue.

In the same volume the court sustained regulation of railroad rates. After referring to the fact that railroads are carriers for hire, are incorporated as such, and given extraordinary powers in order that they may better serve the public, it was said that they are engaged in employment "affecting the public interest," and therefore, under the doctrine of the Munn case, subject to legislative control as to rates. And in another of the group of railroad cases then heard it is said that the property of railroads is "clothed with a public interest" which permits legislative limitation of the charges for its use. Plainly the activities of railroads, their charges and practices, so nearly touch the vital economic interests of society that the police power may be invoked to regulate their charges, and no additional formula of affection or clothing with a public interest is needed to justify the regulation. And this is evidently true of all business units supplying transportation, light, heat, power, and water to communities, irrespective of how they obtain their powers.

The touchstone of public interest in any business, its practices and charges, clearly is not the enjoyment of any franchise from the state. . . .

Many other decisions show that the private character of a business does not necessarily remove it from the realm of regulation of charges or prices. The usury laws fix the price which may be exacted for the use of money, although no business more essentially private in character can be imagined than that of loaning one's personal funds. . . . Insurance agents' compensation may be regulated, though their contracts are private, because the business of insurance is considered one properly subject to public control. . . . Statutes prescribing in the public interest the amounts to be charged by attorneys for prosecuting certain claims, a matter ordinarily one of personal and private nature, are not a deprivation of due process. . . . A stockyards corporation, "while not a common carrier, nor engaged in any distinctively public employment, is doing a work in which the public has an interest," and its charges may be controlled. . . . Private contract carriers who do not operate under a franchise and have no monopoly of the carriage of goods or passengers may, since they use the highways to compete with railroads, be compelled to charge rates not lower than those of public carriers for corresponding services, if the state, in pursuance of a public policy to protect the latter, so determines.

So far as the requirement of due process is concerned and in the absence of other constitutional restriction, a state is free to adopt whatever economic policy may reasonably be deemed to promote public welfare and to enforce that policy by legislation adapted to its purpose. The courts are without authority either to declare such policy or, when it is declared by the legislature, to override it. If the laws passed are seen to have a reasonable relation to a proper legislative purpose and are neither arbitrary nor discriminatory, the requirements of due process are satisfied, and judicial determination to that effect renders a court functus officio. "Whether the free operation of the normal laws of competition is a wise and wholesome rule for trade and commerce is an economic question which this court need not consider or determine." *Northern Securities Co.* v. *United States*, 193 U.S. 197, 337–38. And it is equally clear that if the legislative policy be to curb unrestrained and harmful competition by measures which are not arbitrary or discriminatory it does not lie with the courts to determine that the rule is unwise. With the wisdom of the policy adopted, with the adequacy or practicability of the law enacted to forward it, the courts are both incompetent and unauthorized to deal. The course of decision in this court exhibits a firm adherence to these principles.

Tested by these considerations we find no basis in the due process clause of the Fourteenth Amendment for condemning the provisions of the Agriculture and Markets Law here drawn into question.

Roger C. Cramton (1929–   )

❧ 48

The Effectiveness of Economic Regulation: A Legal View*

Cramton poses the simplest and most important question about regulation: What are its effects?

Some time ago I came across a quotation which ever since has been weighing on my mind. It is reported to have been spoken by an aged West Coast Indian, sitting on a rock and looking out to sea, under circumstances which I do not know. It reads as follows: "Lighthouse, him no good for fog. Lighthouse, him whistle, him blow, him ring bell, him flash light, him raise hell; but fog come in just the same." . . .

The most basic question one can ask about economic regulation is whether it makes a difference in the behavior of the regulated industry. . . . The net effect of the busy humming of the regulatory machinery may be only to irritate entrepreneurs and to enrich their lawyers, without effecting a fundamental alteration in the state of affairs that would have existed in the absence of regulation.

A moment's thought will indicate why the economic effect of regulation is essentially independent of the content of formal regulation. The regulation may prohibit conduct which no one desires to engage in or it may encourage conduct which will take place anyway. Even if the regulation deals with conduct that would take a different course in the absence of regulation, it is always possible that the objective so devoutly desired by the regulators will not be achieved. The regulatory machinery may be too cumbersome or the ingenuity of circumvention too great. In order to determine whether the observed economic behavior in a particular industry is due to the existence of regulation, the possible effect of regulation must be isolated from other factors influencing behavior.

The significance of individual regulatory actions cannot be judged by the number of lawyers or regulators engaged in the fray, the heat of the

*Roger C. Cramton, "The Effectiveness of Economic Regulation: A Legal View," *American Economic Review*, May 1963, excerpted from pp. 182–89. Cramton is now Dean of the Cornell Law School.

battle, or the length of the struggle. These external indicia have little relationship to the economic significance of the proceeding. It is a safe generalization that many of the most time-consuming and expensive controversies in regulatory annals have had little economic or social significance—other than as tribal rites which lend legitimacy to conduct that otherwise might be viewed as antisocial behavior. On the other hand, some regulatory actions, which may or may not be accompanied by formal proceedings, elaborate trappings, and controversial publicity, are of great economic importance.

There are inherent limitations on the effectiveness of economic regulation even where public policy is fairly clear and the regulatory task, relatively speaking, is confined and manageable. The simpler case of economic regulation—the determination of maximum rates of a conventional public utility—has not been performed with obvious success. I do not assert that public utility regulation has been a failure. I do maintain, however, that unqualified assertions of its effectiveness would be unwarranted. The lesson of a half-century of experience is that the environment generates enduring problems which limit the potential effectiveness of rate regulation.

The regulation of interstate telephone rates by the Federal Communications Commission during the period 1953 through 1962 illustrates the general proposition. The objectives are clear and limited; and the methods are traditional and well established. Yet a detailed look at the methods and mechanics of regulation suggests strong doubts concerning its effectiveness: Disputed issues have been compromised by the Commission after private negotiation with the Bell System; standards for determining allowable expense, items includible in investment, and cost of capital have never been determined; and a relatively high rate of return of 7.5 percent over an extended period has encouraged investors to treat AT&T stock as a growth rather than as an income security. The FCC has never even explained or attempted to justify this state of affairs.

I do not offer this as a demonstration of the ineffectiveness of federal telephone regulation. My thesis is that this pattern is typical, that doubts of similar dimension could be raised concerning the performance of nearly all regulatory schemes. Why is this so? What are the limiting conditions on the effectiveness of economic regulation that emerge from the task itself or that are imposed by the environment in which it operates?

I have spoken of the relative simplicity of conventional public utility regulation in that its purposes are fairly clear and its methods well established. . . . Even so, the complexity of the regulatory task is staggering. The treatment of joint costs in the telephone industry or the explanation of the toll rate disparity between interstate and intrastate rates are problems that tax the abilities of able economists. It is easy to underestimate the difficulty of the problems if one is not responsible for the results nor embarrassed by an overabundance of information.

Inadequacies of personnel and appropriations constitute a second limiting factor that seems to be endemic. A handful of poorly paid employees are asked to perform complex tasks of regulation requiring zeal and imagination. Before long nearly all of the available manpower is tied down in the processing or review of routine matters. Once the immediate needs which produced regulation have been assuaged, the public loses interest, and the agency falls into a routine in which day-to-day accommodations are made with those subject to the regulation.

After the first years of regulation when the initial enthusiasm has been replaced by a convenient reliance on routine solutions, the vague mandate—expressed in terms of some undefined "public interest"—is likely to produce a timid and unimaginative approach. Agency members, who are readily identifiable and exposed to attack, are reluctant to assume tasks of national planning which they or others may feel are beyond their competence or commission. Lack of a clear legislative mandate stultifies administration.

The so-called independence of the regulatory agency is a source of weakness when the agency is not implementing policies that find strong support in a democratic consensus. Isolated from the sources of political power, forced to evolve working arrangements with those it regulates, dependent on Congress for funds and on the President for reappointment, and harassed by an unending succession of congressional investigations and industry pressures, the agency withdraws from committing itself on decisive issues of policy. It drifts along, responding to the most urgent pressures as they arise and perpetuating, for the most part, regulatory patterns which were created in the past to meet different problems. In short, the agency becomes passive, backward-looking, and resistant to change.

An important implication of these general tendencies is that the more passive functions of protectionism are more effectively implemented than the affirmative functions of planning, development, and coordination.

*   *   *   *   *

B. ECONOMIC CRITERIA AND EFFECTS

―――――――――――――― ✳ ――――――――――――――

Early regulation lacked clear economic guidelines. The *Smyth* v. *Ames* decision was an attempt to set good criteria, but it failed. Only some 46 years later did the *Hope* decision end the confusion and near-paralysis of regulation by giving regulators a free hand.

The basic pricing criteria are stated by Alfred E. Kahn in his landmark textbook. As the selection here shows, marginal cost is central. Various exceptions may be needed, but the basic role of marginal cost remains. Regulation may induce the utility firm to use too much capital. This "rate-base effect" was first clearly analyzed by Averch and Johnson in 1962. Many utilities and regulators deny that a rate-base effect occurs, but its validity has withstood intense debate. The remaining question is whether the effect is large or small from case to case.

✳ 49

Smyth v. *Ames*
U.S. Supreme Court
169 U.S. 466 (1898)

The criteria for regulation were here garbled and confused so much that regulation was virtually stalled for several decades. Which criteria listed here are (1) inappropriate on economic grounds, (2) unworkable, and or (3) mutually conflicting?

. . . We hold, however, that the basis of all calculations as to the reasonableness of rates must be the fair value of the property being used by it for the convenience of the public. And in order to ascertain that value, the original cost of construction, the amount expended in permanent improvements, the amount and market value of its bonds and

243

stock, the present as compared with the original cost of construction, the probable earning capacity of the property under particular rates prescribed by statute, and the sum required to meet operating expenses are all matters for consideration and are to be given such weight as may be just and right in each case. We do not say that there may not be other matters to be regarded in estimating the value of the property. What the company is entitled to ask is a fair return upon the value of that which it employs for the public convenience. On the other hand, what the public is entitled to demand is that no more be exacted from it for the use of a public highway than the services rendered by it are reasonably worth. . . .

✳ 50

Federal Power Commission et al. v. Hope Natural Gas Co.

U.S. Supreme Court
320 U.S. 591 (1944)

Here the Court cut through the confusion to give commissions power to regulate on any clear and reasonable criteria.

Mr. Justice Douglas.   The primary issue in these cases concerns the validity under the Natural Gas Act of 1938 (52 Stat. 821, 15 U.S.C., 717) of a rate order issued by the Federal Power Commission reducing the rates chargeable by Hope Natural Gas Co., 44 P.U.R. (N.S.) 1. . . .

Hope is a West Virginia corporation organized in 1898. It is a wholly-owned subsidiary of Standard Oil Co. (N.J.). Since the date of its organization, it has been in the business of producing, purchasing, and marketing natural gas in that state. It sells some of that gas to local consumers in West Virginia. But the great bulk of it goes to five customer companies which receive it at the West Virginia line and distribute it in Ohio and in Pennsylvania. In July 1938 the cities of Cleveland and Akron filed complaints with the Commission charging that the rates collected by Hope from East Ohio Gas Co. (an affiliate of Hope which distributes gas in Ohio) were excessive and unreasonable. Later in 1938 the Commission on its own motion instituted an investigation to determine the reasonableness of all of Hope's interstate rates.

On May 26, 1942, the Commission entered its order and made its findings. Its order required Hope to decrease its future interstate rates so as to reflect a reduction on an annual basis of not less than $3,609,857 in operating revenues. And it established "just and reasonable" average rates per million cubic feet for each of the five customer companies.

Hope contended that it should be allowed a return of not less than 8 percent. The Commission found that an 8-percent return would be unreasonable but that 6½ percent was a fair rate of return. That rate of return, applied to the rate base of $33,712,526, would produce $2,191,314 annually, as compared with the present income of not less than $5,801,171.

The Circuit Court of Appeals set aside the order of the Commission for the following reasons. (1) It held that the rate base should reflect the "present fair value" of the property, that the Commission in determining the "value" should have considered reproduction cost and trended original cost, and that "actual legitimate cost" (prudent investment) was not the proper measure of "fair value" where price levels had changed since the investment. (2) It concluded that the well-drilling costs and overhead items in the amount of some $17,000,000 should have been included in the rate base. (3) It held that accrued depletion and depreciation and the annual allowance for that expense should be computed on the basis of "present fair value" of the property, not on the basis of "actual legitimate cost."

We held in *Federal Power Commission* v. *Natural Gas Pipeline Co., supra,* that the Commission was not bound to the use of any single formula or combination of formulae in determining rates. Its rate-making function, moreover, involves the making of "pragmatic adjustments." And when the Commission's order is challenged in the courts, the question is whether that order "viewed in its entirety" meets the requirements of the Act. . . . Under the statutory standard of "just and reasonable" it is the result reached not the method employed which is controlling. . . . It is not theory but the impact of the rate order which counts. If the total effect of the rate order cannot be said to be unjust and unreasonable, judicial inquiry under the Act is at an end. The fact that the method employed to reach that result may contain infirmities is not then important. Moreover, the Commission's order does not become suspect by reason of the fact that it is challenged. It is the product of expert judgment which carries a presumption of validity. And he who would upset the rate order under the Act carries the heavy burden of making a convincing showing that it is invalid because it is unjust and unreasonable in its consequences. . . .

The rate-making process under the Act, i.e., the fixing of "just and reasonable" rates, involves a balancing of the investor and the consumer interests. Thus we stated in the *Natural Gas Pipeline Co.* case that "regulation does not insure that the business shall produce net revenues." But such considerations aside, the investor interest has a legitimate concern with the financial integrity of the company whose rates are being regulated. From the investor or company point of view it is important that there be enough revenue not only for operating expenses but also for the capital costs of the business. These include service on the debt and dividends on the stock.

. . . By that standard the return to the equity owner should be commensurate with returns on investments in other enterprises having corresponding risks. That return, moreover, should be sufficient to assure confidence in the financial integrity of the enterprise, so as to maintain its credit and to attract capital. The conditions under which more or less might be allowed are not important here. Nor is it important to this case to determine the various permissible ways in which any rate base on which the return is computed might be arrived at. For we are of the view that the end result in this case cannot be condemned under the Act as unjust and unreasonable from the investor or company viewpoint.

In view of these various considerations we cannot say that an annual return of $2,191,314 is not "just and reasonable" within the meaning of the Act. Rates which enable the company to operate successfully, to maintain its financial integrity, to attract capital, and to compensate its investors for the risks assumed certainly cannot be condemned as invalid, even though they might produce only a meager return on the so-called fair value rate base. In that connection it will be recalled that Hope contended for a rate base of $66,000,000 computed on reproduction cost new. The Commission points out that if that rate base were accepted, Hope's average rate of return for the four-year period from 1937–40 would amount to 3.27 percent. During that period Hope earned an annual average return of about 9 percent on the average investment. It asked for no rate increases. Its properties were well maintained and operated. As the Commission says, such a modest rate of 3.27 percent suggests an "inflation of the base on which the rate has been computed." . . . The incongruity between the actual operations and the return computed on the basis of reproduction cost suggests that the Commission was wholly justified in rejecting the latter as the measure of the rate base.

Alfred E. Kahn (1917–   )

✻ 51

The Economics of Regulation*

> *Kahn here treats marginal-cost pricing and then argues that the Averch-Johnson "rate-base effect" (see below) is probably a good thing, not a cause of waste.*

THE CENTRAL ECONOMIC PRINCIPLE: MARGINAL COST PRICING

The central policy prescription of microeconomics is the equation of price and marginal cost. If economic theory is to have any relevance to public utility pricing, that is the point at which the inquiry must begin.

As almost any student of elementary economics will recall, marginal cost is the cost of producing one more unit; it can equally be envisaged as the cost that would be saved by producing one less unit. Looked at the first way, it may be termed incremental cost—the added cost of (a small amount of) incremental output. Observed in the second way, it is synonymous with avoidable cost—the cost that would be saved by (slightly) reducing output. . . .

If consumers are to make the choices that will yield them the greatest possible satisfaction from society's limited aggregate productive capacity, the prices that they pay for the various goods and services available to them must accurately reflect their respective opportunity costs; only then will buyers be judging, in deciding what to buy and what not, whether the satisfaction they get from the purchase of any particular product is worth the sacrifice of other goods and services that its production entails. If their judgments are correctly informed in this way, they will, by their independent purchase decisions, guide our scarce re-

*Excerpted from *The Economics of Regulation,* Alfred E. Kahn, vol. I, pp. 65–66, 75, 83–85, 95, 98–100, and vol. II, pp. 106–107. Copyright © 1971 John Wiley & Sons, Inc. Reprinted by permission of John Wiley & Sons, Inc. Something of a universal force in the field, Kahn has written widely on antitrust, patents, the oil industry, and even the British economy, as well as producing this major text. He has also been Dean of the Cornell University faculty, Chairman of the New York Public Service Commission (1974–77), and Chairman of the Civil Aeronautics Board during 1977–78.

sources into those lines of production that yield more satisfaction than all available alternatives—which means that total satisfaction will be maximized.

. . . The economic principles are clear-cut. They are two. First, the essential criterion of what belongs in marginal cost and what not, and of which marginal costs should be reflected in price, is causal responsibility. All the purchasers of any commodity or service should be made to bear such additional costs—*only* such, but also *all* such—as are imposed on the economy by the provision of one additional unit. And second, it is short-run marginal cost to which price should at any given time— *hence always*—be equated, because it is short-run marginal cost that reflects the social opportunity cost of providing the additional unit that buyers are at any given time trying to decide whether to buy.

Specifying the Incremental Block of Output

The level of incremental cost per unit depends, also, on the size of the increment. Consider the passenger airplane flight already scheduled with the plane on the runway, fueled up and ready to depart, but with its seats not completely filled. The incremental unit of service in this case might be defined as the carrying of an extra passenger on that flight—in which case, the marginal cost would be practically zero. It was just such a marginal cost calculation, involving the smallest possible number of additional units and the shortest possible run, that underlay the introduction of standby youth fares by some American airlines in 1966— half-price for young people willing to come out to the airport and take their chances of finding an empty seat on their flight ten minutes before departure time.

Or is the incremental unit in question the particular scheduled flight, taken as a whole, involving the carrying of 50 or 100 passengers between a particular pair of cities at a particular time? If the plane must fly anyhow as long as the flight is scheduled, the additional cost of taking on all the passengers is still practically zero. But schedules can be changed in the comparatively short run, in which event the relevant marginal costs of a particular flight include all the costs of flying the plane as compared with not flying it. Or is the incremental unit of sales the provision of regular service between a pair of cities, involving an entire schedule of flights? In this case, still more costs enter into the marginal calculation—airport rentals, ticket offices, the cost of advertising in local newspapers, indeed the cost of the planes themselves, which need not be acquired or can be used in other service. The larger the incremental unit of service under consideration, the more costs become variable. . . .

TEMPERING PRINCIPLE WITH PRACTICALITY—OR ONE PRINCIPLE WITH ANOTHER

The outcome of this entire discussion about the problems of defining (as contrasted with actually measuring and applying) marginal cost is that neither the choice between short- and long-run, nor the problem of defining the incremental unit of sale, nor the prevalence of common and joint costs raises any difficulties in principle about the economically efficient price. It is set at the short-run marginal cost of the smallest possible additional unit of sale. Common costs do not preclude separable marginal production costs, and joint products have separate marginal opportunity costs.

But, as we have already suggested, short-run marginal costs (SRMC) are the place to begin. There are situations in which it is both efficient and practical to base rates on them, as we shall see. Typically, this is not the case; principle must be compromised in various ways in the interest of practicality, for a number of interrelated reasons:

1. It is often infeasible or prohibitively expensive for businesses to make the necessary fine calculations of marginal cost for each of their numerous categories of service.

2. Marginal costs will vary from one moment to the next in a world of perpetually changing demand as firms operate at perpetually changing points on their SRMC functions (unless marginal costs happen to be constant, that is, horizontal) and between far wider extremes than either average variable or average total costs. [They] will vary also because cost functions themselves are constantly shifting. Thus, it would be prohibitively costly to the seller to put into effect the highly refined and constantly changing pricing schedules, reflecting in minute detail the different short-run marginal costs of different sales. It would also be highly vexatious to buyers, who would be quick to find discrimination in departures from uniform prices, who would be put to great expense to be informed about prices that were constantly changing, and whose ability to make rational choices and plan intelligently for the future would be seriously impaired.

3. For these reasons the practically achievable version of SRMC pricing is often likely to be pricing at *average* variable costs (AVC), themselves averaged over some period of time in the past and assumed to remain constant over some period in the future—until there occurs some clear, discrete shift caused by an event such as a change in wage rates. But since short-term AVC (in contrast with SRMC) are never as large as average total costs, . . . universal adoption of this type of pricing is infeasible if sellers are to cover total costs, including (as always) a minimum required return on investment. This in turn produces a strong

tendency in industry to price on a "full cost" basis—usually computed at AVC (really *average* AVC over some period of time) plus some percentage mark-up judged sufficient to cover total costs on the average over some time period—a far cry, indeed, from marginal cost pricing.

4. SRMC can be above or below ATC, as we have seen; but whether it is above often enough for businesses pricing on that basis to cover total costs on the average depends on the average relationship over time between demand and production capacity. As J. M. Clark has often pointed out, excess capacity is the typical condition of modern industry, and we would probably want this to be the case in public utilities, which we tend to insist be perpetually in a position to supply whatever demands are placed on them. In these circumstances, firms could far more often be operating at the point where SRMC is less than ATC than the reverse, and if they based their prices exclusively on the former, they would have to find some other means of making up the difference. Partly for this reason and partly because of the infeasibility of permitting prices to fluctuate widely along the SRMC function, depending on the immediate relation of demand to capacity, the practically achievable benchmark for efficient pricing is more likely to be a type of average long-run incremental cost, computed for a large, expected incremental block of sales, instead of SRMC, estimated for a single additional sale. This long-run incremental cost (which we shall loosely refer to as long-run marginal cost as well) would be based on (1) the average incremental variable costs of those added sales and (2) estimated additional capital costs per unit, for the additional capacity that will have to be constructed if sales at that price are expected to continue over time or to grow. Both of these components would be estimated as averages over some period of years extending into the future.

5. The prevalence of common costs has similar implications. Service A bears a causal responsibility for a share of common costs only if there is an economically realistic alternative use of the capacity now used to provide it or if production of A requires the building of additional capacity. The marginal opportunity cost of serving A depends on how much the alternative users would be willing to pay for devoting the capacity to serving them instead. The sum of the separable marginal costs will therefore cover the common costs only if at separate prices less than this the claims on the capacity exceed the available supply.

6. Long-run marginal costs are likely to be the preferred criterion also in competitive situations. Permitting rate reductions to a lower level of SRMC, which would prove to be unremunerative if the business thus attracted were to continue over time, might constitute predatory competition—driving out of business rivals whose *long-run* costs of production might well be lower than those of the price-cutter. . . .

Public utility companies do employ peak-responsibility pricing to some degree. The telephone companies charge lower rates for night than for daytime long-distance calls; electric companies frequently have low night rates for hot-water heating; both they and natural gas companies—local distributors and interstate pipelines alike—offer at lower rates service that the customer will agree may be interrupted if capacity is being taxed by other users and try to promote off-peak sales in numerous ways; railroads charge lower rates for return-hauls of freight, when the greater flow is in the opposite direction; airlines offer special discount fares—family plans, youth fares, and so forth—for travel on unfilled planes or in slack seasons or days of the week.

Although most public utility executives and regulators recognize that peak responsibility pricing has some validity, probably most would also vigorously resist its wholehearted acceptance. William G. Shepherd's survey disclosed that the majority of American electric utilities practice little or no explicit marginal cost pricing, and among those that do, the main emphasis is on raising off-peak sales by charging them something less than average capacity costs instead of purposefully imposing all the capacity charges on the peak users.[1] He found, moreover, that publicly owned companies, if anything, follow marginalist and peak responsibility principles even less than private; and that electric utilities in states with "tough" regulatory commissions, such as New York and California, similarly incorporate little marginalism in their rate structures.

An outstanding illustration of the resistance of strong regulatory commissions is provided by the Federal Power Commission's formula for natural gas pipeline rate-making specified in its famous *Atlantic Seaboard* decision of 1952. The distinctive feature of the *Atlantic Seaboard* formula is that it requires that capacity costs be distributed 50–50 between the demand and commodity charges instead of incorporated exclusively in the former. Since the demand costs are distributed among customers in proportion to their shares in the volume of sales at the system's (three-day) peak, while the commodity costs are borne in proportion to their annual volume of purchases, the consequence of the 50–50 formula is to shift a large proportion of capacity costs to off-peak users. This produces an uneconomic encouragement to sales at the peak (whose price falls short of the true marginal costs of peak service) and an uneconomic discouragement of off-peak. (In fairness, it should be pointed out that the FPC has permitted departures from this strict formula when it appeared that the pipelines would suffer large losses of interruptible, off-peak sales at the inflated commodity charges it produced—permitting them instead to "tilt" the rate schedule downward on the commodity side of the balance. Among other alleged harmful

---

[1] "Marginal Cost Pricing in American Utilities," *Southern Economic Journal*, July 1966, pp. 58–70.

consequences of *Atlantic Seaboard* has been a tendency to discourage distribution companies from installing storage capacity: demand and commodity charges more fully reflecting the true respective marginal costs of peak and off-peak purchases would have increased their incentive to "shave" their purchases at the former by installing storage which they could fill by low-cost purchases off-peak and draw on at the peak.

We present two last examples of the pervasive uneconomic departure from peak responsibility pricing. First, commutation books and other such devices that give commuters quantity discounts on passenger trains and toll bridges have the consequence that occasional travelers, who usually travel off-peak, pay a higher rate than commuters, who concentrate their traveling in the rush hours. Second, airplane landing fees do not reflect the enormous variations in airport congestion from one time of day, day of the week, or one airport to another. These variations themselves doubtless tend to induce air travelers and airplane companies to rearrange their traveling plans and schedules to avoid peak hours and locations and make fuller use of off-peak time; equivalently varying landing fees could make a further contribution. . . .

[The Averch-Johnson (A–J–W) "Rate Base" Effect]

If regulation were instantaneously effective, it would eliminate this restrictive effect of monopoly; and that is precisely what it is supposed to do. The economic purpose of holding price to average total cost, including only a competitive return on investment, is to produce the competitive level of investment and output. . . .

But the fact is, as we have seen, that regulation is not instantaneously effective. Public utility companies therefore do have some opportunity to choose between higher and lower rates of profit at correspondingly lower and higher respective rates of output. . . .

As an offset to monopoly, the A–J–W distortion probably does more good than harm. It encourages risk-taking and output-expanding investment. We have earlier suggested that one possible manifestation of the A–J–W effect is some reluctance of public utilities to adopt thoroughgoing peak-responsibility pricing: If peak users can be charged less than the full capacity costs for which they are (marginally) responsible, this "justifies" a greater capacity and a larger rate base, the costs of which can then be recouped partially from off-peak users. But it is precisely with respect to such investments that monopoly has heretofore been accused of producing excessive conservatism.

*   *   *   *   *

Harvey A. Averch
Leland L. Johnson (1930–   )

✦ 52

Behavior of the Firm under Regulatory Constraint*

The "Averch-Johnson effect" sprang full-grown from this landmark article in 1962. There are really two effects: Regulation may induce the firm (1) to waste capital and (2) to capture adjacent markets by pricing for low or even negative profitability ("cut-throat" pricing). Despite efforts to refute or dilute these points, they stand largely intact. The second effect, though neglected, may be the more important.

The purpose here is (a) to develop a theory of the monopoly firm seeking to maximize profit but subject to such a constraint on its rate of return, and (b) to apply the model to one particular regulated industry—the domestic telephone and telegraph industry. We conclude in the theoretical analysis that a "regulatory bias" operates in the following manner: (1) The firm does not equate marginal rates of factor substitution to the ratio of factor costs; therefore, the firm operates inefficiently in the sense that (social) cost is not minimized at the output it selects. (2) The firm has an incentive to expand into other regulated markets, even if it operates at a (long-run) loss in these markets; therefore, it may drive out other firms, or discourage their entry into these other markets, even though the competing firms may be lower-cost producers. Applying the theoretical analysis to the telephone and telegraph industry, we find that the model does raise issues relevant to evaluating market behavior.

I. THE SINGLE-MARKET MODEL

First we shall consider a geometrical and a mathematical framework showing the effect of the regulatory constraint on the cost curves of the

*Harvey A. Averch and Leland L. Johnson, "Behavior of the Firm under Regulatory Constraint," *American Economic Review,* December 1962, excerpted from pp. 1052–59 and 1068. A brief retrospect by Johnson is also included: "A Reassessment," *American Economic Review,* May 1973, excerpted from pp. 91 and 95–96. A RAND staff member, Johnson is a leading expert on the economics of telecommunications, including satellites and cable TV as well as more traditional issues. Averch has also done research on economic development.

firm employing two factors. The essential characteristic to be demonstrated is: If the rate of return allowed by the regulatory agency is greater than the cost of capital but is less than the rate of return that would be enjoyed by the firm were it free to maximize profit without regulatory constraint, then the firm will substitute capital for the other factor of production and operate at an output where cost is not minimized.

FIGURE 1

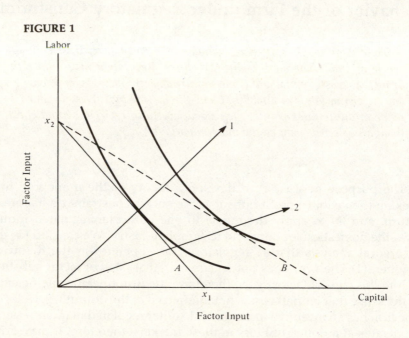

Figure 1 denotes the firm's production where capital x_1 is plotted on the horizontal axis and labor x_2 on the vertical axis. The market or "social" cost of capital and labor generates the isocost curve A and the *unregulated* firm would move along expansion path 1 where market cost is minimized for any given output. With regulation, however, the cost of capital to the firm—the "private" cost—is no longer equal to market cost. For each additional unit of capital input, the firm is permitted to earn a profit (equal to the difference between the market cost of capital and rate of return allowed by the regulatory agency) that it otherwise would have to forego. Therefore, private cost is less than market cost by an amount equal to this difference. The effect of regulation is analogous to that of changing the relative prices of capital x_1 and labor x_2: isocost curve B becomes relevant and the firm moves along expansion path 2—a path along which market cost is not minimized for any given output.

FIGURE 2

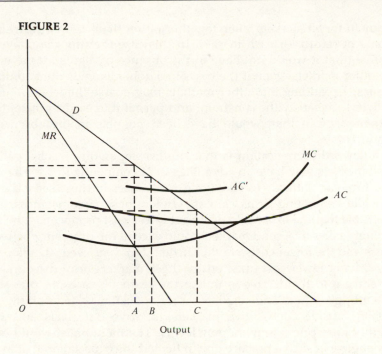

Output

The firm finds path 2 advantageous simply because it is along that path that the firm is able to maximize total profit given the constraint on its rate of return. . . .

The firm adjusts to the constraint, then, by substituting capital for the cooperating factor and by expanding total output. Comparative equilibrium outputs are shown in Figure 2. If the regulated firm were constrained to move along the socially efficient expansion path 1 in Figure 1, it would operate at OC in Figure 2. Here price is slightly above average cost AC to reflect the fact that $s_1 > r_1$ (profit is not entirely eliminated). Since the regulated firm moves along path 2, the social cost curve rises from AC to AC', and the regulatory constraint is satisfied at the lower output OB. The effect of regulation is to force the firm to expand output from the unregulated position OA, but output does not expand to C because a portion of what would otherwise be profit is absorbed by cost. The extent to which regulation affects output depends upon the nature of the production function.

II. THE MULTIMARKET CASE

Suppose that in addition to operating in a single market the firm can also enter other regulated markets and that the regulatory agency bases its "fair rate of return" criterion on the firm's overall value of plant and equipment for all markets taken together rather than computing a separate rate of return for each market. In this case the firm may have an incentive (that it would not have in the absence of regulation) to enter these other markets, even if the cost of so doing exceeds the additional revenues. Expanding into other markets may enable the firm to inflate its rate base to satisfy the constraint and permit it to earn a greater total constrained profit than would have been possible in the absence of second markets.

A noteworthy implication is that the firm operating in oligopolistic second markets may have an advantage over competing firms. The regulated firm can "afford" to take (long-run) losses in these second markets while competing firms cannot. Under these circumstances, it is conceivable that the firm could drive out lower-cost producers—the loss it willingly takes in second markets could exceed the difference between its costs and the lower costs of other firms. It may succeed, therefore, in either driving lower cost firms out of these markets or of discouraging their entry into them. This is unlike the textbook case of "predatory price-cutting" where the regulated monopolist may temporarily cut prices in outside competitive markets to drive out rivals and subsequently raise prices to monopoly levels. The monopolist would ordinarily engage in such a practice only if he had the expectation that in the long run he would make a positive profit in these additional markets; but here even in the case of a long-run loss the regulated firm may find operations in such markets to be advantageous as long as the firm is permitted to include its capital input in these markets in its rate base.

. . . While the unregulated firm would be indifferent about operating in market 2, the regulated firm in this example finds market 2 attractive because it can add capital to the rate base at "no loss"; i.e., for any capital input in market 2 the output generates revenues just equal to factor cost. Since in market 2 the actual cost of capital is below the allowed rate of return, the firm can apply the difference in satisfying the constraint in market 1 and thereby enjoy additional profit equal to $s_1 - r_1$ for each unit of capital in market 2.

This analysis suggests that even if the firm suffers a loss in market 2 (measured in terms of social costs r_1 and r_2) it may still operate there provided the value of x_{12} ($s_1 - r_1$) exceeds this level of loss. If it suffers a loss it would no longer operate in market 1 at the profit-maximizing output OA in Figure 1; seeking to equate the marginal value product of capital in both markets, it would move toward OB.

III. THE TELEPHONE AND TELEGRAPH INDUSTRY

Turning to the domestic telephone and telegraph industry, we find that the market structure and the regulatory setting are consistent with those described in the model. And the implications drawn from the model, concerning relative factor inputs and incentives to operate in some markets even at a loss, raise issues relevant to assessing market behavior of firms in the industry. . . .

IV. CONCLUSIONS

The preceding analysis discloses that a misallocation of economic resources may result from the use by regulatory agencies of the rate-of-return constraint for price control. The firm has an incentive to substitute between factors in an uneconomic fashion that is difficult for the regulatory agency to detect. Moreover, if a large element of common costs exists for the firm's outputs in the various markets, the widely used "fully allocated" cost basis for rate-of-return computation is likely to prove satisfactory in determining whether the firm is operating at a loss in any given market, or whether its activities in some markets tend to restrict competition in an undesirable manner. At the same time, regulatory practices that provide an incentive for the firm to operate in some markets even at a loss may constitute a convenient mechanism through which certain activities of the firm judged to be in the "public interest" can be subsidized.

*   *   *   *   *

[From Johnson, "A Reassessment" (1973)]

In light of the extensive discussion over the past decade, it seems fair to say that the Averch-Johnson analysis, given its assumptions, remains valid on theoretical grounds. But the question remains about the importance of overcapitalization and cross-subsidization in reality. Are the Averch-Johnson effects merely an intellectual curiosity, or do they describe serious distortions in the behavior of regulated firms? Unfortunately the answer is not clear. It is not enough to compare the behavior of regulated and unregulated firms because, as mentioned above, the capital-labor ratio of the regulated firm is not necessarily greater than that of the unregulated monopolist. The search for goldplating and obviously wasteful use of capital is likely to prove fruitless since, within the regulatory constraint, the firm does seek to use capital in a manner that produces additional revenue.

To the extent that Averch-Johnson effects operate, they do so subtly: The firm can engage in activities for a number of reasons that seem plausible; to separate the real from the merely plausible reasons is not easy. . . .

With respect to regulatory lags, as [Elizabeth] Bailey and Roger Coleman point out, the longer the firm must wait for an increase in rates to bring the allowable rate of return to a point above the market cost of capital, the less incentive the firm has to add to rate base in the interim; for during the time lag it suffers a loss that only eventually will be compensated.

However, it is useful to distinguish between two kinds of regulatory lags. The first I shall call Type I to describe the situation in which the firm is caught in a general inflationary spiral leading eventually to rate increases. It is this kind of lag that would dampen incentives to over-capitalize, and it is this kind of lag with which so many utilities are faced today as a consequence of the strong inflationary forces that have persisted since the mid-1960s. Under a second kind of lag, which I shall call Type II, the firm is able to enjoy technological advances of such magnitude and/or such large economies of scale in the face of growing demand that its unit costs fall in spite of inflationary forces. This situation leads eventually to rate decreases rather than increases. It is under Type II lags that one would expect overcapitalization to emerge most clearly. In the extreme case, by sufficient overcapitalization, the firm could remain within the range of a fair rate of return and postpone indefinitely pressures by the regulatory agency to reduce rates.

The differences in the cases in which firms seek or avoid capital investment are, I would conjecture, traceable in part to whether Type I or Type II lags are at work. Today, Type I lags are far more evident than they were a decade ago. Hence the potential for overcapitalization is probably less than it was in 1962 when the Averch-Johnson model was formulated.

C. THE POWER SECTOR

There have been rapid changes in both electricity and gas, making several earlier landmark cases obsolete. One broad change is toward time-of-day electric prices, in line with marginal cost principles. Wisconsin's Commission has been a leader in this direction, and the decision excerpted here (in the *WEPCO* case) shows the main lines of the new rate design.

Another issue is whether a small town publicly owned electric system can be denied fair access to power supply by the surrounding large private electric firm. In the *Otter Tail* decision of 1973, the Court said no. The issue affects many hundreds of comparable systems across the country. In fact, a degree of competition in wholesale (or "bulk") electric power could be directly encouraged, according to Leonard W. Weiss. His analysis shows that such competition could be vigorous, perhaps improving the efficiency of the sector.

In gas pipelines, also, competition can be valuable. The marathon *El Paso* case ensured that a new entrant, Pacific Northwest, would not be captured by a preexisting dominant gas supplier in the Pacific coast area. (The case took nearly 20 years to complete, including 5 times up to the Supreme Court.) Natural gas production at the well-head is far from a natural monopoly, but it has been under federal regulation since 1954. A complex area system of pricing was developed by the Federal Power Commission in the *Permian Basin* case of 1963. Later, uniform national prices were set. In 1978, Congress was on the verge of acting to remove regulation. Yet there may be substantial monopoly power in that market, as John W. Wilson points out. The issue is still open.

Stephen Breyer and Paul W. MacAvoy suggest that the FPC's regulation of electricity and gas gives the public little net benefits. Good term-paper topics are: Are Breyer and MacAvoy correct? (Work through the procedure in their book and reestimate the magnitudes) and Have changes since then improved the agency's value?

❊ 53

Before the Public Service Commission of Wisconsin: *Wisconsin Electric Power Co.* *

Finding of Fact and Interim Order
Docket 6630–ER–2, 6630–ER–5 (1977)

This case offers three special features. First, it is much more lucidly written than the typical state commission order. Second, it covers the standard categories of a rate decision clearly (rate base, cost of capital, rate of return, revenue requirement, and rate structure). Third, this is one of the leading cases in applying time-of-use pricing, fitted to cost patterns. Note the differences among rates for the customer classes.

The main points are explained nicely, and the reader can gain a good feel for the tone and parts of a skillful state-commission electric rate case of the late 1970s. Still one can ask: Are these rates as efficient as possible? Are they fair? What refinements might be needed? The Concurring Opinion by Chairman Cicchetti sums up the effects of the decision.

On April 26, 1977, applicant filed an application, docketed as 6630–ER–5, with the commission for retail electric service rate relief pursuant to § § 196.03, 196.20 and 196.37, Wis. Stats. The amount of the requested increase was not set forth in the application, but the record as subsequently developed disclosed the requested increase in retail electric rates to be $11,244,000.

Pursuant to due notice, hearings were held in docket no. 6630–ER–2 at Milwaukee on January 6, 1976, before Examiner James A. Spiegel. Hearings continued in Milwaukee on August 1, 2, 3, and 4, 1977, and in Madison on August 5, 8, 15, 16, and 18, 1977.

Also pursuant to due notice, hearings were held in docket no. 6630–ER–5 at Milwaukee on July 12 and on September 6 and 7, 1977, at Madison before Examiner Spiegel.

At such hearings, applicant, staff, and intervenors presented and cross-examined testimony and exhibits concerning cost of service, rate design, revenue requirement, and the cost of capital.

The request for rate relief is granted on an interim basis in the amount of $11,244,000, a 3-percent increase.

---

*Wisconsin's Commission has been a leader in revising electric rate structures along marginal-cost pricing lines. Charles J. Cicchetti, appointed chairman in 1976, has been a leading economic expert on rate design.

FINDINGS OF FACT

The Commission Finds:

Applicant and Its Business

Wisconsin Electric Power Company is an electric public utility as defined in § 196.01, Wis. Stats., engaged in the production, transmission, distribution, and sale of electric energy to approximately 650,000 retail customers in southeastern Wisconsin. The territory served includes the city of Milwaukee and its surrounding area, the cities of Racine, Kenosha, Waukesha, Fort Atkinson, Watertown, West Bend, Whitewater, and various areas of southeastern Wisconsin and parts of upper Michigan. Applicant also sells energy at wholesale to municipal utilities operating in Cedarburg, Deerfield, Elkhorn, Hartford, Jefferson, Kiel, Lake Mills, Oconomowoc, Slinger, and Waterloo. The rates applicable to sales of electric energy at wholesale to municipal utilities for resale, being in interstate commerce, are not subject to the jurisdiction of this commission but are regulated by the Federal Energy Regulatory Commission and hence not affected by these proceedings. Applicant also operates as a steam-heating utility in certain areas of Milwaukee.

A wholly-owned subsidiary, Wisconsin Natural Gas Company, operates as a natural gas distribution utility in various areas in northeastern and southeastern Wisconsin. Applicant and the former Wisconsin Michigan Power Company, a wholly-owned subsidiary, were merged effective December 31, 1977.

Need for Interim Rate Relief

The application in docket no. 6630–ER–5 was filed several months ago and was based on test year 1977. . . .

. . . [I]t is reasonable and just that rate relief be granted at this time, subject to refund, in order to help negate the adverse effects of a revenue deficiency. The estimated income statement for the test year 1977 considered reasonable and just for determining interim revenue requirement in this proceeding is as follows:

Income Statement

	(000)
Operating revenues	$417,117
Operating expenses:	
Fuel expense	$128,735
Pooled power expense	(13,215)
Other operations	77,182
Maintenance expense	43,666
Total Operation and Maintenance Expense	$236,368

Amortization of storm losses	576
Depreciation expense	47,579
Taxes other than income taxes	23,163
Income taxes:	
State	5,142
Federal	21,778
Investment tax credit adj.	9,101
Total operating expenses	$343,707
Net operating income	$ 73,410
Less income tax effect of elimination of interest on debentures allocated to subsidiary	(325)
Adjusted Net Operating Income	$ 73,085

Net Investment Rate Base

The estimated average net investment rate base for the test year 1977 for applicant's electric operations, found reasonable and just for purposes of determining interim rate relief in this proceeding, is as follows:

	(000)
Utility plant in service	$1,158,195
Less: Accumulated provision for depreciation	442,616
Net utility plant	$ 715,579
Add: Materials and supplies	66,941
Less: Contributions in aid of construction	$ 8,500
Net Investment Rate Base	$ 774,020

Earned Rate of Return

Estimated operating income of $73,085,000, when applied to the average net investment rate base of $774,020,000, results in an earned rate of return of 9.44 percent.

Cost of Capital

Applicant's corporate capital structure on December 31, 1977, consists of 43.02 percent common stock equity, 9.15 percent preferred stock, 46.23 percent long-term debt and 1.60 percent notes payable.

Applicant's outstanding issues of preferred stock and debentures are, in part, applicable to its investment in its wholly-owned subsidiary, Wisconsin Natural Gas Company. The commission in past proceedings involving rates for the three utility companies in the Wisconsin Electric Power Company system has properly allocated capital on a consolidated basis so as to follow the commission's procedure for all holding company systems wherein a determination is made as to the source of equity capital in subsidiaries.

WEPCO has requested a return on common stock equity of 13 percent, which was the amount allowed in its last rate order, docket no. 6630–ER–1, dated August 5, 1976. Accordingly, capitalization ratios, annual cost rates and a composite cost of capital rate applicable to electric utility operations of Wisconsin Electric Power Company, which are reasonable and just for purposes of determining interim rates in this proceeding, are as follows:

	Capitalization Ratios	Annual Cost Rate	Weighted Cost
Common stock equity ...	43.02%	13.00%	5.59%
Preferred stock	9.15	7.06	.65
Debt:			
Long-term			
Bonds	43.43	6.66	2.88
Debentures	2.80	7.00	.20
Short-term	1.60	8.00	.13
Composite cost of capital rate	100.00%		9.45%

Rate of Return

Once the composite cost of capital rate has been determined, it is necessary that this rate be translated into a rate of return to be applied to net investment rate base to establish an overall interim return requirement in dollars.

Here the average net investment rate base, plus construction work in progress, is 102.62 percent of capital applicable primarily to utility operations. This figure is reasonable and just in translating the composite cost of capital into a return requirement applicable to net investment rate base.

Applicant presently uses a 7-percent interest during construction rate applied to that portion of construction work in progress which exceeds 10 percent of net investment rate base. The commission has considered this procedure under current conditions and has found in this and other proceedings involving rates of Wisconsin public utilities that it is reasonable and just. The ratio of construction work in progress to electric net investment rate base is 11.65 percent for the test year 1977. An adjustment has been properly included below for this factor.

Accordingly, the rate of return on net investment rate base reasonable and just for the purposes of establishing interim revenue requirement in this proceeding, computed on the basis of the above findings, with an allowance of .05 percent for contributions and miscellaneous corporate expenses, is as follows:

	Electric Utility
Composite cost of capital	9.45%
Average percent of utility net Investment rate base to capital applicable primarily to utility operations	102.62%
Percent return requirement Applicable to net investment rate base (9.45%/102.62%)	9.21%
Adjustment to overall return Requirement of net investment rate base from effect of cost of capital on construction work in progress in excess of recorded interest during construction of 7%	
Electric construction work in progress as percent of net investment rate base	11.65%
Electric construction work in progress bearing interest during construction of 7% as percent of net investment rate base	1.65%
Adjustment to return requirement to provide return on construction work in progress (11.65% x 9.21%) − (1.65% × 7%)	.96%
Allowance for miscellaneous corporate expenses	.05%
Adjusted percent return requirement on net investment rate base	10.22%

Revenue Requirement

On the basis of the above findings, the increase in electric utility revenue for retail electric service under the jurisdiction of this commission considered reasonable and just for purposes of determining interim rates in this proceeding is $11,244,000, computed as follows:

	Electric Utility
Return earned on net investment rate base at present rates	9.44%
Percent rate of return requirement of net investment rate base	10.22%
Deficiency in earnings as a percent of net investment rate base	.78%
Amount of earnings deficiency	$ 6,037,000
Amount of revenue deficiency to provide for earnings deficiency plus increased federal and state income taxes	$12,527,000
Amount of revenue deficiency applicable to jurisdiction of this commission	$11,244,000

Electric Rate Design

Time-of-Day Historical Discussion. This commission has previously made a commitment to time-of-day pricing principles.[1] The lan-

---

[1]Commission Order, *Madison Gas and Electric Co. (Madison Gas)*, docket no. 2–U–7423 (Wis. Public Serv. Comm., Aug. 8, 1974); Commission Order, *Wisconsin Power and Light*, docket no. 2–U–8085 (Public Service Commission Wisconsin 11/12/76)

guage in its August 15, 1975, notice in rule-making docket no. 01–ER–1 contains the following excellent statement of those principles:

> 2. Time-of-day tariff proposals. (1) Any application and evidence submitted by a utility applicant requesting a change in its electric service tariffs shall be considered presumptively deficient if they do not include;
> A proposal for time-of-day tariffs for those customers having existing metering capabilities or present metering capability which can economically be modifiable for time-of-day measurement. Customers included in these categories would be primarily those industrial and large commercial classes.

The time-of-day policy statement and notice of proposed rules, docket no. 01–ER–1, emphasized the need and the benefits obtained by adopting time-of-day pricing.

> The adverse features of rates which are established on the basis of average monthly usage can be greatly mitigated by a time-of-day pricing structure which is not promotional and which properly recovers the cost caused by those customers, both new and old, responsible for the substantial burden of meeting system peaks.[2]

Time-of-day rates are one form of time-of-use rates. There is no disagreement among economists or rate engineers that the cost of providing electricity may vary from minute to minute, from hour to hour, day to day, and by seasons of the year depending on the extent to which the utility's facilities are being utilized. Because the demand for electricity varies widely from one part of the day to another and from season to season, much of the generation and transmission capacity lies idle for substantial periods of time. In addition, utility fuel costs per unit of production vary with the level of demands; as demand increases, the production cost of additional generating capacity increases because the utility dispatches the generating units in the order of increasing unit production costs.

Time-of-use rates give price signals to the customer as to the cost of producing units of electricity according to the time it is used. Seasonal rates are one form of time-of-use rates. A more complicated form of time-of-use rates recognizes changes in costs by time of day (time-of-day rates).

Wisconsin Electric Power Company Time-of-Day Rates

Wisconsin Electric Power Company's rates authorized herein represent a major implementation of time-of-day rates in Wisconsin. Table 1

---

[2]*Policy Statement and Notice of Proposed Rule,* docket no. 01–ER–1 (Wis. Public Serv. Comm., August 15, 1975).

shows the scope of the authorized Wisconsin Electric Power Company time-of-day rates in terms of applicant's Wisconsin retail total number of customers, system coincident peak, and total megawatt-hour consumption. Approximately 38 percent of the power (Wisconsin retail coincident peak) and 47 percent of the energy (Wisconsin retail total megawatt-hour consumption) are affected by the authorized time-of-day rates.

TABLE 1: Wisconsin Electric Power Company Authorized Time-of-Day Rates

Customer Class	Time-of-Date Rates Number of Customers	Coincident Peak Demand MW	Usage MWH
Large residential July 1, 1978	500	5	30,174
General primary January 1, 1978	438	703	4,445,283
Large commercial (general secondary rate code 45)			
July 1, 1978	825	210	901,401
January 1, 1979	825	74	510,513
July 1, 1979	825	37	272,947
Total time-of-day		1,029 (38%)	6,160,318 (47%)
System Total		2,735	13,161,292

Rate Design Considerations.   Rate design is essentially an exercise in opinion and judgment in which the commission is bound by statutory requirements to be nondiscriminatory, reasonable, and just. The commission has consistently followed certain rate design guidelines and principles which have been developed over time and are widely used. Such rate design criteria include:

1.   Cost-based rates.
2.   Simplicity and ease of understanding.
3.   Freedom from interpretation controversy.
4.   Yielding of the revenue requirement.
5.   Revenue stability from year to year.
6.   Historical rate structure continuity.
7.   Fair apportionment of the cost of service.
8.   Avoidance of discrimination.
9.   Discouraging of wasteful use while promoting justified types and quantities of use.

This list is far from exhaustive. The criteria for a sound or desirable rate structure are difficult to apply precisely. Formulating a rate structure is both an art and a science, requiring a judgmental weighing of the various rate design criteria. This proceeding also considers the economic, social, and physical environmental impact of rate design.

Customer Class Revenue Levels

Customer class revenue levels were adjusted to yield total revenues of approximately $409,235,784. The rates authorized herein provide a $11,221,322 revenue increase for the test year. Total retail revenues are increased by 2.8 percent. The authorized rates result in approximately equal increases in class revenue levels.

Staff's and Wisconsin Electric Power Company's class revenue level proposals are shown in Table 2, columns 6 and 7 respectively. Staff proposed to move the class revenue levels toward cost in a step-by-step fashion. According to the staff's proposal, it would take three rate cases to align class revenue levels with the cost range. Wisconsin Electric Power Company proposed a uniform surcharge to avoid distorting the time-of-day pricing signal.

The cost-of-service studies, presented in the combined 6630–ER–2 and 6630–ER–5 proceeding, indicate that the residential class is not paying its full cost of service. Table 2, columns 3, 4, and 5, compares the percentage increases necessary to align class revenue levels to the results from the various cost-of-service methods.

The authorized rates herein provide for increases to customer classes of service in approximately the same percentage amounts. The commission finds such rates reasonable and just because the authorized rates are designed to give a proper price signal to all customers within the various classes. To price residential service higher as recommended by staff could cause price increases in the winter rate period at the time we are primarily (desperately) interested in reducing peak demand in the summer and changing use patterns throughout the year. We are compelled in our judgment, not to cloud the rates with changes of revenue but to seek clear price signals to all rate classes on an equal basis at this time.

TABLE 2: Indicated Percent Increase

(1) Customer Class	(2) Authorized Percent Increase*	(3) Embedded Cost of Service†	(4) LRIC†	(5) Marginal Peaker Method†	(6) Staff Proposed Increase†	(7) WEPCO Proposed Increase†
Residential	2.88%	20.20%	32.90%	30.61%	6.20%	2.99%
General secondary.......	2.90%	(6.08)	(19.34)	(16.09)	2.99	2.99
General primary.........	2.68%	(11.20)	(11.47)	(12.62)	(1.68)	2.99

*Includes: .347¢/kWh fossil production cost in the base rates.
†Includes: .260¢/kWh fossil production cost in the base rates.

Time-of-Day Rates.   Two different time-of-day rate proposals were presented in this proceeding, one by the applicant and another by the commission's Utility Rates Division staff. The staff's and the applicant's time-of-day proposals may be discussed in terms of three issues.

1.   Availability.
2.   Peak periods.
3.   Pricing.

"Availability" refers to the scope of the time-of-day pricing proposal. For instance, time-of-day pricing may be applied only to those customers who exceed a specified level of demand. "Peak periods" refers to the determination of the on-peak, off-peak pricing periods. "Pricing" refers to the allocation of costs between the on-peak, off-peak periods. The impact of any given time-of-day proposal may be tempered or increased by changing the scope of the availability, the duration of the peak periods, and/or the magnitude of the on-peak rate.

Availability

Residential Time-of-Day Rates.   The commission authorized mandatory time-of-day rates for the 500 largest kWh-usage residential customers. This time-of-day rate will be placed into effect on July 1, 1978. Wisconsin Electric Power Company may add additional large residential customers to the time-of-day rate if the required meters are available and such change is economically feasible. Both staff and applicant recommended mandatory time-of-day rates for the largest residential customers.

General Secondary (Cg–1) Time-of-Day Rates.   The commission authorizes mandatory time-of-day rates for those general secondary customers with monthly consumption in excess of 30,000 kWh for three consecutive months (rate code 45). The time-of-day rate will be implemented in three phases to accommodate meter availability beginning July 1, 1978, for the one-third largest rate code 45 customers. The second phase will place the next one-third group of rate code 45 customers on time-of-day rates effective January 1, 1979. The remaining rate code 45 customers will be placed on a time-of-day rate effective July 1, 1979.

Staff proposed mandatory time-of-day rates for all rate code 45 customers one year following the effective date of the 6630–ER–2 order; an optional time-of-day rate was proposed for the remaining general secondary customers. Wisconsin Electric Power Company proposed a time-of-day rate for the large general secondary customers (80,000 kWh) to be implemented at some future date in conjunction with the proposed general primary rate.

General Primary Time-of-Day Rates.   Mandatory time-of-day rates are authorized for all general primary (Cp–1) customers. Both the staff and applicant recommended mandatory time-of-day rates for the general primary class.

Peak Periods

The record indicates that the staff and the applicant agree as to definition of the on-peak, off-peak pricing periods and the seasonal pricing periods.

Seasonal periods:
  a. Usage during the billing months of July through October will be billed at the *summer* rate.
  b. Usage during the billing months of November through June will be billed at the *winter* rate.
Pricing periods:
On-Peak:
  a. Residential—7:00 A.M. to 7:00 P.M. (CST) Monday through Friday including holidays.
  b. General secondary—9:00 A.M. to 9:00 P.M. (CST) Monday through Friday including holidays.
  c. General primary—8:00 A.M. to 8:00 P.M. (CST) Monday through Friday, including holidays.
Off-Peak: All times not designated as on-peak.

The peak-period determination is based on an examination of applicant's available capacity, load duration curves, and loss of load probability, which taken together are measures of system reliability for different time periods during the year. Consideration was also given to the stability of the pricing periods, and a period of sufficient duration was selected so that an opportunity would be provided for customers to reduce or shift their consumption during designated on-peak periods.

Pricing: Time-of-Day Rates

The authorized time-of-day rates are based on the cost of providing service. Various cost-of-service studies were presented in the combined 6630–ER–1 and 6630–ER–2 proceedings. These studies established a framework for designing the authorized time-of-day rates.

The authorized time-of-day rates were designed in four steps:

1. Class revenue levels were set at adjusted current revenue levels.
2. The off-peak energy rate reflects four considerations:
    a. System lambdas (a measure of the operating cost of the next unit of production).

    b.   Average fuel cost.

    c.   Operating characteristics.

    d.   Voltage losses.

3.   The on-peak energy rate is based on the cost differential indicated by the system lambdas.

4.   The demand charge and the customer facilities charge were adjusted to equal the class revenue level. The demand charges were designed to reflect the seasonal differential of the cost of providing service.

Residential and General Primary Time-of-Day Rates. The residential and general primary time-of-day rates reflect marginal cost as closely as possible, considering revenue constraints.

General Secondary Time-of-Day Rates. The commission is not authorizing a Cg–1 time-of-day rate at this time for the code 44 customers. The commission has not reached a conclusion relative to the appropriateness of a three-part rate (Demand, Energy, and Customer Charge) or a two-part rate (Energy and Customer Charge). Hearings will be held early in 1978 to determine the appropriate general secondary rate design.

Rate Design. The rates were designed to reflect appropriate costs to the extent that the commission considers feasible at this time.

Residential Rate Design—Rg–1. The following revisions were made to the residential rate:

1.   A flat energy rate is authorized, thereby eliminating the existing declining blocks.

2.   A seasonal differential is applied to all consumption. The summer rate is approximately 50 percent higher than the winter rate.

3.   The special rate block for water heating is eliminated. Testimony was given by Wisconsin Electric Power Company that the load characteristics of the water heating customers are similar to non-water heating residential customers.

4.   The number of kWh's included in the minimum charge is reduced from 100 kWh's to 50 kWh's.

General Secondary Cg–1 Rate Design. The following revisions were made to the Cg–1 rate:

1.   A flat two-part rate is authorized for all Cg–1 customers.

2.   The Cg–1 customers in rate code 45 will be placed on the Cp–1 time-of-day rate schedule over the next 18 months.

3.   The hours-of-use credit was eliminated for customers using less than 80,000 kWh per month.

4.   A seasonal differential is incorporated into the rate. The summer rate is approximately 40 percent greater than the winter rate.

General Primary Cp–1 Rate Design.   The following revisions were made to the general primary rate:

1.   Both the energy and demand charges are flat for both the winter and summer. All declining blocks have been eliminated.
2.   All customers served on the Cp–1 rate are now placed on a mandatory 3-part time-of-day rate.
3.   The on-peak energy charge is twice the off-peak energy charge.
4.   The minimum monthly bill for Cp–1 customers is the charge for 300 kW billed demand plus the facilities charge.

Other Rate Classes.   A specific rate design was not discussed for rate classes other than Rg–1, Cg–1 and Cp–1. All other rates were increased by the authorized revenue increase and adjusted for the present fuel adjustment clause. . . .

Load-Management Report.   The applicant is required to submit a load-management report to the commission one year and one month from the effective date of the authorized time-of-day rates. This report will focus on the impact of applicant's time-of-day rates and of its off-peak excess demand provision on:

1.   Customer acceptance.
2.   Load shift.
3.   System planning.
4.   Future load-management applications.
5.   Utility cost benefit analysis.
6.   Other relevant information.

*   *   *   *   *

Charles J. Cicchetti, Chairman, Concurring:

General Assessment

As one of the nation's advocates of time-of-use pricing I am pleased to sign my pen to endorse this order. We have not completely achieved our stated goals of complete tariff reform, but we have progressed significantly. . . .

. . . While this is an important, and to some even a bold step, it is not enough to accomplish the job. We must vigorously pursue those metering entrepreneurs who claim that they can bring to electric metering reduced costs and increased performance so that time-of-use pricing and load management will be available to all, even the medium consumption residential customers. We must first induce WEPCO to implement: (a) time-of-use pricing for its commercial customers, (b) interruptible tariffs for industrial customers, and *(c)* more extensive load management for its commercial customers. If nudging fails, we as a commission must be prepared to use all of our regulatory apparatus to require WEPCO's full compliance.

I remain optimistic about our progress in this order.

Residential customers will no longer find that when they reduce electric use their monthly bills will shrink less proportionately than their efforts. Now residential rates are flat, and conservation efforts will mean a proportional reduction in the monthly bill.

Residential bills will decline for most customers compared to existing bills in the eight nonsummer months of the year. Prices in the summer months when electricity is most expensive will be 50 percent higher. Customers will learn that conserving electric use in the summer will mean an even greater reduction in their monthly bills. Conversely, continued high or even increased use in the summer will be a sharply higher monthly bill. Nevertheless, the typical or average residential user (about 500 kWh per month) will actually have an annual reduction in electric costs compared to existing electric prices.

Residential winter heating customers will not be particularly hard hit by the changes since winter electric rates will be lower. Additionally, turning their thermostats down and conserving in other ways will lead to bigger savings than under existing tariffs.

It is the summer air conditioning customer who will face sharply higher bills. Regrettably, this is the reality of the costs facing WEPCO. To ignore these facts would mean that the commission condoned the subsidy of residential air conditioning. It cannot. The only solace I can give to the air conditioning customer is that, contrasted to existing tariffs, conserving a single kWh of summer electric use will mean almost two times the reduction on the customer's monthly electric bill (a 4.2¢ saving versus 2.35¢ saving).

Larger volume of usage commercial customers will be on a full time-of-use pricing system within 18 months. When this occurs, 38 percent of WEPCO's current power or peak capacity requirements and 47 percent of WEPCO's sales of energy will be priced under a time-of-use pricing system. Volume discount pricing is being fully eliminated in Wisconsin. It is being replaced by a more rational mixture of time-of-use penalties and discounts.

The new tariffs, which will be applied immediately to large industrial users will include a two-to-one day-night differential (day means 8 A.M. to 8 P.M., Monday through Friday) in the energy charge. When added to the fact that peak period capacity charges will also be assessed against daytime maximum demands, industrial customers will experience about a six-to-one day-night difference in the summer and about a four-to-one day-night difference in the nonsummer. . . .

Class of Service	Residential

Effective in	All Areas Served

AVAILABILITY

To residential customers contracting for electric service for domestic purposes for a period of one year or more.

RATE

Customer Charge, including one meter	$3.39 per month	
	Billing Periods	
Energy Charge	July-October	November-June
First 50 kWh per month	0.00¢	0.00¢
Over 50 kWh per month, per kWh	4.20¢	2.80¢

Subject to adjustment for cost of fossil production. See sheet 13.

Meter Charge

The monthly meter charge for each meter in excess of one shall be $1.00.

Class of Service	Residential - Time-of-Use

Effective in	All Areas Served

AVAILABILITY

To residential customers contracting for electric service for domestic purposes for a period of one year or more.

RATE

Customer Charge, including one meter	$5.00 per month	
	Billing Periods	
Energy Charge per kWh	July-October	November-June
On-peak energy (a)	8.20¢	5.20¢
Off-peak energy (b)	1.30	1.30

Subject to adjustment for cost of fossil production. See sheet 13.

Meter Charge

The monthly meter charge for each meter in excess of one shall be $2.50.

(a)   Residential on-peak energy usage is the energy in kilowatt-hours delivered between 7:00 A.M. and 7:00 P.M. Central Standard Time, Monday through Friday, including holidays.
(b)   Residential off-peak energy usage is the energy in kilowatt-hours delivered during all hours other than during on-peak hours.

Class of Service	General Secondary

Effective in	All Areas Served

AVAILABILITY

To customers contracting for secondary electric service for one year or more for general commercial, industrial, or governmental purposes.

RATE

Customer Charge		$5.50 per month
Energy Charge		Billing Periods
	July-October	November-June
All kWh per month, per kWh	4.60¢	3.31¢

Class of Service	General Primary—Time-of-Use

Effective in	All Areas Served

AVAILABILITY

To customers contracting for 3-phase 60 hertz power service at approximately 3,810 volts or higher for periods of one year or more.

RATE

Customer Charge		$645.00 per month
		Billing Periods
Demand Charge	July-October	November-June
All billed total demand, per kW	$3.60	$2.65

Energy Charge per kWh

On-peak energy (a)	2.12¢
Off-peak energy (b)	1.06¢

(a) General primary on-peak energy usage is the energy in kilowatt-hours delivered between 8:00 A.M. and 8:00 P.M., Central Standard Time (CST), Monday through Friday, including holidays.

(b) General primary off-peak energy usage is the energy in kilowatt-hours delivered during all hours other than during on-peak hours.

(continued from preceding page)

DETERMINATION OF DEMAND

1. Measured Demands
   (a) Measured maximum demand shall be the maximum rate at which energy is used for a period of 15 consecutive minutes as ascertained by a recording wattmeter and an associated tape recorder or other standard measuring device.
   (b) Measured on-peak demand shall be the average of the weekly measured maximum demands occurring in the two calendar weeks in which the highest and second highest demands occurred which are established during on-peak hours for the calendar weeks ending within the billing period. Unless specified to the contrary in writing by six months prior written notice to customers, provided the on-peak period does not exceed 12 hours per day, on-peak hours shall be from 8:00 A.M. to 8:00 P.M., Central Standard Time (CST), Monday through Friday, including holidays.
   (c) Measured off-peak demand shall be the average of the weekly measured maximum demands occurring in the two calendar weeks in which the highest and second highest demands occurred which are established during off-peak hours for the calendar weeks ending within the billing period. Off-peak hours are those hours not designated as on-peak hours.
   (d) Measured total demand shall be the measured off-peak demand or on an optional basis 75 percent of the measured off-peak demand, whichever is the greater.

✷ 54

Otter Tail Power Co. v. United States

U.S. Supreme Court
410 U.S. 366 (1973)

Mr. Justice Douglas.   In this civil antitrust suit brought by appellee against Otter Tail Power Co. (Otter Tail), an electric utility company, the District Court found that Otter Tail had attempted to monopolize and had monopolized the retail distribution of electric power in its service area in violation of § 2 of the Sherman Act, 26 Stat. 209, as amended, 15 U.S.C. § 2. The District Court found that Otter Tail had attempted to prevent communities in which its retail distribution franchise had expired from replacing it with a municipal distribution system. The principal means employed were (1) refusals to sell power at wholesale to proposed municipal systems in the communities where it had been retailing power; (2) refusals to "wheel" power to such systems, that is to say, to transfer by direct transmission or displacement electric power from one utility to another over the facilities of an intermediate utility; (3) the institution and support of litigation designed to prevent or delay establishment of those systems; and (4) the invocation of provisions in its transmission contracts with several other power suppliers for the purpose of denying the municipal systems access to other suppliers by means of Otter Tail's transmission systems.

Otter Tail sells electric power at retail in 465 towns in Minnesota, North Dakota, and South Dakota. The District Court's decree enjoins it from refusing to sell electric power at wholesale to existing or proposed municipal electric power systems in the areas serviced by Otter Tail, from refusing to wheel electric power over the lines from the electric power suppliers to existing or proposed municipal systems in the area, from entering into or enforcing any contract which prohibits use of Otter Tail's lines to wheel electric power to municipal electric power systems, or from entering into or enforcing any contract which limits the customers to whom and areas in which Otter Tail or any other electric power company may sell electric power.

The decree also enjoins Otter Tail from instituting, supporting, or engaging in litigation, directly or indirectly, against municipalities and their officials who have voted to establish municipal electric power systems for the purpose of delaying, preventing, or interfering with the establishment of a municipal electric power system. 331 F. Supp. 54. Otter Tail took a direct appeal to this Court under § 2 of the Expediting Act, as amended, 62 Stat. 989, 15 U.S.C. § 29; and we noted probable jurisdiction, 406 U.S. 944.

In towns where Otter Tail distributes at retail, it operates under municipally granted franchises which are limited from 10 to 20 years. Each town in Otter Tail's service area generally can accommodate only one distribution system, making each town a natural monopoly market for the distribution and sale of electric power at retail. The aggregate of towns in Otter Tail's service area is the geographic market in which Otter Tail competes for the right to serve the towns at retail.[1] That competition is generally for the right to serve the entire retail market within the composite limits of a town, and that competition is generally between Otter Tail and a prospective or existing municipal system. These towns number 510 and of those Otter Tail serves 91 percent or 465.

Otter Tail's policy is to acquire, when it can, existing municipal systems within its service areas. It has acquired six since 1947. Between 1945 and 1970, there were contests in 12 towns served by Otter Tail over proposals to replace it with municipal systems. In only three—Elbow

---

[1]Northern States Power Co. also supplies some towns in Otter Tail's area with electric power at retail. But the District Court excluded these towns from Otter Tail's area because the two companies do not compete in the towns served by each other. Of the 615 remaining towns in the area, 465 are served at retail by Otter Tail, 45 by municipal systems, and 105 by rural electric cooperatives.

Lake, Minnesota, Colman, South Dakota, and Aurora, South Dakota —were municipal systems actually established. Proposed municipal systems have great obstacles; they must purchase the electric power at wholesale. To do so they must have access to existing transmission lines. The only ones available belong to Otter Tail. While the Bureau of Reclamation has high-voltage bulk-power supply lines in the area, it does not operate a subtransmission network, but relies on wheeling contracts with Otter Tail and other utilities to deliver power for its bulk supply lines to its wholesale customers.

The antitrust charge against Otter Tail does not involve the lawfulness of its retail outlets, but only its methods of preventing the towns it served from establishing their own municipal systems when Otter Tail's franchises expired. The critical events centered largely in four towns— Elbow Lake, Minnesota, Hankinson, North Dakota, Colman, South Dakota, and Aurora, South Dakota. When Otter Tail's franchise in each of these towns terminated, the citizens voted to establish a municipal distribution system. Otter Tail refused to sell the new systems energy at wholesale and refused to agree to wheel power from other suppliers of wholesale energy.

Colman and Aurora had access to other transmission. Against them, Otter Tail used the weapon of litigation.

As respects Elbow Lake and Hankinson, Otter Tail simply refused to deal, although according to the findings it had the ability to do so. Elbow Lake, cut off from all sources of wholesale power, constructed its own generating plant. Both Elbow Lake and Hankinson requested the Bureau of Reclamation and various cooperatives to furnish them with wholesale power; they were willing to supply it if Otter Tail would wheel it. But Otter Tail refused, relying on provisions in its contracts which barred the use of its lines for wheeling power to towns which it had served at retail. Elbow Lake after completing its plant asked the Federal Power Commission, under § 202 (b) of the Federal Power Act, 49 Stat. 848, 16 U.S.C. § 824a (b), to require Otter Tail to interconnect with the town and sell it power at wholesale. The Federal Power Commission ordered first a temporary and then a permanent connection. Hankinson tried unsuccessfully to get relief from the North Dakota Commission and then filed a complaint with the federal commission seeking an order to compel Otter Tail to wheel. While the application was pending, the town council voted to withdraw it and subsequently renewed Otter Tail's franchise.

It was found that Otter Tail instituted or sponsored litigation involving four towns in its service area which had the effect of halting or delaying efforts to establish municipal systems. Municipal power systems are financed by the sale of electric revenue bonds. Before such bonds can be sold, the town's attorney must submit an opinion which includes a statement that there is no pending or threatened litigation which might impair the value or legality of the bonds. The record amply bears out the District Court's holding that Otter Tail's use of litigation halted or appreciably slowed the efforts for municipal ownership. "The delay thus occasioned and the large financial burden imposed on the towns' limited treasury dampened local enthusiasm for public ownership." 331 F. Supp. 54, 62.

I

Otter Tail contends that by reason of the Federal Power Act it is not subject to antitrust regulation with respect to its refusal to deal. We disagree with that position.

"Repeals of the antitrust laws by implication from a regulatory statute are strongly disfavored and have only been found in cases of plain repugnancy between the antitrust and regulatory provisions." *United States* v. *Philadelphia National Bank,* 374 U.S. 321, 350–51. See also *Silver* v. *New York Stock Exchange,* 373 U.S. 341, 357–61. Activities which come under the jurisdiction of a regulatory agency nevertheless may be subject to scrutiny under the antitrust laws. . . .

The District Court determined that Otter Tail's consistent refusals to wholesale or wheel power to its municipal customers constituted illegal monopolization. Otter Tail maintains here that its refusals to deal should be immune from antitrust prosecution because the Federal Power Commission has the authority to compel involuntary interconnections of power pursuant to § 202 (b) of the Federal Power Act. The essential thrust of § 202, however, is to encourage voluntary interconnections of power. See S. Rep. No. 621, 74th Cong., 1st Sess., 19–20, 48–49; H. R. Rep. No. 1318, 74th Cong., 1st Sess., 8. Only if a power company refuses to interconnect voluntarily may the Federal Power Commission, subject to limitations unrelated to antitrust considerations, order the interconnection. The standard which governs its decision is whether such action is "necessary or appropriate in the public interest." Although antitrust considerations may be relevant, they are not determinative.

There is nothing in the legislative history which reveals a purpose to insulate electric power companies from the operation of the antitrust laws. To the contrary, the history of Part II of the Federal Power Act indicates an overriding policy of maintaining competition to the maximum extent possible consistent with the public interest. As originally conceived, Part II would have included a "common carrier" provision making it "the duty of every public utility to . . . transmit energy for any person upon reasonable request. . . ." In addition, it would have empowered the Federal Power Commission to order wheeling if it found such action to be "necessary or desirable in the public interest." H. R. 5423, 74th Cong., 1st Sess.; S. 1725, 74th Cong., 1st Sess. These provisions were eliminated to preserve "the voluntary action of the utilities." S. Rep. No. 621, 74th Cong., 1st Sess., 19.

It is clear, then, that Congress rejected a pervasive regulatory scheme for controlling the interstate distribution of power in favor of voluntary commercial relationships. When these relationships are governed in the first instance by business judgment and not regulatory coercion, courts must be hesitant to conclude that Congress intended to override the fundamental national policies embodied in the antitrust laws. See *United States* v. *Radio Corp. of America, supra,* at 351. This is particularly true in this instance because Congress, in passing the Public Utility Holding Company Act, which included Part II of the Federal Power Act, was concerned with "restraint of free and independent competition" among public utility holding companies. See 15 U.S.C. § 79a (b) (2).

Thus, there is no basis for concluding that the limited authority of the Federal Power Commission to order interconnections was intended to be a substitute for, or to immunize Otter Tail from, antitrust regulation for refusing to deal with municipal corporations.

II

The decree of the District Court enjoins Otter Tail from "[r]efusing to sell electric power at wholesale to existing or proposed municipal electric power systems in cities and towns located in [its service area]" and from refusing to wheel electric power over its transmission lines from other electric power lines to such cities and towns. But the decree goes on to provide:

> The defendant shall not be compelled by the Judgment in this case to furnish wholesale electric service or wheeling service to a municipality except at rates which are compensatory and under terms and conditions which are filed with and subject to approval by the Federal Power Commission.

So far as wheeling is concerned, there is no authority granted the Commission under Part II of the Federal Power Act to order it. . . . [P]rovision in the original bill and the power to direct wheeling were left to the "voluntary coordination of electric facilities." Insofar as the District Court ordered wheeling to correct anticompetitive and monopolistic practices of Otter Tail, there is no conflict with the authority of the Federal Power Commission.

As respects the ordering of interconnections, there is no conflict on the present record. . . .

III

The record makes abundantly clear that Otter Tail used its monopoly power in the towns in its service area to foreclose competition, or gain a competitive advantage, or to destroy a competitor, all in violation of the antitrust laws. See *United States* v. *Griffith*, 334 U.S. 100, 107. The District Court determined that Otter Tail has "a strategic dominance in the transmission of power in most of its service area" and that it used this dominance to foreclose potential entrants into the retail area from obtaining electric power from outside sources of supply. 331 F. Supp., at 60. Use of monopoly power "to destroy threatened competition" is a violation of the "attempt to monopolize" clause of § 2 of the Sherman Act. *Lorain Journal* v. *United States*, 342 U.S. 143, 154; *Eastman Kodak Co.* v. *Southern Photo Materials Co.*, 273 U.S. 359, 375. So are agreements not to compete with the aim of preserving or extending a monopoly. *Schine Chain Theatres* v. *United States*, 334 U.S. 110, 119. In *Associated Press* v. *United States*, 326 U.S. 1, a cooperative news association had bylaws that permitted member newspapers to bar competitors from joining the association. We held that that practice violated the Sherman Act, even though the transgressor "had not yet achieved a complete monopoly." Id., at 13.

When a community serviced by Otter Tail decides not to renew Otter Tail's retail franchise when it expires, it may generate, transmit, and distribute its own electric power. We recently described the difficulties and problems of those isolated electric power systems. See *Gainesville Utilities* v. *Florida Power Corp.*, 402 U.S. 515, 517–20. Interconnection with other utilities is frequently the only solution. Id., at 519 n. 3. That is what Elbow Lake in the present case did. There were no engineering factors that prevented Otter Tail from selling power at wholesale to those towns that wanted municipal plants or wheeling the power. The District Court found—and its findings are supported—that Otter Tail's refusals to sell at wholesale or to wheel were solely to prevent municipal power systems from eroding its monopolistic position.

Otter Tail relies on its wheeling contracts with the Bureau of Reclamation and with cooperatives which it says relieve it of any duty to wheel power to municipalities served at retail by Otter Tail at the time the contracts were made. The District Court held that these restrictive provisions were "in reality, territorial allocation schemes," 331 F. Supp., at 63, and were per se violations of the Sherman Act, citing *Northern Pacific R. Co.* v. *United States*, 356 U.S. 1. Like covenants were there held to "deny defendant's competitors access to the fenced-off market on the same terms as the defendant." Id., at 12. We recently reemphasized the vice under the Sherman Act of territorial restrictions among potential competitors. *United States* v. *Topco Associates*, 405 U.S. 596, 608. The fact that some of the restrictive provisions were contained in a contract with the Bureau of Reclamation is not material to our problem for, as the Solicitor General says, "government contracting officers do not have the power to grant immunity from the Sherman Act." Such contracts stand on their own footing and are valid or not, depending on the statutory framework within which the federal agency operates. The Solicitor General tells us that these restrictive provisions operate as a "hindrance" to the Bureau and were "agreed to by the Bureau only at Otter Tail's insistence," as the District Court found. The evidence supports that finding.

*   *   *   *   *

V

Otter Tail argues that, without the weapons which it used, more and more municipalities will turn to public power and Otter Tail will go downhill. The argument is a familiar one. It was made in *United States* v. *Arnold, Schwinn & Co.*, 388 U.S. 365, a civil suit under § 1 of the Sherman Act dealing with a restrictive distribution program and practices of a bicycle manufacturer. We said: "The promotion of self-interest alone does not invoke the rule of reason to immunize otherwise illegal conduct." Id., at 375.

The same may properly be said of § 2 cases under the Sherman Act. That Act assumes that an enterprise will protect itself against loss by operating with superior service, lower costs, and improved efficiency. Otter Tail's theory collided with the Sherman Act as it sought to substitute for competition anticompetitive uses of its dominant economic power.

The fact that three municipalities which Otter Tail opposed finally got their municipal systems does not excuse Otter Tail's conduct. That fact does not condone the antitrust tactics which Otter Tail sought to impose. Moreover, the District Court repeated what we said in *FTC* v. *National Lead Co.*, 352 U.S. 419, 431, "those caught violating the Act must expect some fencing in." The proclivity for predatory practices has always been a consideration for the District Court in fashioning its antitrust decree. See *United States* v. *Crescent Amusement Co.*, 323 U.S. 173, 190.

We do not suggest, however, that the District Court, concluding that Otter Tail violated the antitrust laws, should be impervious to Otter Tail's assertion that compulsory interconnection or wheeling will erode its integrated system and threaten its capacity to serve adequately the public. As the dissent properly notes, the Commission may not order interconnection if to do so "would impair [the utility's] ability to render adequate service to its customers." 16 U.S.C. § 824a (b). The District

Court in this case found that the "pessimistic view" advanced in Otter Tail's "erosion study" "is not supported by the record." Furthermore, it concluded that "it does not appear that Bureau of Reclamation power is a serious threat to the defendant nor that it will be in the foreseeable future." Since the District Court has made future connections subject to Commission approval and in any event has retained jurisdiction to enable the parties to apply for "necessary or appropriate" relief and presumably will give effect to the policies embodied in the Federal Power Act, we cannot say under these circumstances that it has abused its discretion.

Except for the provision of the order discussed in part IV of this opinion, the judgment is

Affirmed.

Mr. Justice Stewart, with whom The Chief Justice and Mr. Justice Rehnquist join, concurring in part and dissenting in part.

*   *   *   *   *

The Court in this case has followed the District Court into a misapplication of the Sherman Act to a highly regulated, natural-monopoly industry wholly different from those that have given rise to ordinary antitrust principles. In my view, Otter Tail's refusal to wholesale power through interconnection or to perform wheeling services was conduct entailing no antitrust violation. . . .

In considering the bill that became the Federal Power Act of 1935, the Congress had before it the report of the National Power Policy Committee on Public Utility Holding Companies.

*   *   *   *   *

. . . In the face of natural monopolies at retail and similar economies of scale in the subtransmission of power, Congress was forced to address the very problem raised by this case—use of the lines of one company by another. One obvious solution would have been to impose the obligations of a common carrier upon power companies owning lines capable of the wholesale transmission of electricity. Such a provision was originally included in the bill.

*   *   *   *   *

. . . Yet, after substantial debate, the Congress declined to follow this path. . . .

*   *   *   *   *

As the District Court found, Otter Tail is a vertically integrated power company. But the bulk of its business—some 90 percent of its income—derives from sales of power at retail. Left to its own judgment in dealing with its customers, it seems entirely predictable that Otter Tail would decline wholesale dealing with towns in which it had previously done business at retail. If the purpose of the congressional scheme is to leave such decisions to the power companies in the absence of a contrary requirement imposed by the Commission, it would appear that Otter Tail's course of conduct in refusing to deal with the municipal system at Elbow Lake and in refusing to promise to deal with the proposed system at Hankinson, was foreseeably within the zone of freedom specifically created by the statutory scheme.[1] As a retailer of power, Otter Tail asserted a legitimate business interest in keeping its lines free for its own power sales and in refusing to lend a hand in its own demise by wheeling cheaper power from the Bureau of Reclamation to municipal consumers which might otherwise purchase power at retail from Otter Tail itself.

The opinion of the Court emphasizes that Otter Tail's actions were not simple refusals to deal—they resulted in Otter Tail's maintenance of monopoly control by hindering the emergence of municipal power companies. The Court cites *Lorain Journal* v. *United States*, 342 U.S. 143, for the proposition that "[u]se of monopoly power 'to destroy threatened competition' is a violation of the 'attempt to monopolize' clause of § 2 of the Sherman Act." This proposition seems to me defective. *Lorain Journal* dealt neither with a natural monopoly at retail nor with a congressionally approved system predicated on the existence of such monopolies. In *Lorain Journal*, a newspaper in Lorain, Ohio, used its monopoly position to discourage advertisers from supporting a nearby radio station seen by the newspaper to be a competitor. The theory of the case was that competition in the communications business was being foreclosed by the newspaper's exercise of monopoly power. Here, by contrast, a monopoly is sure to result either way. If the consumers of Elbow Lake receive their electric power from a municipally owned company or from Otter Tail, there will be a monopoly at the retail level for there will

---

[1]The District Court was persuaded that the restrictions on wheeling contained in Otter Tail's contracts with the Bureau of Reclamation were "in reality, territorial allocation schemes." 331 F. Supp., at 63. I think this finding was clearly erroneous. Territorial allocation arrangements that have run afoul of the antitrust laws have traditionally been horizontal and have involved the elimination of competition between two enterprises that were similarly situated in the market. *United States* v. *Topco Associates*, 405 U.S. 596; *Timken Roller Bearing Co.* v. *United States*, 341 U.S. 593; cf. *White Motor Co.* v. *United States*, 372 U.S. 253, 261–64. Otter Tail and the Bureau of Reclamation stand in a vertical, not a horizontal, relationship. Furthermore, though Otter Tail refused to wheel power to towns whose consumers it formerly served at retail, it did not exact from the Bureau a promise that the latter would not provide power to such towns by alternative means. Hence, I cannot see how these contracts operate as territorial-allocation schemes. If Otter Tail had demanded that the Bureau not sell to former Otter Tail customers or if Otter Tail had combined with other retailers of electricity and undertaken mutual noncompetition agreements, this would be a different case.

in any event be only one supplier. The very reason for the regulation of private utility rates—by state bodies and by the Commission—is the inevitability of a monopoly that requires price control to take the place of price competition. Antitrust principles applicable to other industries cannot be blindly applied to a unilateral refusal to deal on the part of a power company, operating in a regime of rate regulation and licensed monopolies.

*   *   *   *   *

With respect to decisions by regulated electric utilities as to whether or not to provide nonretail services, I think that in the absence of horizontal conspiracy the teaching of the "primary jurisdiction" cases argues for leaving governmental regulation to the Commission instead of the invariably less sensitive and less specifically expert process of antitrust litigation. I believe this is what Congress intended by declining to impose common carrier obligations on companies like Otter Tail, and by entrusting the Commission with the burden of "assuring an abundant supply of electric energy throughout the United States" and with the power to order interconnections when necessary in the public interest. This is an area where "sporadic action by federal courts" *can* "work mischief." Cf. *United States* v. *Radio Corp. of America*, 358 U.S., at 350.

*   *   *   *   *

Leonard W. Weiss (1925–   )

✳ 55

Antitrust in the Electric Power Industry*

Can bulk electric power be converted —at least in part —to an effectively competitive industry? Weiss maintains that it can and should, if the rigidities which regulation now embodies could be relaxed. The conditions and the needed policy changes are fairly complex, but their main features are given here.

Electric power is often pictured as a "natural monopoly." Yet some competition exists in the industry today, and the possibility of more competition might well be enhanced if the structure of the industry were changed. In recent years, the Antitrust Division of the Department of Justice has adopted an active policy toward the industry. This chapter evaluates the possibilities both for more competition and for various types of antitrust action.

THE POTENTIAL ROLE OF COMPETITION

The Electric power industry is conventionally subdivided into generation, transmission, and distribution components. Generation accounts for about 53 percent of the total costs of the industry, transmission about 12 percent, and distribution about 35 percent. The possibilities for competition vary among the three sectors.

Generation

Most important regions could support enough generating plants to permit extensive competition if the plants were under separate ownership and had equal access to transmission and distribution. The physical

*Leonard W. Weiss, "An Evaluation of Antitrust in the Electric Power Industry," chap. 5 in A. Phillips, *Competition and the Regulation of Industry* © 1975 by The Brookings Institution. A tireless and perceptive researcher, Weiss has treated a wide range of industrial and policy issues. His textbooks are also well known. During 1969–70 he was Special Economic Assistant to the Assistant Attorney General for Antitrust, U.S. Department of Justice. He is on the faculty at the University of Wisconsin.

limits on the size of the market are set by transmission costs, which vary approximately in proportion to distance and inversely with the square of transmission voltages. As the power load has grown, extra-high-voltage transmission (currently 230 to 765 kilovolts) has become profitable, thus greatly reducing the impediment to long-distance transmission. One result has been such spectacular developments as the 850-mile, 750-kilovolt Pacific Northwest-Pacific Southwest, intertie, connecting the Columbia River with Los Angeles, and the 600-mile, 500-kilovolt line running from the Four Corners site in New Mexico to Los Angeles. In the more populous parts of the country, the possibility of high-voltage networks makes it technologically feasible for plants anywhere in a wide region to supply any consuming center connected with the network, though costs will still vary with the supplier's location. Much of the new capacity intended to supply the largest load centers is, in fact, being constructed at points more than 100 miles away in order to use local fuel supplies and to reduce air pollution in the more congested areas.

Table 1 gives estimates of concentration among bulk-power producers within 100 or 200 miles of ten of the thirteen largest load centers.[1] Although there are at least two bulk-power producers within 100 miles, and several within 200 miles, of each of these cities, the markets are highly concentrated. Their oligopolistic character is reinforced by the present regulatory blockade to entry by large private bulk-power producers.

Some features of bulk-power transactions, however, tend to make tacit collusion difficult. Sales among bulk-power producers or to distribution utilities or large industrial users (that is, customers that can receive power at high voltage) are often for large blocks of power over long periods of time, and the transactions are very diverse in character. They include long-term sales of blocks of capacity from particular units; long-term sales of blocks of firm power from the supplying system as a whole; sales of interruptible energy; spot sales of "economy" energy arising from the allocation of a region's load among units on the basis of short-run marginal costs; exchanges of "diversity" power to take advantage of different peaks; and sales or exchanges of emergency assistance with varying limits on the seller's commitments. Marginal costs vary among the types of transactions, among producers for any given type of transaction, and even within a firm according to the size, timing, and duration of the transaction. Since these sales are large (some in the hundreds of megawatts) and individually negotiated, substantial price

---

[1]Seattle–Tacoma, Portland, Oregon, and Knoxville–Oak Ridge are excluded because the predominance of federal power in those areas makes concentration measures unrepresentative.

TABLE 1: Estimated Concentration in Electric Generating Capacity within 100 and 200 Miles of Ten Major Load Centers, 1968*

	Within 100 Miles			Within 200 Miles		
Load Center	Number of Firms with Greater Than 100-Megawatt Capacity	Share of Largest Firm (percent)	Share of Four Largest Firms (percent)	Number of Firms with Greater Than 100-Megawatt Capacity	Share of Largest Firm (percent)	Share of Four Largest Firms (percent)
New York	12	29	75	18	21	57
Chicago	7	61	93	17	43	67
Los Angeles	6	67	97	8	55	93
San Francisco	2	97	100	8	76	89
Detroit†	8	48	90	13	30	75
Philadelphia	9	29	79	19	21	57
Houston	2	79	100	7	44	81
St. Louis	5	52	94	15	24	59
Washington	8	38	79	11	16	57
Boston	6	26	79	14	32	65

*All members of a holding company are treated as a single firm, but members of pools are treated as separate firms. Where data are available, joint ventures are allocated among owners within the specific market in the proportions reported; on an equal-shares basis otherwise. The portion of joint ventures within a market owned by firms otherwise outside the market is considered a single firm. All federal capacity and individual municipals in a market are also treated as owned by a single firm.

†Includes Hydro-Electric Power Commission of Ontario.

Sources: For firms that operate entirely within the market, specified total capacity is from Federal Power Commission, *Statistics of Privately Owned Electric Utilities in the United States, 1968: Classes A and B Companies* (1969), and FPC, *Statistics of Publicly Owned Electric Utilities in the United States* (1969). Where only part of a firm's capacity is within the market only the capacities reported in FPC, *Steam-Electric Plant Construction Cost and Annual Production Expenses, Twenty-First Annual Supplement—1968* (1969), and FPC, *Hydroelectric Plant Construction Cost and Annual Production Expenses, Twelfth Annual Supplement, 1968* (1970), are included. Ontario capacities are from Hydro-Electric Power Commission of Ontario, *Annual Report, 1968.*

competition seems possible in many of the load centers shown in Table 1, where regulatory and ownership conditions permit.

In practice, competition among generating companies is impeded by the ownership of transmission and distribution systems by individual generating firms. Transactions involving "wheeling" do occur, but they are voluntary and of minor importance at present.[2] If the owners of

[2]Wheeling refers to transmission by one firm of energy generated by another firm and delivered to a third party—that is, the generating company inputs energy into the transmission system of the intermediate utility, which delivers the same amount of energy to the third firm. The generating company is paid by the customer for the power, and the intermediate firm receives a wheeling charge for the use of its transmission lines. Wheeling differs from a sale of power to and resale by the intermediate firm in that it is the generating company that controls the price. Although the FPC requires voluntary wheeling agreements to be filed with it, it has never regulated wheeling charges. In 1968, privately owned utilities generated 1,022 billion kilowatt-hours, sold 175 billion for resale, and wheeled 33 billion (*Statistics of Privately Owned Utilities, 1968*, p. xliii).

transmission lines or systems were treated as common carriers, the generating firms of a region could compete for the loads of independent distribution systems and, conceivably, large industrial users throughout the region. Where generation costs and environmental considerations are similar throughout a region, plants would still tend to supply neighboring load centers, but generating companies would have only limited local monopoly because of potential competition from more distant plants whose costs would exceed theirs by only the extra transmission expense. . . .

Other Effects of Competition

Increased competition would have a mixed effect on the extent of rate discrimination. More competition for industrial load would presumably lead to lower industrial rates relative to residential rates; this could mean higher, lower, or unchanged residential rates, depending on whether long-run marginal generation and transmission costs are respectively increasing, decreasing, or constant. If residential rates were limited by regulation, the Averch-Johnson argument would imply higher residential rates as industrial demand became more elastic. However, if, as Moore suggests, residential rates are set at approximately profit-maximizing levels already, any further Averch-Johnson effect would be nil. In any event, since competition for large industrial load is already intense, further reductions in industrial rates relative to residential rates would be limited. The major effect of procompetitive policy on discrimination is thus likely to be simply to preserve the opportunities for competition that already exist.

Intermodal competition would lead to discrimination in favor of uses of electricity that compete closely with gas. While such discrimination at the residential level could cause Averch-Johnson rate increases on the inelastic elements of demand, the main effects of intermodal competition would be to make large segments of residential demand more elastic, thus reducing the opportunity to discriminate between industrial and residential customers, and to make discrimination between gas and electric customers impossible.

Increased competition for the load of distribution utilities might result in some uneconomic geographic rate differences, but the main effect would be to reduce residential rates generally.

There could be conflict between the effects of increased competition and the goals of environmental protection. Intermodal competition and competition for industrial load encourage the increased use of energy, while some environmentalists have proposed flat or even inverted rate structures to discourage it. There would be no conflict between flat or inverted rates and competition among generation companies for the loads of distribution utilities, however, and a system of effluent charges would be fully consistent with all forms of competition in the power industry. The shift of generating facilities away from densely populated areas for environmental reasons would, in fact, increase the possibilities for competition.

If the separation of generation and distribution functions caused widespread bilateral monopoly, the result could conceivably be wholesale rates above the internal marginal generating and transmission costs of an integrated company with higher retail rates as the ultimate effect.[3] A competitive wholesale market would prevent such a development. For vertical disintegration to be unequivocally beneficial to consumers, it should be accompanied by free access to interconnection and wheeling and by the absence of mergers that greatly increase regional concentration.

The classic concern about "cream skimming" is given little attention today in the electric power industry, but it might well become a problem if regionwide competition for industrial and retail utilities' loads should develop. It could be argued that the capture of large industrial loads by more distant bulk-power suppliers would result in high costs and hence higher residential rates in the service area of the original supplier. But because of the transmission costs involved, such a result is likely only where the distant utility has a large cost advantage. In that case, the high-cost utility could reduce costs by buying power to supply its own load, an option that would be available to it in a competitive market. If generation and distribution utilities were separate, the high-cost generating company would also be forced into some such adjustment. Even with no vertical divestiture, the generator would still be under pressure to adjust because of the threatened loss of bulk-power customers and the conceivable loss of retail business caused by the formation of new municipals. Cream skimming would therefore seem to be a minor problem at worst and might even have beneficial effects in encouraging vertical disintegration and a more rational geographic rate pattern.

Summary

The question posed at the beginning of this section—what would be the net effects of increased competition?—can now be tentatively answered. The economies of gas and electric combination are probably small. Those of vertical integration have not been investigated thoroughly but are also likely to be small. Any net losses from increased competition due to the advantages won by municipals and REA

---

[3]See Fritz Machlup and Martha Taber, "Bilateral Monopoly, Successive Monopoly, and Vertical Integration," *Economica, U.S.* (May 1960), pp. 101–19.

cooperatives, to discrimination, successive monopoly, or cream skim-ming are problematical. The net effects of these changes might, in fact, be socially useful in and of themselves. The main concern about the effect of competition on the power industry's performance must thus be the conventional one—the industry's ability to attain economies of scale. The crucial question is whether pools or contracts among independent firms can achieve such economies as efficiently as the multiunit firm. Experience with pooling or bilateral contracting where there is extensive high-voltage interconnection among independent firms has been too brief and incomplete, however, to warrant a final assessment at present of the desirability of large-scale horizontal mergers. . . .

AN EVALUATION OF COMPETITIVE POLICY ALTERNATIVES

Given the costs and consequences of increased competition explored above and the implications of various antitrust positions toward the industry, what ought public policy toward the electric power industry to be?

Maximum Competition

Maximum competition consistent with low costs, though possibly an unattainable ideal, would require a restructuring of the power industry to include: (1) the separation of generation-transmission companies from distribution companies; (2) the dissolution of combination utilities; (3) the elimination of public and private territorial restrictions on sales to distributors or large industrial customers; (4) a general requirement of interconnection and wheeling at reasonable charges; (5) the elimination of preferential access to federal power and preferential tax and capital-cost treatment for municipals and cooperatives; (6) the elimination of legal restrictions on entry into bulk power; and (7) the limitation of horizontal mergers among generation-transmission companies to cases where the partners are too small to negotiate effectively with other bulk-power producers of a region. The last of these stipulations is the least certain. As more information accumulates, large-scale mergers may be needed to attain reasonable economies of scale. On the other hand, in a more competitive setting bilateral contracts by unaffiliated firms or less restrictive pooling agreements may offer the same economies as either large single-owner systems or closely coordinated pools.

Modified Competition

Such a thorough restructuring of the industry may not be practically or politically possible in the foreseeable future. A more limited set of policy goals may be more nearly attainable [and] would involve (1) the elimination of private and public territorial restrictions on sales for re-sale, and possibly private restrictions on sales to large industrial custom-ers, as well; (2) a general requirement of interconnection and wheeling; (3) control of horizontal and vertical mergers; and (4) at least some dives-titure of gas properties in connection with further mergers. These changes would effect further reduction in vertical integration because of the increased access of municipals and cooperatives to power at com-petitive prices and the increased competitive pressure on small utilities that are presently integrated. If such policies resulted in a large-scale expansion of municipals, political circumstances might allow the elimina-tion of some of their special advantages as well. A more general dissolu-tion of combination utilities under the structures of the Sherman Act may also be within the range of possibility; the country has once, after all, accepted such a change for a large part of the industry.

Under these second-best policies, the public could still benefit from increased wholesale competition and, to the extent that combination utilities could be dissolved, intermodal competition. The increase in wholesale competition might be substantial or minor, depending on whether economies of scale are attainable short of large-scale merger or, even better, short of closely coordinated pooling. Since complete elimi-nation of the special advantages of municipals and cooperatives seems unlikely, industry reorganization might lead to some uneconomic ex-pansion by such utilities and probably would bring about a redistribu-tion in favor of their customers. On the other hand, municipals and cooperatives would probably be less prone to invest in suboptimal capacity than they are now. . . .

The Role of Regulation

Even with the most thorough reorganization of the industry, regula-tion would still have a role. Transmission would continue to be a mo-nopoly, so the requirement of interconnection and wheeling and the regulation of wheeling charges would be essential. The determination of reasonable wheeling charges could be a difficult problem because the decreasing costs of transmission result in marginal costs that are below average costs. How effective regulation of these charges would be is not certain, but it is to be hoped that the FPC could at least prevent charges that were designed to be prohibitive.

Retail distribution would also remain monopolistic, except perhaps for large industrial loads and under intermodal competition, so conven-tional state regulation of retail rates would still be in order. Such regula-tion might well be more effective than it is now because pure distribu-tion utilities would be less complex and thus easier to regulate and because intermodal competition and competition for industrial load would reinforce regulatory controls in important areas.

If territorial and wheeling restrictions were removed, vertical integration disbanded, and substantial numbers of firms maintained at the generation level, much of the need for regulation at wholesale would be obviated. Since this falls under FPC jurisdiction, a national policy of partial deregulation would seem appropriate. Controls over interconnections and wheeling charges would still be necessary, and the industry would still be subject to public actions with respect to environmental matters, but entry and rate questions could be left to the marketplace. If regulation were retained (as might happen if large mergers are permitted), the increased competition should serve to reinforce rather than weaken its impact.

The continuation of widespread integration between retail and generation utilities seems likely under present policies. If so, competition will continue to have only a peripheral effect on a large part of bulk-power supply, and widespread regulation at both retail and wholesale levels will still be necessary. Even under those conditions, however, a pro-competitive policy would probably help to offset some of the manifest imperfections in regulation.

✺ 56

United States v. *El Paso Natural Gas Co.*
U.S. Supreme Court
376 U.S. 651 (1964)

El Paso is a classic "big case": a massive cumulation of facts and litigation, and a remarkable series of delaying actions. It also is a landmark extension of antitrust into a "regulated" sector. More than 16 years have passed as re-appeals and remands have proliferated.

Justice William O. Douglas.   This is a civil suit charging a violation of Section 7 of the Clayton Act by reason of the acquisition of the stock and assets of Pacific Northwest Pipeline Corp. (Pacific Northwest) by El Paso Natural Gas Co. (El Paso). The District Court dismissed the complaint after trial, making findings of fact and conclusions of law, but not writing an opinion. The case is here on direct appeal. . . .

The ultimate issue revolves around the question whether the acquisition substantially lessened competition in the sale of natural gas in California—a market of which El Paso was the sole out-of-state supplier at the time of the acquisition.

In 1954, Pacific Northwest received the approval of the Federal Power Commission to construct and operate a pipeline from the San Juan Basin, New Mexico, to the State of Washington to supply gas to the then unserved Pacific Northwest area. Later it was authorized to receive large quantities of Canadian gas and to enlarge its system for that purpose. In addition, Pacific Northwest acquired Rocky Mountain reservoirs along its route. . . . By 1958 one half of its natural gas sales were of gas from Canada.

In 1954 Pacific Northwest entered into two gas exchange contracts with El Paso. . . .

El Paso, however, could not get Commission approval to build the pipeline. . . . Consequently, a new agreement on that aspect was negotiated in 1955. . . . Pacific Northwest, still obligated to take 300 million cubic feet per day from Westcoast, disposed of the balance in its own market areas.

Prior to these 1954 and 1955 agreements Pacific Northwest had tried to enter the rapidly expanding California market. It prepared plans regarding the transportation of Canadian gas to California, where it was to be distributed by Pacific Gas & Electric (PGE). That effort—suspended when the 1954 agreements were made—was renewed when the new agreement with El Paso was made in 1955; and the negotiation of the 1955 contract with El Paso was conceived by Pacific Northwest as the occasion for "lifting of all restrictions on the growth of Pacific." In 1956 it indeed engaged in negotiations for the sale of natural gas to Southern California Edison Co. (Edison). The latter, largest industrial user of natural gas in Southern California, used El Paso gas purchased through a distributor. It had, however, a low priority from that distributor, being on an "interruptible" basis, i.e., subject to interruption during periods of peak demand for domestic uses. Edison wanted a firm contract and, upon being advised that it was El Paso's policy to sell only to distributors, started negotiations with Pacific Northwest in May 1956. The idea was for Pacific Northwest to deliver to Edison at a point on the California-Oregon border 300 million cubic feet of Canadian gas a day. In July 1956 they reached a tentative agreement. Edison thereupon tried to develop within California an integrated system for distributing Canadian gas supplied by Pacific Northwest to itself and others. El Paso decided to fight the plan to the last ditch and succeeded in getting (through a distributor) a contract for Edison's needs. Edison's tentative agreement with Pacific Northwest was terminated. Before Edison terminated that agreement with Pacific Northwest, Edison had reached an agreement with El Paso for firm deliveries of gas; and while the original El Paso offer was 40¢ per Mcf, the price dropped to 38¢ per Mcf, then to 34¢ and finally to 30¢. Thereafter, and while the merger negotiations were pending, Pacific Northwest renewed its efforts to get its gas into California.

El Paso had been interested in acquiring Pacific Northwest since 1954. The first offer from El Paso was in December 1955—an offer Pacific Northwest rejected. Negotiations were resumed by El Paso in the summer of 1956, while Pacific Northwest was trying to obtain a California outlet. The exchange of El Paso shares for Pacific shares was accepted by Pacific Northwest's directors in November 1956, and by May 1957 El Paso had acquired 99.8 percent of Pacific Northwest's outstanding stock. In July 1957 the Department of Justice filed its suit charging that the acquisition violated Section 7 of the Clayton Act. In August 1957 El Paso applied to the Federal Power Commission for permission to acquire the assets of Pacific Northwest. On December 23, 1959, the Commission approved and the merger was effected on December 31, 1959. In 1962 we set aside the Commission's order, holding that it should not have acted until the District Court has passed on the Clayton Act issues. . . . Meanwhile (in October 1960) the United States amended its complaint so as to include the asset acquisition in the charged violation of the Clayton Act.

. . . On review of the record—which is composed largely of undisputed evidence—we conclude that "the effect of such acquisition may be substantially to lessen competition" within the meaning of Section 7 of the Clayton Act.

There can be no doubt that the production, transportation, and sale of natural gas is a "line of commerce" within the meaning of Section 7. There can also be no doubt that California is a "section of the country" as that phrase is used in Section 7. The sole question, therefore, is whether on undisputed facts the acquisition had a sufficient tendency to lessen competition or is saved by the findings that Pacific Northwest, as an independent entity, could not have obtained a contract from the California distributors, could not have received the gas supplies or financing for a pipeline project to California, or could not have put together a project acceptable to the regulatory agencies. Those findings are irrelevant. . . .

Pacific Northwest, though it had no pipeline into California, is shown by this record to have been a substantial factor in the California market at the time it was acquired by El Paso. At that time El Paso was the only actual supplier of out-of-state gas to the vast California market, *a market that expands at an estimated annual rate of 200 million cubic feet per day*. At that time Pacific Northwest was the only other important interstate pipeline west of the Rocky Mountains. Though young, it was prospering and appeared strong enough to warrant a "treaty" with El Paso that protected El Paso's California markets.

Edison's search for a firm supply of natural gas in California, when it had El Paso gas only on an "interruptible" basis, illustrates what effect Pacific Northwest had merely as a potential competitor in the California market. Edison took its problem to Pacific Northwest, and as we have seen, a tentative agreement was reached for Edison to obtain Pacific Northwest gas. El Paso responded, offering Edison a firm supply of gas and substantial price concessions. We would have to wear blinders not to see that the mere efforts of Pacific Northwest to get into the California market, though unsuccessful, had a powerful influence on El Paso's business attitudes within the State.

This is not a field where merchants are in a continuous daily struggle to hold old customers and to win new ones over from their rivals. In this regulated industry a natural gas company (unless it has excess capacity) must compete for, enter into, and then obtain Commission approval of sale contracts in advance of constructing the pipeline facilities. In the natural gas industry pipelines are very expensive; and to be justified, they need long-term contracts for sale of the gas that will travel them. Those transactions with distributors are few in number. For example, in California there are only two significant wholesale purchasers—Pacific Gas & Electric in the north and the Southern Companies in the south. Once the Commission grants authorization to construct facilities or to transport gas in interstate commerce, once the distributing contracts are made, a particular market is withdrawn from competition. *The competition then is for the new increments of demand that may emerge with an expanding population and with an expanding industrial or household use of gas.*

The effect on competition in a particular market through acquisition of another company is determined by the nature or extent of that market and by the nearness of the absorbed company to it, that company's eagerness to enter that market, its resourcefulness, and so on. Pacific Northwest's position as a competitive factor in California was not disproved by the fact that it had never sold gas there. Nor is it conclusive that Pacific Northwest's attempt to sell to Edison failed. That might be weighty if a market presently saturated showed signs of petering out. But it is irrelevant in a market like California, where incremental needs are booming.

. . . Had Pacific Northwest remained independent, there can be no doubt it would have sought to exploit its formidable geographical position *vis-à-vis* California. No one knows what success it would have had. We do know, however, that two interstate pipelines in addition to El Paso now serve California—one of the newcomers being Pacific Gas

Transmission Co., bringing down Canadian gas. So we know that opportunities would have existed for Pacific Northwest had it remained independent.

Unsuccessful bidders are no less competitors than the successful one. The presence of two or more suppliers gives buyers a choice. Pacific Northwest was no feeble, failing company nor was it inexperienced and lacking in resourcefulness. It was one of two major interstate pipelines serving the trans-Rocky Mountain States; it had raised $250 million for its pipeline that extended 2,500 miles through rugged terrain. It had adequate reserves and managerial skill. It was so strong and militant that it was viewed with concern, and coveted, by El Paso. If El Paso can absorb Pacific Northwest without violating Section 7 of the Clayton Act, that section has no meaning in the natural gas field. For normally there is no competition—once the lines are built and the long-term contracts negotiated—except as respects the incremental needs.

Since appellees have been on notice of the antitrust charge from almost the beginning—indeed before El Paso sought Commission approval of the merger—we not only reverse the judgment below but direct the District Court to order divestiture without delay.

Reversed.

John W. Wilson (1943–   )

✂ 57

Competition and Regulation in Natural Gas*

Many experts (see Breyer and MacAvoy below) have urged deregulating natural gas production because it has "effectively competitive" conditions. Wilson argues, instead, that natural gas is highly monopolistic and needs tight public controls. How competitive would the industry be if it were deregulated: Is current policy sound?

I would like to thank the Chairman and Members of this Subcommittee for once again inviting me to appear before you to present testimony on a most important national economic policy matter. . . .

CONCENTRATION

. . . Initially, it should be observed that when we address the "natural gas producing industry" we are really discussing the "petroleum industry." The dominant firms are the same, and these firms have fully integrated gas and oil producing and marketing operations which can not be analyzed intelligently in isolation. As shown in Table 1, the top 14 natural gas producers in 1970 were also among the top 15 oil and liquids producers and among the top 17 petroleum refiners. These 14 leading gas producers were also among the 17 largest sellers of gasoline and other refined petroleum products and among the 17 largest sellers of natural gas to interstate pipelines.

Perhaps a better impression of actual concentration can be obtained from Table 2. The four-firm and eight-firm ratios shown there are based on an actual survey by the FPC of available uncommitted gas supplies as of December 31, 1971, and June 30, 1972. These ratios are extremely high, and they tend to be rather stable from one period to the other. . . .

Also, . . . concentration appears to be quite high even in a prospec-

*John W. Wilson, "Competition and Regulation in Natural Gas," Testimony before the Senate Subcommittee on Antitrust and Monopoly, *Hearings on the Industrial Reorganization Act,* June 27, 1973 (Washington, D.C.: U.S. Government Printing Office), excerpted. Wilson is an expert on energy markets and policy, with his own consulting firm. In 1973 he was Chief of the Division of Economic Studies at the FPC.

TABLE 1: Rankings of Largest Firms in the Petroleum Industry (1970)

	Natural Gas Producers	Oil and Gas Liquids Producers	Petroleum Refining	U.S. Refined Product Sales	Natural Gas Sales to Interstate Pipelines
1.	Exxon	1	1	1	1
2.	Texaco	2	2	2	7
3.	Amoco	6	6	4	4
4.	Gulf	3	5	7	2
5.	Phillips	12	11	9	5
6.	Mobil	8	3	6	6
7.	Shell	4	7	3	3
8.	Atlantic-Richfield	7	8	8	8
9.	Sun	11	9	10	12
10.	Chevron	5	4	5	11
11.	Union Oil	9	10	11	9
12.	Getty	10	15	17	17
13.	Continental	13	14	14	10
14.	Cities Service	15	17	13	14

TABLE 2: Concentration of the Available New Gas Supplies as of 12/31/71 and 6/30/72* (percentage of reported uncommitted reserves controlled by four and eight largest producers)[1]

	12/31/71		6/30/72	
Producing Area	Four Largest	Eight Largest	Four Largest	Eight Largest
Permian Basin	63.6%	86.4%	80.6%	94.2%
Hugoton Anadarko	76.6	94.5	62.6	83.3
Other Southwest	93.3	98.6	94.4	99.3
South Louisiana				
Onshore	96.9	99.6	92.3	98.4
Offshore (federal)	57.0	83.3	49.6	74.9
Offshore (state)	84.5	100.0	94.9	100.0
Texas Gulf Coast				
Onshore	89.4	96.7	84.4	92.4
Offshore (federal)	98.5	100.0	100.0	100.0
Offshore (state)	100.0	100.0	100.0	100.0
Rocky Mountain	63.4	82.9	70.4	86.0
Appalachian	99.6	100.0	100.0	100.0
Unclassified				
Michigan	100.0	100.0	—	—
California	95.4	100.0	94.3	100.0
Miscellaneous	87.7	99.9	98.0	100.0
Alaska‡	93.9	99.9	93.9	99.9
Total U.S.‡	51.4	75.9	51.0	73.9

*Concentration ratios are based on individual company reserve reports. To the extent that two or more companies report pro rata ownership shares of jointly held leases for which there is a single operation, the concentration ratios tend to underestimate the actual degree of seller concentration.

†Reports were obtained from 79 large producers. These producers provide most of the gas sold to interstate pipelines (e.g., in 1971 the top 22 supplied over 70 percent of all interstate gas). Nevertheless, to the extent that nonreporting small producers may have had significant volumes, the ratios reported here tend to overstate slightly actual market concentration.

‡Does not include certain North Slope reserves reported in the aggregate for all companies by one producer.

tive sense. Over 80 percent of the federal offshore leases acquired (weighted by bonus dollars paid) in each of three recent lease sales were accounted for by the top eight bidders and their bidding partners. In all three sales combined, the top eight accounted for 70 percent of the successful bids. As shown below, these bidding partnerships generally become producing partnerships, and consequently future prospects, for our offshore areas at any rate, are for continued high levels of supply concentration.

JOINT VENTURES, INTERTIES, AND INTERLOCKS

There is substantial direct evidence of mutual interdependence between virtually all of the major firms in the petroleum industry. This interdependence includes joint ventures, interlocks, and institutional interties in the following general areas of activity:

1. Joint lease acquisition (bidding combines).
2. Banking interlocks (directorates and common stock ownership).
3. Joint ownership of pipelines and gathering systems.
4. Joint ownership and production from oil and gas leases.
5. International joint ventures.
6. Vertical relationships between the producing, transporting, processing, and marketing sectors of the industry.

Bidding Combines

In any given sale, it is obvious that when four firms such as the CATC group, each able to bid independently, combine to submit a single bid, three interested, potential bidders have been eliminated; i.e., the combination has restrained trade. This situation does not differ materially from one of explicit collusion in which four firms meet in advance of a given sale and decide who among them should bid (which three should refrain from bidding) for specific leases and, instead of competing among themselves, attempt to rotate the winning bids. The principal difference is that explicit collusion is illegal. [1]

The logic of this observation is unexceptionable, and though it was made some six years ago, the situation which it describes has grown substantially since then so that today bidding combines tend to dominate even the acquisition of federal offshore leases. Table 3 lists the major bidding combines which participated in federal offshore lease sales in 1970 and 1972. Because various majors belonged to two or more

---

[1]Walter Mead, "The Competitive Significance of Joint Ventures," *Antitrust Bulletin,* Fall 1967, p. 839; quoted in the Federal Power Commission staff's reply brief in *Belco Petroleum Corporation et al.,* docket no. C173–293, *et. al.,* April 20, 1973.

TABLE 3: Major Bidding Combines Which Participated in Recent Federal Offshore Lease Sales

1. Tenneco*, Texaco
2. Cities Service, Tenneco*, Continental
3. Atlantic Richfield, Cities Service*, Continental, Getty
4. Phillips, Skelly (Getty), Allied Chemical, American Petrofina
5. Getty, Placid, Superior
6. Superior, Placid, Hunt, Transocean*, Ashland
7. Superior, Chevron, Murphy, Pelto, General American
8. Chevron, Mobil, Pennzoil*
9. Chevron, Mesa, Burmah
10. Mobil, Gulf, Pennzoil*
11. Mobil, Gulf, Chevron
12. Ashland, Mesa, Pennzoil*
13. Mobil, Burmah, Mesa, Pennzoil*
14. General American, Burmah, CNG*
15. Burmah, General American
16. Amoco, CNG*, Shell, Transco*
17. Amoco, Union, Texas Eastern*
18. Amoco, Southern National*, Champlin
19. Texas Gas*, Union, Florida Gas*
20. Signal, La. Land, Amerada, Marathon, Texas Eastern*
21. Shell, Florida Gas*

*An affiliate of a major interstate gas pipeline company.

of these combines, the web of interdependence is far more pervasive than the membership of any single combine would suggest. . . .

My own view is that the offshore leasing program, as currently administered by the Interior Department, has become one of the most onerous anticompetitive cartelization devices at work in our domestic gas producing industry. Not only is it a vehicle for further joint ventures and the integration of intercorporate interests, it has also become an effective entry blockade for all but the very largest firms in the industry. As the president of an established oil company with annual revenues of over $100 million recently testified in an FPC hearing, it would now take a consortium of 15 or more firms like his to surmount the offshore entry barriers which have been erected under Interior's watchful eye. Consequently, his company and others like it have been effectively precluded from entering these producing areas except by obtaining limited farmouts of unwanted acreage from the dominant majors or perhaps by joining one of the established combines as a junior partner. Neither is likely to have much of a procompetitive effect, and that is most critical because our federal domain contains a large portion of our nation's remaining oil and gas reserves.

*   *   *   *   *

Banking Interlocks

A listing of certain interlocking directorates in the petroleum industry by major banks, as of 1968, is provided in Table 4. This situation is a

TABLE 4: Bank Director Interlocks between Major Firms in the Petroleum Industry (1968)

La. Land and Exploration Co.	
Belco Petroleum Corp.	
Texas Gulf Sulphur*	
Continental Oil	Morgan Guaranty
Cities Service Co.	Trust Co.
Atlantic Richfield	
Columbia Gas System	
Allied Chemical	
Monsanto Co.	
W. R. Grace Co.	First National
Standard Oil of N.J.	City Bank
Mobil Oil	
Sinclair Oil	
Standard Oil of N.J.	
Standard Oil of Ind.	Chase Manhattan
Diamond Alkali	
Texaco, Inc.	
Marathon Oil	National City Bank
Standard Oil of Ohio*	(Cleveland)
Consolidated Natural Gas	
General Crude Oil Co.	
Texas Gulf Sulphur	Manufacturers
Union Carbide	Hanover Trust
W. R. Grace Co.	
Amerada Petroleum	
Freeport Sulphur Co.	
Texaco, Inc.	Chemical Bank
Cities Service Co.	
Texas Gas Transmission Co.	

*The bank specified also owns a substantial equity interest in this oil company.

Source: *Commercial Banks and their Trust Activities*, Staff Report for the Subcommittee on Domestic Finance, Committee on Banking and Currency, House of Representatives, 90th Congress, 2d Session, July 8, 1968.

threat to effective competition among these petroleum companies not only because the interlocks create a commonality between their boards, but even more so because of the critical role of the financial community in providing the capital which will be needed to expand energy production to meet future needs. . . .

Joint Ownership of Oil Pipelines

Virtually all of the major integrated petroleum companies hold joint interest with others in the transportation network that moves crude oil and products from producing regions to refineries and markets. . . . Whereas early in this century Standard's control of the pipeline network gave it a distinct upper hand over all of its rivals, today's joint venture arrangements, which dominate the oil pipeline industry, draw ostensibly independent firms together into the common pursuit of a mutual purpose. Moreover, these jointly owned transportation links between producing, refining, and marketing operations (about three fourths of all crude and one fourth of refined products move through pipelines) require that producing and processing operations of the various partners be coordinated with each other so that the whole vertically integrated system functions smoothly. . . .

Joint Production

Only 4 of the 16 largest majors with interests in federal offshore producing leases own 50 percent or more of their leases independently. Conversely, 10 of the 16 own 80 percent or more of their offshore properties jointly with each other. In addition, very few companies outside of the top 16 have any independent holdings at all. In addition to the top 16, 23 medium- to large-size producers were surveyed. Of these, only 2 held as much as 25 percent of their leases independently and 17 had no independently owned leases at all. . . .

TABLE 5: Four Joint Ventures in the Oil Pipeline Industry

Pipeline Company	Co-Owners and Percent Held by Each	
Dixie Pipeline Co.	Amoco	12.1
(Assets—$46.4 million)	Atlantic-Richfield	7.4
	Cities Service	5.0
	Continental	4.1
	Exxon	11.1
	Mobil	5.0
	Phillips	14.5
	Shell	5.5
	Texaco	5.0
	Gulf	18.2
	Transco	3.6
	Allied Chemical	8.6
Laurel Pipeline Co.	Gulf	49.1
(Assets—$35.9 million)	Texaco	33.9
	Sohio	17.0
Colonial Pipeline Co.	Amoco	14.3
(Assets—$480.2 million)	Atlantic-Richfield	1.6
	Cities Service	14.0
	Continental	7.5
	Phillips	7.1
	Texaco	14.3
	Gulf	16.8
	Sohio	9.0
	Mobil	11.5
	Union Oil	4.0
Plantation Pipeline Co.	Exxon	48.8
(Assets—$176.1 million)	Shell	24.0
	Refiners Oil Corp.	27.1

TABLE 6: Joint Production in the Permian Basin, Texas (matrix shows number of joint unitization agreements)

		1	2	3	4	5	6	7	8	9	10	11	12	13	14	15	16
		Amerada	Atlantic	Cities	Continental	Getty	Gulf	Marathon	Mobil	Phillips	Shell	Amoco	Exxon	Sohio	Sun	Texaco	Union
Amerada	1																
Atlantic	2	16															
Cities	3	14	32														
Continental	4	8	18	15													
Getty (Skelly)	5	17	32	19	9												
Gulf	6	5	3	12	8	17											
Marathon	7	7	10	6	4	8	6										
Mobil	8	9	25	14	10	20	12	8									
Phillips	9	13	33	20	15	20	12	6	13								
Shell	10	9	28	15	11	17	11	8	10	16							
Stand. of Ind. (Amoco)	11	18	36	30	20	29	21	9	24	29	25						
Stand. of N.J. (Exxon)	12	12	29	14	13	18	20	6	18	17	15	29					
Stand. of Ohio (Sohio)	13	4	10	4	6	6	5	2	6	6	2	8	8				
Sun	14	12	29	20	13	23	15	5	14	21	15	33	17	6			
Texaco	15	12	42	23	19	25	23	8	19	22	18	30	22	10	23		
Union	16	5	18	12	5	13	13	4	13	11	5	21	12	7	17	11	

In addition to these studies of the ownership of federal offshore producing leases and State of Louisiana leases, a study has also been made of producing units in the Permian Basin in West Texas. Again, what emerges is a picture of extensive intercorporate interties. As shown in the following matrix, Table 6, literally every one of the 16 large major oil companies studied had a significant number of joint producing arrangements with every other major. . . .

International Joint Ventures

In addition to the interrelated domestic operations of the major American petroleum companies, we should not lose sight of the fact that it is largely these same corporate entities or their affiliates which make up the international oil cartel. . . .

Other Interties

The evidence presented above was obtained entirely from public sources. In addition, American Petroleum Institute records indicate that there are substantial crude oil exchange agreements among the majors, ranging from more than 50 percent of their total domestic liquid hydrocarbon production for some companies down to only a few percentage points for others. . . .

POLICY PROPOSALS

As shown above, market control in the petroleum industry, including the natural gas producing sector, is held by a closely knit consortium comprised of the large fully integrated oil companies and their jointly interlocked affiliates. These firms, working in cooperation with each other, have the ability to control petroleum supplies and, in so doing, to maneuver for monopolistic market price levels.

Federal regulation of the field price of natural gas was supposedly designed to deal with this problem. Apparently, it is not working well. As in the case of fuel oil and gasoline, natural gas supplies are short and prices are rising rapidly. No one can deny that policy changes are needed. The prescription offered by the petroleum industry and its various spokesmen is for unrestrained "market freedom"—a situation wherein the industry (not the public) would be "free"; free, that is, to extract the maximum possible price that the market will bear. Unless capitulation to the monopoly power of private economic interests is now viewed as a national policy alternative, this prescription makes no sense. Certainly, from the consuming public's view, it cannot be described as a rational stratagem.

Stephen Breyer (1938–   )
Paul W. MacAvoy (1934–   )

⚹ 58

Energy Regulation by the Federal Power Commission*

This careful attempt by skeptics to appraise the results of FPC regulation finds scant benefits for the public. It is a good example of the post-1960 efforts to find regulation's real effects.

MAJOR EFFORTS

The commission's major efforts went into regulating the profits and prices of natural gas pipeline companies, setting the field price of natural gas, and promoting coordinated planning among firms engaged in interstate electric power transmission. On the average, 25 percent of the FPC's annual budget had to do with pipelines and about 20 percent had to do with gas producers. The share of FPC budget allotted to electric power planning was relatively small. The activity, nevertheless, was important, for it was the commission's most serious and sustained effort to foster increased production efficiency. . . .

RESULTS

From the account given of the commission's work in each of the stipulated areas, it is possible to show approximately the total direct expense of regulation during a typical year in the late 1960s. Table 1 sets forth a single column for FPC expenditures, derived from budget information. Two columns are offered for company expenditures. One lists a "most probable" figure in each category of activity; the other shows the range within which the precise amount could fall. Some recordkeeping

---

Stephen Breyer and Paul W. MacAvoy, Energy Regulation by the Federal Power Commission. © 1974 by The Brookings Institution, Washington, D.C., excerpted from pp. 4, 3–15, 122–23 and 132–34. Breyer teaches at Harvard Law School and was legal assistant to the Antitrust Division chief during 1965–67. MacAvoy has analysed regulation from many angles, with books on natural gas and railroad regulation (both concluding that regulation has been superfluous and/or harmful). He has also done a major study of breeder reactors and is the editor of the *Bell Journal of Economics and Management Service.* He is at Yale.

The Federal Power Commission was in 1977 renamed the Federal Energy Regulatory Commission.

and reporting expenses are routinely imposed on the companies by FPC regulations. Other administrative expenses are "initiated" by the companies on the supposition that the decisions obtained thereby may benefit them. Both forms of company expense count as costs of regulation in Table 1. . . .

The combined agency and private expenditures set the minimum value of the benefits that regulatory activities must "buy" if the game is to be worth the price of admission. From the public's standpoint, regulation is not worthwhile unless it produces benefits greater than the total regulatory expense. . . .

Unfortunately the reader *cannot* take the utility of the Federal Power Commission for granted or assume that the remaining chapters merely cover technicalities and fine points. On the contrary, economic analysis reveals that in the late 1960s, with the commission operating at full steam, results were dismal: Prices collected by the pipeline companies were not perceptibly lower than they would have been without regulation; setting field prices for natural gas did the residential consumer more harm than good by affecting the market so as inadvertently to bring on a gas shortage; and with federally regulated sales constituting only a minor portion of electricity sales, manifold opportunities to shift costs tended to render federal pricing ineffective. Commission planning efforts faltered. . . .

Three conclusions emerge from this study. First, commission activity benefited the consumer very little if at all. The administrative costs of operating the commission, including the costs to litigants, ranged between $31 million and $95 million per year and probably averaged approximately $35 million. Although this expenditure is small when compared with gas and electricity revenues, it did not buy much. Measures of the effectiveness of gas pipeline price regulation indicate that pipeline prices were not lower than they would have been without regulation. Gas producer price regulation, which accounted for the largest portion of the administrative expense attributable to commission operation, caused more harm than good. Ceiling prices at the wellhead were set too low, creating a reserve shortage and a production shortage. In all probability, the gas shortage hurt residential consumers more than lower prices helped them. Efforts to plan for increased efficiency in electricity production achieved a few minor successes but did not gain for the consumer the considerable benefits that increased coordination might have provided. The full array of these calculations is shown in Table 1. Perhaps the commission's secondary activities—gathering statistics, reviewing construction plans, providing a forum for complaints—justified the administrative expenses shown there. But certainly FPC regulation did not achieve direct gains to consumers.

Second, the study adds support to the growing suspicion that regula-

TABLE 1: Estimated Expenses for FPC Regulation during a Typical Year in the 1960s (millions of dollars)

Activity	Federal Power Commission	Expenditures Companies Estimate	Expenditures Companies Range	Combined	Benefits from Regulation for Consumers Direct	Benefits from Regulation for Consumers Indirect or Long-Term Benefits
Gas pipeline price and systems regulation	3.5	2.5	2.0 to 3.0	6.0	1–10	Insignificant
Gas field price regulation	3.1	18.0*	18.0 to 76.0	21.1	Negative	Negative
Electric power						
Price regulation	1.6	1.6	0.2 to 3.1	3.2 }		
Systems evaluation	1.3	1.9	1.4 to 2.4	3.2 }	Insignificant	Insignificant
General FPC administration	1.1	—	—	1.1		
Total	10.6	24.0	21.6 to 84.5	34.6		

*Area rate proceedings only; excludes certification expenses and individual price cases.

Sources: Col. 1 derived from data in *The Budget of the United States Government—Appendix*, various issues; cols. 2 and 3 estimated on the basis of information discussed in the text.

tion by commission is at best a clumsy tool for achieving economic goals. In each instance, the FPC responded slowly and inefficiently to changing conditions. . . .

Third, the study shows the serious risks that flow from an agency's single-minded pursuit of lower prices. . . .

STEPS TOWARD REFORM

The behavior of the Federal Power Commission indicates the immediate desirability of three specific changes in regulatory policy. First, efforts to regulate the prices charged by natural gas producers should be abandoned. Deregulation in all likelihood would end the gas shortage, while competition among producers probably would keep prices near market-clearing levels. Competition prices would be higher than recent ceiling prices by several cents per Mcf. The government should consider changes in tax policy, such as abolition of the depletion allowance, rather than rely upon regulatory policy to capture any inordinately high producer rents that might follow from the price increases.

Second, the commission should consider relaxing, rather than tightening, its supervision of pipeline prices and profits. Our findings suggest that the pipelines face a certain amount of competition in many of their regulated markets. Such competition limits the extent to which they can raise prices above costs. That fact, together with the near impossibility of regulating prices in such a way as to eliminate monopoly profit, makes it most unlikely that regulation provides benefits worth its administrative cost. The commission should consider abandoning the cost-of-service price setting method and instead investigate the extent to which various pipeline markets are competitive. Where competition exists—where there are more than two gas pipelines and there are close substitute sources of energy—it could deregulate. Where effective competition does not exist, it could set prices based upon costs and prices in the more competitive markets. Such a "comparative" price-setting technique, though approximate, is likely to be as effective as present rate-setting methods and to require less extensive supervision. The commission should begin to explore the details of such an alternative.

Third, energy policy planners, who are now groping with the problems posed by the need for economy, reliability, and environmental protection, ought not to look to traditional regulation for solutions. The need for coordination in planning and operating electricity systems is great. Electric power should be provided through unified systems that each serve several states and include several companies. Yet, the Federal Power Commission's history suggests that it cannot be relied upon to bring about any major change in industry structure, and chapter 4 suggests that the reasons lie in the nature of the regulatory process itself.

Policymakers should begin to study the desirability of injecting the government more directly into the planning process. Such governmental involvement might take a variety of forms, ranging from the creation of special task forces with power to order the building of particular lines and plants to the creation of industry/government regional power authorities with direct planning and operating responsibilities. Our study does not indicate to what extent such systems are preferable to the status quo; it indicates only that the status quo and similar forms of regulation will not solve the coordination problem. Thus policymakers must begin the study of very different institutional alternatives.

These three changes do not constitute a detailed program. Our basic objective here has been to assess the effectiveness of past commission action. That assessment indicates that it is expecting too much to ask a commission to undertake profit regulation or complex planning. As A. E. Kahn notes in *The Economics of Regulation,* some critics of the regulatory agencies suggests that "the present institution embodies the worst of both possible worlds—monopoly without effective control, private enterprise without effective incentive or stimulus, governmental supervision without the possibility of effective initiative in the public interest." The performance of the FPC adds support to this view.

D. TELECOMMUNICATIONS

The two main types of services are *point-to-point* (namely telephone and data communication) and *broadcasting* (namely television, radio, and cable-casting). The economic issues and cases have clustered mainly around the telephone system. Though that industry is partly a natural monopoly, it also has growing areas of natural competition. The FCC has had to settle the margin of competition in a series of difficult cases.

Formed in 1934, the FCC went 30 years without a formal case on telephone prices and rates of return, relying instead mainly on private negotiations with the Bell System. As the Johnson-Dystel excerpt notes, the FCC is usually overwhelmed by a mass of issues to decide, many of them secondary matters. In 1965 it finally began a formal case on prices, profits, and competitive issues in the Bell System.

The competitive issues divide into two main groups. One is the provision and pricing of high-volume trunk-route services. A key step was the Bell System's monopolization of microwave transmission (by those towers with reflectors at the top which you see at intervals between cities) in 1948–50. The Beelar reading presents that episode. When in 1959 the FCC's "Above 590" decision let in some competition in the area, one Bell response was "TELPAK," a sharp volume discount for large business customers. In 1965 the FCC found TELPAK rates to be too low, a form of "predatory pricing" to keep out new competition (recall Part I above). Yet appeals and further actions by the Bell System kept TELPAK in being through 1977.

In 1969 the FCC moved to let new firms set up competitive systems to transmit data between major cities. The *MCI* decision also reversed Bell's longstanding refusal to let competitors interconnect with its system. A category of "specialized common carriers" was created, and some 20 firms had entered by 1975. Yet few made profits and by 1978 several had gone bankrupt.

The other area of possible competition is in selling equipment to the operating firms. The Bell System's Western Electric Company has always supplied virtually all of the system's equipment. This amounted to a tie-in of far greater scope than Jerrold's (recall Part I above). In 1969 the FCC finally decided that users could attach other apparatus to Bell equipment, under suitable safeguards. The *Carterfone* decision involved a small device made by a tiny firm, but it set the precedent for a variety of larger equipment. In ten years, this new market had grown, but it still left the main Bell dominance intact. A lengthy FCC task force report in 1975 recommended separating Western Electric from AT&T (recall the Antitrust suit in Part II above). The FCC turned down the proposal in 1977, but it also ordered the Bell System to develop more open purchasing, involving outsiders on a fair basis. The policy statement is excerpted here.

The FCC does not regulate the prices or profits of broadcasters, but it does seek to promote diversity and local interests in programming. Peter O. Steiner discusses the difficulty of balancing monopoly and competition to get better broadcasting fare.

Nicholas Johnson (1934–   )
John J. Dystel

59

A Day in the Life: The Federal Communications Commission*

The flood of issues, large and small, which the FCC must "decide" is graphically portrayed here, and the dubious results are bluntly appraised. Johnson was an outstanding maverick FCC commissioner during 1966–73, alert to the economic issues and to the political forces beating upon—and within—the agency. These excerpts give only a small part of the whole. Other commissions have much the same experience: struggling to cope.

"I read the news today, oh boy!"—The Beatles, "A Day in the Life"

For seven years I have struggled with the FCC in an effort to inject some rationality into its decision-making process and to reveal its workings to the public. There is reason enough to assert that everything the FCC does is wrong.[1] But, like contributions to the literature detailing disasters in given areas of Commission responsibility, such assertions are almost universally dismissed as exaggerations.

And so it is that I have come to try to describe the agency one more time, but from a unique perspective: "A day in the life" of the Federal Communications Commission.[2] The day—Wednesday, December 13, 1972—was selected from the Commission's meeting days in 1972. It is neither better nor worse than any other day during the past seven years.

---

*Nicholas Johnson and John J. Dystel, "A Day in the Life: The Federal Communications Commission." Reprinted by permission of The Yale Law Journal Company and Fred B. Rothman & Company from *The Yale Law Journal*, vol. 82, pp. 1575–79, 1582, 1586–89, 1595, 1626, 1633–34. Johnson was bounced over to his seat on the FCC after attempting to shake up the Federal Maritime Commission as Commissioner during 1965–66. He is now in political eclipse but is active in policy groups. Dystel was his assistant at the FCC.

[1]There are many who have bemoaned what may aptly be described as the FCC's analytical void. For example, Newton Minow, a former FCC Chairman, complained upon leaving the Commission that the FCC is "a quixotic world of undefined terms, private pressures, and tools unsuited to the work." Drew, *Is the FCC Dead? Atlantic*, July 1967, at 29. For a somewhat different view, however, see Cox, *Does the FCC Really Do Anything?* 11 *Broadcasting* 97 (1967).

[2]Numerous books, articles, and government reports have been written about the FCC. See H. Friendly, *The Federal Administrative Agencies* (1962); J. Landis, *Report on Regulatory*

It is typical. This article is an effort to describe what the FCC did on that typical Wednesday.

Professors and students of administrative law tend to concentrate on a particular agency decision—usually one that has gone to the appellate courts. But a look at one day's events may well be more instructive than a close examination of a single event in determining why an agency is failing at its job or why it acts in a consistently unprincipled manner.[3]

The seven FCC Commissioners meet weekly, on Wednesdays,[4] to vote on the items brought to their attention by the Commission's various bureaus.[5] It is not clear who decides what matters will be considered. The agenda is the product of industry pressures, staff idiosyncrasies, and political judgments. If he chooses, however, the Chairman is in a position to control the flow of items to the Commission.

Most matters are not handled at FCC meetings but are delegated by the Commission to the staff for action. In theory these items are in areas of settled Commission policy, but in fact, the Commission has not so limited the scope of its delegations. During my term the majority has been unwilling to examine its delegation orders or to enunciate what standards control the delegation of decision-making authority.

Those issues which do reach the Commissioners each week often take them by surprise. Opening a new agenda (the stack of mimeographed staff memos and accompanying recommended opinions for a Wednesday meeting) is like Christmas morning. All too often the agenda includes a long, detailed staff document dealing with a controversial and complicated matter in which: (1) numerous alternatives are presented (or excluded) after extensive staff work, (2) the proposed resolution is

---

Agencies to the President-Elect, Senate Comm. on the Judiciary, 86th Cong., 2d Sess. (1960); Drew, supra note 1; Kalven, Broadcasting, Public Policy and the First Amendment, 10 J. Law & Econ. 15 (1967); Zeidenberg, Is the FCC Obsolete? Television, October 1966, at 27, 51.

[3]There are some shortcomings in this expository device. Considerable background material must be included in order to analyze the Commission's actions. Moreover, although one day does include a range of Commission activities, such concentration runs the risk inherent in any evaluation based on a random sample.

[4]Most Commission meetings last for a day or less. If several important matters must be resolved, however, the meetings may last as long as two days. The meeting which constitutes the subject matter of this article began on Wednesday, December 13, and ended the following day. These meetings are closed to the public.

[5]The FCC has a number of major regulatory responsibilities including regulation of broadcast and cable television (CATV), allocation of the nongovernmental portion of the radio spectrum, regulation of interstate telephone, telegraph, miscellaneous radio common carriers, e.g., land mobile radio users, domestic satellites, and international communications services.

To deal with these primary areas of concern, the Commission is divided into four substantive bureaus: the Broadcast Bureau, the Cable Bureau, the Safety and Special Radio Services Bureau, and the Common Carrier Bureau. The Chief Engineer's Office and General Counsel's Office are comparable to bureaus. Each bureau, in turn, has various divisions to which I shall refer throughout this article.

endorsed by all of the Commission's bureau chiefs, (3) an immediate decision is required, and (4) any alteration in the proposed resolution will mean considerably more staff work and costly delay. As a result, rational decision-making suffers.

On December 13, 1972, the Commission was presented with 59 items.[6] In each case the staff made a recommendation to the Commissioners. If a majority votes to approve the staff's recommendation, it adopts the proposed Commission opinion as well. If one of the Commissioners questions a particular item, there is a discussion with the staff prior to a vote. On December 13, 28 of the 59 items were discussed.[7]

Each week's agenda is divided into 13 substantive categories: Hearing, General, Safety and Special, Common Carrier, Personnel, Classified, CATV, Assignment and Transfer, Renewals, Aural, Television, Broadcast, and Complaints and Compliance—in that order.[8]

Briefing for Commissioners

In recent months the Commissioners have scheduled briefings during regular agenda meetings by each Bureau and Office on its work, resources, and problems. Such briefings often consist of a superficial review of an organizational chart or may deteriorate into a discussion of a pending case. They seldom involve consideration of any innovative changes and amount to little more than the Commissioners' collective nod toward fulfillment of their management responsibilities.

Measured by past briefings the Cable Bureau's December 13 briefing was excellent. It focused on the growth and geographic distribution of the CATV industry, developments in the industry's ownership structure, bureau backlog problems, reports filed with the Commission but as yet unprocessed, and bureau organization.

The Cable Bureau's Chief noted, "The trouble we are in now will only

---

[6]Fifty-seven of these items had been distributed to each Commissioner's office at the close of the preceding week. Two, however, did not reach the Commissioners until just prior to the meeting. These latter items are called "walk-in items," and because they are rushed to the Commission for resolution, the Commission's analysis is often extremely superficial.

[7]Twenty-four of the remaining items were adopted without discussion in what is called the "consent agenda." On December 13, the consent agenda lasted one half hour. The remaining seven items were simply passed over for future consideration. Of the 28 items which the Commissioners discussed, 11 were deferred for future resolution.

[8]There is a final category of agenda materials which can be called information items. Some are copies of previous agenda items which were acted upon before a regular distribution of materials could be completed. Others are matters acted upon by circulation: The item is passed from one Commissioner's office to the next for the recording of votes. Some are staff memos (or occasionally Commissioner memos) that contain important information—among them staff papers on major policy proceedings underway at the Commission, reports on meetings attended by staff, or reports on work underway in the Commission.

deepen." Backlogs were growing, the toughest certification cases were yet to come, and time lost due to inadequate staff could not be recouped. The Commissioners were advised that there was no staff to process and analyze the annual reports from CATV systems.

The discussion turned to mergers within the Cable industry. The Cable Bureau saw no harmful effects from growing concentration of control within the industry and attempted to rationalize recent mergers by analogy to companies in other communications industries which serve more subscribers than the largest cable corporation. No rule yet governs multiple ownership of cable systems by a single corporation and adoption of such a rule now would probably be too late.

The Bureau presented no written recommendations on any of these issues and the Commission gave no orders, designated no one to study the problems further, and scheduled no future meetings; nothing, in short, has been done. Some of these matters will come before the Commission again only if the briefings continue and the Bureau Chief thinks it worthwhile to mention them.

Finally, the Bureau Chief and the Commissioners discussed some consulting work on Bureau resource needs performed by Harbridge House, Inc. It is common practice to pay consultants to "recommend" that an agency do what it wants to do anyway, the report being used only to convince the budgeting authority. Based on a draft report and the Cable Bureau's recommendation, the Commission proposed large increases in the Cable Bureau Budget for Fiscal Year 1974. . . .

The General Agenda

The General Agenda consists of matters not contained in other substantive agenda categories. On December 13, the Commissioners considered 12 such matters. Resolution of at least one required a level of expertise which the Commissioners lack. On other matters, the majority, presumably capable of comprehending the issues, reached bizarre conclusions or no conclusions at all. . . .

An item involving common carrier issues appeared on the General rather than Common Carrier Agenda because more than one bureau was involved. For years the FCC has struggled with the problem of whether a customer has the right to attach his own accessory equipment to the common carriers' communications networks. Customers prefer to use their own equipment and independent equipment manufacturers are happy to supply it, but common carriers, particularly if they own very profitable equipment manufacturers, oppose such arrangements.

The FCC has furthered the carriers' interests in this controversy by delay and selective approval of the carriers' tariffs. Tariffs describe the rates and practices which govern the services offered by the carrier. In

1968 the Commission struck down AT&T's tariffs on the ground that they were an unreasonable barrier to the connection of customer equipment.[9] Bell then filed new tariffs and the lengthy review process began again. The Commission has still not resolved this matter, though the tariffs have gone into effect. Delay has obviously worked to the carriers' benefit.[10]

The Commission has also delayed taking affirmative action to assist customers in the exercise of their right to connect personally owned equipment. The Chief Engineer's report on that subject (recommending a program for customer-interconnection) was considered by the Commission at the December 13 meeting. The majority, obviously sympathetic to AT&T's interests, temporized, assuring those of us concerned about further delay that the Chief Engineer's proposals would receive consideration within 30 days. Four months later, when the Commission issued a further notice, no action had been taken, and it seems clear that final resolution of this question will take several more years. . . .

The Commissioners' deliberations in this proceeding illustrate the problems inherent in FCC policy formulation. The Commission lacks data, makes no independent analysis, relies heavily on information provided by interested parties, considers broad questions piecemeal, defers to industry interests, postpones difficult decisions, hopes for compromises that the agency can ratify, and fails to anticipate major problems before they arise. Had the FCC been more prescient, it might have been prepared to handle the massive "hotelvision" problem that presented itself on December 13. Instead, the Commission simply drifted.

The Cable Television Agenda

Cable television, a new industry, could have an impact upon the American people rivaling that of the telephone or the automobile. The Commission, however, very solicitous of the interests of the commercial

---

[9]*Carterfone*, 13 F.C.C.2d 420 (1968).

[10]The FCC can reject a carrier's tariff as unlawful (47 C.F.R. § 61.69 (1972)) or take no action and let the tariff go into effect. In between these extremes there are two other possibilities. First, the tariff can be suspended for up to 90 days and a hearing on its lawfulness ordered. The implementation of the tariff is thus merely delayed 90 days since there is almost no possibility that the Commission can complete hearings in that period. Second, the Commission can require carriers to ask permission to file additional tariff changes which could affect existing proceedings that have been underway for a long period of time. This permission may be withheld if the tariff filing would disrupt the Commission's deliberations. *AT&T*, 33 F.C.C.2d 522, aff'd, 36 F.C.C.2d 484 (1972). My own view is that the Commission has the authority to suspend tariffs for as long as is necessary to litigate major issues raised by them. *AT&T*, 37 F.C.C.2d 754, 761 (1972). On rare occasions a carrier will "voluntarily" postpone a tariff at the Commission's request. Usually, however, a new carrier tariff goes into effect 90 days after the carrier scheduled it to become effective.

broadcasting industry, and hence, of that industry's fear of cable television, has for years been antagonistic toward Cable. Such bureaucratic intransigence cannot last forever—especially in view of the broadcast industry's rush to buy cable systems. In February 1972, the Commission "opened up" the cable industry by promulgating a set of complex rules which, while allowing Cable to begin operating on a national scale, nevertheless prevented the industry from fully developing. . . .

Television Station License Renewals

*   *   *   *   *

On December 13, after a seemingly routine investigation had uncovered a multitude of violations, the FCC designated the renewal application of WHBI, a medium-size operation, for hearing on 15 issues. Thus another blow was struck on behalf of what a former Commission General Counsel calls the "three outhouses policy of broadcast regulation—any broadcaster with three outhouses or fewer will be far more likely to bear the full brunt of Commission regulatory fervor than his larger broadcast colleagues.

It is ironically in the case-by-case and unsystematic atmosphere of the Complaints and Compliance Agenda that the Commissioners engage in their most sensitive and best known form of regulation, i.e., regulation of programming content. It is therefore at the end of a grueling day that the Commissioners are confronted with questions requiring the most difficult balancing of competing interests. The FCC's regulation of programming content has long been of greatest concern to broadcast licensees. While the broadcaster communicates the same ideas as publishers or private speakers, he finds himself clothed in a different set of First Amendment obligations. He alone must deal with the rights of listeners and speakers who have no financial or corporate interest in his venture.

*   *   *   *   *

Several conclusions emerge.

First, it seems evident that the FCC deals each week with an incredibly broad range of communications matters. On December 13, the FCC considered everything from personnel decisions to significant issues of international consequence. The Commission delved into areas surely beyond its expertise and into issues simply beyond its ken.

Second, as the Hearing Agenda reveals, the Commission, burdened with so much work and having so few resources, takes years to resolve important cases.

Third, as both the Cable and Aural Agendas illustrate, the FCC is manipulated daily by the industries it is supposed to regulate and by its own staff. As a result the Commissioners often make precedents which return to haunt them.

Fourth, if the FCC no longer approves of its own rules and precedents, it simply ignores them—either by waiving them to death or otherwise evading them. In short, the concept of principled decision making does not exist at the FCC.

Fifth, the FCC not only disdains its own administrative principles, but it also ignores those established by the judiciary. Thus, on December 13 the FCC simply turned its back on numerous decisions construing the National Environmental Policy Act and relied on a construction of a recent case involving programming "format changes" not justified by the language of that case.

Sixth, as the General and Common Carrier Agendas show especially well, the Commissioners often decide cases they do not understand.

Finally, the Commission has not developed rational communications policies for governing its day-to-day decisions.

Perhaps it is easier to understand the Commission's sloppy work, its serious gaffs, when one sees an individual decision in the context of the burdensome "day in the life" on which it was voted. Yet much of the burden is of the Commission's own making. It is neither necessary nor advisable to divide up the FCC's workload between a "Broadcasting Commission" and a "Communications Common Carrier Commission." First semester business school principles would suggest that the Commission should formulate *some* statements of national communication policy for the benefit of itself, its staff, the business community, the Congress, the press, and the public. Having done this, it should prepare precise delegation orders to its staff, allow the staff to handle individual cases as they come up, and create a management information reporting system whereby the Commission is able to follow the processing of cases, modifying policy and delegation orders as warranted.

Another purpose of this piece is to offer the public some information concerning the operation of one of its administrative agencies, one which has struggled to keep its activities secret. The FCC is a *public* agency, receiving public funds for the purpose of regulating "in the public interest" communications industries whose services are crucial to the continued vitality of a democratic society. Ironically, though the agency keeps the public in the dark, the communications interests learn all the details of Commission actions through information services provided by lawyers, lobbyists, and the trade press.

Neither the Commission majority nor its staff is troubled by the agency's treatment of the public. Whether because they adhere to notions of "laissez faire" economics or because they sympathize with communications industry interests, a majority of the staff at the FCC exploit the lack of public representation day after day.

Donald C. Beelar (1903–   )

60

Cables in the Sky and the Struggle for Their Control*

> *Utility markets often embrace both "natural monopoly" parts and competitive activities. A key instance is microwave transmission, which the Bell System has controlled since 1950. Since 1965, the gradual opening of the microwave market has involved small but ambitious entrants, strenuous Bell resistance, and landmark FCC decisions. The initial closure during 1948–50, as analysed by Beelar, is typical of utility moves into many other markets which have long-lasting effects.*

The struggle for control of microwave which began more than 20 years ago was in every way as hard fought as that now involving satellites. And the similar potentialities of microwave and domestic satellites—each in its own time—indicate why. Microwave in the 1940s emerged as a competitive threat to the wire line and cable transmission modes; domestic satellites in the 1960s pose a new threat to both wire line and cable and microwave systems. Both developments in turn have raised broad policy issues, namely *(a)* monopoly or competition between common carriers or between different modes of transmission; *(b)* private system competition; *(c)* captive or free enterprise manufacturing markets; *(d)* interconnection restraints and *(e)* the permissible common carrier rate base for the lower cost new communication mode.

These are the issues which, with respect to microwave, remain largely unresolved and which, as to domestic satellites, should be decided before authorization of any initial system. A consideration of these issues in the context of the domestic satellite technology may provide an opportunity to review and complete the unfinished business of microwave regulation. The microwave story, heretofore untold, is the subject of this article.

---

*Donald C. Beelar, "Cables in the Sky and the Struggle for Their Control," *Federal Communications Bar Journal*, January 1967, excerpted from pp. 26–33, and 40–41. Beelar is an attorney.

319

ROUND ONE: CHECKMATE IN MICROWAVE

The struggle for control of the new microwave industry in the late 1940s, as seen from the perspective of the 1960s, may be likened to a chess game. Not one between two players, but one in which multiple opponents were taken on by one master, AT&T. The contestants in that encounter were the leading electronic manufacturers and the communications carriers; the trophy at stake was the emerging television network market and the franchise for a nationwide microwave system of unprecedented broad-band channel capacity, not necessarily a part of the wire line public telephone network.

The Contestants

1. *Philco* was the first in the field with an operational video relay system, applied for in the fall of 1944 and put into operation between Washington, D.C., and Philadelphia, Pennsylvania, in the spring of 1945. The inauguration of this system, as well as the events which forced it out of business three years later, is described later.

2. *Raytheon's* was far and away the most ambitious and imaginative proposal, and it was the most active challenger throughout the 1944–48 period. In early 1945, Raytheon announced its intention to construct and operate a transcontinental microwave relay system for television, broadcasting, aviation, weather, press, and other business uses. By 1947, it had license authorizations for a microwave system from Boston to New York to Chicago paralleling that of AT&T. A year later Raytheon withdrew from the scene.

3. *Western Union* placed a microwave system in operation between New York and Philadelphia in 1945. It had ideas about constructing a transcontinental microwave system and getting into the video network business. It got as far west as Pittsburgh, Pennsylvania, in the 1940s where it came to a ten-year halt. Western Union's dream of owning a transcontinental microwave system was not realized until the 1960s.

4. *General Electric* joined with *IBM* in obtaining experimental licenses in November 1944 for a microwave system from Schenectady to New York to Philadelphia to Washington. Their proposal emphasized a system for the transmission of modern business machine data. This system was expressly restricted to experimentation.

5. *AT&T,* as of the end of World War II, was a wire line and cable company and wire line minded, but in June 1944, it did obtain experimental licenses for a microwave system between New York and Boston which became operational November 11, 1947. AT&T proposed to use microwave relay stations for television, facsimile, sound programs, and multiplex telephony, eventually over nationwide networks.

6. *DuMont*, one of the pioneers in television broadcasting, was the last entry in the contest for intercity microwave relay facilities. Its proposal, a five-station relay system between New York and Washington, D.C., filed in June 1947, was in a large measure a protest against what it considered excessively high AT&T rates for video transmission service ($5.15 per hour per station for 28 hours a week).

So much for the principal contestants and their proposals. The scene is now set for the play-by-play account of the microwave chess game which shaped the destiny of this new industry during its first decade.

Move One

In the beginning the wire line common carriers, AT&T and Western Union, were outnumbered 5 to 2. The opening gambit was deceptively innocent. In the FCC's landmark 1945 frequency allocation proceeding, which made eight bands of frequencies available for microwave relay systems, AT&T took the position that it was undesirable for frequencies used by public relay telephone systems to be shared with other services. AT&T's request was initially rejected on the ground that all microwave assignments at that time were on an experimental basis. A bit later, however, the position sponsored by AT&T was adopted by the FCC, and this became the cornerstone of the microwave regulatory structure. The effect of setting aside bands of microwave frequencies for use only by a "common carrier" operated, in fact, as a reservation of frequencies for the exclusive use of the Bell System. This in turn put the free enterprise sector of the infant microwave industry into a captive market situation.

Move Two

The second move further solidified control over the microwave market in the wire line common carriers. When IBM and General Electric filed applications for a Schenectady-New York-Washington microwave system, Western Union protested on the ground that the experimental authorization should be limited to experimental purposes and precluded from handling any commercial operations. The FCC agreed and imposed a condition on these licenses expressly prohibiting any commercial use of the system, either as a common carrier or otherwise. The effect of this action was strictly to limit the five nonwire line companies to experimental operations in the strict sense of that term and to make it impossible for these operations to ripen into any form of commercial service without further FCC authority. At this early stage of the contest, therefore, the battle lines appeared to be drawn between the established wire line common carriers, AT&T and Western Union, and the would-be newcomers to the microwave field. In reality, as made apparent by subsequent events, the contest was one between AT&T and the rest of the field.

Interlude. The significance of the next move is highlighted by reference to intervening events in the market place. Philco's six-station system between Washington and Philadelphia was dedicated at a banquet in the Statler Hotel in Washington on the night of Tuesday, April 16, 1945. On that occasion, the image and speech of then FCC Chairman Paul Porter and Dr. Karl Compton, President of MIT, were transmitted over the Philco microwave system from Washington to Philadelphia and there broadcast over TV station WPTZ with excellent technical quality, it was reported. Chairman Porter observed that this event marked "a historic milestone in our progress towards a nationwide system of television" and "this demonstration is a harbinger of exciting things to come." These remarks were indeed prophetic, except that Philco, an active pioneer in the microwave field, was soon to lose out as a contender for the TV video market. By 1947, the microwave capability for video program transmission, which required a very wide band carrier channel of four megacycles, or the equivalent of 1,000 voice transmissions, was confined to the northeast sector of the United States and the facilities of AT&T, Western Union, Raytheon, Philco, IBM, and General Electric.

Move Three

In 1948, AT&T revealed its intention to be the sole supplier of video network program service. It proceeded to challenge all comers, both in proceedings before the FCC and in the market place. On March 29, 1948, AT&T filed a video transmission tariff to be effective May 1, 1948.[1] Western Union joined in the proceeding a day later by filing a similar tariff for program transmission service, also effective May 1, 1948, between New York and Philadelphia. These tariffs were formally challenged by the Television Broadcasters Association (TBA), which raised various issues, including the validity of the provision in AT&T's tariff precluding interconnection with the facilities of any other company. An investigation was ordered April 28, 1948.

While this hearing before the FCC was under way, AT&T administered a mortal blow to the Philco system. On September 9, 1948, AT&T refused to transmit an NBC-TV program from New York to Boston over its facilities which originated in Philadelphia and was carried over the

---

[1]The fact that AT&T's microwave station licenses were still experimental did not preclude it from launching a commercial service by a public tariff offering, in contrast to the FCC restraints imposed on GE and IBM. See "Move Two," *supra*.

Philco microwave system. On another occasion, AT&T refused to carry an NBC telecast of an Army football game from West Point to New York City which NBC proposed to transmit from New York City to Philadelphia via the Philco microwave system. Philco went to court to enjoin AT&T, but this proved unsuccessful. Thereafter Philco's vice president of engineering in testimony before the FCC announced Philco's withdrawal from the intercity microwave relay service because of interconnection refusal. AT&T's victory over Philco showed AT&T's willingness to take on any and all would-be newcomers to the microwave market and signaled the retreat or surrender of all the original contestants, except Western Union.

Move Four

Television broadcasters appeared unexpectedly as a late challenger to AT&T's position as the sole source of TV network service. In the late 1940s, many television broadcasters could not get video network channels from AT&T for network television programs, a serious handicap to a rapidly expanding TV industry. Accordingly, several television broadcasters undertook to construct microwave facilities to other cities where physical connection could be made with common carrier facilities. AT&T, however, had by tariff precluded the interconnection of private microwave systems with its own facilities. In its December 23, 1949, decision in the tariff investigation in docket no. 8963, the FCC required AT&T, over its objection, to interconnect with TV broadcasters' private microwave facilities. Otherwise, it was pointed out, the Commission's grant of license to TV broadcasters for the operation of interim microwave video program transmission facilities would be rendered a nullity.

While the broadcasters had won the battle, it was AT&T which had nonetheless won the war. For previously, on February 20, 1948, the FCC had rather casually made a policy determination that frequencies for video network facilities would be only for service furnished by common carrier facilities and that broadcasters operating interim private microwave stations would be required to abandon such systems whenever service became available from a common carrier, i.e. AT&T. Hence, while the broadcasters were accorded interim interconnection rights, the long-term result was to give AT&T the green light to displace private microwave systems of broadcasters whenever it was ready, willing, and able to do so. This eliminated the threat to AT&T of the broadcasting sector. Thus, AT&T entered the 1950s with only one remaining opponent of those originally seeking entry into the microwave field five years earlier—Western Union.

Move Five and Checkmate

In the spring of 1950, hearings were commenced in docket no. 9539 on Western Union's effort to require AT&T to interconnect with the former's microwave system between New York and Philadelphia. Previously, Western Union found itself in the middle between the TV broadcasters and AT&T on interconnection, and it was promised a separate proceeding on that issue. Two and one half years later AT&T emerged as the victor in this controversy in a split decision, the majority holding that Western Union had failed to make out a sufficient showing warranting compulsory interconnection on the facts of that case. The real significance of this decision was made apparent in the opening paragraph of the dissenting opinion of two Commissioners, Rosel H. Hyde, now Chairman of the FCC, and Frieda B. Hennock, which stated:

> The decision of the majority, while it states in its conclusions that "it is not intended to support any claim which the Bell System may have made to a monopoly in the field of intercity video transmission," effectively does grant such a monopoly to Bell. Moreover, this de facto monopoly is granted without specific recognition by the Commission of such effect and without a finding that such a result would be in the public interest.

With the defeat or elimination of Philco, GE, IBM, Raytheon, and DuMont, and the containment of Western Union to the New York-Philadelphia-Pittsburgh route without interconnection arrangements, the infant microwave industry was completely under AT&T's control by 1950. . . .

On these basic issues the Commission's approach to date has either been negative, passive, or piecemeal. Without ever having conducted a general investigation on interconnection or rendering a decision on that issue, the Commission has permitted AT&T to use interconnection to defeat common carrier competition and to restrict private microwave competition, thereby limiting the utility and services of competing microwave systems. Without specifying the issue, conducting a hearing, or rendering a decision, the FCC permitted AT&T to convert from a privately owned cable and wire plant to a public domain radio spectrum resource without providing that the investment in the lower unit cost microwave system would be the rate base for its use. Without specifying the issue, conducting a hearing, or rendering a decision, the Commission allowed the noncompetitive public telephone network to impose the traditional noncompetitive characteristics on an otherwise potentially competitive private line market. Without specifying the issue, conducting a hearing, or rendering a decision, the Commission has allowed Western Union's high capacity, east-west transcontinental and north-south, western, central, and eastern microwave plant to remain largely unused and unavailable for low cost video and other bulk private line services by reason of restrictive pricing policies controlled by the rate base of the wire line telephone network.

✳ 61

Federal Communications Commission, In the matter of *American Telephone & Telegraph Company, Long Lines Department (TELPAK)*

Revisions of Tariff FCC No. 260 Private
Line Services, Series 5000 (TELPAK) Docket No. 18128
Memorandum Opinion and Order
Adopted: September 23, 1976

Faced with new competition in large-scale business data transmission, the Bell System in 1961 provided sharp price cuts in a new "TELPAK" tariff. The FCC examined TELPAK and in 1964 found its prices to be too low. Further changes, hearings, orders, and appeals kept the issue going into 1978.* The issues and interests are summarized here in the FCC's 1976 decision, which tried to terminate TELPAK. What are good criteria for judging such price cuts?

I. INTRODUCTION AND SUMMARY

1. The issues involved in this proceeding can be traced to the early 1960s with the inception of docket 14251 (the original TELPAK investigation) and docket 14650 (an inquiry into Western Union's domestic telegraph and other services). Docket 18128 originally concerned the lawfulness of TELPAK rate increases of March 25, 1968. However, through consolidation of certain issues extant in docket 16258 (which concerned

*The parties to the proceeding included: 1. The Bell System, 2. The airlines (users of TELPAK), 3. The U.S. Department of Defense and other government agencies (users of TELPAK), 4. an Ad Hoc Telecommunications Committee (of many industrial users of TELPAK). Naturally, all of these favored the TELPAK discounts.

Meanwhile, 5. Microwave Communications, Inc. (MCI), 6. Data Transmission Co. (Datran), and 7. Western Union Co., all competitors of Bell, argued that the price cuts were too deep.

appropriate interstate service revenue contributions) and docket 18684 (which concerned revised video transmission rates), the scope of this proceeding now includes the issue of the general lawfulness of overall rate levels[1] and interservice rate level relationships of Bell's major categories of interstate service. (Findings in this proceeding apply to those services of Western Union which exhibit matching rate levels.) Implicit in the determination of appropriate earnings relationships of Bell's services is our parallel determination of the proper methodology by which each service's contribution to total earnings is to be measured.

2. It is Bell's position that each category of service should yield revenues, at a minimum, to cover its forward-looking, long-run incremental costs (LRIC). Actual rates should exceed such minimums so that aggregate revenues from all services yield the overall interstate revenue requirement. Bell has employed a "basic service philosophy" with regard to determining how total revenue requirements are to be recovered by its private line and monopoly services (MTS and WATS). That is, private line service rates are to yield an "optimum" contribution to earnings above minimum LRIC levels. MTS and WATS rates are to cover residual revenue requirements not met by private line service revenues. Bell has proposed an incremental, prospective "burden test" allegedly to show that its rates are free from cross-subsidization and a "retrospective accountability" test for purposes of providing comparative information concerning forecast and actual results.

3. The Chief of the Common Carrier Bureau released a Recommended Decision (RD) herein on January 19, 1976. The case is before us on exceptions filed to the RD. The RD did not accept Bell's LRIC-oriented basic service philosophy, but supported Fully Distributed Costs (FDC) Method 1 to determine each service's relevant costs. The RD relied on individual service deviations from the Method 1 computed return on investment as an indication of the existence of cross-subsidization and to determine the lawfulness of rate levels and rate level relationships. (The RD held that MTS rates should be designed so as to yield earnings no more than the lesser of Bell's maximum allowed rate of return or the overall rate of return actually being realized. Private line categories of service rates should be designed to yield no less than the minimum allowable overall rate of return).

4. We find it encumbent to select the costing methodology which best reflects our statutory mandate (see Section VIII). Our prior policy supports the position that actual costs of providing service underlie the statutory requirement that rates be just, reasonable, and nondiscriminatory, albeit this does not mean that costs are the *only* criterion useful in determining whether rates are lawful under the Act. Further, we

---

[1]"Rate levels" and "return levels" are generally used interchangeably herein.

conclude that the public interest is not generally served by interservice cross-subsidization, but recognize that statutory and social policies may lend sanction to some intraservice subsidies. Finally, we make findings regarding proper cost standards, measures of cross-subsidization, and acceptable departures from cost of service as a criterion of the justness and reasonableness of return levels and relationships.

5. We hold that Bell's use of LRIC and, generally, its basic service philosophy do not satisfy the constructs of true marginal cost pricing principles. Indeed, we note that it is not possible to make a strict translation from neoclassical marginal costing theory to the pragmatic world of telecommunications. On the basis of these determinations, we have concluded that no "optimal" social welfare or beneficial public interest characteristics could be imputed to Bell's costing methodology. To the contrary, we find Bell's basic service philosophy merely a variant of a full costing approach.

6. We determine that an FDC costing approach is most consistent with our objectives and responsibilities under the Act and should be the basic standard by which the justness and reasonableness of rates will be judged. Of the seven FDC methods of record, Method 7's historical cost causation basis of allocating costs is determined to be most consistent with our mandate to ensure just, reasonable, and nondiscriminatory rates. However, we recognize that such factors as demand fluctuations and varying growth patterns between services could cause distortions between historical causation and actual cost patterns. For this reason, we require that revised Method 1 data be filed concurrent with that of revised Method 7 to document comparative current relative use cost patterns and to establish the veracity of the cost patterns determined under the historical cost causation approach. Revisions are found to be necessary in the case of both Method 1 and Method 7 to correct certain infirmities in these methods as they have previously been implemented. These revisions are to be made before these methods are used as the basis of revised interstate rates, supportive data for subsequent rate changes, or continuing surveillance.

7. We find that Method 1 and Method 7, full cost data currently available from the record provide an adequate "zone of reasonableness" for purposes of drawing conclusions concerning the lawfulness of Bell's past and present rate levels. On the basis of a zone of reasonableness defined by Method 1 and Method 7 data, we find the current MTS return level lawful under Section 201 (b) and that since 1969, at least, MTS has earned a level of return that has not been unduly excessive. Present WATS return levels appear, on the data in this record, excessive and indicative of the presence of cross-subsidization. Past WATS levels of return likewise appear excessive, inclusive of the period from the Seven-Way Cost Study (1964) to the present. However, as we note

below, we are uncertain as to the actual costs of providing WATS and will await a refiling and cost justification of new WATS rates in accordance with our recent *WATS* decision. We also find that the present return levels for Bell's other services (private line telephone, private line telegraph, audio/radio, television, and the "other" service classifications) are deficient and, as such, are being subsidized by other services. Past return levels for these services are generally also found to have been unlawfully low, although in some years the return level of certain services could have been considered to have approached the zone of reasonableness.

8. We have investigated the lawfulness of Bell's rate levels for its interstate services under Section 202 (a). Consistent with the Commission's TELPAK decision we find that the RD correctly recognized that competitive necessity may justify what might otherwise be considered as unlawfully discriminatory rates. However, we disagree with the RD's conclusion, relying on the *TELPAK Sharing* proceeding, that discriminatory pricing based on competitive necessity is permissible only if the carrier meets the three criteria enunciated in that proceeding. We also depart from the RD by concluding that the competitive necessity criteria need not be applied to *all* Private Line Services.

9. We find that only two of the three competitive necessity criteria are pertinent and should be applied to Bell's TELPAK offering to determine if there are violations of Section 202(a): (1) that those benefitting from the discrimination have an alternative supply source which will be utilized in the absence of discrimination and, (2) that the discrimination benefits users discriminated against. We find the record shows that the threat from private microwave and indeed from competing terrestrial and satellite carriers has not and still does not warrant the extent of discrimination manifested by Bell in its TELPAK category of service. There has been no showing that this specific TELPAK bulk rate response is commensurate with any *real* competitive threat. Nevertheless, we recognize that a bulk rate offering of some other nature and magnitude may be warranted. We therefore order Bell to refile its TELPAK offering.

10. Under our guidelines, we direct Bell to assign all extant facilities to its services to provide a facility "datum." Such a datum will provide the distributive basis for related cost assignments and will ensure carrier accountability and nondiscriminatory treatment of all users. Nevertheless, we conclude that certain demand and supply conditions may warrant the offering of less than full cost ("discount") rates. This might be permissible if the carrier can make a definitive and clear showing of recovery of full recorded costs by the service involved within a reasonable time certain and if such departures are in the public interest and consistent with the Commission's basic mandate. Further, we have di-

rected Bell to develop acceptable forecasting techniques in conjunction with the Bureau Staff for use in Method 7 procedures and that the Staff, in consultation with Bell, revise Method 7 and Method 1 procedures to correct certain infirmities. These revisions will permit the use of these methods as the foundation of our basic evaluative procedures. Finally, we direct the staff to complete the methodological revisions within three months and direct Bell to file rates for all its services based on a revised Method 7 analysis (supplemented by revised Method 1 data) within eight months, both from the effective date of this order.

II. HISTORY OF THE PROCEEDINGS

11. This docket is an outgrowth and consolidation of several significant and complex proceedings before the Commission over the past 15 years. Consequently, we believe it helpful to present an abridged case history to facilitate an understanding of its evolution. We note that the RD contains a more elaborate history.

12. On September 7, 1961, we instituted docket no. 14251, an investigation into Bell's original TELPAK tariff.[2] TELPAK, a bulk private line offering, was filed in anticipation of competition from private microwave arising from our *Above 890* decision.[3] On March 18, 1964, we issued our Tentative Decision in docket 14251, concluding that:

a. Services furnished under the TELPAK tariff and those furnished under the various other private line tariffs are like communications services.

b. There are no material cost differences attributable to furnishing a number of channels of one customer under TELPAK as opposed to furnishing the same number of channels to several customers under the other private line tariffs.

c. There is no justification for TELPAK A and TELPAK B in terms of competitive necessity, inasmuch as the rates for the equivalent number of channels offered under ordinary private line tariffs are reasonably competitive with the costs of private microwave systems.

d. There is apparent justification for TELPAK C and D classifications in terms of meeting competition from private microwave systems having channel capacities comparable to those offered by such TELPAK classifications. However, we are unable to determine on this record that the rates for TELPAK C and D classifications are compensatory in relation to the costs of furnishing the services offered

---

[2]FCC 61–1039 (1961).

[3]27 FCC 359 (1959); reconsideration denied, 29 FCC 825 (1960).

thereunder, and therefore are unable to find that the other users of AT&T services will benefit and not be burdened by the application of such rates.[4]

We affirmed these conclusions by a final decision adopted December 23, 1964. However, we held that the record should be reopened to allow Bell to furnish probative cost data showing that the TELPAK C (60 voice-grade channels)[5] and TELPAK D (240 voice-grade channels) offerings are compensatory and do not burden other users of Bell's services. We ordered Bell to file tariffs to eliminate the unlawful discrimination found to exist between TELPAK A (12 voice-grade channels) and TELPAK B (24 voice-grade channels) and private line rates.[6]

13. In 1962, while the *TELPAK* proceeding was underway, we instituted docket no. 14650, a broad inquiry into Western Union's domestic telegraph and other services.[7] In response to allegations by Western Union that Bell had historically used its monopoly voice services to subsidize its competitive services, the Commission's Telephone and Telegraph Committees requested Bell to perform a study to ascertain Bell's interstate investment, revenues, and expenses, and net earnings among its seven categories of service: MTS, wide area telephone service (WATS), teletypewriter exchange service (TWX), private line telephone service, private line telegraph service, TELPAK, and all others.[8]

14. Bell submitted study results known as the "Seven-Way Cost Study," on September 10, 1965. The study showed that for the 12-month period ending August 31, 1964, the return on Bell's investment ranged from 10.1 percent for WATS to 0.3 percent for TELPAK. Further, Bell's return on its competitive services were significantly below its systemwide average, while its return on monopoly services, MTS and WATS, were above the average.[9] However, the Commission did not address the questions of compensativeness and cross-subsidy in docket 14650.

15. As a result in part of the Seven-Way Cost Study we instituted docket no. 16258 on October 27, 1965.[10] This proceeding was a general investigation into the rate levels and rate level relationships existing with respect to Bell's interstate services. We noted the importance of such investigation, stating that:

---

[4]38 FCC 270, 395 (1964).

[5]The bandwidth of a single voice-grade channel is generally regarded as 4 kHz.

[6]37 FCC 1111, 1117–1118 (1964), aff'd sub. nom., *American Trucking Assn.* v. *FCC*, 377 F.2d 121 (1966), cert. denied, 386 U.S. 943 (1967).

[7]FCC 62–533.

[8]Report of the Telephone and Telegraph Committees in the Domestic Telegraph Investigation, docket no. 14650, p. 200.

[9]Id. at 200–204.

[10]2 FCC2d 871 (1965).

Certain of the services involved are furnished by the Bell System in direct competition with services offered by other carriers. To the extent that these services may be underpriced by the Bell System, this may have a competitive impact on such other carriers.[11]

16. Following affirmation of our *TELPAK* decision,[12] we terminated docket no. 14251 and amended our designation order in docket no. 16258 to include the issue of whether TELPAK C and D were compensatory. We ordered the record in docket no. 14251 incorporated by reference into docket no. 16258. We also stressed that if Bell were to submit additional tariff filings with respect to its TELPAK offerings, such filings should be examined in a separate proceeding, not as a part of the general issues of docket no. 16258.[13]

17. On March 25, 1968, Bell filed certain rate increases in its interstate private line TELPAK tariffs. By Order adopted April 10, 1968, we suspended such revised tariffs for the statutory period and instituted docket no. 18128, an investigation into the lawfulness of the tariff increases.[14] . . .

19. As a result of the "Statement of Ratemaking Principles and Factors," Bell filed new proposed TELPAK tariff rate increases on October 1, 1969, based on updated studies. On October 29, 1969, these tariffs were suspended and set for hearing in this proceeding.[15] Additionally, we directed that the hearings herein be removed from deferred status and that they proceed as expeditiously as possible. Western Union matched AT&T's TELPAK increases; these rates were also suspended and set for hearing herein.[16]

20. On February 18, 1970, Phase 1–B of docket no. 16258 was procedurally terminated. However, we stated that the various rate revisions made by Bell, allegedly in conformity with the "Statement of Ratemaking Principles," and the lawfulness of the rate levels of each of AT&T's service categories including MTS and WATS would be reviewed in the context of this proceeding and in docket no. 18684.[17]

21. Docket no. 18684 was instituted on September 24, 1969, as an investigation into the lawfulness of AT&T's revised video transmission

---

[11]Id. at 872.

[12]*American Trucking Assn.* v. *FCC,* 377 F.2d 121 (1966), cert. denied 396 U.S. 943 (1967).

[13]7 FCC2d 30, 31 (1965); 6 FCC2d 177, 180 (1966).

[14]FCC 68–388 (1968).

[15]20 FCC2d 383, 388 (1969), petitions for reconsideration denied, 21 FCC2d (1970). We also set for hearing Bell's Series 11000 wide-band service. This service was terminated on May 1, 1973. On Petition for Review, the United States Court of Appeals for the District of Columbia Circuit affirmed our decision not to reject the TELPAK increases. *Associated Press* v. *FCC,* 448 F.2d 1095 (D.C. Cir. 1971).

[16]FCC 69–1345 (1969).

[17]21 FCC2d 495, 496–497 (1970).

rates.[18] Bell also filed revised tariffs on September 25, 1969, for its audio program transmission service. These too, were set for hearing in docket no. 18684.[19] Through informal conferences the issues concerning the audio services were resolved.[20] However, the lawfulness of the video private line services continued unresolved. On June 10, 1970, we consolidated docket no. 18684 with this proceeding in order to "view the totality of costs for all of AT&T's interstate services so that the question of interstate burden can be examined and if necessary corrected. . . ."[21] Hearings commenced on September 28, 1970, following three prehearing conferences.

22. On November 20, 1970, AT&T filed tariffs designed to increase rates for MTS in order to achieve a higher overall return on total investment. At our request, Bell postponed the effectiveness of these tariff revisions pending an expedited rate hearing. As an interim measure the Commission granted special permission to AT&T to file lesser rate increases. These were suspended and set for hearing with an accounting order in docket no. 19129.[22] However, certain of the issues raised by the MTS rate increases were designated as issues to be determined herein. In particular, Bell was required to show that its claimed additional interstate revenue requirement should be met solely through increased charges to the MTS customer and further that the rate increases at issue in docket no. 19129 did not involve cross-subsidization of any other service.[23]

23. On December 6, 1971, AT&T filed revised private line tariffs, increasing rates for TELPAK and private line telephone and telegraph services. These increases were suspended and the lawfulness of the revision designated for hearing in this proceeding.[24] Similar increased rates filed by Western Union were also placed in issue in this docket.[25] . . .

25. Evidentiary hearings herein began on September 28, 1970, and were concluded on August 8, 1972. Fifty-three witnesses presented testimony and evidence. There are now approximately 27,000 pages of

---

[18]FCC 69–1038 (1969).

[19]FCC 69–1197 (1969).

[20]See *Orders of the Examiner*, FCC 70–M–808, June 5, 1970, and FCC 70–M–941, July 1, 1970.

[21]23 FCC2d 503, 509. By this Order we also denied various petitions for reconsideration of our February 18, 1970, action which included the lawfulness of the rate levels of all of Bell's major services as an issue herein. 23 FCC2d at 507.

[22]27 FCC2d 149 (1971).

[23]27 FCC2d 151, 156–57 (1971). AT&T later agreed to consider further rate increases for services other than MTS subject to final determination in docket no. 18128. 30 FCC2d 503 (1971).

[24]33 FCC2d 522 (1972).

[25]34 FCC2d 839 (1972).

transcript and exhibits before us in this docket alone, in addition to the record from docket 16258. The Administrative Law Judges closed the record herein on December 11, 1972.[26] Proposed Finding of Facts and Conclusions were filed on March 12, 1973, and Replies thereto on May 14, 1973. The Recommended Decision of the Chief, Common Carrier Bureau was released on January 19, 1976. The parties' Exceptions and Supporting Briefs were submitted one month later. We entertained oral argument on July 14, 1976.

✖ 62

Federal Communications Commission, In the matter of Applications of
Microwave Communications, Inc.
18 F.C.C. 953 (1969)

New entry into bulk transmission in the main routes is regarded as especially threatening by Bell System officials, who assert that such "cream-skimming" undermines the financing of the entire network. Despite this landmark FCC decision, rehearings and further tactics have yielded only slow compliance.

Commissioner Bartley for the Commission: This proceeding involves applications filed by Microwave Communications, Inc. (MCI), for construction permits for new facilities in the Domestic Public Point-to-Point Radio Service at Chicago, Ill., St. Louis, Mo., and nine intermediate points. MCI proposed to offer its subscribers a limited common carrier microwave radio service, designed to meet the interoffice and interplant communications needs of small business. . . . MCI, however, does not plan to provide its subscribers with a complete microwave service. The proposed service would be limited to transmissions between MCI's microwave sites, making it incumbent upon each subscriber to supply his own communications link between MCI's sites and his place of business (loop service).

MCI contends that it will offer its subscribers substantially lower rates

---

[26]FCC 72–M–1528.

than those charged for similar services by the established carriers and that subscribers with less than full-time communication needs will be able to achieve additional savings through the channel sharing and half-time use provisions of its proposed tariff. Up to five subscribers will be permitted to share each channel on a party-line basis with a pro-rata reduction in rates. . . . MCI further asserts that its proposed tariff contains fewer restrictions than those of the existing common carriers, so that greater flexibility of use will be possible, particularly with respect to channel bandwidth, splitting channels for voice and data transmissions, and in the attachment of customer equipment.

MCI's applications are opposed by Western Union Telegraph Co. (Western Union), General Telephone Co. of Illinois (General), and the Associated Bell System Cos., American Telephone and Telegraph Co., Illinois Bell Telephone Co., and Southwestern Bell Telephone Co. (Bell), which presently provide microwave services to the geographical area which MCI proposed to serve. In a memorandum opinion and order, on February 11, 1966, we designated the MCI applications for hearing on issues to determine inter alia: (a) whether the established common carriers offer services meeting the needs which MCI proposes to meet in the area which MCI proposes to serve; (b) whether the grant of MCI's applications would result in wasteful duplication of facilities; (c) whether MCI is financially qualified to construct and operate its proposed facilities; (d) whether there is need for MCI's proposal; and (e) whether operation of MCI's proposed system would result in interference to existing common carrier services.

The evidentiary hearings commenced on February 13, 1967, and were concluded on April 19, 1967. In an initial decision, Hearing Examiner Herbert Sharfman recommended the grant of MCI's applications. The examiner found that the proposed MCI system would not generate harmful electrical interference to the receivers of the existing carriers or receive harmful interference from their stations. Although he indicated that serious questions exist concerning the reliability of MCI's proposal, the examiner nevertheless found no reason to believe that the system would not work, and he concluded that MCI had established that it is technically qualified. The examiner also found that MCI is financially qualified and that it would offer its subscribers a more economical rate structure, additional savings through the utilization of the shared and half-time use provisions of its tariff, and greater flexibility of use which would permit MCI's subscribers to adapt the system to their particular needs. The examiner noted that the proposed Chicago-St. Louis route is served by a wide range of common carrier services, that there is a duplication of facilities, and that the MCI proposal would result in additional duplication. However, he concluded that MCI's lower rates and more flexible use would enable it to serve a market whose needs are unful-filled by the available common carrier services; that consequently there would be no unnecessary or wasteful duplication; and that the public interest would be served by authorizing MCI's proposed microwave system.

Upon release of the initial decision, we recognized that the questions raised at the hearing involved important policy considerations respecting the entry of new licenses into the communications common carrier field. . . . We have considered the initial decision in light of the record, pleadings, and oral argument. Except as modified below, . . . we adopt the hearing examiner's findings and conclusions.

*   *   *   *   *

NEED FOR MCI'S PROPOSALS

This is not a rate proceeding . . . and we are not called upon to make specific findings concerning the reasonableness of MCI's proposed rates or whether they are compensatory. . . .

The significant fact remains that the existing carriers do not offer a 2-kc. voice channel and MCI will; so that a subscriber may achieve a substantial savings in his communications costs by utilizing MCI's services. Further savings may be effected by the sharing and part-time provision of MCI's proposal. . . .

Additional advantages to MCI's subscribers are afforded by the flexibility of its system. In contrast to the protesting carriers which will lease no less than a nominal 4-kc. channel for voice use, MCI will lease and subdivide its channel into bandwidths in increments of 2-kc. and permit multiple terminations of channels. Furthermore, MCI imposes fewer restrictions on the nature of the subscribers' terminal equipment and on the use of its channels. The absence of restrictions gives each MCI subscriber the same flexibility to vary its stations' capability and use as if it were its own private system. Thus, each subscriber may adapt the system to its particular needs and equipment, lease shelter and tower space from MCI, and use the MCI trunk system for the carriage of voice, facsimile, and high speed or lower speed data transmissions, or a combination thereof in a manner which best suits its business requirements. No comparable degree of flexibility is offered by the existing carriers. . . .

The carriers argue that even if lower rates for MCI communications services have been shown that factor may not properly be considered in resolving the issue of need. They assert that they are required by the Commission to serve both high-density high-profit and low-density low-profit areas and in order to maintain rates which are relatively uniform, all rates are based on a cost averaging principle. Claiming that MCI is "cream skimming," i.e., proposing to operate solely on high density routes where lower fixed costs per channel permit lower rates with higher profits, the carriers state that in order to compete with MCI they will be forced to abandon their cost averaging policies with a resultant increase in rates for subscribers on lightly used routes.

MCI is offering a service intended primarily for interplant and interoffice communications with unique and specialized characteristics. In these circumstances we cannot perceive how a grant of the authorizations requested would pose any serious threat to the established carriers' price averaging policies. Lower rates for the service offered is not the sole basis for our determination that MCI has demonstrated a need for the proposed facilities, but the flexibility available to subscribers and the sharing and the part-time features of the proposal have been considered to be significant factors as well. . . . It may be, as the telephone companies and Western Union argue, that some business will be diverted from the existing carriers upon the grant of MCI's applications, but that fact provides no sufficient basis for depriving a segment of the public of the benefits of a new and different service.

Moreover, if we were to follow the carriers' reasoning and specify as a prerequisite to the establishment of a new common carrier service that it be so widespread as to permit cost averaging, we would in effect restrict the entry of new licensees into the common carrier field to a few large companies which are capable of serving the entire Nation. Such an approach is both unrealistic and inconsistent with the public interest. Innovations in the types and character of communications services offered or economies in operation which could not at once be instituted on a nationwide basis would be precluded from ever being introduced. In the circumstances of this case, we find the cream skimming argument to be without merit. . . .

RELIABILITY OF SERVICE

No specific standards have been enunciated by the Commission as to what constitutes a minimum degree of reliability which is acceptable for a common carrier communications service, and we believe it would be inconsistent with the public interest, in view of the need for the proposed service and the valuable information to be obtained from the operation of the system, to defer action in this proceeding until such standards are adopted. On the basis of the evidence before us, however, we find that the MCI proposal may reasonably be expected to achieve a degree of reliability which, while not matching the high degree of reliability claimed by the major carriers, will provide an acceptable and a marketable common carrier service. . . .

EFFICIENT UTILIZATION OF THE FREQUENCY SPECTRUM

We recognize, as the carriers argue, that MCI will not make the fullest possible use of the frequencies which it seeks. . . . We have found that by reason of its low-cost, sharing and part-time use provisions, MCI can reasonably be expected to furnish an economical microwave communications service to a segment of the public which presently cannot avail itself of such a service; and that its flexibility features will enable potential users to make more efficient use of their business equipment. These are substantial benefits which, in our view, outweigh the fact that MCI will not make the fullest possible use of its frequencies. When frequencies are used to meet a significant unfulfilled communications need, we do not believe that such use may be considered as "inefficient."

THE FEASIBILITY OF LOOP SERVICE

The testimony of MCI's public witnesses and the findings of the Spindletop survey show that, in general, MCI's potential subscribers have no interest in providing their own communications link between their facilities and MCI's transmitter sites. Therefore, MCI's ability to market its services will be dependent on the ability of its subscribers to secure loop service from the other common carriers serving the service area.

What seems a more likely obstacle in interconnection is, as the hearing examiner indicated, the "carriers' intransigence, manifested in this case. . . ." In these circumstances, the carriers are not in a position to argue that consideration of the interconnection question is premature. Since they have indicated that they will not voluntarily provide loop service, we shall retain jurisdiction of this proceeding in order to enable MCI to obtain from the Commission a prompt determination on the matter of interconnection. Thus, at such time as MCI has customers and the facts and details of the customers' requirements are known, MCI may come directly to the Commission with a request for an order of interconnection. We have already concluded that a grant of MCI's proposal is in the public interest. We likewise conclude that, absent a significant showing that interconnection is not technically feasible, the issuance of an order requiring the existing carriers to provide loop service is in the public interest. . . .

SUMMARY

This is a very close case and one which presents exceptionally difficult questions. We have found MCI to be financially qualified, but we realize that any unforeseen circumstances requiring a sizable expenditure may impair the applicant's financial capacity. We have found, based on the weight of the evidence, that there is a substantial likelihood that the communications of its subscribers will arrive promptly, in accurate form, and without extended interruptions due to failures in the system. We wish to make clear, therefore, that the findings and conclusions reached herein apply only to the frequencies specified and for the areas described in the applications now pending before us. Should MCI seek to obtain additional frequencies or to extend its microwave service to new areas, our action on its application will be based on a close scrutiny of its operations, the rules then governing the grant of applications for common carrier microwave frequencies and all other applicable policy considerations. Likewise, in connection with an application for renewal of license, we may deny the application if circumstances so warrant or grant renewal on such conditions as we deem essential to insure that MCI's subscribers receive a reliable transmission service of acceptable quality. However, it would be inconsistent with the public interest to deny MCI's applications and thus deprive the applicant of an opportunity to demonstrate that its proposed microwave facilities will bring to its subscribers the substantial benefits which it predicts and which we have found to be supported by the evidence in this proceeding. We conclude, on the basis of the record as a whole, that the public interest will be served by a grant of MCI's application.

Dissenting Statement of Chairman Rosel H. Hyde:

The decision of the majority is diametrically opposed to sound economics and regulatory principles. It likewise is designed to cost the average American ratepayer money to the immediate benefit of a few with special interests. . . .

Why does the majority condone this obviously grossly inefficient use of the spectrum? Because, they say, of the low cost and flexibility of the facilities proposed by applicants. It should be noted that the so-called flexibility cited by the majority is here, as it was in the *TELPAK* case, a mere euphemism connoting lower rates. But how is it that applicant is able to propose lower rates than the existing common carriers for private line service? For no other reason than that it is proposing a typical "cream-skimming" operation. Thus, it has selected a major route, Chicago to St. Louis, with heavy traffic density characteristics and the concomitant lower unit costs. The existing common carriers, on the other hand, have been encouraged by the Commission, primarily for social reasons, to base their rates both for message toll and private line services on nationwide average costs. Thus the small users in the hinterlands are afforded the same rates as the large users in the major cities. The evidence in this record tends to show, and there is no basis in our experience to believe otherwise, that AT&T and Western Union could offer lower rates for private line service between Chicago and St. Louis than those proposed by MCI were they to base such rates on their costs for that route alone.

The chances are, and the record so indicates, that AT&T and Western Union will be constrained to lower their private line rates to meet the competition of MCI. This, however, means that other users, either the small private line users who are not so fortunate as to live in large cities, or message toll users, or both, will have to make up the difference if total revenue requirements are to be met. . . .

Separate Statement of Commissioner Nicholas Johnson:

What do the proponents of regulation fear about this radical experiment with competition? "Cream-skimming." Once an honorable enough agricultural undertaking, the expression is now used as an economic pejorative. The suggestion is that if competition were ever to be extended to such a sensitive area as pricing then the correct prices might not be charged. The services for which costs are low might be priced lower than those for which costs are high. The currently exorbitantly high profits from the low-cost services would be "skimmed" by a company that would fail to provide the higher cost services as well. . . .

An additional problem with a cream skimming argument at this time is that it is a little too late. To make the argument is to suggest that any deviation from present pricing policies is somehow immoral, illegal, and unprecedented, and will result in higher prices to all consumers. It is none of the above. The telephone rate system is riddled with subsidies. In the first place, the telephone company itself deals in cream skimming. The really high-cost low-revenue subscribers—those who live in rural America—would never have had telephone service had they waited for Bell to ring. They had to get government assistance through the Rural Electrification Administration, their own cooperative telephone services, and non–Bell microwave carriers. In the second place, Bell has notoriously undercharged for those services in which it is engaged in competition—making up the differences by soaking those subscribers over whom it has a monopoly. . . . Finally, Congress has just given its approval to the principle of free or reduced cost service to educational radio and television interconnection—over the protests of the telephone company. . . .

✖ 63

Federal Communications Commission, In the matter of *Use of the Carterfone Device in Message Toll Telephone Service*
13 F.C.C. 420 (1968)

> Carterfone *and* MCI *(see above) reversed the FCC's long acquiescence in Bell System policies excluding competition from its various markets. A rapid growth in terminal equipment followed with improved variety and little adverse effect on the whole system's performance.*

By Commissioner Nicholas Johnson for the Commission: This proceeding involves the application of American Telephone and Telegraph Co. tariffs to the use by telephone subscribers of the Carterfone.

The Carterfone is designed to be connected to a two-way radio at the base station serving a mobile radio system. When callers on the radio and on the telephone are both in contact with the base station operation, the handset of the operator's telephone is placed on a cradle in the Carterfone device. A voice control circuit in the Carterfone automatically switches on the radio transmitter when the telephone caller is speaking; when he stops speaking, the radio returns to a receiving condition. A separate speaker is attached to the Carterfone to allow the base station operator to monitor the conversation, adjust the voice volume, and hang up his telephone when the conversation has ended.

The Carterfone device, invented by Thomas F. Carter, has been produced and marketed by the Carter Electronics Corp., of which Mr. Carter is president, since 1959. From 1959 through 1966, approximately 4,500 Carterfones were produced and 3,500 sold to dealers and distributors throughout the United States and in foreign countries.

The defendant telephone companies, acting in accordance with their interpretation of tariff FCC No. 132, filed April 16, 1957, by American Telephone and Telegraph Co., advised their subscribers that the Carterfone, when used in conjunction with the subscriber's telephone, is a prohibited interconnecting device, the use of which would subject the user to the penalties provided in the tariff. The tariff provides that:

> No equipment, apparatus, circuit or device not furnished by the telephone company shall be attached to or connected with the facilities furnished by the telephone company, whether physically, by induction, or otherwise.

* * * * *

We agree with and adopt the examiner's findings that the Carterfone fills a need and that it does not adversely affect the telephone system. They are fully supported by the record. We also agree that the tariff broadly prohibits the use of interconnection devices, including the Carterfone. Its provisions are clear as to this. Finally, in view of the above findings, we hold, as did the examiner, that application of the tariff to bar the Carterfone in the future would be unreasonable and unduly discriminatory. However, for the reasons to be given, we also conclude that the tariff has been unreasonable, discriminatory, and unlawful in the past and that the provisions prohibiting the use of customer-provided interconnecting devices should accordingly be stricken.

. . . [O]ur conclusion here is that a customer desiring to use an interconnecting device to improve the utility to him of both the telephone system and a private radio system should be able to do so, so long as the interconnection does not adversely affect the telephone company's operations or the telephone system's utility for others. A tariff which prevents this is unreasonable; it is also unduly discriminatory when, as here, the telephone company's own interconnecting equipment is approved for use. The vice of the present tariff, here as in Hush-A-Phone, is that it prohibits the use of harmless as well as harmful devices.

AT&T has urged that since the telephone companies have the responsibility to establish, operate, and improve the telephone system, they must have absolute control over the quality, installation, and maintenance of all parts of the system in order effectively to carry out that responsibility. Installation of unauthorized equipment, according to the telephone companies, would have at least two negative results. First, it would divide the responsibility for assuring that each part of the system is able to function effectively, and second, it would retard development of the system since the independent equipment supplier would tend to resist changes which would render his equipment obsolete.

There has been no adequate showing that nonharmful interconnection must be prohibited in order to permit the telephone company to carry out its system responsibilities. The risk feared by the examiner has not been demonstrated to be substantial, and no reason presents itself why it should be. No one entity need provide all interconnection equipment for our telephone system any more than a single source is needed to supply the parts for a space probe. We are not holding that the telephone companies may not prevent the use of devices which actually cause harm or that they may not set up reasonable standards to be met by interconnection devices. These remedies are appropriate; we believe they are also adequate to fully protect the system.

Nor can we assume that the telephone companies would be hindered in improving telephone service by any tendency of the manufacturers and users of interconnection devices to resist change. The telephone companies would remain free to make improvements to the telephone system and could reflect any such improvements in reasonable revised standards for nontelephone company provided devices used in connection with the system. Manufacturers and sellers of such devices would then have the responsibility of offering for sale or use only such equipment as would be in compliance with such revised standards. An owner or user of a device which failed to meet reasonable revised standards for such devices would either have to have the device rebuilt to comply with the revised standards or discontinue its use. Such is the risk inherent in the private ownership of any equipment to be used in connection with the telephone system. . . .

In view of the unlawfulness of the tariff there would be no point in merely declaring it invalid as applied to the Carterfone and permitting it to continue in operation as to other interconnection devices. This would also put a clearly improper burden upon the manufacturers and users of other devices. The appropriate remedy is to strike the tariff and permit the carriers, if they so desire, to propose new tariff provisions in accordance with this opinion. We make no rulings as to damages since that relief has not been requested. As noted above, the carriers may submit new tariffs which will protect the telephone system against harmful devices, and may specify technical standards if they wish.

Accordingly, we find that tariff FCC 263, paragraphs 2.6.1 and 2.6.9 are, and have since their inception been, unreasonable, unlawful, and unreasonably discriminatory under sections 201(b) and 202(a) of the Communications Act of 1934, as amended.

❧ 64

Federal Communications Commission, In the matter of *American Telephone and Telegraph Company: Charges for Interstate Telephone Service*
Docket No. 19129
(Phase II)
Final Decision and Order
(February 23, 1977)

> *An FCC task force recommended that the Commission require the Bell System to divest Western Electric. (Recall from Part I that the Antitrust Division's suit, filed in 1974, also sought this change.) In 1977 the FCC refused to decide the issue either way, but it did require the Bell System to shift toward more open purchasing methods. Its reasoning is summed up in this section from the 125-page Final Decision and Order.*

1. This case is before us on exceptions from the Initial Decision (ID) of the presiding Administrative Law Judge (ALJ) released August 2, 1976. Oral argument was held before us *en banc* on December 13, 1976, and the record is before us for decision.

*   *   *   *   *

98. **Summary.**   In sum then, this record shows that the result of the entire Bell System procurement and make/buy decision processes is that the preponderant portion of the Bell Operating Companies' (BOCs') telecommunications equipment requirements would be provided by Western, not necessarily due to product superiority in terms of quality and price, but merely as a result of the present organization and functioning of the Bell System entities themselves. This resultant bias in favor of Western products limits not only the autonomy and independence of the BOCs to procure equipment and better serve their ratepayers, but also precludes a fair opportunity for the general trade to serve BOCs' equipment needs.

99. Bell argues that "[t]here can be no reasonable doubt . . . that general trade manufacturers have been able to sell a great deal of equipment to the Bell operating companies when the general trade has successfully developed better or less expensive equipment." In this regard, total Western sales to the Bell System during 1972 amounted to $5.5 billion. In the same year, Western purchased $550 million worth of equipment from the general trade for the BOCs. In addition, in 1972 the

BOCs purchased $250 million worth of such equipment directly from the general trade.[1] In both 1973 and 1974 Bell bought approximately $900 million in products from the general trade. Thus, the dollar value of general trade products purchased by Bell is not unsubstantial. However, Western provides some 80–90 percent of the BOCs' equipment needs, and under such circumstances one can hardly contend that Western is not the predominant supplier of the BOCs' equipment market. Further, as long as Western maintains its present influence and role in Bell System equipment procurement for BOCs, we cannot be assured that even the present level of general trade products purchased for BOCs will continue, much less that it will increase. It appears from this record that the amount of general trade sales to BOCs could be expected to increase in the presence of an evaluation and price comparison procedure which given the BOCs greater autonomy and independence, both jointly and individually, in equipment procurement and which is less biased toward the selection of Western products.

100. Bell also argues that it has taken sufficient steps to insure fair general grade access to BOCs, citing primarily its creation of the Bell System Purchased Products Division (BSPPD). For reasons already given this assertion is without merit. Moreover, the ALJ had BSPPD and other Bell actions before him for consideration but nevertheless expressly concluded in the ID that further formal and publicly announced actions were required by Bell to broaden the "autonomy (centrally enforced)" to BOCs in procurement and to permit a fair opportunity for access by the general trade to BOCs. If the ALJ agreed with Bell at the time of the ID the BSPPD and other Bell actions were sufficient, he could easily have stated so in the ID. This he did not do. In any event, we are not satisfied from our own consideration of this record that Bell has taken sufficient steps to assure that the BOCs have the necessary autonomy and independence, both jointly and individually, to procure equipment or to provide for fair general trade access to BOCs. Thus, upon considering the ID, the parties' exceptions to the ID, and the record as a whole, we cannot be assured, as we must, that the BOCs and their ratepayers are being provided the best quality and least costly equipment under present Bell System policies and practices governing BOCs' equipment procurement. We now turn to what we believe may be a reasonable and practical means to achieve the desired improvements.

101. We conclude that the potential for approaching the BOCs' equipment procurement in an optimal manner, thereby assuring that

---

[1]As noted above, the fact that individual BOCs may make decisions to procure general trade equipment does not militate against the need for the BOCs to have greater autonomy and independence through consolidated centralized procurement.

BOCs and their ratepayers utilize the best quality and least costly equipment, has not been, and is not likely to be, achieved under present Bell System procurement policies and practices. We rely primarily on the findings and conclusions of the ALJ noted herein; the ITT, GE and Trial Staff evidence (primarily the case studies); and the additional evidence relating to the Bell System make/buy decision process, which we have considered and it appears that the ALJ did not fully discuss. Our conclusion is based primarily on our analysis of the Bell organizational structure and the manner in which the entities of the Bell System presently interact in procurement matters. The major problem, as we see it, is that the BOCs have insufficient autonomy and independence, both jointly and individually, from Western in equipment procurement and make/buy decision. Thus, although Bell has a BSPPD (which is itself subject to the deficiencies noted herein),[2] we find that Western is ubiquitous in its participation in the BOCs' equipment procurement process—from the make/buy decision, to purchasing, to inspection. We have noted the "chilling effect" this has had, or is likely to have, on general trade suppliers which may seek to serve BOCs' equipment needs and the resultant actual or potential impact on BOCs and ratepayers.

102. In addition, with respect to Western's charges to the BOCs, we have other concerns. Under the provisions of the current standard supply contract between Western and the BOCs, Western unilaterally determines prices paid by BOCs to Western and is committed to serve all the BOCs' equipment needs. Moreover, Western's policy is not to sell to Independents, except in exceptional circumstances. Thus, we see the possibility for actual and potential impact to ratepayers emanating from two additional sources: Western prices for equipment which it traditionally supplies on a sole source basis may be too high; and the prices for competitive equipment provided to BOCs—that which may also be provided to BOCs by the general trade—can be set artificially low. We are compelled to take actions herein which will improve this situation in the future.

103. We are not attempting to prescribe herein a reorganization of the Bell System. We have, however, noted in this Decision certain aspects of BSPPD and the existing procurement and make/buy decision processes overall of the Bell System and in the BOCs' relationships with Western

---

[2]As noted above, the BOCs are given virtually no managerial control and little influence in BSPPD; the BSPPD itself conducts invalid and unfair price comparison studies of Western and general trade products; the BSPPD does not make quantity commitments for BOCs; the BSPPD does not solicit competitive bids; the BSPPD and BOCs utilize the Western Purchasing Organization; and the BOCs are likely to rely on BSPPD recommendations regarding what products to purchase. We have found that these factors and others taken together result in a bias in favor of Western products.

that need improvement. We further note, in our opinion, there reside within the General Department and the Bell System in general, effective organizational entities which are capable of providing the guidance support functions which we believe would be required to permit the BOCs to have maximum independence and autonomy to arrive at rational make/buy and procurement decisions while procuring equipment on a consolidated centralized basis. Such decisions can be equally fair to the general trade and Western alike, while treating Western as a competitive supplier on an arm's length basis.

104. We believe it is unlikely that arm's length dealing between the BOCs and Western in BOCs' equipment procurement will work to the disadvantage of the BOCs, the ratepayers, or Western. If indeed Western makes the highest quality and least costly products, as Bell claims, then it is likely that even under arm's length dealing the BOCs will continue substantial purchases from Western. Indeed, Western is for all intents and purposes the sole manufacturer of a substantial number of products. Moreover, we do not propose herein an alteration in Bell Labs' role in providing product development and basic research support to Western or the BOCs. While it could be argued there may be some disadvantage to the BOCs because they will no longer have available for use the Western Purchasing Organization and thus the alleged economies which may result from its use could be lost, this record convinces us that the competitive benefits to BOCs and ratepayers which are likely to result from the changes in the Bell policies and practices governing BOC equipment procurement we are requiring herein far outweigh any of the possible disadvantages. In any event, it is likely that the BOCs could expect to realize certain economies of their own while conducting their own centralized purchasing and inspection functions. Finally, even if Western loses some BOC business to general trade competitors, it has the option, as we noted previously, of selling to Independents if it so chooses.

105. Moreover, Western is not unique in its role as a manufacturing subsidiary in a telecommunications conglomerate. Based upon our experience, we believe it may be useful to consider other telecommunication companies such as International Telephone and Telegraph Corporation and RCA Corporation which also have an ownership position in common carrier subsidiaries as well as in separate manufacturing entities. To varying degrees, the manufacturing subsidiaries of each of these entities function as independent profit and loss centers, working toward annual sales and profit targets set by management. There is extensive use of competitive bidding for major procurements. The manufacturing companies compete vigorously in meeting their targets. Their status as an accountable profit and loss center exerts beneficial pressures when trying to sell to a sister common carrier—which must also meet

certain financial performance criteria. The proffered prices will not be artificially high—since the carrier must meet certain cost control criteria. Similarly, the prices cannot be artificially low, since the manufacturer must meet its revenues and profit target. Although competitive bidding is widespread in these holding companies, sole source procurement within the corporation is not prohibited where such arrangements may be concluded for reasons not based entirely upon price and perform-ance. While it may be argued that Western's *modus operandi* has much in common with those other manufacturing entities Bell has taken contrary positions on the record.[3]

106. Accordingly, pursuant to the statutory authority vested in the Commission under the Communications Act, we are ordering the Bell System to submit a proposal to achieve optimal separation of its equip-ment procurement and manufacturing functions within the framework of the following guidelines. The BOCs should have centralized capabilities and mechanisms for performing, independent of Western, the functions which include (a) make/buy and procurement decisions; (b) issuing of requests for proposals and evaluation of responses in com-petitive bidding and other procurement situations;[4] (c) purchasing; and (d) inspection. The make/buy and procurement decisions should be made by a centralized entity at a level of management authority which is at least equal to that of the top executive level of the BOCs. While we expect the BOCs equipment needs to be met primarily through consoli-dated centralized procurement, the BOCs should retain autonomy to make procurement decisions of their own choice apart from centralized procurement as is the case today. This individual autonomy could in-clude their own purchasing, product evaluation organizations, etc. It will be necessary for this Commission to determine at periodic intervals that the BOCs and Western are indeed operating on an arm's length basis in accordance with these guidelines and with the findings and conclusions cited throughout this Decision. We shall therefore also rec-

---

[3]It appears that Western may not always be under a constraint to set charges to BOCs at a specified level of profitability either on a companywide or individual product basis. For example, Bell Counsel stated in oral argument, TR. 22139:

> Western Electric does not have a separate manufacturing goal of maximizing profits from manufacturing. These are all part of an integrated enterprise with one goal. The one goal is better service at lower costs.

Further, in discussing Western's role in the integrated Bell System structure the ALJ, relying on Bell evidence, found that Western's manufacturing activity is subservient to the needs of the BOCs and Western gears up in advance of hard orders from BOCs. Id, paras. 52–53. Also, the ALJ found that Western has wide latitude and flexibility in pricing its products. Id, para. 281. All of these policies and practices are not normally undertaken by a manufacturing firm operating as an independent profit and loss center.

[4]We believe competitive bidding may be appropriate for some, but not necessarily all, of the equipment that BOCs and their ratepayers may require. Thus, we disagree with Bell's view that it is inappropriate under all circumstances.

ommend that the internal financial reporting procedures for Western and the BOCs be refined to the extent that this compliance can be readily perceived.

107. We expect Bell to respond within 90 days of the release of this Decision with a detailed proposal, including a time frame for implementation, for effectuating the necessary improvements in the present Bell System policies and practices which govern how BOCs and their ratepayers obtain equipment. It is our expert judgment that the BOCs will have an enhanced opportunity to better satisfy their own equipment needs and those of their ratepayers if such improvements are made in accordance with the guidelines set forth herein. Upon our receipt and study of Bell's proposal we will initiate appropriate procedures to provide an opportunity to the public for comment. Bell, of course, is free to submit alternative proposals if it believes those will meet our concerns and those of the ALJ as stated in this Decision.

*   *   *   *   *

Peter O. Steiner (1922–)

⚞ 65

Monopoly and Competition in Television: Some Policy Issues*

What conditions foster "good" television broadcasting? How many channels? Private or public ownership? Fees, taxes, or advertising funds? Steiner lays out some of the main issues in these policy choices. Is there now reasonable balance in programming? Does public broadcasting help to fit the variety of viewer interests?

The new debate upon public policy toward television has centered on the award of broadcasting rights for a third channel. Should it go to the BBC, to a new public corporation, to a new or existing commercial organization, or to toll television? More is at stake than the nature of the new channel since the additional service may fundamentally alter the behavior and performance of the existing services and thus affect the pattern of development of the whole broadcasting system. This is one of those rare moments when the public has a real opportunity to choose among alternatives; the purpose of this paper is to explore them. . . .

THE CHARACTER OF AMERICAN TELEVISION

Three national network organizations (NBC, CBS, ABC) dominate American television. Each offers its affiliated stations about twice as many hours of programs per week as BBC television. Some of these programs are sponsored, some not; of the former some are network produced, some produced by advertising agencies or independent producers. While the networks own a few key stations, most stations are independent, private, commercial organizations that have voluntarily affiliated with the networks, yielding to the networks options on a significant portion of their time, the major share of the revenue from the sale of their time, the major share of the revenue from the sale of their time to network advertisers, and much of their jurisdiction over pro-

*Peter O. Steiner, "Monopoly and Competition in Television: Some Policy Issues," Manchester School of Economic and Social Studies, May 1961; excerpted. Steiner's research also includes basic work on cost-benefit analysis and the economics of mergers. He is Professor of Law and Economics at the University of Michigan.

gramming. In return they are provided with the cable interconnection that makes simultaneous national broadcasting possible with a stream of programs of all types and with the minor share of the revenue from the sale of their time as part of the network. The two biggest networks are enormously profitable by any standard; ABC is less profitable but is above the average of American corporations of its size. Stations typically enjoy moderate profits and are clearly better off with network affiliation than without it.

Stations, rather than networks, are licensed by the Federal Communications Commission and renewal, while subject to standards of overall performance, is virtually automatic. Stations receive additional revenue from spot commercial announcements and from sale of their time for local or nonnetwork "national spot" broadcasting. Nonnetwork sources account for perhaps a quarter of the total time of stations and more than half of their revenue. These fractions should not lead one to underestimate the importance of network programming for two reasons: Firstly, virtually all of the high budget programs, entertainment and public service alike, are network, and their drawing power creates the audience at which both spot commercial announcements and the adjacent programs aim; secondly, with only two or three stations in the typical market area, virtually all stations are affiliated to one of the networks and rely heavily on their network programs for the "quality" programming with which they justify themselves to the FCC.

COMPETITION, MONOPOLY, AND THE PUBLIC INTEREST: PROTOTYPES COMPARED

1. An Ample, Unbiased Source of News and an Open Forum for Commentary and Public Discussion. The arguments against monopoly power in these areas need no rehearsing here. Nor is it the fear of outrageous abuse of freedom of thought or expression that motivates opposition to a benevolent and public spirited monopoly like that of the BBC in sound broadcasting. It is, rather, that the centralization of authority over the selection and presentation of public issues imposes an awesome responsibility for a benevolent monopoly; it must be prudent and it must be studiously impartial. This responsibility leads, apparently inevitably, to paternalism. At best, and the BBC frequently achieves this best, it produces the broadcasting equivalent of a superbly balanced book. But this is not the equivalent of a balanced library. The brilliance of individual items may obscure the fact that there is no appeal from the decision *not to cover* a particular story or to give it merely routine coverage. This can, of course, occur under any system but is less likely if there are several independent decision units than if there is one. This is a major objection to monopoly in broadcasting.

How does American experience compare? With respect to news reporting it is by usage free from advertisers' preview or editing. Both unsponsored and sponsored broadcasts are common, at both the station and network level; selection and production decisions reside with the broadcasters in all cases. The frequency of such news broadcasts is great, and because of the diversity of the selection, the number of stories reported in a given day is substantially larger than on the BBC. News commentary is also frequent and exhibits substantial range of opinion—from the extreme right to the middle left. While punditry far outweighs polemic, both are present. In the field of public discussion, panel interviews and documentary coverage in depth are frequent—once in a while in bad taste, typically informative, and occasionally superb.

2. Existence of a Sufficient Number of Independent Sources of Employment.   The market for television performers, directors, producers, and technical personnel is necessarily discontinuous and imperfect. The advantages of having even two or three potential employers rather than one are obvious. They are particularly compelling where artistic judgments are involved. Blacklisting, favoritism, and discrimination may occur, but they may also be imagined if there is no real alternative source of employment. Pluralism of decision making provides an essential element of protection.

Because skills are specialized and markets are imperfect, appropriate levels of compensation are difficult to determine. It is clear that introduction of independent television in Britain has led to a significant increase in the pay scales of the BBC as a response to the loss of personnel to its competitor. This suggests that monopoly, public or private, exercises significant monopsony power as well.

If one accepts the view that these considerations are important, it is clear that competition—even competition limited to a few competitors—has a major advantage over monopoly.

3. Public Service Responsibility.   A semipublic monopoly has one enormous asset: It is free to undertake a wholehearted commitment to public service. Freed from any crass scratching for revenue, freed from competition for listeners, and insulated from pressure groups; it may consciously and conscientiously pursue its image of the public interest. The BBC's worldwide reputation and its many programming triumphs attest to the public benefits that can be achieved.

These benefits are not without costs. The image served is that of the monopoly. That it may be paternalistic, that it may identify too closely with the Establishment, that it may resist changes in itself and become impervious to changes in the public climate are real rather than phantom dangers. They are the hazards of power wherever it is found. Complete lack of power, the characteristic of atomistic competition, while avoiding the dangers, negates the benefits as well in cases where public service is not identical with private interest. The challenge is to find the mixture of monopoly and competition that gives the best balance.

The American mixture does not. Not that the conscious pursuit of public service is absent; the networks do have such an image and it is reflected in news and documentary programs, and elsewhere as well. But even networks can afford to be "uneconomic" in some areas only if they attend to the business of collecting revenue most of the time. If one makes a rough distinction between entertainment and other programming, it is only slightly unfair to say that networks abdicate public service responsibility in the former and embrace it in the latter. As to entertainment, the creed is to "give them (the listeners and/or the advertisers) what they want." (How well they do this is discussed below.) For the other they can be magnificent.

But these activities are inversely related to competition. ABC has gained both listeners and profits by leaving prestige programming to its rivals and developing "adult" Westerns. National spot programming eschews it entirely, and individual stations frequently reject unsponsored network prestige programs in favor of national spot or locally sponsored film series if they have an option. Subjecting the networks to fiercer and more compelling competition, a goal frequently advocated and fruitlessly pursued by the FCC, would work against, rather than for, public service responsibility.

The successes of the networks should not detract from the question of whether enough of the networks' time is devoted to programs of this sort. This is the problem of the program mix.

4. The Provision of a Rich and Varied Program.   Here the disadvantages of limited competition are most pronounced. This fact, and the reasons for it, are very important but only dimly appreciated. It is convenient to consider the problem in stages.

Consider first a situation in which there are three channels operating concurrently for a single period (say 30 minutes) broadcasting to a population of potential listeners whose tastes vary in the following very simple way; out of every 100 potential listeners, 80 want a program of type A (e.g., Western), 18 want a program of type B (e.g., dramatic show), and the remaining 2 want a program of type C (e.g., discussion of current events). Further assume to start with that a listener will turn on his set only if a program of the type he wants is broadcast.

A monopoly interested in maximizing the number of listeners (which in this case is the same as satisfying the largest number of people) will clearly produce one program of each type, one on each channel, and both capture and satisfy the whole audience. Three competing firms, each trying to get as many listeners *for itself* as it can, will probably *all* produce a program of type A for the simple reason that each one's share of the mass audience will be larger than the whole of the potential audience for programs of types B or C. If we assume that two or more stations producing the same program type will share the audience equally, it is easily seen that a fourth channel will also produce type A (20 percent of the audience) rather than type B (18 percent). Indeed, one would need 5 stations before one could expect type B to be produced, and at least 48 channels before type C would appear attractive. Duplication is a consequence of competition for listeners, and if choices are varied and the number of channels limited, duplication will leave some listeners unnecessarily dissatisfied. While each of the duplicating program producers can claim that "we give people what they want," this is not so in the aggregate.

If viewers will accept (if grudgingly) less-preferred programs rather than none at all, the tendencies for duplication under competition are increased. To see this quickly, suppose 70 percent of the audience prefer type A and 30 percent type B but will listen to either. If there are only two channels, both will produce type A and each will get 50 percent of the audience. A third channel has a choice of producing type B and getting 30 percent of the listeners or duplicating type A and getting one third of the total. If it aims strictly at maximizing its audience, it will choose type A. (If viewers had not been shiftable, it would have chosen type B.)

When attention is directed to variation over time rather than to a single period, there are clearly substantial opportunities for increased variety. But there are major forces tending toward duplication as well, and a clear overrepresentation of the most popular program types. This can be shown theoretically, but the argument is somewhat complex, even tedious, and it will be omitted.[1] Empirically, duplication of program types by channels at the same time, and also over time, are perhaps the most clearly visible features of the American system. The near-saturation of prime evening hours on all networks with Westerns, "private eye" shows, and situation comedies has been noted by many critics. The cost is less coverage of minority tastes than their place in the reference pattern of the population warrants.

So far, then, as satisfying as many listeners as is possible is a sensible objective, and so far as choice is only between program types, it is clear that complete monopoly is, in principle, a more effective instrument than maximum competition when there are binding limits on the number of competitors possible. Monopoly, even private monopoly, is motivated to avoid duplication; competitors are not. . . .

Viewers select specific programs as well as program types. A choice

---

[1]For extended theoretical treatment of this and other complications, see P. O. Steiner, "Programme Patterns and Preferences and the Workability of Competition in Radio Broadcasting," *Quarterly Journal of Economics*, vol. 76 (May 1952), pp. 194–223.

between two Western (or two religious programs, or two variety shows) is, after all, better than no choice. Not only do tastes vary within program types but competition between programs imposes standards of competence on program producers. But such choice is expensive if it precludes the wider alternatives. Further, the same forces that tend toward duplication of program type lead to imitative programming where competition for listeners is the spur. . . .

In summary, the comparison between the prototypes—public monopoly and private, commercial, limited competition—shows:

1. The advantages of pluralism in providing an open forum for news and discussion and in providing alternative sources of employment give competition a decisive edge.

2. Public service responsibility flows from two sources: power and motivation. The public monopoly has both and has the advantage. But the form of limited competition considered leaves substantial monopolistic power in the hands of the competitors who can (and do) choose to compete for public esteem as well as for audience. In either case the existence of a protected position provides the opportunity for conscious public service.

3. Monopoly is inherently motivated to provide the complementary programming that leads to maximum variety; competitors are not so motivated and a significant restriction on choice owing to both duplication and imitation is to be expected.

4. Competition, if it generates substantial additional resources for programming, can do some things better than a (relatively) underfinanced public monopoly, and (while it should not be overstressed) the need to compete for audiences may have a beneficial effect on the particular programs of the kinds most heavily demanded.

If choice is limited to one or the other of these prototypes, judgment as to a "balance of advantage" is required. The challenge is to find a mixture that can tap the advantages of both. . . .

E. TRANSPORTATION

The ICC and CAB have long supported the cartel-like actions of the rate bureaus among railroads, truckers, and airlines. The result has often been to prevent price cutting. Ceiling price limits have become price floors, even though there has been a growing area of natural competition in all three transport modes. In a leading case—*Ingot Molds*, decided by the Supreme Court in 1968—the ICC prevented a price-cutting innovation by a southern railroad. The price must be above "fully distributed cost" (i.e., average cost), even though long-run marginal cost was much lower. The point relates to "predatory pricing"; in this case, barge lines claimed that the new railway prices would be unfairly low, taking traffic from them. (Compare with the "TELPAK" case, above.) A century ago railroads often practiced selective price cutting in predatory fashion, but they have much less scope to do so now. The bad economics in this decision continues in current ICC policy, though a moderate range of discretion is now permitted in changing prices.

The CAB has shifted since 1975 toward more efficient pricing rules and toward freer competition. The Chairman's speech excerpted below gives the Board's rationale. Discount fares rapidly proliferated after 1976, and the evolving fare structure reflected both costs and the elasticities of demand.

🚂 66

American Commercial Lines, Inc. et al. v. Louisville & Nashville Railroad Co. et al.

The *Ingot Molds* Case
U.S. Supreme Court
392 U.S. 571 (1968)

> Ingot Molds *was a leading effort to inject "efficient"—marginal cost—pricing so that railroads could compete more effectively. Yet the Court chose instead to stress "inherent advantages," much to the criticism of most economists. Who is right?*

Justice Marshall.   The basic issue in these cases is . . . the action of the Interstate Commerce Commission in disallowing a rate reduction proposed by the appellee railroads, [in 1965] Section 15a (3) of the Interstate Commerce Act, 49 U.S.C. Section 15a (3), added by 72 Stat. 572 (1958), which governs ratemaking in situations involving intermodal competition. . . .

Since 1953, the movement of ingot molds from Neville Island and Pittsburgh, Pennsylvania, to Steelton, Kentucky, has been almost exclusively by combination barge-truck service and since 1960, the overall charge for this service has been $5.11 per ton. In 1963, the Pennsylvania Railroad and the Louisville & Nashville Railroad lowered their joint rate for this same traffic from $11.86 to $5.11 per ton. The competing barge lines, joined by intervening trucking interests, protested to the ICC that the new railroad rate violated Section 15a (3) of the Interstate Commerce Act because it impaired or destroyed the "inherent advantage" then enjoyed by the barge-truck service. The Commission thereupon undertook an investigation of the rate reduction.

In the course of the administrative proceedings that followed, the ICC made the following factual findings about which there is no real dispute among the parties. The fully distributed cost[1] to the railroads of this service was $7.59 per ton, and the "long-term out-of-pocket costs"[2]

---

[1]Fully distributed costs are defined broadly by the ICC as the "out-of-pocket costs plus a revenue-ton and revenue ton-mile distribution of the constant cost, including deficits, [which] indicate the revenue necessary to a fair return on the traffic, disregarding ability to pay." *New Automobiles in Interstate Commerce*, 259 I.C.C. 475, 513 (1945).

[2]The long-term out-of-pocket costs were computed under an ICC-sponsored formula which generally holds that 80 percent of rail operating expenses, rents, and taxes are out-of-pocket in that they will vary with traffic. To this is added a return element of 4 percent on a portion of the investment (all the equipment and 50 percent of the road property), which is apportioned to all traffic on a proportional basis.

were $4.69 per ton. The fully distributed cost to the barge-truck service
was $5.19 per ton. The out-of-pocket cost[3] of the barge-truck service was
not separately computed but was estimated without contradiction to be
approximately the same as the fully distributed cost and higher, in any
event, than the out-of-pocket cost of the railroads. The uncontroverted
shipper testimony was to the effect that price was virtually the sole
determinant of which service would be utilized but that, were the rates
charged by the railroads and the barge-truck combination the same, all
the traffic would go to the railroads.

The railroads contended that they should be permitted to maintain
the $5.11 rate, once it was shown to exceed the out-of-pocket cost at-
tributable to the service, on the ground that any rate so set would enable
them to make a profit on the traffic. The railroads further contended that
the fact that the rate was substantially below their fully distributed cost
for the service was irrelevant, since that cost in no way reflected the
profitability of the traffic to them. The barge-truck interests, on the other
hand, took the position that Section 15a (3) required the Commission to
look to the railroads' fully distributed costs in order to ascertain which of
the competing modes had the inherent cost advantage on the traffic at
issue. They argued that the fact that the railroads' rate would be profitable was merely the minimum requirement under the statute. The railroads in response contended that inherent advantage should be determined by a comparison of out-of-pocket rather than fully distributed
costs, and they produced several economists to testify that, from the
standpoint of economic theory, the comparison of out-of-pocket, or incremental, costs was the only rational way of regulating competitive
rates.

The ICC rejected the railroads' contention that out-of-pocket costs
should be the basis on which inherent advantage should be determined.
The Commission observed that it had in the past regularly viewed fully
distributed costs as the appropriate basis for determining which of two
competing modes was the lower cost mode as regards particular traffic.
It further indicated that the legislative history of Section 15a (3) revealed
that Congress had in mind a comparison of fully distributed costs when
it inserted the reference to the National Transportation Policy into that
section in place of language sought by the railroads.

Having decided to utilize a comparison between fully distributed
costs to determine inherent advantage, the Commission then concluded

---

[3]Out-of-pocket costs have been regarded generally in these cases as equivalent to what
economists refer to as "incremental" or "marginal" costs. Accordingly we shall equate the
terms likewise, although we have no intention of vouching for the accuracy of that equation as a matter of pure economics. . . . Such costs are defined generally as the costs
specifically incurred by the addition of each new unit of output and do not include any
allocation to that unit of preexisting overhead expenses.

that the rate set by the railroads would undercut the barge-truck combination's ability to exploit its inherent advantage because the rate would force the competing carriers to go well below their own fully distributed costs to recapture the traffic from the railroads. Moreover, since the result sought by the railroads was general permission to set rates on an out-of-pocket basis, the Commission concluded that eventually the railroads could take all the traffic away from the barge-truck combination because the out-of-pocket costs of the former were lower than those of the latter and, therefore, in any rate war the railroads would be able to outlast their competitors. Accordingly, the Commission ordered that the railroads' rate be canceled.

The District Court read the statute and its accompanying legislative history to reflect a congressional judgment that inherent advantage should be determined in most cases by a comparison of out-of-pocket costs and that, therefore, railroads should generally be permitted to set any individual rate they choose as long as that rate is compensatory.[4] The court also held that the Commission had failed adequately to articulate its reasons for deciding that the proper way of determining which mode of transportation was the more efficient was by comparison of fully distributed costs rather than out-of-pocket costs.

II.

This court has previously had occasion to consider the meaning and legislative history of Section 15a (3) of the Interstate Commerce Act. . . .
So far as relevant here, Section 15a (3) provides that:

[r]ates of a carrier shall not be held up to a particular level to protect the traffic of any other mode of transportation, giving due consideration to the objectives of the national transportation policy declared in this Act.

The National Transportation Policy, states that it is the intention of the Congress:

to provide for fair and impartial regulation of all modes of transportation subject to the provisions of this act, so administered as to recognize and preserve the inherent advantages of each. . . .

The District Court apparently believed that the Commission was required to exercise its judgment in the direction of using out-of-pocket costs as the rate floor because that would encourage "hard" competition. We do not deny that the competition that would result from such a decision would probably be "hard." Indeed, from the admittedly scanty

---

[4]A rate is compensatory in the sense used by the District Court any time it is greater than the out-of-pocket cost of the service for which the rate is set. The term fully compensatory is sometimes used to describe a rate in excess of fully distributed costs.

evidence in this record, one might well conclude that the competition resulting from out-of-pocket ratemaking by the railroads would be so hard as to run a considerable number of presently existing barge and truck lines out of business.

We disagree, however, with the District Court's reading of congressional intent. The language contained in Section 15a (3) was the product of a bitter struggle between the railroads and their competitors. One of the specific fears of those competitors that prompted the change from the original language used in the bill was that the bill as it then read would permit essentially unregulated competition between all the various transportation modes. It was argued with considerable force that permitting the railroads to price on an out-of-pocket basis to meet competition would result in the eventual complete triumph of the railroads in intermodal competition because of their ability to impose all their constant costs on traffic for which there was no competition.

The economists who testified for the railroads in this case all stated that such an unequal allocation of constant costs among shippers on the basis of demand for railroad service, i.e., on the existence of competition for particular traffic, was economically sound and desirable.

The simple fact is that Section 15a (3) was not enacted, as the railroads claim, to enable them to price their services in such a way as to obtain the maximum revenue therefrom. The very words of the statute speak of "preserv[ing]" the inherent advantages of each mode of transportation. If all that was meant by the statute was to prevent wholly noncompensatory pricing by regulated carriers, language that was a good deal clearer could easily have been used. And, as we have shown here, at least one version of such clear language was proposed by the railroads and rejected by the Congress. If the theories advanced by the economists who testified in this case are as compelling as they seem to feel they are, Congress is the body to whom they should be addressed. The courts are ill-qualified indeed to make the kind of basic judgments about economic policy sought by the railroads here. And it would be particularly inappropriate for a court to award a carrier, on economic grounds, relief denied it by the legislature. . . .

The Commission stated here that it intended to exercise its informed judgment by considering the issues presented here in the context of a rulemaking proceeding where it could evaluate the alternatives on the basis of a consideration of the effects of a departure from a fully distributed cost standard on the transportation industry as a whole. Until that evaluation was completed, the Commission took the position that it would continue to follow the practice it had observed in the past of dealing with individual rate reductions on a fully distributed cost basis.

. . . In any event, regardless of the label used, it seems self-evident that a carrier's "inherent advantage" of being the low cost mode on a fully distributed cost basis is impaired when a competitor sets a rate that forces the carrier to lower its own rate below its fully distributed costs in order to retain the traffic. In addition, when a rate war would be likely eventually to result in pushing rates to a level at which the rates set would no longer provide a fair profit, the Commission has traditionally, and properly, taken the position that such a rate struggle should be prevented from commencing in the first place. Certainly there is no suggestion here that the rate charged by the barge-truck combination was excessive and in need of being driven down by competitive pressure. We conclude, therefore, that the Commission adequately articulated its reasons for determining that the railroads' rate would impair the inherent advantage enjoyed by the barge-truck service.

The judgment of the District Court is reversed and the cases are remanded to that court with directions to enter a judgment affirming the Commission's order.

It is so ordered.

Alfred E. Kahn (1917–   )

✴ 67

The Moves toward Deregulation by the Civil Aeronautics Board*

> *A leading scholar of antitrust and regulation, Kahn was made chairman of the CAB in 1977, after several years in which the former chairman, John R. Robson, had begun liberalizing the CAB's approach. Kahn moved the shift forward with a firm but careful program of changes. He explains their complexities here: Deregulation is not a simple process. The shift is a remarkable exception to the usual hardening of regulation along protective lines.*

I didn't come into this job with a grand strategy. But I did come in with a strong sense of the imperfections of regulation, a healthy respect for the efficiency of markets, and a predilection in favor of relying on the latter wherever effective competition appears to be feasible. . . .

I do not want to draw overly simplified lessons from what has been a very complicated—and, incidentally, extremely rewarding—experience, but for the most part the last seven months have reinforced those general views. For one thing, I could not possibly have imagined the number and variety of ways in which I was going to be called upon every single day to give my consent before a willing buyer and a willing seller could get together: May an airline pick up some celebrities from various points to an assembly point and carry them on a triumphal preinaugural flight along some newly certificated route? May a freight forwarder receive commissions from a cargo carrier? To how many travel agents may a tour operator give free passage to inspect an all-inclusive tour? And must those agents then visit and inspect every one of the accommodations in the package? May an air taxi acquire a 50-seat plane? May a supplemental carrier carry horses from Florida to somewhere in the Northeast? Should we let a scheduled carrier pick up stranded charter customers and carry them on seats that would otherwise be empty at charter rates? May an air taxi operate a single round-trip passenger

---

*Excerpted from a speech to the New York Society of Security Analysts, February 2, 1978. Alfred E. Kahn is a leading scholar of antitrust and regulation, as well as chairman of the CAB during 1977–78.

charter flight between two points in substitution for a supplemental? Should we take review of an order by our Bureau of Enforcement dismissing this or that complaint, even though no party has appealed the dismissal? May a carrier introduce a special fare for skiers that refunds the cost of their return ticket if there is no snow? May the employees of two financially affiliated airlines wear similar-looking uniforms? May a cargo carrier serve city X from airport Y while X's airport is under construction? May a scheduled carrier fly over some city on Saturdays? May it fly nonstop between two points when its certificate says it must make at least one stop along the way? Or fulfill that one-stop obligation at city A rather than city B? May a carrier already certificated to fly between A and C via B pick up passengers going only from A to B? Is it any wonder that I ask myself every day: Is this action necessary? Is this what my mother raised me to do?

*   *   *   *   *

So what I am trying to do, to put it in the broadest possible terms, is to remove the meddling, protective, and obstructionist hand of government and to restore this industry, insofar as the law permits, to the rule of the market. This law constrains us to do so gradually, case by case and within the prescription of due process. . . .

THE PROGRAM

Let me begin by simply outlining, without explanation or justification, the main components of the program that we have been evolving during the last several months. . . .

Entry

Freedom of entry is the heart of competition; and route certification by the CAB has therefore been the critical instrumentality for the cartelization of this industry. The extreme exemplification of this policy was the route moratorium of the early 1970s, during which the Board simply refused to entertain the hundreds of applications that came into it for new route authority; less obvious but equally effective is the indescribably intricate maze of restrictions on the operating rights of each of the existing carriers.

Our program of liberalization involves the following:

1. A greater receptivity to applications for new operating authority by existing carriers and new ones.

2. A particular receptivity to applications that are accompanied by proposed new low-fare options—not the mere verbal promise of low

fares that may come to be regarded as *de rigeur* in future applications, but the offer of a plan of operation that backs up that promise with a credible expectation of low costs.[1]

3. A willingness to make route awards temporary, with renewal dependent on performance. In our recent *Trans-Atlantic Routes* decision, for example, we made the awards good for only five years, promising to take into account in deciding whether to renew the extent to which the carriers had continued to offer the low fares they had recently introduced, purportedly in response to the Laker Skytrain.[2]

4. Permitting existing carriers with increasing liberality to realign their routes and slough off the restrictions that limit their operating flexibility.[3]

5. Making more of the certificated authority we grant permissive and

6. Nonexclusive, and/or

7. Accompanied by a provision for backup authority.[4]

If one or more carriers are applying for a particular market whose ability to support an additional carrier is questionable or whose traffic, it appears, is large enough to justify only one; or if it can clearly take at least one at present prices but might conceivably take more if prices were reduced—in those various situations, we are experimenting increasingly with admitting one, permissively, but in the same case naming a second and even a third with authority to move in if the first does not; or

------

[1]Both of these policies are clearly reflected in the high priority we have given to four major route proceedings in which innovative low fare services have been proposed. On Tuesday hearings began in the first of these, the *Chicago-Midway Low-Fare Route Proceeding* (docket 30277), in which we have set August 1 as the deadline for Board decision (Orders 76–12–149, 77–5–81, and 77–8–10). Last November, we adopted a procedural schedule giving priority to the other three cases (Order 77–11–126). They are the *Transcontinental Low-Fare Route Proceeding* (docket 30356) (which includes a consideration of World Airways' 10-year old application), in which we intend to reach a final decision by March 8, 1979 (Orders 77–1–94, 77–6–23, and 77–11–39); the *California-Nevada Low-Fare Route Proceeding*, scheduled for final decision by April 26, 1979 (docket 31574, Orders 77–10–136 and 78–1–16); and the *Miami-Luxembourg Low Fare Service Investigation*, October 18, 1979 (docket 30790). Those of you not familiar with CAB procedures and the rigors of due process cannot begin to appreciate how tight those deadlines really are. Or how clearly their setting reflects our determination to rearrange our business so that applications promising substantial public benefits will be heard as quickly as the law and our staff resources permit.

[2]Opinion of October 21, 1977, at 32 (docket 25908).

[3]Order 77–11–74, involving the Western Airlines realignment.

[4]Only a few examples of our new approach have reached final decision. In the *Cincinnati-Washington Subpart M Proceeding*, Order 77–10–4, we made multiple nonstop awards in a relatively small market. Just last week we granted permissive authority to one applicant, with a backup award to a second, in the *Phoenix-Des Moines/Milwaukee* route proceeding, Order 78–1–116. And at our Board meeting yesterday, we considered the award of authority to two additional carriers—rather than just one as would have been likely in the past—in several major Atlanta markets. *Midwest-Atlanta Competitive Service* case, docket 28115.

certificating more than one even at the outset but, again, requiring neither to enter. As a result, we are proliferating situations in which there are carriers with authority to enter markets in which they do not yet operate—standing in the wings and ready to enter whenever in their judgment the market situation justifies it. Our comprehensive route realignments are having the same effect.

8. A more permissive attitude toward market exit in situations where entry has been liberalized. This attitude is of course implicit in our increasing willingness to grant permissive and backup authority, both of which reflect a willingness to see second and third carriers in a particular market not exercise the licenses we give them. In a competitive regime, there is no room for governmentally imposed obligations on sellers to serve markets that they think cannot economically support them—provided others are free to enter if they think otherwise—or for internal subsidization. It is the essential function of competitive entry to eliminate the supernormal profits on hitherto sheltered routes that have served in part to subsidize service on uneconomic routes: Erosion of the former privileges must carry with it as a logical counterpart relaxation of the latter obligations. Certainly one major historical reason for the financial problems of the railroads has been their subjection to increasingly intense intermodal competition, while continuing to be required to serve uneconomic markets. . . . .

The corollary of a liberal attitude on our part toward market exit is our devising of a plan, the essentials of which are embodied in the major regulatory reform statutes now before Congress, for the explicit, direct taxpayer-financed subsidization of markets that are too thin to be served on a strictly economic basis by private unsubsidized carriers.

9. A relaxation of the functional and operational restrictions on the various categories of carriers and on the services they are permitted to offer. The most obvious and dramatic instance has been our liberalization of charter rules—making charter travel available to nonaffiliated groups, reducing the advance purchase requirements, permitting additional fill-up sales and substitutions as flight time approaches, and reducing the minimum group sizes. Symmetrically, we have relaxed the limitations on the right of scheduled carriers to run charters off their certificated routes; declared our willingness in principle to let them transfer customers from charters onto empty seats of scheduled flights; and permitted them with greatly increased freedom to appeal to the same economy-minded public as charters do and in much the same way with sharply discounted fares for off-peak and standby services, conditional reservations, capacity-restricted advance sales of seats that would otherwise go empty, and the like.

Equally logical components of a program of removing the shackles on different kinds of carriers—step by step, and synchronously—will be our sympathetic consideration of applications by supplemental carriers to engage in scheduled service (I'd like to think that if this kind of application had come to us in 1977 it wouldn't have required a Court of Appeals decision to make us do so); by combination carriers and all-cargo carriers to compete with one another; by airlines traditionally restricted to international routes to enter domestic markets, as we have already been permitting domestic carriers to move in the opposite direction, and of foreign flag carriers to have access to additional U.S. gateways in exchange for reciprocal relaxations by foreign governments, particularly in their willingness to receive our charters and low-fare scheduled flights.

Pricing

I need hardly describe to you at length the similarly permissive attitude we have been taking toward more flexible, discretionary pricing. Historically, the Board has insisted on second-guessing decisions by individual carriers to offer price reductions in terms not only of whether they might result in reduced profits for the industry as a whole—thus playing the role of grand cartelizer for the industry—but even of whether the proposing carrier had correctly gauged its own interest. During the last several months, we have been abandoning this paternalistic role, leaving the introduction of discount fares increasingly to management discretion.

We are contemplating a codification of our new procompetitive policies in a comprehensive revision of the industry pricing standards promulgated just a few years ago in the Domestic Passenger Fare Investigation. Among other changes, these could involve abandoning the following aspects of the DPFI:

1. Its fundamental disapproval or at least critical attitude toward discount fares, except on a temporary basis and in the presence of excess capacity (I am told that this is an overly simplified characterization of that policy; I believe there is no doubt, however, that the Board's attitude toward discount fares has become much more tolerant during the last year or two);

2. Its required cross-subsidization of short-haul by long-haul traffic;

3. Its imposition of uniform rates per mile in all markets, thick and thin, low-cost and high;

4. Its prescription of a minimum mark-up of first-class over coach fares and a maximum discount of economy from coach;

5. Its requirement of uniform rates, based on industry cost, to be charged by all carriers, regardless of their own individual modes of operations and costs—which, by excluding possible differences in fares, has ensured the resolution of contests for route awards only on the basis

of such considerations as the kinds of service that the competing applicants promise to offer, their comparative need of "route strengthening,"
which one got an award last time, if not by the toss of a coin; and, in
general,

6. Its insistence that rates be judged primarily in terms of their
coverage of fully allocated costs, almost regardless of the direction of
travel or its relation to the system peak, except for quite restricted and
rigid allowances of night coach rates—from almost all of which principles the Board has already departed in important ways.

*   *   *   *   *

DANGERS, REAL AND IMAGINARY,
AND THEIR IMPLICATIONS

The most general fear about such a program is that when the CAB
withdraws its protective hand from the doorknob the door will open to
destructive competition—to wasteful entry and cut-throat pricing—that
will depress profits, render the industry unable to raise capital, and so
cause a deterioration in the service it provides—on the whole, it must be
admitted, good service. This dire prediction has at least two aspects, one
short-term, the other chronic. The first has to do with the dangers of
taking a delicate plant that has been raised to maturity in a hot house
and setting it suddenly out in the cold. The other is a belief that for some
inherent reason the kind of competitive regime under which most industries in our economy have grown and prospered is unsuited to airlines.
(There are other aspects to which I will allude only indirectly—such as
the expectation, almost certainly justified, that the pressures of competition on costs will necessarily result in deterioration of service quality, at
least for those customers that opt for the lower-fare options, but perhaps
for others as well.)

The Fear of Sudden Change

So far as the first prognosis is concerned, the simple prescription
would seem to be gradualness: Adjust the conditions of the overgrown
infant's incubator only gradually to those of the outside world; give the
delicate organism time to adjust.

On the other hand, as I have already emphasized, this prescription
will never work unless the commitment to gradualness is accompanied
by a resolution to make the change. This industry must know what its
future regulatory environment is going to be like. So long as its management continues to hope or believe that it can stay in the incubator,
that its prospects of success will continue to be best assured by fighting
in the halls of the CAB and Congress against the eventual necessity for

emerging into the adult world, it will refuse to begin the process of fundamental reorientation that is the key to ultimate survival in that world. If the CAB and Congress are best advised to be cautious, they must equally be advised to be resolute.

Distortions and Inefficiencies of Free Entry

Turning to the more fundamental fear: There seems to be a general belief among defenders of the present regulatory regime that there is something about airplanes that drives businessmen crazy—that once the CAB removes its body from the threshold, they will rush into markets pell-mell en masse without regard to the size of each, how many sellers it can sustain, and how many others may be entering at the same time. I don't believe it. I suspect, on the contrary, that once it becomes clear entry is genuinely free of government restraint, the reaction is likely to be cautious, with each carrier and would-be carrier holding back in order to see what the others do. If I am right, the entries that do take place will be the result of careful advance calculation and selection by managements of the opportunities that are most promising for their particular companies.

These fears are probably inspired partly by the avid competition for route authorizations that now takes place before the CAB: At the moment, we have something like 280 applications for domestic route authority filed largely within the last three years and, it is quite clear, with varying degrees of sincerity. But of course there will always be heavy competition for government franchises, so long as they confer some degree of exclusivity. There is no way of knowing how many of these applications before us would be prosecuted if competition were transferred from the corridors of the CAB to the market place. Carriers file applications in part to gain the value, especially the future value, of the certificate in an otherwise closed system, to prevent other carriers from getting authority, and on the theory that they will gain more authority if they participate in a large number of cases, albeit as losers most of the time. If entry were genuinely free and if, therefore, the pieces of paper for which the companies are vying carried no exclusivity—had no inherent value except perhaps as certifications of financial and technical fitness—this particular, regulatorily-induced application filing and entry would cease.

* * * * *

I will not attempt to assess all these expectations in a priori terms. Instead, I will try to explain how our program takes them into account—is indeed in some ways specifically designed to meet them. I do not pretend to certainty that these precautions will suffice; they will certainly not take the place of intelligent company planning. But in my judgment they, plus the discipline of market competition, should do the job.

1. The best answer to the inefficient entry and operations that are artificially induced by a desire to obtain and to hold a valuable certificate is to diminish and eventually wipe out the scarcity value of the certificate; and the way to do this is to make entry *free* and *permissive*. Eliminating the door prize will eliminate that artificial inducement to go through the door; it will also eliminate the incentive to stay inside and engage in uneconomic operations merely in order to hold on to the prize.

2. The best answer I can think of to the differential handicaps to which carriers are subject because of the comparative efficiencies of their existing route systems is to give them freedom to improve those systems by route realignments, new entries, and market exits. I do not mean by this to dismiss as unimportant the preexisting advantages and handicaps with which carriers enter the new and more competitive era. Route structure is, indeed, the dominant influence on relative unit costs: the longer the haul and the greater the traffic density, the lower the costs. But carriers compete over *particular* routes: The distance and density of traffic between Kansas City or Charlottesville and Washington is no greater or less for carrier A with a preponderance of long hauls and dense markets on the rest of its system than for carrier B with a lot of short hops over sparse routes. Of course, B will worry about A's ability to draw on a deeper purse than it has available to it. But, first, the notion that the larger carriers with the longer, denser routes are typically richer than the smaller ones is obviously wildly off the mark. And, second, what reason is there to think that a business will transfer funds from a profitable operation to subsidize ventures in others in which it enjoys no advantage except the possession of more money to lose than its competitors there—particularly if it will itself be subject to the constant threat of entry in the latter markets if it should succeed in driving those competitors out and then attempt to recoup its initial losses?

Moreover, costs also vary significantly among carriers with roughly the same route structures. A statistical analysis made several years ago showed carriers with almost identical route systems but widely differing unit costs, clearly suggesting that differences in efficiency stemming from differences in management quality have at least as important an impact on the relative abilities of different carriers to compete on particular routes as the quality of their overall route structures.

These considerations provide no simple answer either to the possibility that free entry will permit the bigger airlines with ample feeder and beyond operations to funnel intermediate traffic on competitive routes into their own aircraft, making it impossible for smaller, more specialized carriers to compete on those routes. To the extent this advantage exists, it may represent in part a genuine economy of integration: If a carrier can attract passengers because it gives them single-plane or single-carrier service, that is, at least in part, a genuine social advantage and one that should weigh favorably in the struggle for competitive success.

But also, experience has already amply demonstrated if there are such advantages of integration there are also powerful economies of specialization. A lack of feeder and beyond traffic did not prevent PSA from becoming the dominant carrier in the Los Angeles to San Francisco route or Southwest Airlines from duplicating that success between Dallas and Houston; and it is interesting to observe at least one of Eastern Airlines' most profitable routes is the shuttle between Washington, New York, and Boston, in which it has surrendered any possible advantages of single-plane service, feeder, or beyond operations. A concentration on turnaround service between a pair of cities will, if true origination and destination traffic between them is sufficiently great, permit optimum scheduling for that single market, without the need for compromises to accommodate a combination of other markets for through flights. It should also permit better on-time performance by avoiding down the line delays. And perhaps most important it permits optimum use of the aircraft best adapted for that particular route—a powerful determinant of costs—whereas a carrier operating a more diversified network has to compromise in order to accommodate the needs of markets of differing sizes or peaking characteristics.

So far as I know there is no objective basis for deciding which of these situations is more likely to prove typical—the one in which the integrated typically larger carrier can out-compete its more specialized rivals because of the network economies it enjoys from the multistop and on-line traffic flows at its command, or the one in which the specialized carrier will have clear advantages. There will undoubtedly be situations of both kinds with all sorts of gradations and combinations in between: There is no reason to expect most markets to fit neatly into one category or the other. In market after market, carriers of widely varying sizes and degrees of integration co-exist today. I understand that where local service carriers and trunks meet in head-to-head competition there is no systematic tendency for the former to have lower load factors than the latter. Perhaps the only conclusion one can and need draw is that under a competitive regime where all suppliers are free to try to take advantage of the opportunities presented by free entry and exit to augment their advantages and shed their handicaps and to have their qualifications tested in the market place these various kinds of market situations can be expected to sift themselves out automatically, with various kinds of suppliers emerging successful on the basis of their respective advantages and handicaps in each. I admit to the slightest feeling that this conclusion may be just a little glib, but it seems to me the only one justified by the experience with market competition in this industry and in the economy at large.

Moreover, if we cannot *predict* how these offsetting advantages and handicaps of the several carriers are likely to work out under a regime of free entry, it seems to me even less likely that we can hope to achieve the most efficient performance of the transportation function by *prescribing* how the thousands of markets should be served through a comprehensive regulation of entry. I find it difficult to see how these uncertainties tilt the balance in the direction of a reliance on ignorant regulation in preference to an uncertainly predictable market process.

3. And the answer to the fear of excessive capacity and low load factors, I am convinced, is to reverse the process that produces this kind of wasteful, cost-inflating service competition by opening the door to price competition. The observation is by now commonplace—and the airline industry is its prime exemplar—that an industry that is deterred from price competition, whether because of oligopolistic self-restraint or by cartel-like controls, will, if there remain incentives to compete, do so instead in service; that if, for one reason or another, price is prevented from falling to marginal cost, then marginal cost will adjust upward to price; and if supernormal profits consequent on restriction of entry cannot be competed away through price reductions, they will be competed away through service rivalry.

Service competition is up to a point desirable: Load factors can be too high as well as too low. It is objectionable only where customers are not presented with choices of better and poorer service, with corresponding cost-based differences in price—i.e., when the amount of service provided is not subjected to a market test.

And the solution is already inherent in our program: Our particular receptivity to entry accompanied with plans to provide genuinely new low-price options is intended to provide exactly this wider range of choice and, in so doing, to limit cost-inflating service competition to what sufficiently large groups of customers, given a genuine choice, are willing to pay for. Once price competition is possible, there is far less need to assume that competitive entry will mean only lower load factors and wasteful use of fuel: On the contrary, as I will explain more fully in a moment, low-fare options will mean higher break-even load factors and, therefore, more efficient use of fuel.[5]

Destructive Price Competition

But may not the competition of low-fare options destroy scheduled service—the very result protective CAB regulation is intended to avert

---

[5]We have explicitly spelled out this expectation in setting down our Miami-Los Angeles low fares proceeding, largely *because* of the very low load factors prevailing in that market.

—by causing a loss of business to charters, and/or by the competitive responses of the scheduled carriers so filling their planes as to eliminate the one essential characteristic of such service: the ability of regular fare-paying customers to make reservations on convenient flights on relatively short notice? Is not the flood of discounting that has beset the industry during the last year or so the best demonstration of the threat of destructive price competition?

I do not have the complete answer: Any industry that operates on the average at something like 55 percent of capacity and whose marginal costs are therefore well below average costs can never be said to be totally free of this danger. But there are a number of partial answers:

1. First of all, almost all of this industry's markets can support only a single carrier or a few: Their natural structure, therefore, is monopolistic or oligopolistic. This kind of structure could still be conducive to highly effective competition if only the government would get out of the way: The ease of potential entry into these individual markets and the constant threat of its materializing could well suffice to prevent monopolistic exploitation. Still, that kind of market situation—particularly when exit is likewise easy—is simply not conducive to bitter end price competition.

Indeed, if I had to decide which is the greater danger, I think it would be that because carriers are few, even in the so-called competitive markets, each will take into account the probable responses of its rivals to its fare reductions and fearing retaliation, will refrain from initiating any. The carrier with a small share of one market and, therefore, with the most to gain and least to lose from a price cut is likely to be deterred from engaging in all-out price competition there by the likelihood that it will be meeting those same competitors in other markets in which, more than likely, the situation will be reversed. This kind of situation is more conducive to a diplomatic policy of live-and-let-live than to continuous price warfare.

2. This industry has long ago evolved a method of pricing that takes advantage of its low marginal costs while limiting the danger of undermining the entire market. I refer, of course, to the intricate maze of special fares, carefully—but not always successfully, to be sure—defined to avoid spoiling the market for regularly scheduled service while yet picking up the additional traffic at prices well in excess of marginal cost. Like others, I have tended to regard the complexity and variety of these fares, each with its own set of sadistic restrictions, as an abomination. To some extent I still do. But I recognize that they also represent a rational response to the situation I have described, much superior from the social standpoint than no response at all.

I have attempted to analyze the character of these discount fares more fully elsewhere. It probably suffices to observe here, first, that they undoubtedly embody very substantial elements of price discrimination—representing largely successful efforts to reduce prices selectively to the price-conscious, demand-elastic customers, while continuing to hold the demand-inelastic passengers to levels reflecting the average costs of operation at something like 55 percent of capacity. But they also represent efforts to tailor the various discount services in such a way as to ensure that they will indeed have the lower marginal costs, both short and long-run, that characterize the filling of empty seats. Albeit discriminatorily, they embody the basic principles of peak responsibility pricing. This is obviously the case with charters, standbys, and conditional reservations. But it is also true of capacity-controlled discount fares: The capacity controls are analogous to the interruptibility of service that enables gas and electric distribution companies to offer extremely low rates for customers who, being willing to suspend taking at times of peak demand, bear no marginal causal responsibility, either short- or long-run, for the incurrence of capacity costs.

*   *   *   *   *

. . . The essential economic implication and consequence of low fares is that by reducing average net revenue yields per passenger they raise the break-even load factor—the point at which adding capacity becomes marginally profitable. Unless, therefore, managements are totally irrational—and competition and capital markets have a way of disciplining any such—this means that equipment acquisition and scheduling decisions will reflect those reduced average yields by ensuring continuation of those higher load factors.

3. For this reason, I do not expect intensified price competition to result in the feared disappearance or debilitation of scheduled service. I see the offer of discount fares by the scheduled carriers, with our encouragement and under intelligent management planning, as pushing them toward a new equilibrium of lower average yields, higher load factors, and consequently lower average costs. This equilibrium need not at all be achieved by sparser scheduling: The effect of scheduled airlines taking advantage of the low short- and long-run marginal costs of empty seats should be to improve the viability of scheduled as compared with charter service and possibly even to permit increased frequency of scheduling, depending on how elastic demand proves to be.

4. Increased competition should make for a leaner, more efficient scheduled operation in more than one way. Filling empty seats with discount fares reduces average costs. Even more important, I think, increasing intensity of price competition should exert powerful pressures on airlines, who have for too long been operating in a regime of protectionism and cost-plus pricing, to intensify their efforts to rationalize their operations, hold down input prices, and improve the efficiency with which they use those inputs.

Withal, I do not presume to guarantee you that the industry will be a model of prosperity in the transition to a more intensely competitive regime. May I be permitted to whisper, however, that the industry's financial record has not exactly been *eclatant* under the CAB's protection? I cannot believe, in any event, that it requires governmentally imposed cartelization to make this or any other industry creditworthy. There is something marvelously effective and responsible about a market system, in which whoever seeks to seize an opportunity to profit bears the risk of loss. It does not require an all-powerful government agency to make these investment decisions responsible. . . .

Questions for Review II: Regulation

1. How can we tell whether an industry is a "public utility" and therefore should be regulated?

2. The goal of regulation is often thought to be "to simulate the patterns of competition." What problems is such an approach likely to run into?

3. Public utility regulation has been compared to the cost-plus method for buying military supplies. In both cases, it is said, public policies remove incentives for efficiency. Is this a fair appraisal?

4. Is a "comparable earnings" criterion appropriate for setting regulatory profit-rate ceilings?

5. A. "Value-of-service pricing has two great virtues. It charges users according to their ability to pay. And it encourages the maximum use (and growth) of the service. Therefore value of service pricing promotes both equity and efficiency."
    B. "Value of service is simply a euphemism to cloak a system of charging what the traffic will bear. It also encourages too much expansion by the utility. Therefore value of service pricing violates both equity and efficiency."
    Who's right, A or B? Or are they both wrong?

6. Under what conditions do "marginal-cost pricing" and "value-of-service pricing" prescribe the same rate structure? Use a diagram, if you think it helpful.

7. Give a practical example of a conflict between an *efficient* price and an *equitable* (fair) price.

8. Can an economist determine if a particular utility price is "just and reasonable"? Explain.

9. Would a utility usually prefer that its yearly depreciation allowance be large or small? Explain.

10. Outline the reasons why public utility regulation may induce too large a share of resources into the public utility industries.

11. How does the Averch-Johnson hypothesis now stand in point of (1) logic and (2) quantitative importance?

12. You have been assigned to test for the presence of the Averch-Johnson "rate base effect" in regulated utilities. What criteria will guide your selection of possible cases? That is, under what conditions is the A–J effect likely to be strong and observable?

13. Reconcile the purported "Averch-Johnson effect" according to which utilities should overinvest in capital with the existence of electricity shortages in many areas.

14. Define these and indicate their importance for regulation (5 minutes each): Efficient allocation. Replacement cost depreciation. Fair value. Second-best.

15. "The cost of capital is simply a weighted average based on the company's capital structure. The commission can measure this cost."
     "The cost of capital is the minimum the utility must offer to attract new capital funds, and this depends on the rate of return permitted by the commission. The commission cannot measure this cost; it is *making* it."
     Which one is right? Explain.

16. Is regulatory lag really a good way to achieve "incentive regulation?" Explain.

17. Name two of the "tougher" state regulatory commissions. How can one judge this?

18. What is marginal-cost pricing, and why may it be important? In what circumstances is it *not* important? Give a practical example of marginal-cost pricing.

19. For what two main reasons might electric companies set lower prices to industrial users than to households?

20. "Businesses are charged *more* for phone service than are households; e.g., $12 per month compared to $4.25. But businesses pay *less* for electricity than households are charged; e.g., 1¢ per kilowatt hour compared to 2¢." What *economic* factors affecting price discrimination may explain this strange apparent contrast in price differentials?

21. Why might utility regulation cause inefficiency? *Does* it? You have been commissioned to do a comprehensive study evaluating the performance of the privately owned, regulated part of the electric power industry. (a) What performance standards would you use? (b) What do you expect your general conclusions would eventually be (excellent, poor, mediocre, and so on on specific standards)? (c) Why are performance appraisals such as these usually difficult to make?

22. Have Bell System earnings been "comparable" in recent years to those elsewhere? Explain the criteria you use in reaching an answer.

23. What main effects has regulation had in telecommunications, electric power, railroads *or* airlines (choose only one)? Distinguish between *structural* (or strategic) regulation and controls on *behavior*. In the case you discuss, what main changes, if any, would you recommend in regulation?

24. "Competition between gas and electric utilities is intense." Does this mean that regulation is no longer necessary?

25. What is the key difference between price regulation by (1) the CAB, on the one hand, and (2) the FCC and FPC, on the other?

26. There are several areas (such as natural gas production) where the proper coverage of regulation is in question. Note *three* of these areas (excluding natural gas production). Appraise the issues and give your recommendation.

27. The possibility of "destructive competition" has been used to justify the "regulation" of such sectors as air transport, stock trading, and commercial banking. Summarize the theory of destructive competition. Evaluate whether the possibility of destructive competition justifies actual policies now in being.

Part III

PUBLIC ENTERPRISE

THE LITERATURE ON public enterprise is sparse for several reasons. American ideology has been adverse. Research support on the topic is scanty.

Yet the United States contains a remarkable variety of public enterprises, some of them important to economic and cultural life. "Fannie Mae" is just one of them. Many others help the financial, utility, and agricultural sectors to function well. The great majority of cities rely on public enterprises for transit, waste disposal, water and sewage, library, and other services. William Vickrey notes that the traditional marginal-cost criteria need to be applied thoroughly by them.

Abroad, there is even more experience and variety of public enterprise. James Nelson discusses efficient pricing in French electricity. John Sheahan draws some lessons about several French and Italian public firms which compete with private firms. Yugoslav "worker-managed firms" are a special type, which may be adopted more widely as time passes. Two excerpts portray the activities of such firms, suggesting that they can be efficient, innovative, and flexible.

Gurney Breckenfeld

✖ 68

Nobody Pours It Like Fannie Mae*

The Federal National Mortgage Association (FNMA: "Fannie Mae") is now a large, active quasi-public firm, as this report attests. It plays a key role in housing finance, and it is as entrepreneurial as many private firms. But like most public firms in the United States, it is little noticed. Note how it mingles commercial and social objectives.

Even people who ought to know better sometimes mistake Fannie Mae, the world's largest mortgage bank (assets at the end of 1971: $18.6 billion), for Fannie May, the Chicago-based candy manufacturer. . . .

Anyone who is confused about Fannie Mae has some pretty good excuses. The company is, first of all, neither a purely private enterprise nor a purely government agency but, rather, a curious combination of the two. It is ultimately controlled by the President of the United States (who, in fact, appointed Hunter after firing his predecessor), and it is charged with major responsibilities in implementing U.S. housing policies; but it is also supposed to seek profits for its stockholders (who have, in fact, done rather well in recent years). It has been renamed once and restructured three times, and its mission has been redefined twice.

FNMA's principal mission these days is to provide lenders and builders with mortgage money for housing when such funds are difficult to obtain from traditional private sources: the savings and loan associations, banks, and insurance companies. During 1970, the most recent year in which mortgage money was in short supply, Fannie Mae financed nearly a quarter of the nation's new housing. By doing so, the association minimized the decline in housing starts, thus tempering the severity of the last recession.

Fannie Mae wields enormous influence over the housing industry and, indeed, over the whole U.S. economy. Her decisions about how and where to pump money into housing finance can diminish or multiply the fortunes of thousands of entrepreneurs in building and allied fields. To a lesser but still interesting degree, the association's policies

---

*Gurney Breckenfeld, "Nobody Pours It Like Fannie Mae," *Fortune* magazine, June 1972, excerpted from pp. 86–89 and 136, 140, and 145. © 1972 Time, Inc. Breckenfeld is a staff writer at *Fortune*.

also affect the interest rate on money that many consumers borrow to buy or build homes.

RESHAPING A $70-BILLION BUSINESS

During most of her lifetime, Fannie Mae has limited her financing to government-backed mortgages. But last February she took a portentous step: The association began dealing in conventional mortgages—those not insured by the Federal Housing Administration or guaranteed by the Veterans Administration. In entering this new field, Fannie Mae is confronting some lively competition. The Federal Home Loan Mortgage Corporation, a new arm of the Federal Home Loan Bank Board, has entered the same field, and in March the wholly private MGIC Investment Corp. started a similar enterprise. . . . All three rivals aim to reshape the $70-billion-a-year residential-mortgage business by creating an enormous trading market in conventional loans, which account for three quarters of the total. One result of this competition should be a marked increase in the availability of 95 percent mortgage loans, of as much as $40,000, for buyers of both new and existing houses.

Fannie Mae has risen to her present preeminence among mortgage lenders because she managed, at least in some respects, to escape from federal captivity. As a government agency, created in 1938, FNMA naturally found it easy to borrow money in the private market to make mortgage loans. But the borrowed funds went on the Treasury's books in red ink, increasing the federal deficit. In order to keep those funds out of the deficit and to free her from the restraints imposed by the government's debt limit, the 1968 Housing Act transformed Fannie Mae from a government agency into a private corporation. In May 1970, control of the company's board of directors moved into the hands of 7,300 (now 14,880) private stockholders.

The stockholders elect ten of the association's directors, but the President of the United States appoints the other five, and he may remove any of the fifteen from office "for good cause shown." The congressional charter also grants . . . [the] Secretary of Housing and Urban Development, "general regulatory powers" over FNMA affairs; decisions involving dividends, stock issues, total debt, and borrowing must have [his] explicit approval. In addition, the Secretary of the Treasury must approve the timing, maturity, and amount of all debt securities that the company sells.

The government's stranglehold over Fannie Mae's finances has not yet interfered with her operations, but the potential is there because the company runs almost entirely on borrowed money. The allowable ratio of debt to equity, . . . raised to twenty-five to one, far exceeds that of any other major financial company in the U.S.; Fannie Mae has roughly one third as much capital, in relation to liabilities, as a typical commercial bank. Last year the company floated $13 billion of loans, including refinancing—a volume second only to that of the Treasury.

A PRIVILEGED BORROWER

The financial controls are intended, as Congress made clear in the Senate and House Committee reports accompanying the 1968 legislation, to ensure that Fannie Mae operates in the public interest. Specifically, she is supposed to promote an increased flow of mortgage credit and to help finance housing for low- and moderate-income families. And because of Fannie Mae's public purpose, Congress let her retain the privileged borrowing status of a government agency—which means lower interest charges and a broader market for her debentures and notes. To further enhance her credit standing, the lawmakers also gave Fannie Mae the power, in an emergency, to borrow up to $2.25 billion from the U.S. Treasury.

Thus enjoying the benefits of federal sponsorship, Fannie Mae has become a gigantic money-transfer machine, using her government credit rating to borrow billions on Wall Street and relending the funds at higher interest rates to finance homes and apartments. During the past four years the company has more than tripled in size; its $18.6 billion of assets at the end of 1971 made it, by that measure, the eighth largest company in the U.S., just behind Jersey Standard and just ahead of General Motors. (AT&T, with $54.5 billion of assets, is the largest company of all.) Over the same four-year span, Fannie Mae's mortgage holdings rose from $5.5 billion to $17.8 billion and her debt increased even faster, from almost $5 billion to $17.7 billion. Profits climbed 686 percent, from $7,779,000 to $61,181,000, and per-share earnings (adjusted for two stock splits) more than trebled, from 41 cents to $1.43. . . .

In the long search for alternative methods to bring a larger, more reliable flow of money into housing, attention gradually turned toward the vast pool of capital in the nation's bond and money markets. To be sure, a small link between housing and the securities market had been forged a generation ago by Fannie Mae herself and the privately owned government-run Home Loan Bank System (which supervises the nation's s. and l.'s and lends them money raised on Wall Street in much the same way as FNMA). But until the last half of the 60s, their operations remained so small, compared with the total volume of residential lending, as to have only a minor impact. . . .

Many large investors consider mortgages to be a cumbersome and undesirable outlet for their money, and the legislation that turned Fannie Mae private also made an effort to attract more of this money into mortgages. Congress created a new agency, the Government National Mortgage Association, nicknamed Ginnie Mae, which took over Fannie Mae's job of making mortgage loans with Treasury money for HUD's galaxy of subsidized housing programs. The law provided Ginnie with an entirely new device to snare capital for both subsidized and unsubsidized FHA and VA loans. Ginnie stamps her guarantee, pledging the full faith and credit of the government to pay both principal and interest, upon "mortgage-backed securities." These represent pools of FHA and VA loans (minimum amount: $2 million) that are, of course, already insured or guaranteed by the government.

Fannie Mae by herself has, of course, far more impact on housing and the U.S. economy than Ginnie Mae and Freddie Mae combined. Yet the company remains almost invisible to most Americans because it deals with the public entirely through 1,500 middlemen, principally mortgage bankers. These companies make loans to builders and home buyers, resell the loans to FNMA, and thereafter collect the monthly payments, forwarding to the association the principal and interest, minus a fee (currently ⅜ of 1 percent).

To sell loans on one- to four-family homes to Fannie Mae, they must submit bids at the company's weekly auctions. What Fannie Mae auctions off at these remarkable events is in effect a four-month "put." Each bidder names the dollar amount he would like to sell and the interest yield he will accept on mortgages to be delivered within four months.

The auctions take place on Mondays, normally alternating between FHA and VA loans one week and conventional loans the next. Bidders telephone their offers to a battery of 16 skilled clerks at Fannie Mae headquarters in Washington. From the opening at 10:00 A.M. to the closing at 3:00 P.M., the auction staff feverishly jots down the amount and price of each bid, reads the figures back for verification, and simultaneously tape-records each message to permit a subsequent double check. Only after all the bids are in and computers have analyzed the offerings do Fannie Mae's top officers decide which ones to accept. Fannie Mae calls this procedure a "free-market system auction; however, many mortgage bankers argue with the characterization, complaining that the agency can rig the average yield of accepted bids (i.e., by rejecting those they consider too low).

Each winner receives a contractual commitment that the agency will buy all, or a stated part, of its offering if it is delivered to the agency within four months; in exchange for this commitment the winner must pay a nonrefundable fee of ¼ of 1 percent of the amount of the loan. A winner is not required to go through with the sale; he may dispose of the loan elsewhere and is apt to do so if interest rates fall (and the value of his mortgage rises) during the four-month period. The rules are different for loans on multifamily dwellings. Fannie Mae buys only FHA-insured mortgages, offers two-year commitments at fixed prices, and requires delivery of the loans.

The auctions attract an enormous amount of business. Last year the company received $10.4 billion in auction offers, rejected $6.8 billion, and accepted $3.6 billion. This year Hunter expects Fannie Mae to issue $7 billion in commitments, mostly through the weekly auctions, and to purchase $5 billion of loans, enough to finance 270,000 homes and apartment units.

NEW LIFE IN A PLODDING BUREAUCRACY

The auction was devised by mortgage banker Raymond H. Lapin, an aggressive innovator who, in two and a half years as Fannie Mae president, transformed the organization from a plodding civil-service bureaucracy into a major force in the mortgage market. . . .

Perhaps the largest management problem facing any Fannie Mae chief executive is the recurrent conflict between the company's need to earn profits and its obligation to support housing. For example, when mortgage money grew scarce three years ago, the company borrowed heavily at high and rising interest rates in order to expand its loans and prop up housing starts. As a result, for the sixteen months from May 1969 to February 1971, FNMA earned less from its loan portfolio than it spent for borrowed funds. In February 1970, the month that Hunter calls "the blackest period of our cost-price crisis," the company paid an average of 7.59 percent on $11.7 billion of debt and collected only 6.59 percent on $12.1 billion of mortgages. Only a sharp increase in income from commitment fees kept the company from slipping into the red. Even so, net income fell from $16,400,000 in 1969 to $6,700,000 in 1970, or from 63 cents to 19 cents per share. . . .

There is no clear-cut answer to the perennial question about whether Fannie Mae should place more emphasis on profits or on helping the mortgage market. The company's congressional charter admonishes it to be self-supporting, which means that profits must be adequate to attract private capital; but the law also says that support of the residential mortgage market is the company's prime aim, and this may require it to run in the red at times. "FNMA is nothing but one big conflict of interest," says Director Robert Pease, a prominent Chicago mortgage banker.

William S. Vickrey (1914–)

❧ 69

Pricing in Urban and Suburban Transport*

Long a leading advocate of marginal cost pricing, Vickrey outlines what could be done in pricing city transport services rationally. Instead, he notes, actual practices are often sharply—even hilariously—inefficient, with severe social costs. Though his examples are from New York City, they are lamentably fitting for many cities everywhere. Is improvement possible?

I will begin with the proposition that in no other major area are pricing practices so irrational, so out of date, and so conducive to waste as in urban transportation. Two aspects are particularly deficient: the absence of adequate peak-off differentials and the gross underpricing of some modes relative to others.

In nearly all other operations characterized by peak load problems, at least some attempt is made to differentiate between the rates charged for peak and for off-peak service. Where competition exists, this pattern is enforced by competition: Resort hotels have off-season rates; theaters charge more on weekends and less for matinees. Telephone calls are cheaper at night, though I suspect not sufficiently so to promote a fully efficient utilization of the plant. Power rates are varied to a considerable extent according to the measured or the imputed load factor of the consumer and, in some cases, usually for special-purpose uses such as water heating, according to the time of use. . . . But in transportation, such differentiation as exists is usually perverse. Off-peak concessions are virtually unknown in transit. Such concessions as are made in suburban service for "shoppers tickets" and the like are usually relatively small, indeed are often no greater than those available in multitrip tickets not restricted to off-peak riding, and usually result in fares still far above those enjoyed by regular commuters who are predominantly peak-hour passengers.

*   *   *   *   *

*William S. Vickrey, "Pricing in Urban and Suburban Transport," *American Economic Review*, May 1963, excerpted from pp. 452–58. A Columbia University professor, Vickrey has also written extensively on microeconomic theory.

But while suburban and transit fare structures are seriously deficient, the pricing of the use of urban streets is all but nonexistent. Superficially, it is often thought that since reported highway expenditures by the state and federal government are roughly balanced by highway tax and license revenues, the motorist is on the whole paying his way. But what is true on the average is far from true of users of the more congested urban streets. Much of the expenditure on such streets is borne by city budgets supported slightly if at all by explicit contributions from highway sources in most states. More important, much of the real economic cost of providing the space for city streets and highways does not appear in the accounts at all, being concealed by the fact that this space has usually been "dedicated" to the public use at some time in the past. It is extremely difficult to make close evaluations from the scanty and scattered data available, but very roughly it appears to me that if we take the burden of all the gasoline and other vehicular taxes borne by motorists by reason of their use of city streets this amounts to only about a third of the real economic cost of the facilities they use. In current terms, the high marginal cost of increased street space becomes painfully apparent whenever a street widening scheme is evaluated. Even in terms of long-range planning, urban expressways cost many times as much as expressways in rural areas built to comparable specifications, and while the flow of traffic may be greater, this is not enough to come anywhere near amortizing the cost out of the taxes paid by the traffic flowing over the urban expressways. Even when tolls are charged in conjunction with special features such as bridges or tunnels, these seldom cover the cost of the connecting expressways and city streets. And except where the street layout is exceptionally favorable, such tolls usually have an unfavorable effect on the routing of traffic.

The perversity of present pricing practices is at its height, perhaps, for the East River crossings to Long Island and Brooklyn. Here the peculiar political logic is that the older bridges are in some sense "paid for," and hence must be free, while tolls must be charged on the newer facilities. The result is that considerable traffic is diverted from the newer facilities that have relatively adequate and less congested approaches to the older bridges such as the Manhattan and the Queensboro bridges, which dump their traffic right in the middle of some of the worst congestion in New York. The construction of the proposed expressway across lower Manhattan from the Holland Tunnel to the Manhattan and Williamsburgh bridges would be at least less urgent, if not actually unwarranted, in view of its enormous cost, if, as would seem possible, traffic could be diverted from the Manhattan Bridge to the Brooklyn-Battery tunnel by imposing tolls on the Manhattan and other East River bridges and reducing or removing the toll on the tunnel. The delusion still persists that the primary role of pricing should always be that of financing the service rather than that of promoting economy in its use. In practice there are many alternative ways of financing; but no device can function quite as effectively and smoothly as a properly designed price structure in controlling use and providing a guide to the efficient deployment of capital.

The underpricing of highway services is even more strongly pronounced during peak hours. Even if urban motorists on the average paid the full cost of the urban facilities, rush hour use would still be seriously underpriced; moreover, this underpricing would be relatively more severe than for transit or commutation service. This is because off-peak traffic on the highways and streets is a much larger percentage of the total than is the case for either transit or commutation traffic; and therefore in the process of averaging out the costs, much more of the costs properly attributable to the peak can be shifted to the shoulders of the off-peak traffic than can be thus shifted in the case of transit or commutation service. The effect of this is that while the commutation fare problem is chiefly one of the overpricing of off-peak travel, and to a minor extent if at all one of underpricing of peak travel, the problem of the pricing of automobile travel is chiefly that of remedying the underpricing of peak travel, and to a relatively minor extent if at all of the overpricing of off-peak travel. These two relationships combine to give the result that even if motor traffic and commuter train traffic each on the whole fully paid their way on the basis of a uniform charge per trip, the proportion by which the peak-hour motorist would be subsidized by the off-peak motorists would be far greater than the proportion by which the peak-hour commuter is subsidized by the off-peak commuter.

A quantitative indication of the seriousness of the problem of peak-hour automobile traffic is derivable from some projections made for Washington, D.C. Two alternative programs were developed for taking care of traffic predicted under two alternative conditions, differing chiefly as to the extent to which express transit service would be provided. The additional traffic lanes required for the larger of the two volumes of traffic would be needed almost solely to provide for this added rush hour traffic, the less extensive road system being adequate for the off-peak traffic even at the higher overall traffic level. Dividing the extra cost by the extra rush hour traffic, it turned out that for each additional car making a daily trip that contributes to the dominant flow, during the peak hour, an additional investment of $23,000 was projected. In other words, a man who bought a $3,000 car for the purpose of driving downtown to work every day would be asking the community, in effect, to match his $3,000 investment with $23,000 from general highway funds. Or if the wage earners in a development were all to drive downtown to work, the investment in highways that this development would require would be of the same order of magnitude as the entire investment in a moderate-sized house for each family. It may be that the affluent society will be able to shoulder such a cost, but even if it could there would seem to be many much more profitable and urgent uses to which sums of this magnitude could be put. And even if we assume that staggering of working hours could spread the peak traffic more or less evenly over three hours, this would still mean $8,000 per daily trip, even though achievement of such staggering would represent an achievement second only to the highway construction itself. At 250 round trips per year, allowing 10 percent as the gross return which a comparable investment in the private sector would have to earn to cover interest, amortization, and property and corporate income taxes, this amounts to over $3.00 per round trip, or, on a one-hour peak basis, to $9.00 per round trip, if staggering is ruled out. This is over and above costs of maintenance or of provision for parking. When costs threaten to reach such levels, it is high time to think seriously about controlling the use through pricing. . . .

But talk of direct and specific charges for roadway use conjures up visions of a clutter of toll booths, an army of toll collectors, and traffic endlessly tangled up in queues. Conventional methods of toll collection are, to be sure, costly in manpower, space, and interference with the smooth flow of traffic. Furthermore, unless the street configuration is exceptionally favorable, tolls often contribute to congestion over parallel routes. However, with a little ingenuity, it is possible to devise methods of charging for the use of the city streets that are relatively inexpensive, produce no interference with the free flow of traffic, and are capable of adjusting the charge in close conformity with variations in costs and traffic conditions. My own fairly elaborate scheme involves equipping all cars with an electronic identifier which hopefully can be produced on a large-scale basis for about $20 each. These blocks would be scanned by roadside equipment at a fairly dense network of cordon points, making a record of the identity of the car; these records would then be taken to a central processing plant once a month and the records assembled on electronic digital computers and bills sent out. Preliminary estimates indicate a total cost of the equipment on a moderately large scale of about $35 per vehicle, including the identifier; the operating cost would be approximately that involved in sending out telephone bills. Bills could be itemized to whatever extent is desired to furnish the owner with a record that would guide him in the further use of his car. In addition, roadside signals could be installed to indicate the current level of charge and enable drivers to shift to less costly routes where these are available.

*   *   *   *   *

James R. Nelson (1915–   )

✸ 70

Practical Applications of Marginal Cost Pricing in the Public Utility Field*

Marginal cost pricing is equally appropriate under public and private ownership, but public firms in France and Britain have done it most thoroughly. Nelson here outlines the French "green tariff," which carefully fits marginal costs rather than price discrimination. With more recent refinements, French and British electricity pricing has become more efficient than American pricing. This has eased their problems of capacity shortages, ecological impacts, and national energy policy.

The word "Applications" in my title has shrunk all the way from plural to singular. For, so far as I know, the only public utility enterprise in the world to proceed from the theory of marginal cost pricing to both a schedule of rates and a series of rules for investment policy is Electricité de France (or E.D.F., hereafter)—a public corporation which is the dominant factor in the generation, transmission, and distribution of electricity in France. . . .

What are the marginal cost principles which have already been mentioned so often? In brief:

1. The first step in the short-run cost analysis proceeds from the fact that Paris is the heaviest center of electricity consumption—and at a great distance from major sources of hydro supply. Therefore, at any given hour of any day, the short-run marginal cost of electricity delivered in the Paris area is the cost of fuel for an extra unit of output from the least efficient thermal plant which must be in service to enable the total demand at that hour to be met. A price which covers the marginal cost of this least efficient plant will, of course, produce a surplus over the fuel cost of all other plants in service.

2. The exception to this general rule that the marginal price should just cover marginal fuel cost occurs at the peak. The peak kilowatt-hour

*James R. Nelson, "Practical Applications of Marginal Cost Pricing in the Public Utility Field," *American Economic Review*, May 1963, excerpted from pp. 474–81. A brilliant analyst, Nelson has written about nearly all economic aspects of utilities, private and public, in the United States, western Europe, and Latin America. He is Professor of Economics at Amherst College.

is responsible for the installation of new generating capacity. Here we begin to pass from short-run to long-run marginal cost analysis. But note that the long-run marginal cost is not the total cost of a new base-load generating plant. It is the lesser of two costs, neither of which is as high as the baseload cost: The unit cost of a plant specially designed for peak loads or the net cost of the base-load plant after subtracting fuel economies because installation of the new baseload plant permits a reduction of the output required from older, less efficient plants.

3. These thermal conclusions must be modified in two ways to allow for French hydro production:

a. Since Paris is the residual deficit market, always ready to soak up hydro production when it is available, Paris is the key to the geographical price structure appropriate for the industry. Consuming areas closer to hydro surpluses than Paris should enjoy a price equal to marginal thermal cost at Paris minus transmission cost. In the limit, the value of the electricity at the site of the hydro plant itself is determined by the cost of a kilowatt-hour from the marginal thermal source at Paris minus transmission costs from the hydro site to the capital.

b. Since hydro supplies depend on variable water conditions, they involve more uncertainty than thermal supplies. Moreover, since hydro supplies reach their peak in France in the summertime, eking out the uncertain winter supply requires substantial investment in reservoir capacity. Thus the familiar problem of supplying peak use is complicated by the further problem of assuring winter supplies of electricity.

E.D.F. has assembled these theoretical ingredients into a new tariff for larger industrial users, the *tarif vert*, which was introduced during 1957.

The structure of the *tarif vert* in a mainly hydro area may be illustrated by actual rates charged in the departments of the lower Rhone valley. The original annual fixed charge was 4,000 francs per kilowatt, or the equivalent of just under $10 at the exchange rate then prevailing.

The price per kilowatt-hour was varied through five standard periods: peak hours in winter, heavy-use hours in winter, slack hours in winter, heavy-use hours in summer, and slack hours in summer. The kilowatt-hour price from the 150-kilovolt transmission system ranged from 7.50 francs, or just under 2 cents, at the winter peak, down to 2.13 francs, or less than 4/10ths of a cent, in the slack hours of summer. If the slack-hour rate in summer is arbitrarily equated to 100, then the other four rates, three winter and one summer, are: 352, 253, 130, and 157. For the smallest customer eligible for the *tarif vert*—one supplied by the 5-kilovolt distribution system—the range of kilowatt-hour rates was from 13.41 franc to 2.31 francs. With the lowest rate as 100, the other rates were 581, 323, 129, and 160. The 5-kilovolt consumer was asked to pay only 15 percent more than the 120-kilovolt consumer in summer, and only 7½ percent more in the slack hours of winter; but the smaller user had to pay 70 percent more in the heavy-use hours in winter and almost 80 percent more at the winter peak.

E.D.F. has estimated that improvement in load factors due to the *tarif vert* permitted an initial saving in capacity equal to six months' investment program. . . .

The French system has adopted the only possible economic rule for marginal cost pricing: In an industry in which costs decrease in any dimension, the economic case for making any sales at less than marginal cost is especially weak. The consistent emphasis in the E.D.F. analysis on at least covering marginal cost provides not only a powerful reason for knowing the exact magnitude of these costs but also a long-run protection against certain types of political pressure. . . .

Although the French electrical rate structure is a product of a special relationship between hydro and thermal resources, the idea of combining peak costs and relatively high rates on the plateau of heavy winter use is doubly useful; it provides partial safeguards against future demand shifts and it establishes principles on which the rate structure itself may be altered if need be. The *tarif vert* might still be hovering in the wings if it had not been for the unsatisfactory rate level and structure produced by the interplay of specific freezes and general inflation. But, once on the scene, it offers more prospect for flexibility than the familiar rigid "on-peak-off-peak" structure of rates. . . .

John B. Sheahan (1923–   )

✵ 71

Active Competition by Public Enterprise*

Public firms often compete directly with private firms in industrial markets. Several such cases in France and Italy are appraised here. Sheahan finds that the public firms often do quite well without special assistance or favors.

Particular public firms have in several cases proven to be distinctly more dynamic than the private firms with which they were in competition, especially in the sense of using more active investment policies and moving into new fields. Perhaps the most important examples have been Finsider in the Italian steel industry, ENI, Renault in the French automobile industry, and in some ways SNIAS in French aviation. Instances have also been identified in which public firms have exerted pressure on private monopolistic pricing—by price competition in the conventional sense—but this hardly seems to be a widespread or persistent characteristic of their behavior. The advantages of public competition relate more to their ability to lead in new fields than to any great capacity to exert pressure on prices or improve short-run resource allocation.

Finsider. In the Italian steel industry, Finsider went far beyond merely running firms that were previously under private ownership. This branch of IRI converted the industry from a backward set of protected producers into one of the most modern and efficient in the world. At the beginning of the 1950s Italian steel was so expensive that the European Coal and Steel Community was willing to allow Italy to enter the group with a four-year grace period of continued protection. By the end of that period Finsider's new integrated steel plant near Genoa was able to compete without protection, and by the 1960s Italy had become a potent steel exporter.

ENI. ENI's behavior in the petroleum industry under Mattei has been more diversely appreciated. It was certainly independent. Mattei

*John B. Sheahan, "Experience with Public Enterprise in France and Italy," reprinted by permission of the publisher, from William G. Shepherd (ed.), *Public Enterprise: Economic Analysis of Theory and Practice* (Lexington, Mass.: Lexington Books, D. C. Heath and Company. Copyright 1976, D. C. Heath and Company), excerpted from pp. 136–39. Sheahan is Professor of Economics at Williams College and a long-time perceptive observer of public enterprise.

built up a highly professional staff and gave them a certain sense of mission, particularly by casting ENI in the role of the small domestic firm competing against the international petroleum giants. After the initial success in finding good natural gas supplies and bringing them to markets quickly, he turned ENI toward modernization and expansion of oil refining, entry into petrochemical production, expansion of an independent network for gasoline distribution within Italy, and negotiation of rights to explore for oil in Africa and the Middle East. ENI's course was exactly the antithesis of that of public enterprise in the French petroleum industry: Where the French public firms acted as passive participants in that country's cartel, ENI went out to take over markets and upset the international oil industry as much as it possibly could.

On the side of ENI's activity that most directly faced the public—gasoline distribution—AGIP broke away from the dusty model of store-side pumps then common in Europe to build a chain of ultra-modern stations using the best of U.S. techniques plus unbeatable Italian ice cream for hot and hungry children. Beyond that, AGIP cut prices in some periods and forced the international companies to follow suit. AGIP gained a market share of 20 percent by 1952 and 25 percent by 1962. It is probable that at times the company sold gasoline below cost, subsidizing gasoline from natural gas revenues. It is practically certain that Mattei made the company sound more valiantly concerned with the welfare of the Italian public than the facts would warrant. But the company grew and prospered without any French-style control of its rivals' imports to ensure it a safe market share.

On the side of negotiations with foreign countries for oil exploration rights, ENI initiated radically new contract proposals that very much upset the private international petroleum companies. It is possible that the substantive content of the proposals was not a great deal more generous to the developing countries than the contracts then commonly offered by the private companies, but they had an important new flavor. They were phrased in terms of partnership treating the developing countries on terms that were at least formally more equal. And they gained power from being presented as an alternative to domination by collusive private buyers. Paul Frankel concluded in 1966 that the operations had done little for Italian national income because ENI did not have much luck with its concessions, though they did improve the negotiating position of the developing countries and Italian relationships with them. Continued expansion of overseas activities since then makes the initially doubtful results look somewhat better: ENI's crude production outside of Italy had reached only 4.9 million tons by 1963, the year after Mattei's death; it was up to 17.6 million tons by 1973. ENI is still no heavyweight in the world oil industry, but its production has continued to grow, and its more recent development of foreign supplies of natural gas is also fairly promising.

Apart from gas and oil, ENI's activities spread quickly in the 1950s across chemicals, fertilizers, synthetic fibers, woolen fabrics, engineering equipment and services, atomic energy technology and equipment, and newspaper publishing. Its extremely rapid diversification stopped abruptly with Mattei's death in 1962, but its expansion did not. Value added as reported by ENI for the companies in which its ownership interest is over 50 percent was 6 times as high in 1963 as in its initial full year of 1954, and then 4 times again as high in 1973 as in 1963.

Renault.   French public enterprise has been less represented in competitive fields, but at least in the case of Renault it has provided some of the competitive leadership which should be possible in manufacturing. When the company was nationalized, it was given a primary assignment of expanding tractor and truck production under the First Plan. It did develop such production, but management's interest went immediately outside the plan, to competition in the automobile industry. By 1950, Renault accounted for 30 percent of domestic automobile production. This was double the company's share under private ownership in the last prewar year, 1938. By 1960 its share of output reached 40 percent.

In preparing the Second Plan, the Planning Commission asked the company to cut down its ambitious program for expansion of automobile production. The company's director, Pierre Lefaucheux, simply refused: "The worst fault that one can commit against the nationalizations consists precisely of effacing the notion of a responsible head and developing the notion of the state as boss. . . ." Under his management the company raised its share of production from third in the industry to first by effective product innovation, concentration of models for low costs, and somewhat more concern than its private rivals for holding prices down. The company ignored the Planning Commission's appeal to reduce investment but responded enthusiastically to the subsequent request to promote exports. Of the four French producers, Renault was the first and by far the most successful in developing new exports outside of traditional markets in Belgium and Switzerland.

Renault has continued to stress exports and more recently direct investment in developing countries. But it has not been such an independent competitor in the home market as to raise its share any further since 1960. Its market share in truck production, through its subsidiary, Saviem, is about to be raised but only by means of purchasing control of the leading private competitor, Berliet. This purchase is an interesting case of the use of government funds intended for economic development, made available at rates of interest below the market to enable a public firm to acquire control of a private competitor. But it should be noted that government funds were made available at the same time on a much larger scale to enable the number two private automobile producer, Peugeot, to acquire the other private French firm, Citroen. Subsidized credit simultaneously improved the market position of the public firm in trucks and built up the main private rival in automobiles.

SNIAS. The French public firm in aircraft production, SNIAS, has had an interesting record as an international competitor in commercial jet transports. The company led Boeing in the introduction of rear-mounted jet engines with the *Caravelle*. But after getting technical leadership and beginning to establish a strong market position, the firm failed to follow through with improving models that could keep up with the Boeing 727 and then 737. This loss of commercial position after an initial technical lead might possibly be ascribed to unbusinesslike attitudes of public enterprise management, but any presumption in this sense should surely be qualified by consideration of the intensely commercial attitudes and performance of Renault. The difference in the case of SNIAS may be explained rather in terms of an overriding political decision to focus the company's efforts on development of supersonic transport, the *Concorde*. This was not a matter of commercial judgment by the company. It was a political issue at the presidential level, much as with supersonic transport in the United States. The firm has proven itself to be technically capable of carrying out the project at costs which, as seems to be the case in all countries' aircraft development work, far exceeded original expectations.

Although SNIAS has been heavily involved in development of the *Concorde*, it has also become a successful producer and exporter of helicopters, it participates in work on the European Airbus, and it has been developing a new business jet plane on an unsubsidized commercial basis. In terms of technical competence in an extremely fluid area of innovation and rapid change, this public enterprise seems perfectly capable of keeping up with the best of the world's private companies.

Competition in Pricing. As far as straight price competition is concerned, it has at times been important in several fields in Italy. Finsider, the Italian steel producer used price competition to break into the cement market in the 1950s. In that same period, ANIC, within ENI, cut prices on fertilizer to attack Montecatini's dominant position, and AGIP used fairly aggressive price cuts for gasoline to build up its market share. It would be a pleasure to report a long list of further examples, but if there have been many, they have not been brought out publicly. And these examples, like the relatively restrained pricing of Renault in the 1950s, all relate to early periods of market entry or expansion by public enterprise. Once well established in their markets, the public firms have rarely tried to rock the boat. In the last 15 years, the public firms have cooperated rather than competed in their domestic pricing.

*   *   *   *   *   *

Gilbert Burck

❧ 72

A Socialist Enterprise That Acts Like a Fierce Capitalist Competitor*

The Yugoslav firm named "Energoinvest" is a remarkable industrial hybrid that is (1) large, (2) a conglomerate, (3) publicly owned, (4) worker-managed (in part), (5) competitive and (6) successful. In Yugoslavia and other countries (including the United States), there are other hybrids, mixing these and other features in different ways.

Most Americans who know anything about Sarajevo think of it as the Balkan town where Archduke Franz Ferdinand's assassination touched off World War I. Few would imagine it as a modern industrial center. But that's what it is. Among other things, Sarajevo is the headquarters city for an industrial enterprise called Energoinvest, which may be described without undue exaggeration as one of the most ambitious, arresting, edifying, and important conglomerates the business world has ever sprouted. Founded 21 years ago by an entrepreneurial genius named Emerik Blum, Energoinvest has recently been expanding at more than 20 percent per annum. It now emcompasses 41 units turning out a wide range of products dominated by electrical and processing equipment such as heat exchangers, and it plans to become a major aluminum producer. It employs some 22,000 people, maintains sales offices in 32 countries, grosses about $160 million, and spends $5 million to $6 million a year on research, development, and scholarships. As a conglomerate, it is a rare if not unique phenomenon: Because its affiliates can always secede from the group if they choose, the company's very existence depends on doing better for each affiliate than the affiliate can do by itself.

. . . Yugoslavia's Communism is nothing if not flexible, and it practices a kind of market socialism that compels "social" enterprises to operate like private enterprises.

Energoinvest certainly does just that. One of the most enterprising of

---

*Gilbert Burck, "A Socialist Enterprise That Acts Like a Fierce Capitalist Competitor," *Fortune* magazine, January 1972, excerpted from pp. 82–86, 126, and 130–132. © 1972 Time, Inc. Burck is a staff writer at *Fortune*.

Yugoslav enterprises, it scours the world for ideas, pays stiff fees to American management consultants, and exists not merely to make things but to sell them in competitive markets. Along with some other successful Yugoslav firms, Energoinvest has shown that the best way to make socialism work is to subject it to the discipline of the market and put it under good management. It provides an excellent example of a truth now being grasped throughout the whole industrial world: No matter what the political and social bent of a country, the art and science of producing and distributing goods and services efficiently are governed by essentially the same economic laws. . . .

The comrade consumers in the East are just as coy and elusive as the freewheeling buyers in the West. Inflation follows an inordinate expansion of the money supply just as inevitably in a totalitarian state as in representative democracies. . . . Whether socialized or private, production and trade flourish under good management and languish under bad.

THE BIGGER THE PROFITS, THE HIGHER THE WAGE

The key to the Yugoslav economic system is that it recognizes these facts. The system is not as strange and paradoxical as it sounds, nor is it something really new. A brilliant job of improvisation, it resembles very closely the private enterprise system, and it needs good management for the same reason the private system does. The basic difference between the two is that the Yugoslav system is based on so-called self-management (samoupravljanje), which does away with private ownership and invests ownership in "the people," and expects workers and their councils to act as trustees for the people. Self-management is not universal in Yugoslavia; most of the country's farms and hundreds of thousands of small enterprises are privately owned. But the great bulk of the nonagricultural labor force works in "social" enterprises run by worker-elected councils. These workers are the "bosses." Technically they can fire their managers and pull their factories out of a complex like Energoinvest; and they make the final decisions on wages and investment. Their pay depends directly on profits, whereas pay in a private enterprise depends indirectly on them. But the profitability of a Yugoslav firm depends, as it does for enterprises at all times and everywhere, on management. . . .

The Yugoslavs concluded that their own economy had to be decentralized, for true socialism had to be based on motivation, not on command. The obvious way to decentralize without restoring private ownership was to turn to the well-known device of workers' councils—to set up councils in the enterprises and transfer most and eventually perhaps all of the state's economic power to them. But that, of course, meant allowing the enterprises to act freely, subject mainly to the discipline of the market. Without self-government, Yugoslav economists agreed, socialism was impossible. Without free enterprise, by the same token, workers' self-government was impossible.

HIRED HANDS TO BOSS THE BOSSES

The independence of the councils has been intermittently strengthened since 1950, when the era of self-management legally began, and today they are beholden to no one, at least in theory. In every firm with more than five jobs, the workers elect a council by secret ballot. Most councils number anywhere from 15 to 120 members, depending on the size of the enterprise, and they serve for two years. Since the councils generally meet only every month or two, they often choose a managing board which includes the enterprise's director or chief executive to keep the councils in frequent touch with the company's affairs. Each plant boasts at least one council, and large companies with several plants or divisions elect a central council that generally handles broad policy matters. Thus each of the 41 affiliates of Energoinvest elects a council, often supplemented at lower levels by informal discussion groups. And a central council of about 100, elected by all the workers, assembles periodically in Sarajevo.

Legally, the director has a very ambiguous job. As chief executive officer, he is the chief hired hand and implements the council's decisions. Appointed by the council from candidates selected by a committee, he must be re-elected by the council every four years; and the council can sack him if the case against him is strong enough. At the same time, he is charged with seeing to it that the enterprise does nothing contrary to the public interest.

As the Yugoslavs cheerfully explain, they are experimenting and learning from experience. In practice, the original statutes or charters of most enterprises have been rewritten to specify managerial prerogatives and authority. Energoinvest's statute, for instance, has been amended several times. It now empowers the managing director to coordinate the activities of the units or affiliates in the interests of the whole enterprise, to annul decisions made by his executives, to ask the councils to annul acts by their management boards if he considers them unwise, to sign agreements on behalf of the enterprise, and so on. He is also allowed to choose his own collegium or advisory body, composed largely of his chief executives and technical specialists. . . .

JOIN US AND MAKE MONEY

Just to keep itself together, therefore, Energoinvest has had to make each affiliate much better off in the federation than it would be on its own. So it built up an organization that offers prospective affiliates advantages they could get nowhere else. As early as the middle 1950s, Blum decided to develop export markets. The Yugoslav market was too small to allow economies of scale and was still without a really competitive price structure. Blum realized what the Soviet Union and some other East European countries have still to recognize: Modern industrial management in a closed society is a contradiction in terms. The only way to become an economic organization was to fight for business in world markets.

The group's first customers were Czechoslovakia and East Germany. Then, as Yugoslavia developed relations with "nonaligned" countries like itself, the company began to develop markets in the Middle East, the Far East, Africa, Pakistan, and eventually even in Europe and North America. Last year it sold cranes to Krupp and refinery equipment to a U.S. supply house, and competing against the Japanese, it won a $1,500,000 contract to build a penstock for British Columbia Hydro & Power Authority. Exports in 1970 came to nearly 40 percent of revenues; the company's goal is 50 percent.

Energoinvest has also built up staff service departments unmatched anywhere in its part of the world. It maintains four research-and-development centers, including a new high-voltage laboratory; together these centers cost between $4 million and $5 million a year. Other services are provided by a large modern computer center, five designing departments, central export and purchasing departments, and a central financial department complete with a bank that handles all the group's money and financial transactions. And the company had ensured a steady supply of young executive talent, probably the scarcest industrial resource in Yugoslavia, by financing more than 3,100 scholarships at Sarajevo and a few other universities.

So the company's pitch to prospective affiliates can be summed up this way: "We ask you to adhere to our basic program and charge you 4 to 6 percent of your gross, depending on the kinds of products you make. We have access to money, support all kinds of expertise, and can help you export in a way that nobody else can. If we cannot boost your profits in a couple of years, you are free to withdraw from our group."

. . . Yugoslav workers and directors often find themselves taking very different views of what is good for the business. Unlike a capitalist enterprise which tends primarily to maximize the earnings on investment, the self-managed enterprise tends to maximize profit *per worker*. Therefore councils are reluctant to hire people for research, market analysis, or other "unproductive" jobs because these outlays reduce, at least temporarily, profits and hence wages per worker. Thus the council tends to take the short-term point of view, while the conscientious director takes the longer view. Blum has estimated that wages could be raised

across the board by as much as 15 percent if his "investments" in research and other long-term intangibles were abolished. But this means,
as Yugoslavs say, the workers would "eat up their future."

*   *   *   *   *

What is more, Blum argues that the workers' management system
facilitates rather than hinders his job. Speaking before a symposium in
Amsterdam two years ago, he declared flatly that it is easier for a
Yugoslav director to function efficiently than it is for managers in the
West who face the incessant and arbitrary opposition of trade unions or
managers in the Soviet Union who are "subject to the assessments and
wills of government bureaucrats." . . .

The Yugoslav economic press has begun to decry the growing power
of "big business" and the banks, which supply nearly all industrial
capital, and to profess alarm about the growing concentration of the
country's resources. Blum's agreement in effect anticipated more of this
kind of talk by clarifying, sometimes in great detail, just how the affiliates retain their autonomy. For example, the central organization will
handle all financial matters—raise money, pay it out, establish lines of
credit at home and abroad. Each affiliate, however, will make its own
decisions within a broad framework of guidelines about working capital, investment, and the size and disposition of special funds, such as
those for housing.

✖ 73

ISKRA (a Yugoslav enterprise)

Excerpts from the Annual Report, 1977

> *ISKRA is an excellent example of a diversified Yugoslav "worker-man-*
> *aged" enterprise. Its sales are over $1 billion, and its product range is very*
> *wide, as you can see. Though like a U.S. conglomerate firm in many*
> *features, it does have a different basis. Try to interpret its processes from*
> *these passages from a recent Annual Report.*

WHAT IS ISKRA?

Iskra is the largest association in Yugoslavia's electrical industry, and
25 percent of the latter's production value is created by
29,000 Self-Managing Workers. The average number of workers
employed by Iskra was 28,232, including 1,835 with higher or university

education, 3,755 with secondary education, and 6,650 skilled workers. In 1976, Iskra allocated scholarships to/or trained 3,708 persons.

66 Basic Organisations—47 Plants. Iskra comprises 66 basic organisations of associated labour in seven specialized working organisations and four service organisations, i.e., Iskra Commerce, the Institute for Productivity and Metrology, the Automatic Data Processing Centre and Invest Service.

Production. Iskra's production capacities are grouped in seven specialized working organisations: telecommunications, automation, components, electrical parts for motor vehicles, consumer goods, metalware, and capacitors. Last year the output volume increased by 16.8 percent.

Marketing. Iskra has its own domestic and international marketing organisation. Its commercial network abroad numbers 7 commercial firms and 8 agencies, whose total realisation in 1976 exceeded $130 million, including export worth $67 million. The domestic network comprises: 14 branch offices, 27 retail shops, 34 service centres plus over 300 contractual servicing workshops, moreover several engineering offices and numerous on-site assembling units.

Iskra Standard is a specialized division representing foreign companies in Yugoslavia.

Research and Development. In Iskra's production organisations, more than 1,600 experts are engaged in research and development; more than 500 hold university degrees. Besides, Iskra has its own Institute for Quality Control and Metrology where test measurements are carried out, and the functionality, durability, and reliability of the products are tested.

Iskra's industrial and graphic designers have been awarded more than 230 domestic and international prizes and recognitions.

ISKRA'S DEVELOPMENT

The birthday of Iskra, one of the pioneers of the Yugoslav electrical industry, was March 8, 1946. The company was founded in Kranj with a total of 850 employees and started to manufacture electrical and mechanical products. The dynamic development of Iskra can be roughly divided into four periods.

The first period extended from its foundation till 1960 when the organisation was joined by the Ljubljana Telecommunications Institute, which is considered an initiator of the Yugoslav electronics industry, the Electric Apparatus Factory, manufacturers of relays and protection devices—Ljubljana, and Telekomunikacije—Ljubljana, the first manufacturers of radio and TV receivers in the country, each having scattered manufacturing units.

The merger into a united organisation took place following the reali-

sation that, due to the Yugoslav economy's change from a state planned
to a market orientated system, the small self-sufficient companies would
have no chance of survival. Iskra entered upon the second period with
7,000 employees and Din 156 million production output. With the concentration of financial power, technology and knowledge, as well as
with the establishment of its own research and development institute
and a commercial organisation, the acceleration of growth soon became
evident. By further mergers and the construction of new plants Iskra's
capabilities were enlarged in this period by nine factories for electrical
motor vehicle parts, small electric motors, electromechanical and electronic instruments, electronic equipment, foil capacitors, rectifiers,
semiconductors and radio receivers. At the same time consolidation and
specialization of production took place and particular emphasis was
placed on market orientation. This period of development was terminated in 1966 with Din 570 million worth of production and 13,000
workers; but the highly centralized structure was by then an inhibiting
factor. Therefore, the company was reorganised into an association of
units enjoying considerable independence but also sharing the responsibility for a common harmonious development. This reorganisation
brought about an internal consolidation and made it possible for the
Association to strengthen its position in international markets. By
tailoring its manufacturing programme to meet the market requirements
and by setting up an extensive network of companies and representatives abroad an eightfold increase was achieved over the following
period. The same period saw a number of new integrations. New members joining Iskra were the Domestic Appliances Factory Elra—Reteče,
the Antennas Factory—Vrhnika, EMO Enamelled Products and Containers—Celje, Batteries Factory ZMAJ—Ljubljana, Opto-electronics
and Glass Products VEGA—Ljubljana, ELA—Electric Hardware Manufacturers—Novo mesto, and TRENTA Metal Hardware Manufacturers—Bovec.

The fourth period began in 1974 with the adoption of the country's
new Constitution which in the evolution of the Yugoslav socioeconomic
system ushered in a new stage in the development of self-managing
socialist democracy. Thus 65 basic organisations of associated labour
were founded, acting as self-contained technological and/or economic
units each representing a basic unit of our socioeconomic system and
enjoying the status of a legal entity. At the same time, reorganisation
took place, based on the system through which the basic organisations
according to their manufacturing programmes were grouped into six
and later seven specialized divisions, so-called working organisations.
Every basic organisation has one vote in the assembly, which is the
common management body, whereas on decisions on important issues
of common interest a consensus is to be reached.

In 1974, Iskra concluded an agreement in association with the Autoelectrical and Electrical Products manufacturers—Tolmin. With the reorganisation and the occupation of the new central management building in 1975 Iskra was re-named Iskra—Associated Enterprises of the Electrometal Industry, Ljubljana.

ORGANISATION

The basic unit of the Yugoslav self-management system is the basic organisation of associated labour in which the workers are united through technically and technologically complete single phases of a working process that are liable to economic evaluation in market terms or within the working organisation. In such a basic organisation, there are 66 within Iskra, the workers either directly or through their delegates make decisions concerning all the important matters of social reproduction.

The basic organisations within Iskra link up on the basis of production programmes to create working organisations. There are seven such organisations, each specialised in a particular sector of industrial production of electrical goods. . . . The management process takes place directly at assemblies of workers at the level of the basic organisations and working communities, or indirectly through delegates to the workers' councils at the level of the basic organisations, the working organisations and of the entire composite organisation Iskra.

The workers' council of the composite organisation Iskra delegates specific executive functions to the executive committees for development and programme, economic and financial matters, innovations, marketing and information, organisation, personnel, and social matters as well as for social self-defense.

The starting point of the self-management process is the decision making concerning planning documents which serve as the basis for the work of executive and other bodies. The basic planning documents are the five-year medium-term plan and the agreement on the fundamentals of the plan whereby the basic organisations assume mutually binding material and other obligations that have to be met if the plan of each one of them is to be implemented. All the planning documents are renewed annually and further modifications are introduced if marketing, working, and operating conditions so require. Business matters within the composite organisation Iskra are dealt with by the Managing Board, a collegiate executive body. In this body responsibilities are divided by sectors corresponding to major branches of activity. The entire work of the Managing Board is coordinated by its Chairman who also sees to it that the entire operation of the composite organisation Iskra is in accordance with the law.

*   *   *   *   *

MAIN ACTIVITIES

Telecommunications. Public and private automatic telephone exchanges (crossbar switching type); electronic telephone exchanges, public and private; power supply equipment for telephone exchanges; carrier frequency telephone and telegraph equipment; radio relay equipment; shortwave and ultra-shortwave mobile and stationary communication equipment; electro-optical equipment, lasers; radio navigation and location equipment; telephone sets and equipment; telecommunication testing and measuring equipment; telecommunication cable and line-coupling equipment; components for telecommunication equipment and devices (subscribers' meters, relays, electronic components, and other parts, antennas); electric clocks; planning, installation, and maintenance of telecommunication equipment.

Automation. Signalling and protecting equipment for railway and road traffic automation; industrial automation equipment and devices (processors, hydraulic and pneumatic devices and systems); welding equipment; rectifiers; fire and burglar alarms; relays and other devices for protection and generators, transformers, and power networks; relays and parts for signalling and automation; remote control and equipment for power distribution networks; tone frequency receivers; planning, installation, and maintenance of automation equipment.

*   *   *   *   *

Consumer Goods. Electric household appliances (electric and combined electric gas ranges, electric and gas cookers, radiators, fans, vacuum cleaners, floor cleaners, coffee grinders, etc.); gas, oil and electric heaters; electric shavers; TV receivers, stabilizers and antennas; radio receivers; record players; electric power tools (drills, tool sets, concrete vibrators, spray guns, grinders, electric shears, hand and bench type saws, vibration drills, etc.) for industry, handcraft and home use.

*   *   *   *   *

Engineering Activities. Telecommunication; automation of production lines, processing techniques and electric power distribution; railway and road traffic; alarm and protecting equipment in industry, administration, etc.; electric measuring instruments; electric watthour meters; dry cell batteries and rectifiers; electric motor vehicle parts; consumer goods; electromechanical and electronic components and parts; heating and air conditioning equipment; specialized fields of technology.

The following partial or complete services are also being offered: market and economic analysis; drafts and planning of technological processes; co-operation in planning of industrial plants, supervision of construction works; supply and installation of equipment (own and subcontractor equipment); technical documentation, staff training and introduction of new production lines; development and consulting; acquirement and granting of licenses and know-how; other business and technical co-operation; financing of investment works in accordance with Yugoslav regulations.

Questions for Review III: Public Enterprise

1. "Public enterprise is a substitute for *private ownership*, not for antitrust or regulation." Explain this.

2. Under what conditions is public ownership and management the best treatment for all or part of an industry? Illustrate with real cases, if you can.

3. Public ownership of utilities is common abroad, while private ownership under regulation is common in this country. Are there objective standards for deciding in specific cases whether public ownership or regulated private ownership is best? If so, what are these standards?

4. Have public power systems like TVA provided a useful "benchmark" or "yardstick" for evaluating the prices and performance of private power companies? Explain.

5. What criteria are appropriate for pricing and investment decisions in public enterprises? Give instances where these (1) have and (2) have not been followed in actual public enterprises.

6. Are public firms more effective in achieving rational pricing than regulated private firms? Explain.

7. You are chairman of a new Task Force on Public Enterprise. What main changes in the scope of public enterprises in this country would *you* make? Give specific examples of the worst and best instances of public enterprises.

8. "Public enterprises are a costly failure." "Public enterprise is an efficient, flexible policy tool." Which one is correct? Use the practical cases in your explanation.

9. Choose a public enterprise, assess its performance, and specify two main changes in policy or structure which would improve that performance.

10. "Public enterprise has never been properly tried." "Public enterprise is fine in theory but defective in practice." Explain both of these points of view. Are they correct?

11. What advantages do public investment banks offer, compared to the older style of public firms in utility sectors?

12. In what ways might marginal-cost pricing actually be applied to different parts of the urban transportation system?

13. "Each car crossing the George Washington bridge causes 5¢ of wear to the pavement. A flat toll of 5¢ should therefore be charged to equate price with marginal cost." Is this pricing rule correct and complete?

14. "The classic public corporation in a utility sector is only one of many possible forms of public enterprise." What other forms are there?

15. Public firms need not be monopolies. Find five examples of public enterprises that are under competitive pressure.

16. Identify three public enterprises operating in your present locale.

17. Is public ownership merely a last resort, suitable only when all other policies fail?

18. Identify three public enterprises with excellent performance; and three with poor performance. Can you explain why the difference has occurred?

19. Should the U.S. Postal Service be subjected to more competition? On which parts of its business; or all parts; or none?

20. Does uniting city transit operations in one public enterprise help achieve social efficiency? Give pro and con.

21. If you are at a public college or university, how should its pricing policies be improved? Who is benefiting from, and who is paying for, your education?

22. Are there clear criteria to prescribe the profit and pricing behavior of "social enterprises"?

23. Should museums and public libraries charge admission or other fees?